SCIENCE EXPERIENCES FOR THE EARLY CHILDHOOD YEARS
An Integrated Affective Approach

Eighth Edition

Jean D. Harlan

Mary S. Rivkin
University of Maryland–Baltimore County

PEARSON

Merrill
Prentice Hall

Upper Saddle River, NJ
Columbus, OH

Library of Congress Cataloging-in-Publication Data

Harlan, Jean Durgin.
  Science experiences for the early childhood years: an integrative affective approach /
Jean D. Harlan, Mary S. Rivkin.—8th ed.
    p. cm.
  Includes bibliographical references and index.
  ISBN 0-13-038499-2 (pbk.)
    1. Science—Study and teaching (Early childhood) I. Rivkin, Mary S. II. Title.

LB1139.5.S35H37 2004
372.3′5-dc21   2002044456

Vice President and Executive Publisher: Jeffery W. Johnston
Publisher: Kevin M. Davis
Editorial Assistant: Autumn Crisp
Production Editor: Sheryl Glicker Langner
Production Coordinator: Tiffany Kuehn, Carlisle Publishers Services
Design Coordinator: Diane C. Lorenzo
Cover Designer: Jason Moore
Cover Photos: Courtesy of Mary Rivkin
Production Manager: Laura Messerly
Director of Marketing: Ann Castel Davis
Marketing Manager: Amy June
Marketing Coordinator: Tyra Poole

This book was set in Palatino by Carlisle Communications, Ltd. It was printed and bound by R.R.
Donnelley & Sons Company. The cover was printed by Lehigh Press, Inc.

Photo Credits: Hildegard Alder, p. 42; Nancy Alexander, pp. 5, 20, 46, 66, 133, 148, 177, 241, 261, 267, 279,
288, 291, 306; Don Franklin/BM Porter, pp. 87, 135; Gary Goodman, pp. 12, 113, 187, 276; John Harlan, p.
120; Susan Humphries, pp. 24, 256, 258; Jean-Claude LeJeune, p. 77; Janet Brown McCraken/Subjects &
Predicates, pp. 92, 158, 239, 277; Robin Moore, p. 319; Sally Pena, p. 180; Phillips Photo Illustrators, p. 225;
Mary Rivkin, p. 285.

K'nex® is a registered trademark of the K'NEX Industries, Inc. Lego® is a registered trademark of the
LEGO group of companies.

Pearson Education Ltd.   Pearson Education Australia Pty. Limited
Pearson Education Singapore Pte. Ltd.   Pearson Education North Asia Ltd.
Pearson Education Canada, Ltd.   Pearson Educación de Mexico, S.A. de C.V.
Pearson Education–Japan   Pearson Education Malaysia Pte. Ltd.

10 9 8 7 6 5 4 3 2 1
ISBN: 0-13-038499-2

Preface

We have revised this book with the goal of helping you inspire children to care about their world and how it works, to enjoy their investigations, and to proudly remember what they have figured out. It is that kind of emotional involvement which makes any significant learning possible. That crucial element, sadly, is missing from the national mandates decreeing what students *will* learn. We believe that the role of emotion in learning must be recognized to revitalize education in this country.

To reach our goal, we are bringing you the important work of Stanley Greenspan, M.D., defining the emotional origins of intellectual development. We have also added the broadened neuroscience understandings about the complex interactions between emotions, thought processes, and memory. We have recast the learning objectives for the science activities to reflect our convictions about the importance of connecting children's feelings with meaningful explorations for lasting learning.

Other updates in this revision include new classroom experiences with insects, things that move in the air, simple machines, and crystal formation. We continue to value taking science outdoors and, to facilitate this we suggest new ways to improve the schoolgrounds. As usual, we have sorted through the outpouring of new publications to recommend books and other resources to enrich exploration of the topics covered.

During the course of our revision process, we were privileged one afternoon to have tea with Stanley Greenspan, discussing how best to present his insights to you. We also asked his advice for teachers. His answer was clear and impressive. He said, "Engage emotionally with kids, and have a lot of respect for their individual differences." We believe that when you do so, you will find as much satisfaction and pleasure as we found in "doing" science with the children in our classrooms.

ACKNOWLEDGMENTS

Many sources of inspiration make fresh revisions of this book possible. Among them are the children whose curiosity and eagerness to explore are nurtured at the Milwaukee Public Museum and Discovery World. I thank them. I am particularly grateful to Sophia Borghese for sharing her knowledge of mealworms and her passion for science.

Helpful comments for planning our revisions were given by the following reviewers: Cecelia Benelli, Western Illinois University; Marcia Edson, Boston University; Steven H. Fairchild, James Madison University; Wendy Frazier, Old Dominion University; Linda L. Jones, University of Florida; Terrie L. Kielborn, State University of West Georgia; Deborah Moberly, Southeast Missouri State University; and Molly Weinburgh, Texas Christian University.

For unfailing support, love, and lessons in life, I thank my children: Betsy Bales, Anne Strohm, John Harlan, Susan Borghese, and Julie Harlan-Schneider; and my grandchildren: Kate, Rachel, Liz, Christopher, Lauren, Nina, Sophia, Laura, Elinor, and Simone. My deep appreciation for her inquiring turn of mind, depth of knowledge, and wholehearted enthusiasm goes to my co-author, Mary Rivkin, who made our endeavor stimulating, rewarding, and pleasurable.—J.H.

My early childhood education students have helped generously with this book and its revisions; Lynne Cook especially contributed to this edition by reviewing new literature. Donna Neutze and Donna Dieckman at the Elementary Science Integration Project at UMBC aided us in that regard. I thank them all most warmly. Thanks as well to Carol Copple and Nathalie Cavanaugh for their assistance in obtaining new photographs, and to Susan Humphries for her on-going gifts of beautiful images of children learning outdoors.

My young grandchildren, Belden, Maya, Keown, and Wiley, offer new insights and inspiration. I am especially grateful to their parents—Caroline Seckinger, Gustave Carlson, Ina Clark, and Rob Seckinger—for connecting them to the natural world, and to me. Gustave has also given the book his graceful drawings—thank you.

Thanks always to Steve Rivkin and Jesse Rivkin for being very supportive during my interminable hours at the computer. My respect, admiration, and affection for my co-author, Jean Harlan, is unlimited.—M.R.

Discover the Companion Website Accompanying This Book

THE PRENTICE HALL COMPANION WEBSITE: A VIRTUAL LEARNING ENVIRONMENT

Technology is a constantly growing and changing aspect of our field that is creating a need for content and resources. To address this emerging need, Prentice Hall has developed an online learning environment for students and professors alike—Companion Websites—to support our textbooks.

In creating a Companion Website, our goal is to build on and enhance what the textbook already offers. For this reason, the content for each user-friendly website is organized by topic and provides the professor and student with a variety of meaningful resources. Common features of a Companion Website include:

FOR THE PROFESSOR—

Every Companion Website integrates Syllabus Manager™, an online syllabus creation and management utility.

- **Syllabus Manager™** provides you, the instructor, with an easy, step-by-step process to create and revise syllabi, with direct links into Companion Website and other online content without having to learn HTML.
- Students may logon to your syllabus during any study session. All they need to know is the web address for the Companion Website and the password you've assigned to your syllabus.
- After you have created a syllabus using **Syllabus Manager™**, students may enter the syllabus for their course section from any point in the Companion Website.
- Clicking on a date, the student is shown the list of activities for the assignment. The activities for each assignment are linked directly to actual content, saving time for students.
- Adding assignments consists of clicking on the desired due date, then filling in the details of the assignment—name of the assignment, instructions, and whether or not it is a one-time or repeating assignment.

- In addition, links to other activities can be created easily. If the activity is online, a URL can be entered in the space provided, and it will be linked automatically in the final syllabus.
- Your completed syllabus is hosted on our servers, allowing convenient updates from any computer on the Internet. Changes you make to your syllabus are immediately available to your students at their next logon.

FOR THE STUDENT—

- **Introduction**—General information about the topic and how it will be covered in the website.
- **Web Links**—A variety of websites related to topic areas.
- **Timely Articles**—Links to online articles that enable you to become more aware of important issues in early childhood.
- **Learn by Doing**—Put concepts into action, participate in activities, examine strategies, and more.
- **Visit a School**—Visit a school's website to see concepts, theories, and strategies in action.
- **For Teachers/Practitioners**—Access information you will need to know as an educator, including information on materials, activities, and lessons.
- **Current Policies and Standards**—Find out the latest early childhood policies from the government and various organizations, and view state, federal, and curriculum standards.
- **Resources and Organizations**—Discover tools to help you plan your classroom or center and organizations to provide current information and standards for each topic.
- **Electronic Bluebook**—Paperless method of completing homework or essays assigned by a professor. Finished work can be sent to the professor via email.
- **Message Board**—Virtual bulletin board to post and respond to questions and comments from a national audience.

To take advantage of these and other resources, please visit the *Science Experiences for the Early Childhood Years: An Integrated Affective Approach,* Eighth Edition, Companion Website at

www.prenhall.com/harlan

Brief Contents

Contents

11   Magnetism   223

12   The Effects of Gravity   237

13   Simple Machines   251

14   Sound   271

15   Light   287

Note: Every effort has been made to provide accurate and current Internet information in this book. However, the Internet and information posted on it are constantly changing, so it is inevitable that some of the Internet addresses listed in this textbook will change.

PART ONE

THE RATIONALE

An Integrated Approach to Science Learning

THE INGREDIENTS OF LEARNING

"Look, Teacher, my hand!" Jimmy spoke! At last, Jimmy had broken through the stoic silence of his first anxious month in Head Start. Crouched on the carpeted floor to blot up his juice spill, Jimmy was transfixed with wonder at the imprint of his hand on a paper towel. The surprise of encountering the familiar in an unexpected circumstance captured him both intellectually and emotionally. As Jimmy questioned his teacher and experimented with fresh towels, he chattered about his discovery with other children. His own irrepressible curiosity had finally drawn him into the circle of learners at our center.

How can a four-year-old like Jimmy focus with such intensity on a mundane experience with capillary action? Why, for that matter, do children want to know *why?* One part of the answer is that understanding the environment by interacting with it is the natural work of young children. At birth, infants are already equipped with reflexes, senses, and the capacity for emotional responses that gradually link up into information-gathering resources. For example, the separate abilities to see, to grasp, and to mouth objects soon connect into specific, emotionally satisfying ways to recognize and handle different materials.

These linkages and the consequent learning are made possible because of the remarkable way the brain develops as the infant experiences the world. The billions of brain cells (neurons) already in place at birth begin to connect into networks for communicating with other neurons. This happens as neurons branch out in direct response to stimulation from the environment, steadily shaping the infant brain into a thinking mind. Simple discoveries of cause and effect allow babies to solve playpen problems and reach out for new experiences. The new sensations, emotional responses, memories, and actions stimulate more neural branching and connections, allowing the processing of more information in "bootstrapping" fashion (Diamond & Hopson, 1998, p. 115). If children's resulting curiosity and exploring are encouraged, their probing for meaning broadens further as language and locomotion develop. With appropriate stimulation and support, children's inherent need to know continues to deepen and serves as part of their motivation to engage in more complex investigations such as Jimmy's.

When this innate human desire for understanding the world is organized into careful ways of collecting, testing, and sharing information, it is called *science*. Indeed, the word *science* is derived from the Latin root *scire*, meaning "to know." When we offer intriguing science experiences to young children, we nourish their natural human capacity to know. If we do this with sensitivity to their interests and feelings, we help engage the powerful affective component of knowing and learning.

The affective component of knowing and learning is a complex web of interrelated facets, including curiosity, emotional responses to life experiences, and the motivating self-beliefs stemming from our accomplishments: *self-efficacy*. The way children feel about themselves and their world influences their curiosity. There is an energizing reciprocal link between finding out and self-efficacy, between feelings of mastery of the newly learned and the desire to know more. Anxiety about unexplained or frightening events may lure children into finding answers. Pleasure in discovering awesome, delightful, or comforting features of the environment also furthers affective and cognitive growth. This chapter will consider some effects of these interrelationships, their biological basis, and multiple ways to use these interrelationships and biological givens to enhance science learning.

Curiosity

What is this thing called *curiosity?* By definition, *curiosity* is the desire to learn or know about something. Although a desire is an emotion, psychologists consider curiosity to be an *affect:* an activity prompted by emotions. Because the affective system organizes our thoughts and behavior, curiosity is a prerequisite for exploring the environment. With appropriate opportunities, curiosity continues throughout life as an energizing force that helps us reach intrinsically rewarding goals (Kashdan & Fincham, 2002).

Scientists and those in other creative occupations often refer to curiosity as a driving energy in their work. Whether curiosity ultimately leads us to groundbreaking discoveries, or simply enriches our lives by stimulating learning and personal growth, it is a mechanism to respect and encourage in our work with children.

Emotions

A reviewer of the first edition of this textbook in 1975 was startled by its then radical affective-cognitive orientation. He scribbled across one page with exaggerated penstrokes (perhaps revealing strong feelings), "What have feelings got to do with anything? This is a book about science!" Since then, significant advances in the neurosciences have provided a more complete understanding of the complex interactions between emotions, thought processes, and memory. The word *emotion* comes from two Latin root words meaning "to stir up" and "to move." Emotion is now seen as an amazing orchestration of mental functions. In a simplified way, we could think of these processes as a continuous sensory relay system. As we experience our environment with our senses, the information passes to the brain through structures in the midbrain. A reaction to the information registers in this emotion processing area, assessing how the environment is affecting us. This simultaneously integrates with specific reasoning and planning areas of the brain. It also sets in motion a cascade of neuronal and biochemical activities that affect both the brain and the body.

The areas and systems of the brain involved with emotional responses are connected by neurons to the rest of the brain. They form networks as part of the nervous system, communicating with the rest of the body as electrical information carriers.

Numerous biochemicals in the brain also contribute to emotional states. They are exquisitely sensitive to behavioral and environmental stimuli. These biochemical information carriers allow the brain to communicate rapidly with the body by way of the bloodstream. They also affect the neurons associated with learning, shaping our memories as we are forming them (Shonkoff & Phillips, 2000).

Most of this activity occurs beyond our conscious awareness. Our thoughts and emotions usually work together, but sometimes, powerful emotions can drive our actions without us consciously understanding why. Emotions are so important to our lives that, according to Restak, "Without emotions to guide us, we would be incapable of either decisions or plans. Emotions evolved to help us survive" (2001, p. 112).

Pleasure and curiosity combine into lasting learning.

Feelings and Learning

The terms *feelings* and *emotions* are commonly used interchangeably, but neuroscientists now view them as separate entities (Damasio, 1999). Feelings are the way that unconscious emotional responses are encoded and stored in the brain as consciously recognized memories. Those stored feelings influence future behavior, such as engagement in learning (Blair, 2002).

The interplay between thought, feelings, and emotion is of critical importance to learning because one of the functions of emotions is to arouse interest and prioritize what we pay attention to. Also, our emotional state when information is being received determines whether, and how well, we remember it. A positive classroom environment can raise the level of endorphins, the biochemical that induces pleasurable feelings and facilitates memory. The opposite is true of negative environments. Children in stressful childcare situations have shown elevated levels of cortisol, the stress hormone that inhibits memory processes (Greenspan, 2002).

Positive Feelings and Learning

Pleasure in learning awesome, delightful, or comforting features of the environment furthers affective and cognitive growth. A positive feeling about a discovery can motivate a child to continue exploring with renewed curiosity. This was true for six-year-old Amanda during her class visit to a butterfly garden. Amanda's face registered delight, awe, and satisfaction when she coaxed a spectacular blue morpho butterfly onto the back of her hand. As she studied the beautiful creature, her expression suddenly changed to open-mouthed surprise. She whispered to a guide, "Do butterflies pee?" The guide queried back, "What do you notice?"

Amanda thoughtfully examined the tiny orange droplet on her hand. A succession of expressions crossed her face: astonishment, a flicker of dismay, then recognition. "So that's what this is. He's just like us!" She sat, transfixed, quietly observing the placid blue morpho until it was time to leave. She gently transferred the butterfly to a convenient leaf, and slowly backed away. It's safe to surmise that Amanda's memories of this event will maintain her curiosity about butterflies, and etch lasting feelings of connectedness to a fellow creature not entirely unlike herself.

Negative Feelings and Learning

Negative feelings can also stimulate the need to know. Classic psychological studies have shown that when emotionally attached infants felt secure in their mother's presence, spontaneous curiosity and exploratory behaviors were enabled. Conversely, feelings of insecurity and strong fear can interrupt exploration and even paralyze curiosity. Ample research has confirmed that anxious experiences can disrupt attention, memory, and problem solving (Blair, 2002). Other studies by ethologists show that even though overwhelming fear prevents exploration, uncertainty tinged with a bit of fear of the unknown seems to stimulate curiosity and exploring.

This seemed to be true of Jake's ready anticipation of trouble. One of the smallest children in our class, Jake endured regular pummeling by his older brother at home. The boys' parents did not intervene because following their "boys-will-be-boys" beliefs required no action. But Jake brought his resentment to school, moving warily among his male classmates with clenched fists at the ready. Then, Jake became fascinated by our gravity experiences. As often as he could coax a partner, Jake claimed the playground teeter-totter where he could be in control. He could keep a bigger boy dangling above the ground or be in charge of creating a balance between them. In the classroom, he focused long solitary attention on using the balance scale and on finding ways to balance pennies on a ruler placed on a half-circle block fulcrum. Each time he mastered his self-created balance challenges, he exulted, "Now they're even!" Gradually Jake began to let down his guard and cautiously make friendly overtures to a boy about his size. We like to think that his perseverance with the balancing activities helped him grow emotionally and socially.

Anxiety about misunderstood or frightening events also may lure children into finding answers. Occasionally the connection between a child's anxious concern and his or her eagerness to find answers is clearly apparent. For example, the mother of four-year-old Matthew asked for advice on how to help her son get to sleep at night. He was unable to shut his eyes until he had counted all the stars he could see from his window. He needed to count them over and over to make sure they were still all in place. That provided reassurance for him that a star wouldn't fall on him while he was sleeping.

In response to his concern, a series of experiences was provided to build understanding about why things fall to earth, or in this case, why they don't fall. Matthew enjoyed some tangible explorations of the effects of magnetism, an invisible force that could, nonetheless, be felt in the hands of a fascinated boy. After many experiences with magnets, Matthew experimented with some simple effects of the greater invisible force of gravity. He found that the hardest toss by a strong boy couldn't send a ball beyond the pull of the earth's gravity. Even he himself always came back to earth after his highest leaps. Matthew helped build a carton spaceship to play at being an astronaut, floating so far from earth that its gravity could not pull him down. He frequently asked to be read a story about astronauts who traveled three days to reach the moon because it was so far away. He always chimed in at the part that told how stars were even farther away from Earth than the moon.

The day finally came when Matthew's mother reported that it was now easier for him to get to sleep. He only had to do one quick scan of the stars before climbing into bed. He explained confidently to his parents that earth's gravity isn't strong enough to pull down a star. In the years since then, Matthew's fascination with astronomy has continued. He and his family have made many visits to an observatory and a planetarium in a distant city, and he now plans to become a meteorologist. The story of Tony in Selma Fraiberg's classic book *The Magic Years* (1950) is a similar example of how a child's fear led to an enduring interest in science.

Teachers of young children don't often learn how experiences in their classrooms contribute to the long-term shaping of an individual's life. But when feedback like Matthew's story comes our way, it strengthens our convictions that emotionally reassuring or captivating experiences with natural and physical world events can have lasting value for children. Rachel Carson (1998, p. 56) wrote of this in her influential work on nature study, *The Sense of Wonder*: "Once the emotions have been aroused—a sense of the beautiful, the excitement of the new and the unknown, a feeling of sympathy, pity, admiration, or love—then we wish for knowledge about the object of our emotional response. Once found, it has lasting meaning." Surely the influence of feelings on what and how children learn about the world, and subsequently act toward it, is far too important to disregard.

Self-efficacy and Learning

For all of us, *self-efficacy*, the feeling of adequacy and effectiveness in dealing with life, is critical to learning success. With appropriate opportunities, the sense of self-efficacy develops as a belief that we have some degree of control over what happens to us. The way we think and feel about ourselves, and what we can accomplish as learners, influences our ability to focus attention and think strategically (Blair, 2002).

Science experiences have special potential for building a sturdy sense of self-efficacy: the belief in our ability to cope with problems based on our own competence. Martin Seligman's motivation studies (1992, pg. 151) suggest that this belief begins in infancy and develops throughout life as mastery motivation. He believes that if young children are not provided with, or are not allowed to cope with, problems that can be resolved through their own actions, a pattern of helplessness begins. Success that is too easily reached, as well as challenge that is too easily met, produces children with a limited capacity to cope with failure. Therefore, he suggests offering learning challenges in school that children can measure themselves against because meeting challenges helps shape a person's sense of self-worth and self-efficacy.

According to Seligman, our self-esteem and sense of competence do not depend so much on whether good or bad things happen to us, but on whether we believe we have some control over what happens to us. Early science experiences can provide children with some sense of control by allowing them to predict that certain things will happen; for example, "The pan of snow will change to water if we keep it indoors." Through this process, some of the confusion and uncertainty about events occurring around children can be replaced with an awareness of predictability. Children can learn that even they can bring about some of these small occurrences. Science knowledge helps develop the only control children can have over powerful and sometimes unpredictable natural forces. Children can control their *attitudes* through understanding the causes of an event and can control their helpless fear through training to cope safely with events such as earthquakes and violent storms. Science experiences are unique in fostering this strengthening influence on the child's personality.

MULTIPLE LEARNING PATHWAYS

The practice of extending learning through different modes has been followed by nursery and progressive school teachers for nearly a century. New understandings of brain anatomy explain the value of multimodal approaches to learning. Different features of an experience are encoded in different parts of the brain. These separate features are then linked together into more enduring memory systems deeper in the brain. This *elaborative* encoding process allows new information to be integrated with what is already known. The resulting more meaningful information becomes easier to remember (Schacter, 1996, p. 44). The implications for good teaching validate the intuitive understanding of those early nursery school and progressive teachers: that many learning pathways need to be provided for youngsters to develop their enormous intellectual potential most effectively.

Two Ways of Thinking

Cognitive neuroscientists assure us that we have two valid but different ways of thinking that work simultaneously:

1. *Conscious* thinking, which we are aware of doing, because we use language as we acquire and use information.
2. *Nonconscious* thinking, also referred to as *implicit learning* or *unconscious thought*, which goes on continuously beyond our conscious awareness because language is not involved.

Each form of thinking can enhance the other. We regularly draw on both conscious and nonconscious thought in all our mental activities. This is somewhat analogous to the computer that has an unseen DOS (digital operating system) constantly running under the software we are cognizant of using.

Pattern-seeking is one of the key nonconscious thought processes. It is the way young children "pick up" the complex patterns and unspoken rules of social behavior and of learning to talk. It explains three-year-old Caroline's use of her nonconscious knowledge of past-tense formation: "I teached him how to throw." *Imaging* is another nonconscious thought process. For example, we regularly call up mental images when we think nostalgically about a special event. *Metaphor use* is a third well-studied nonconscious thought process. Young Jake seemed to use his fascination with balancing things as a metaphor for making his social relationships come out even.

We all have had unexpected, "Aha, now I've got it!" breakthroughs when our nonconscious processes continued to work out a solution that had stumped our conscious thinking. In the realm of scientific thinking, such intuitive insights, as well as imagination, can be essential both for identifying problems to be solved, and for having hunches about how to pursue a solution. Nonconscious processing takes in vastly more details about what is going on around us than we perceive consciously, and use that information more rapidly than conscious thought can. (Schacter, 1996, pp. 187–191). It is very efficient at creating categories and making relational links to other information (Brandsford, Brown, & Cocking, 1999, p. 112).

When Eli offered a surprisingly sophisticated insight to a class discussion, he considered his words briefly, then said, "Wow! I didn't know I knew that!" Eli couldn't verbally explain how he came up with his sudden burst of understanding, but it was the result of valid mental activity. His teacher didn't dismiss it as a lucky guess. She respected it with, "That was good thinking, Eli." Because, as Damasio (1999, p. 42) says, "The brain knows more than the conscious mind reveals," we need to give credence to the validity of both forms of thought.

Some familiar teaching tools draw upon both forms of thought. For instance, time awareness, such as remembering rhythm patterns, is developed and encoded in memory nonconsciously (Salidis, 2001). When we embed science concepts in well-remembered rhythmic songs, such as pegging the evaporation concept into "The Eency Weency Spider," the consolidation makes for stronger encoding and retrieval of the concept. We strengthen learning when we encourage children to express imaginatively what they are learning with the creative qualities of nonconscious thinking.

Multiple Intelligences Theory

We have long known that there are many ways for our incredible brains to take in and process information into working knowledge. Yet, in 1983, when Harvard educator Howard Gardner described his theory of multiple intelligences in his book, *Frames of Mind,* it stirred controversy among psychologists. But Gardner's theory has steadily gained acceptance among educators because it explains their commonsense observations. It also offers theoretical support for providing a wide variety of media to teach concepts.

Gardner believes that intelligence is more than the single logical-mathematical processing of stored facts that intelligence tests assess. He sees intelligence as problem-solving, problem-creating, and problem-finding across a range of situations. He originally identified seven distinct, interlocking *kinds* of intelligence, possessed by all of us to some degree. They are: *logical-mathematical:* the ability to understand and use mathematical, logical, and scientific concepts; *linguistic:* the capacity to use language to express ideas; *musical:* the ability to think in music and to hear, recognize, and remember patterns; *spatial:* the ability to mentally represent the spatial world; *bodily-kinesthetic:* the capacity to use the body to solve a problem or make something; *interpersonal:* the ability to understand other people; and *intrapersonal:* the capacity to think about one's feelings and to understand oneself (1993). Later, Gardner added an eighth intelligence—*naturalist:* the ability to recognize and classify living things and see patterns in other aspects of the natural world (1997). Gardner proposes that each of us uses different combinations and degrees of these eight intelligences as we learn about and respond to our environment.

Although it is not clear exactly how these intelligences develop independently and interactively, identifying them has provided early childhood educators with a stronger rationale for using integrated curricula. Current research verifies the value of teaching subjects in multiple contexts (Brandsford, Brown, & Cocking, 1999, p. 50). Those multiple approaches help children to effectively construct and use socially valued knowledge, such as science.

AN INTEGRATED LEARNING FRAMEWORK

When we integrate meaningful science experiences with other curricular areas, we help children enhance their mental performance. Different features of an experience are encoded in different parts of the brain. These features are then linked together into more enduring memory systems deeper in the brain. The more fully information is processed over time, the more connections we make. The more consolidation takes place, the better the memory will be. Our teaching needs to provide a range of connections among different styles of absorbing, associating, and applying information. We need to help children reflect on the information they are gathering, relate it to something they already know, and form meaningful associations. We need to help children see that otherwise abstract concepts actually function in their familiar world. Then children with varying intellectual talents can find emotionally satisfying, meaningful paths to learning.

For these reasons a variety of enriching extensions are suggested for each of the major science topics found in Part Two of this book. Each of the learning opportunities described in the following paragraphs draws upon one or more of the multiple forms of intelligence identified by Gardner. The effect is diagrammed in Figure 1–1.

Math activities are an integral part of all science because they provide ways to quantify and record observations. Some of the suggested math activities in this text are necessary parts of a science experience. Others use science themes to provide a new context for using math skills. Both quantifying and numerical reasoning rely on the *logical-mathematical* intelligence identified by Gardner.

Music can strengthen science understanding in many ways. Melody can evoke positive feelings about these concepts. Lyrics can use literal or metaphoric ideas to strengthen recall. Rhythm reinforces song ideas through repetitive patterns. Hearing, in itself, is a sensory system that evokes strong memories. As tunes run through children's minds, they are reminded of the ideas expressed in the lyrics. Catchy melodies, lyrics, and rhythms are routinely used to remind consumers

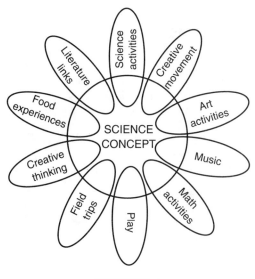

FIGURE 1–1

to buy products because they are such powerful memory cues. Songs and ballads were used to educate for centuries before books and schools existed. Tapping into *musical* intelligence can make learning easier and more durable. Improved spatial-temporal reasoning has been shown when preschool children were provided regular keyboard training in the patterns of rhythm and melody. Spatial-temporal reasoning underlies science and mathematics (Rauscher & Zupan, 2000). A recent brain scan study reveals that music is processed in regions set up to link short-term and long-term memory with sensory, emotional, and motoric associations. (Janata et al., 2002). So, we humans seem to be predisposed to remember and respond both emotionally and physically to music.

Literature links extend science concepts by associating them with fresh language and images, both metaphorically and as narrative. Whether incidentally embedded in fiction or introduced as focal themes of science-based stories and poems, science ideas register emotionally in children's minds as they encounter familiar knowledge in new situations. Encouraging children to write or tell their own stories and poems promotes the creative synthesis of fact, fantasy, and feelings, which uses *linguistic* intelligence. Preschool children also enjoy related fingerplays, which incorporate the *bodily-kinesthetic* form of intelligence into science learning.

Art activities are suggested in the text to stimulate intuitive creative expressions of children's own ideas. They are deliberately open-ended to encourage personal interpretations of science events (Stein, McNair, & Butcher, 2001). As children enjoy drawing, painting, and modeling to represent what they have learned, they

The integrated curriculum easily links science and literacy.

engage both *spatial* and *bodily-kinesthetic* intelligence. Some of the art suggestions incorporate materials used in the science experiences. This encourages divergent thinking because children invent new ways to use the materials. Craft projects that require children to follow specific directions to achieve a certain end-result product are *not* suggested as art activities.

Play situations afford young children chances to test out and apply science ideas imaginatively. Memory is enhanced when concepts can be acted out by the learner (Brown, Craik, & Fergus, 2000). This text suggests two forms of dramatic play: creative drama ideas for impromptu guided dramatization of known stories, and spontaneous play themes for which a few props are supplied to stimulate children's own play ideas. Barbara Biber (1979, p. 6) reminded us that dramatic play has been considered a valid form of learning since the pioneering days of nursery school nearly 75 years ago: "It was seen as a means of deepening insights, integrating knowledge, and finding identification on a personal level." Later research showed that simple spontaneous play and science are complementary aspects of problem solving. Science gives structure to activities, while play encourages creative behaviors and positive attitudes toward solving problems (Wolfe, Cummins, & Myers, 1998). Note, however, that any play loses its value as relaxed, pleasurable activity if adults hover closely, ever ready to capitalize on "teachable moments." Play can draw upon *linguistic, spatial, bodily-kinesthetic,* and *interpersonal* forms of intelligence.

Creative movement is a joyful, relaxing way to increase conceptual understanding and strengthen retention of information. Memory encoding of physical events takes place as abstract ideas are intuitively translated into concrete physical movements of the body. Hannaford (1995, p. 87) tells us, "Before the muscles move the bones, something has to happen in the mind. Attention must be focused to accomplish a physical task well." Spontaneous expression through movement calls forth both *spatial* and *bodily-kinesthetic* forms of intelligence, and sometimes *musical* and *interpersonal* intelligences.

Creative thinking is encouraged through open-ended strategies that reframe concepts with new associations. Using visualization and imagination, science concepts can be tested and clarified by reversing events, taking ideas apart to create fantasy solutions, and looking at ideas from new perspectives. Such activities encourage flexibility in shifting between rational and intuitive styles of thinking and can stimulate new interest in a science topic. Creative thinking activities draw upon *intrapersonal* intelligence.

Food experiences use the sensory input of taste and smell to strengthen the recall of concepts. The pleasure of being involved in preparing or sampling good things to eat provides a heightened emotional state for lasting memories. All of us have vivid connections between particular foods and the memories of the feelings we associated with those foods. Edible science experiences can strengthen concept retention by using *bodily-kinesthetic* intelligence.

Field trips add relevance and validate the science information learned in school (Leary, 1996). Children are proud to recognize that what they know from the classroom has significance in the wider world. It is important to invite visitors into the classroom who are involved in work that applies science concepts that students have learned, thus bringing the field to the school. Classroom windows sometimes become impromptu resources for verifying science learning. For example, the unexpected appearance of a squirrel on the window ledge or the activity of a street repair crew can become a welcome illustration instead of a distraction.

The schoolyard can be a fine location for connecting classroom concepts to the wider world. There is a strong need to make the schoolgrounds as enriching as classrooms, particularly in child-care settings where children spend a preponderance of their waking and learning hours. Recent research corroborates the long advocacy of the outdoors by early childhood educators and environmental/outdoor educators. Children whose education emphasized the outdoor environment as a context for all curricula were found to have higher academic achievement than children in traditional classrooms (Lieberman & Hoody, 1998; Glenn, 2000). Suggestions for improving the schoolyard are offered in each chapter.

This integrated approach to science education weaves physical, sensory, and emotional activities into the total learning process. It encourages the use of both conscious and nonconscious thinking. This approach has been affirmed by the National Association for the Education of Young Children (2001) in its Standards. It is also consistent with the recommendations in the National Science Education Standards that were established by a consensus of hundreds of teachers, scientists, and policymakers. These standards call for a developmentally appropriate curriculum that is connected to other school subjects, coordinated with mathematics programs, and interesting and relevant to children (National Committee on Science Education Standards and Assessment, 1996, see Appendix D).

PROMOTING CONCEPT CONNECTIONS

Children need to reflect on new information and make meaningful associations, relating it to things already known. Two important ways of doing this are less direct than the integrating activities, as they depend upon a teacher's ability to plan ahead to apply them. The methods are (1) *maintaining concepts* by applying them, and (2) *linking concepts* to previously acquired concepts, putting the new information into the context of the larger picture. If the topics to be linked are presented sequentially whenever possible, children can be greatly helped to pull together relationships by themselves. The understandings gleaned from one set of activities can then lead directly or transfer indirectly to those that follow. Each chapter in Part Two of this book offers general suggestions for maintaining concepts and linking *new concepts* to already established concepts. These concept connections surround the integrating activities model as depicted in Figure 1–2.

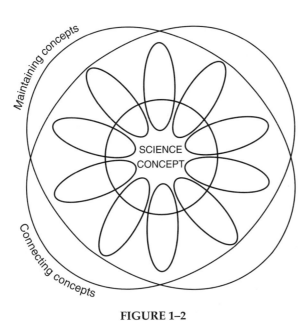

FIGURE 1–2

REFERENCES

BIBER, B. (1979). Thinking and feeling. *Young Children, 35,* 1 (November), 4–16.

BLAIR, C. (2002). Integrating cognition and emotion in a neurobiological conceptualization of children's functioning at school entry. *American Psychologist, 57,* 111–125.

BRANDSFORD, J., BROWN, A., & COCKING, R. (Eds.). (1999). *How people learn: Brain, mind, experience, and school.* Washington, DC: National Academy Press.

BROWN, S., & CRAIK F.I.M. (2000). Encoding & retrieval of memory. In E. Tulvig & F.I.M. Craik (Eds.), *The Oxford handbook of memory* (pp. 137–148). New York: Oxford University Press.

CARSON, R. (1998). *The sense of wonder.* New York: HarperCollins.

DAMASIO, A. (1999). *The feeling of what happens: Body and emotion in the making of consciousness.* New York: Harcourt Brace.

DIAMOND, M., & HOPSON, J. (1998). *Magic trees of the mind: How to nurture your child's intelligence, creativity, and healthy emotions from birth through adolescence.* New York: Dutton.

FRAIBERG, S. (1950). *The magic years.* New York: Norton.

GARDNER, H. (1997). *Extraordinary minds.* New York: Basic Books.

GARDNER, H. (1983/1993). *Frames of mind* (1st/2nd ed.). New York: Basic Books.

GLENN, J. L. (2000). *Environment-based education: Creating high-performance schools and students.* Washington, DC: The National Environmental Education and Training Foundation.

GREENSPAN, S. (2002) *The four-thirds solution: Solving the day care crisis in America.* Cambridge, MA: Perseus Books.

HANNAFORD, C. (1995). *Smart moves: Why learning is not all in your head.* Arlington, VA: Great Oceans Publishing.

JANATA, P., BIRK, J., VAN HORN, J., LEMAN, M., TILLMANN, B., & BARUCHA, J. (2002). The cortical topography of tonal structures underlying western music. *Science, 298,* 2167–2170.

KASHDAN, T., & FINCHAM, F. (2002) Facilitating creativity by regulating curiosity. *American Psychologist, 57,* 373–374.

LEARY, R. (1996). Field trip tips. *Science and Children, 34,* 27–29.

NATIONAL ASSOCIATION FOR THE EDUCATION OF YOUNG CHILDREN. (2001). *2001 standards for the baccalaureate or initial level.* Washington, DC: Author.

NATIONAL COMMITTEE ON SCIENCE EDUCATION STANDARDS AND ASSESSMENT. (1996). *National science education standards.* Washington, DC: National Research Council.

LIEBERMAN, G. A., & HOODY, L. L. (1998). *Closing the achievement gap: Using the environment as an integrating context for learning.* San Diego, CA: State Environment and Education Roundtable.

RAUSCHER, F., & ZUPAN, M. (2000). Classroom keyboard instruction improves kindergarten children's spatial-temporal performance: A field experiment. *Early Childhood Research Quarterly, 15,* 215–228.

RESTAK, R. (2001). *The secret life of the brain.* Washington, DC: Dana Press & Joseph Henry Press.

SALIDIS, J. (2001). Nonconscious temporal cognition. *Memory and Cognition, 29,* 111–119.

SCHACTER, D. (1996). *Searching for memory.* New York: Basic Books.

SELIGMAN, M. (1992). *Helplessness.* San Francisco: Freeman.

SHONKOFF, J. P., & PHILLIPS, D. A. (Eds.). (2000). *From neurons to neighborhoods: The science of early childhood development.* Washington, DC: National Academy Press.

STEIN, M., McNAIR, S., & BUTCHER, J. (2001). Drawing on student understanding. *Science and Children, 38,* 18–22.

WOLFE, C., CUMMINS, R., & MYERS, C. (1998). Dabbling, discovery, and dragonflies: Scientific inquiry and exploratory representational play. In D. Bergen & D. Fromberg (Eds.), *Play: Birth to twelve and beyond* (pp. 68–76). New York: Garland.

Science Participants: Children, Teachers, Families, and Communities

YOUNG CHILDREN AS THINKERS

It is tempting to think of young children's minds as fresh pages to be written on, or clay to be molded by skillful, caring teachers. It is so tempting, in fact, that many inexperienced teachers and parents equate "telling" with teaching. Unfortunately, much writing about education characterizes teaching as "delivery of instruction," as if children's minds were loading docks upon which teachers can deposit boxes of information and skills.

A more realistic view of how children's minds work comes from an ever-widening stream of cognitive psychology research. This view is reinforced by the once-again-appreciated observations of parents and teachers who work daily with children. Both sources see children's minds constantly engaging in sense-making. Consider this story a mother reported to her son's teacher:

Three-year-old Christopher was baking gingerbread with his mother when he asked, "Where is the cinnamon-god?" His surprised mother probed gently to puzzle out the meaning of his question. She learned that the rabbi from a neighboring synagogue had recently visited the children at Christopher's preschool. God, synagogue, cinnamon, cinnamon-god: Christopher had put all the pieces together. He had constructed his own knowledge.

Most likely, Christopher had used previous experiences with cinnamon—something he could touch, smell, taste, and see—as a base of understanding on which to hook the new information. His mother then helped him refashion the connection to conform to more commonly held definitions and pronunciations of *cinnamon* and *synagogue*. Because his mother offered more information, Christopher could form new, more sophisticated knowledge. He could do this without being aware of how marvelously his mind was working. Because at his age he is learning effortlessly about nine new words a day, every experience Christopher has is a source of developing knowledge for him.

Cognition Theories

The role of active experience in learning was both theorized about and demonstrated by John Dewey and Maria Montessori early in the 20th century. Jean Piaget added to their work by focusing on details of the sequencing and content of children's thought development. His explorations led him and his followers to what is today's dominant cognition theory, *constructivism*. This is the view that children build knowledge internally by interacting with the world to learn how it works and to make meaning of it. Constructivism implies that there must be experiences from which to construct knowledge. Piaget especially valued the development of logical-mathematical knowledge, which is identified with science knowledge.

Piaget contributed immeasurably to the development of the early childhood education field by maintaining that young children think differently, in some circumstances, than do older children and adults. He postulated invariant, age-related stages of intellectual development. He believed that young children require a special kind of curriculum because their thinking is more concrete and less logical. However, later research has indicated that young children are not as illogical and concrete in their thinking as Piaget claimed.

It appears that both children and adults—without sufficient experiences, education, and expertise—misconceive aspects of the physical and social worlds, perceiving the world through intuition and common sense. Much of the knowledge so constructed is very resistant to change by schooling (Gardner, 1991). If this is so, in what way do teachers matter? The classic, but newly influential, work of Soviet psychologist Lev Vygotsky (1962) addressed this. It added to Piaget's theories the insight that children are helped and influenced in their knowledge construction by the people around them. For instance, our preschooler, Christopher, will learn to distinguish between cinnamon and a synagogue because his mother shared her society's understanding that these things are distinguishable. She interacted with Christopher in ways that will bring him into that shared understanding.

Currently, the most comprehensive theory of intelligence development is the fresh approach of Stanley Greenspan's work (1999). He has identified the crucial element, missing from earlier theories, that enables the newborn brain to evolve smoothly into a thinking mind. This element is the powerful role that emotions play in thinking and learning from the start of life onward. This can be seen in the earliest reciprocal exchanges between infant and caregiver. The infant learns that smiling in pleasure at seeing the caregiver elicits smiles in return! Such emotion-based, cause-effect learning occurs far sooner than Piaget recognized.

Greenspan notes that each sensation experienced by the infant also produces an emotional response. The experiences are then coded and stored simultaneously in memory for *both* their physical and emotional impact. *These dual codings are the origins of intelligence.*

Greenspan's 25 years of child observation and research have pinpointed six necessary emotional/intellectual, experience-based stages from infancy through the preschool years. These stages build the foundations of intelligence. Intriguingly, neurological research shows that each developmental stage specified by Greenspan coincides with a parallel early brain-growth step (Chugani & Phelps, 1986).

The progressive, emotional/intellectual stages identified by Greenspan are the abilities to (1) calmly focus and attend; (2) engage with others; (3) communicate needs intentionally; (4) engage in complex problem solving; (5) use ideas and words; and (6) combine ideas together with logical bridges as a basis for rational thinking. *Greenspan's fundamental insight is that from the beginning of life, emotional interactions with caregivers enable these abilities to unfold.*

Successful attainment of the six core stages underlies a child's later ability to master challenges, think flexibly and creatively, and maintain curiosity about the world. While the maturing child will continue to go through many additional stages of intellectual development, these initial necessary stages form the groundwork upon which future growth will be built.

According to Greenspan, subsequent mental levels will be constructed as the child experiences new challenges, and integrates ideas and feelings related to them (1977, p. 103). The continuous, interrelated growth of intelligence and emotional health also contributes to the formation of a sense of self. Early emotion-based cause/effect thinking also forms the roots of morality. It leads to awareness of responsibility for one's actions, and to the development of empathy for the needs and rights of others.

Beyond explaining the origins and development of intelligence, this important construct yields a significant therapeutic framework for identifying and remediating children's learning difficulties and emotional problems. Also, by confirming the power of the emotional context of learning to engage the mind, it provides an invaluable key to successful teaching.

For decades, early childhood educators have valued the practice of providing plenty of time and a wide variety of media to teach concepts. Those multiple approaches help children effectively construct and use socially valued knowledge, such as science.

In this text, we try to guide teachers in helping children construct powerful science understandings. By appealing to children's emotional and intellectual interest, by providing multidisciplinary approaches to concepts, and by modeling how teachers can spark and maintain children's engagement with science, we hope to encourage a community of learners. In this community, children and teachers work together to build understanding from their daily efforts.

Young Children as Persons

Earlier, we looked at the influence children's feelings about themselves and their physical world have on their ability to think and learn. Learning, or failing to learn, is also strongly influenced by children's feelings about their place in the social world. The characteristic ways children feel about themselves and relate to others are central parts of their personalities. The classic work of Erik Erikson (1977) identified general developmental trends in personality growth that both contribute to and are enhanced by successful learning. These trends are significant affective components of cognitive development.

Sense of Initiative

If children's earliest experiences have promoted trust in others, and if children have then developed a good sense of autonomy, the next positive personality trend, a

Adam is immersed in quiet insect observation.

sense of initiative, unfolds. Three- and four-year-olds who are developing a sense of initiative have great energy to invest in activity. They want to know what they can do. They are eager for new experiences and new information about their world. Emerging reasoning powers blend with a developing imagination, leading the child to ask searching questions. Children's delightful curiosity in this phase is endlessly expressed as "Why?" A budding behavior control system allows children to slow activity long enough to become immersed in events that capture their attention.

Preschoolers seek the acceptance of children who are like themselves in some way and who have mutual interests. This sociability means that preschool children rarely work alone at the science table, although sharing equipment and materials with others may still be somewhat difficult for them. In general, personality developments in this stage make it an ideal time to explore with children the regularities, relationships, and wonders of the world close at hand.

Sense of Industry

Young school-age children who have succeeded in developing a sense of initiative move toward the next positive personality trend, described by Erikson as the *sense of industry*. Eagerness to do meaningful tasks and to become good at them is evident. Children may persist in working at a task until it is completed, just for the sake of satisfaction in accomplishment. During this phase, mastering challenges enhances children's sense of competence. These children are able to work cooperatively with others because they have good inner control over their behavior. The desire to follow the classroom rules is especially visible in kindergartners. If all goes reasonably well in children's lives, this positive personality trend continues through the remaining early childhood years.

Respecting Personal Development Traits

The natural tendencies to learn where one belongs and what one can do in the social and physical worlds, to create and imagine, to seek answers, to become increasingly effective as an active doer and thinker, and to take pride in independent accomplishment and growing competence all support the interest and persistence needed to learn throughout life. These tendencies and abilities, however, can be misdirected and even diminished to the point of eventual failure in first grade when they are channeled too early into formal training in academic skills and fact memorization (Marcon, 1994). These tendencies are respected and nurtured when preschools and kindergartens allow children to choose whether or not to participate in science explorations.

THE TEACHERS

Who Can Teach Science?

Any teacher who is capable of maintaining a classroom atmosphere of warmth, acceptance, and nurturance meets the basic qualifications for guiding young children in discovery science. The classroom observational studies of Hyson and Molinaro (2000) confirm that children are more engaged in learning activities when teachers are emotionally warm, personal, and involved. In addition, a positive attitude toward science and the ability to carry out the catalyst, consultant, and facilitator roles are needed for good teaching. However, little can be taught when a close rapport between child and teacher is missing. Children learn most from people with whom they feel the bond of personal interest and caring.

Attitude Contagion

Children's long-term attitudes toward science as subject matter begin with the attitudes of teachers whom children encounter in their earliest exposures to science. A teacher's positive attitudes toward science may have a long history. For some teachers, these good feelings accumulated during their own satisfying exposures to science in elementary and secondary schooling situations. Other teachers may have retained strong science interests in spite of inadequate school experiences. They may have had an "answer person" in their lives: a parent, a grandparent, or perhaps a camp naturalist who had interesting information to share and the patience to help a child find answers. People with such fortunate backgrounds feel comfortable teaching science, and they recognize the importance of science in their students' lives.

On the other hand, older children's negative attitudes toward science may have been "caught" from unenthusiastic teachers who relied on textbooks as the only source for gaining information. Those teachers may have been too unsure of themselves to allow children to consider alternatives to the textbook explanations, or to discover science concepts through experimentation. Many female students lost interest in science when they came up against gender bias in the classroom. They observed male students receiving preferential teacher attention because of the stereotyped assumption that males have a stronger aptitude for science. Still others have been discouraged by science courses that emphasized memorizing facts rather than understanding the principles that affect our daily lives.

Negative attitudes toward teaching science can be turned around by opportunities to observe and participate in hands-on science experiences with eager young children. Participation in activity-based science education courses or workshops can restore lost confidence and revitalize faded interest. Classroom follow-up studies of teachers who have participated in activity-based science workshops reflect shifts toward more positive attitudes.

Authentic Interest

The teacher's authentic interest in finding out more about something is a vital part of the positive teaching attitude. This interest implies a willingness to learn along with the children when they lack answers. The ability to admit to not knowing everything is one of the traits of a good teacher.

The teacher's own interest in finding out sustains the children's ready curiosity. It can revive curiosity in children who have been belittled for asking questions, and it can rebuild curiosity that has atrophied in an unstimulating environment. When the teacher's own sense of wonder is alive and active, curiosity behavior is modeled for the children. This important attitude has a fundamental place in the science-teaching framework, as indicated in Figure 2–1. If the teacher is indifferent about how things work, why should the children care?

Teaching Roles

Effective guidance of discovery science calls for four teaching roles:

1. The *facilitator* creates a learning environment in which each child has a chance to grow. Planning, gathering needed cast-off materials, and actually trying experiments are science facilitator tasks. In this role, there is a tolerance for messiness as children work, a willingness to risk new ventures, and an ability to profit from mistakes.

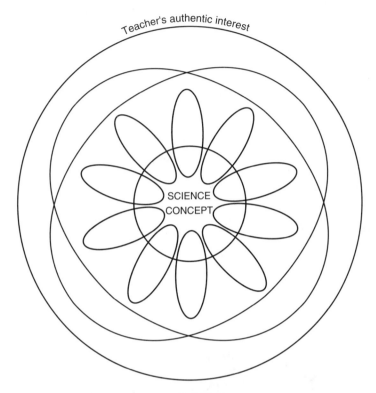

FIGURE 2–1

2. The *catalyst* turns on children's intellectual power by helping them become aware of themselves as thinkers and problem solvers. This role contrasts with the "teacher" image so many of us carry from our own school days in which the teacher seemed to be the ultimate source of all knowledge. A teacher like this can dim children's intellectual power by somehow magnifying the distance between the teacher's knowledge and that of the child. Catalysts, on the other hand, set a positive, encouraging tone by staying in touch with their own excitement in discovery.

3. The *consultant* observes carefully, listens closely, and answers questions simply while children engage in their explorations. In this role, small bits of information can be offered as learning cues, and questions can be asked of a child to help him or her focus on the relevant parts of a problem. The consultant allows each child time to reflect on the new idea and tackle the solution independently. This role often intimidates beginning teachers until they can accept themselves as learners, too. The consultant role is a supportive coaching role rather than a directive one.

4. The *model* deliberately demonstrates to children the important traits of successful learners, such as curiosity, appreciation, persistence, and creativity.

Lillian Katz (1985) defines these characteristics as *dispositions:* habits of mind or tendencies to respond to situations in particular ways. Katz points out that, although these qualities are essential, adults rarely identify and demonstrate these dispositions toward learning; yet, these dispositions are best learned through example. We model these positive learning dispositions when we share our personal experiences and thought processes with children. We model persistence by describing our own efforts; for example: "At first I couldn't make it work, but I just kept on trying until it did work." We model creativity when we reveal a problem we solved in a new way; for example: "I needed a better way to let you see both sides of the moth. Then, I had an idea that worked. I taped these two plastic lids together to make this neat display case for the moth."

Teachers who hold positive attitudes and understand their necessary roles are well rewarded by both personal growth and by the pleasure of sharing the sense of mastery that children find through their science discoveries.

The teacher as consultant observes carefully, listens closely, and answers questions simply.

THE FAMILIES

All parents have information about the world that can be passed on to their children—to their mutual benefit. Daniella's grandmother contributed the cecropia cocoon that, months later, provided us an hour of breathless wonder as the moth struggled free in the full view of 20 children. Four-year-old Maya was able to share solid information about many kinds of boats and their uses because she and her parents watched all the boats in the bay in front of their house. These family members enriched the learning of a whole class. They also intensified the interest of their own children in knowing the world because they endorsed the value of that knowledge.

The teaching role of family members is unique and vital. They, not classroom teachers, have the only continuous opportunity to guide a child's intellectual growth. The earliest imprinting of attitudes of appreciation or disregard for the natural or man-made world takes place within that primary relationship. This teaching by example occurs as part of the child's socialization, whether consciously or not.

The power of parents' supportive interest as motivation for children's immediate learning achievement is well documented. A recent review of the research concluded, "Nothing affects the academic outcome for a child as much as the involvement of a parent or other adult caregiver in that child's education," (Barber, Parizeau, & Bergman, 2002). Early parental encouragement is particularly significant for women and minorities in college math and science (Hammrich, 1997). Bloom's (1985) study of the early development of successful, talented adults (including scientists) consistently revealed parental support for the child's special interest, as well as encouragement to persevere and pursue those interests wholeheartedly. Our own science teaching can help generate parental interest where it might be lacking. When children take home evidence of practical problem-solving ability or share science information that has meaning in the adult world, parents rarely fail to respond positively.

Since its inception, early childhood education has striven for a teaching partnership with families. The National Association for the Education of Young Children, in articulating professional standards for teachers, places the creation of "respectful, reciprocal relationships that support and empower families" as the second of just five standards (2001, p. 14). The U.S. Department of Education encourages parents to prepare their children for school science with its booklet, *Helping Your Child Learn Science.* (See Appendix B.) The National Science Teachers Association (1994) adopted a position statement on parental involvement in science education. It gives priority to encouraging parents to help their children by seeing science everywhere, doing science activities together, and taking advantage of community resources of many kinds—efforts this textbook has been advocating since its first edition in 1976.

Unfortunately, many parents do not realize that they possess science knowledge that could be comfortably shared with their children. They may never have experienced the companionable pleasure of watching an impressive caterpillar with their child. Suggestions from teachers, such as the Family and Community

Support ideas listed in each activity chapter in this text, can draw parents into contributing to classroom inquiries. They can support their children's interest in science by helping with the Exploring at Home projects for each of the major science topics presented in Part Two of this book. They are found in Appendix B.

These projects are intentionally presented in a lighthearted way to avoid inappropriate performance demands by parents that discourage rather than encourage their children's efforts. Each of these related activities may be duplicated by classroom teachers and sent home with the clear intent of offering family fun, rather than required homework. To emphasize the special role the family plays in children's education, most of these activities are those that are best done at home at night, that directly relate to the home, or that are long-term and encompass beginning-to-end cycles that can have special value for families (Furman, 1990). A bibliography listing home-based science project books of special interest to parents appears in Appendix B.

COMMUNITIES

Wonderful resources to enhance science education outside the classroom are flourishing in communities throughout the country. Interactive children's science museums, nature centers, zoos, aquariums, and planetariums offer informal science programs for children and families in pleasurable, noncompetitive settings. Youth groups, churches, libraries, universities, and other municipal organizations are sponsoring recreational science activities to stimulate interest in science. These agencies are creating science linkages with schools through hands-on science as leisure activities, summer camps, family science festivals, traveling museum units, and outreach classes for teachers. Many programs are designed to reach underserved populations where families are less able to encourage their children's curiosity about the world. Through such projects, these youngsters can come to formal school science activities better prepared to enjoy and benefit from them.

Most of this growth has resulted from initiatives and partial funding by the National Science Foundation (NSF) over the past 3 decades. The NSF has pulled together the collaborative efforts of 15 other federal agencies, large corporations, national youth groups, professional science organizations, and the media to improve the quality of science education and to raise the general level of science literacy in this country. Excellent television science programs, such as *Nova* and *Zoom*, are underwritten by these collaborative funding sources.

One strong advocate of informal science learning is the pioneering brain researcher Marion Diamond. It was her work with the effects of enriched environments on brain growth that triggered the infant stimulation movement 25 years ago (Diamond & Hopson, 1998). Her appreciation of the benefits her own children gained at the exciting Lawrence Hall of Science Discovery Center at the University of California-Berkeley prompted her to assume its directorship for many years. Many of these successful Lawrence Hall of Science programs have been published for use in schools as part of the series *Great Explorations in Math and Science* (GEMS).

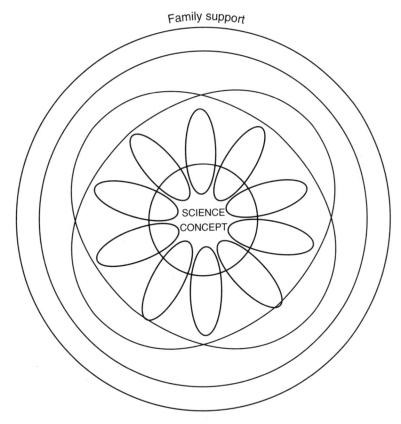

Family support

SCIENCE CONCEPT

FIGURE 2–2

As we write this chapter, at least 50% of American homes are connected to the Internet. This important resource for informal education is growing and changing so rapidly, and the quality is so uneven, that we are very cautious in suggesting specific Web sites. We recommend that you become acquainted with the American Library Association's Web site selection criteria, "How to Tell If You Are Looking at a Great Web site," at *http://www.ala.org/parentspage/greatsites/criteria.html*. These guidelines can help families choose appropriate play and learning sites for their children.

The influence of family and community support completes the science-learning framework, as shown in Figure 2–2.

REFERENCES

BARBER, J., PARIZEAU, N., & BERGMAN, L. (2002). *Spark your child's success in math and science: Practical advice for parents.* Berkeley, CA: Lawrence Hall of Science, University of California, Berkeley.

BLOOM, B. W. S. (Ed.). (1985). *Developing talent in young people.* New York: Ballantine Books.

CHUGANI, H., & PHELPS, M. (1986). Maturational changes in cerebral functioning in infants, determined by positron emission tomography. *Science, 231,* 840–844.

DIAMOND, M., & HOPSON, J. (1998). *Magic trees of the mind: How to nurture your child's intelligence, creativity, and healthy emotions from birth through adolescence.* New York: Dutton.

ERIKSON, E. (1977). *Childhood and society.* New York: Norton.

FURMAN, E. (1990). Plant a potato—learn about life (and death). *Young Children, 46,* 15–20.

GARDNER, H. (1991). *The unschooled mind.* New York: Basic Books.

GREENSPAN, S. (1997). *The growth of the mind.* Cambridge, MA: Perseus Books.

GREENSPAN, S. (1999). *Building healthy minds.* Cambridge, MA: Perseus Books.

HAMMRICH, P. (1997). Yes, daughter, you can. *Science and Children, 34,* (4), 21–24.

HYSON, M., & MOLINARO, J. (2001) Learning through feeling: Children's development, teacher's beliefs and relationships, and classroom practices. In S. Goldbeck (Ed.), *Psychological perspectives on early childhood education: Reframing dilemmas in research and practice* (pp. 107–131). Mahwah, NJ: Earlbaum.

KATZ, L. (1985). *Dispositions in early childhood education.* ERIC/EECE Bulletin, 18.

MARCON, R. (1994). Doing the right thing for children: Linking research and policy reform in the District of Columbia public schools. *Young Children, 49* (7), 8–20.

NATIONAL ASSOCIATION FOR THE EDUCATION OF YOUNG CHILDREN. (2001). *2001 Standards for the Baccalaureate or Initial Level.* Washington, DC: Author.

NATIONAL SCIENCE TEACHERS ASSOCIATION. (August, 1994). *NSTA position statement: Parent involvement in science education.* Washington, DC: Author.

VYGOTSKY, L. S. (1962). *Thought and language.* New York: Wiley.

Guiding Science Learning in the Early Years

GUIDED SCIENCE

Minstrel Tom Hunter was wondering aloud with first and second graders about clouds. He has learned that asking about action leads to fruitful thinking, so had asked, "What do clouds do?" A flurry of answers emerged: They make rain, they move fast, they move slow, they cover the sun, they disappear. One child seemed distant from the conversation, but finally put up her hand. "I know what clouds do—they pretend." "Really?" "Yes, they pretend to be an old man. Or a horse, or a castle, or a tree."

This story illustrates the joy and difficulty of guiding young children to acquire a "foundation for understanding core scientific concepts"(NAEYC, 2001, p. 24). Children observe, listen, reflect, and then invent their own understandings of the world. Some of these understandings are what we can call "science" and others are poetry, ethics, or fantasy, for example. As teachers, one of our goals is to give children access to the widely shared understandings of the natural world that constitute "science," and another is to help them experience the processes that create those understandings: observation, experimentation, careful recording of information, and willingness to think creatively.

In this text, we present "focused exploration of meaningful content" (NAEYC, 2001, p. 24) that will guide teachers in helping children meet national and state standards for science education in content, disposition, and processes. The experiences offered here will encourage children to enjoy science as a school subject and to think of themselves as competent in science. The processes used in these experiences as summarized by NAEYC are as follows.

Raise questions about objects and events around them.
Explore materials, objects, and events by acting upon them and noticing what happens.

Make careful observations of objects, organisms, and events, using all their senses.

Describe, compare, sort, classify, and order in terms of observable characteristics and properties.

Use a variety of simple tools to extend their observations (e.g., hand lens, measuring tools, eye droppers).

Engage in simple investigations, including making predictions, gathering and interpreting data, recognizing simple patterns, and drawing conclusions.

Record observations, explanations, and ideas through multiple forms of representation.

Work collaboratively with others, share and discuss ideas, and listen to new perspectives. (NAEYC, 2001, p. 24.)

These skills have widespread use in the preschool and primary years; competence in them provides a strong basis for ongoing academic success in science as well as other disciplines. In our observation, however, it seems that science as a subject is increasingly ignored in the primary grades, and hence we urge teachers, both new and experienced, to reflect on the powerful reasons to include guided science in their curriculum.

Reasons for Guided Discovery Science

One of the best means of helping children know the world at hand is to organize materials so children can explore, question, reason, and discover answers through their own physical and mental activity. This guided discovery approach to science learning emphasizes *how* to find answers, as well as *what* can be learned. When discovery science experiences are seen as part of the child's continuous search for knowledge, it makes good sense to support and enable that search in the classroom in these basic ways:

- Discovery science values and rewards curiosity as a valid learning tool.
- Discovery science encourages individuality and creativity in children's problem-solving. This leads to better retention of the concepts attained. Interestingly, the four steps of science as a way of knowing and thinking are the same ones used to describe the creative thinking process.
- Discovery science validates the fundamental learning style of direct involvement with materials. It builds upon spontaneous experiencing, touching, and trying by the very young. Active participation remains so important to knowing throughout life that our language uses the term *firsthand* to mean something that is known from the original source.
- Discovery science experiences in early schooling help to gradually replace the young child's intuitive explanations of the unknown. Such experiences demystify bewildering events but respectfully retain the profound and beautiful aspects of natural occurrences.
- Discovery science provides a means of focusing the attention of the restless child, the anxious child who is preoccupied with personal concerns,

and the bored child who is understimulated by less-challenging aspects of the curriculum.

- Discovery science has appeal for resistant learners who have come to protect themselves from inappropriate pressure to perform formal learning tasks. The playlike quality of exploring real materials reduces the stress that more precise paperwork tasks produce. Discovery science allows more physical and social involvement than do the more structured forms of schoolwork. Pressured children can put aside their resistance and restore their sense of themselves as learners when they engage in science activities.

- Discovery science, by its very nature, provides an intriguing path to the goal of developing children's intellectual potential. Any form of learning that includes the manipulation of interesting materials is highly motivating to children. The discovery science activities and cross-curricular extensions in this book lend themselves to programs where language learning and content are integrated, such as the language experience approach, the whole-language approach to reading, and the project approach to curriculum development. The sensory and psychomotor extensions fit well into English as a second language (ESL) programs that emphasize total physical response as a learning strategy.

Guided discovery science recognizes and builds upon the central importance of emotional engagement to thinking, doing, and understanding.

GUIDING LEARNERS

Teaching Styles

At one point in our understanding of constructivism, many teachers hesitated to "interfere" in children's thought processes. They tried not to talk to children about what they were doing. Other more behavioristic teachers continued to consider children to be empty vessels needing to be filled with teacher ideas. Currently, we try to navigate between these polarities, depending on who and what is to be taught. For example, four- and five-year-olds can and do directly observe evaporation as rainy streets become dry. A teacher can supply the term *evaporation* and direct children to further examples, experimentation, and record-keeping. Other natural phenomena, such as those in Part Two of this book, may not be readily observed by children. Then it is essential for teachers to bring them into children's awareness.

A teacher who can empathize with a child's efforts and share a child's feeling of excitement and satisfaction in solving problems is better able to guide and encourage children's intellectual development. Children learn by imitating and interacting with others, as well as through their own exploration and problem solving. The teacher serves as the social facilitator of children's problem-solving abilities (Case, 1986).

Guided discovery learning calls for this social facilitation as direct and indirect guidance. The teacher supplements the child's active exploration of problems by helping the child draw meaning from the experience and by extending conceptual learning. The crucial affective element here is the teacher's belief in the importance of this effort. Without commitment to a central purpose for teaching science, our lesson plans fail to inspire children; our hands-on activities lose vitality. When we are committed to the spirit of sharing with children the powerful constants that make their world more predictable, science comes alive in the classroom. When our focus shifts from teaching *facts* to teaching *children*, the process of helping to uncover enlightening knowledge remains fresh and dynamic.

Organizing Approaches

There are two distinctive approaches to organizing socially facilitated science activities: child-instigated experiences (the incidental approach) and teacher-instigated experiences. The child-instigated approach is ideal for very small classes of preschool children, for nurturing the individual interests of gifted older children, and for creating an atmosphere of inquiry in the classroom.

Incidental science can occur at any time or place, whenever a child's curiosity is aroused by something significant: a sparkling bit of quartz embedded in the sidewalk, the iridescent sheen of a beetle's back, or an evaporating playground puddle. The teacher capitalizes on the child's discovery by asking questions that lead to further discovery, by relating the find to something the child already knows, by extending the experience into other classroom activities, and by offering to help the child locate other resources for expanding his or her information. The confident teacher with a ready interest and strong background in science can do an admirable job of enlarging children's information this way. We urge teachers of young children to make time for these spontaneous investigations. They add freshness to the classroom and create a partnership in the knowledge-business between the children and the teacher. Learning something when you want to learn it—on a "need-to-know" basis—is both memorable and emotionally satisfying.

There are drawbacks to this approach, however. It is difficult to provide the same degree of support for larger classes or to fit spur-of-the-moment activities into a more structured school program. Nor do incidental, child-instigated investigations constitute an adequate conception of science. National standards published by both the American Association for the Advancement of Science (1993) and the National Committee on Science Education Standards and Assessment (1996) lay out cohesive sets of science concepts, skills, and dispositions that children should acquire. Furthermore, many states now have science standards. The teacher-instigated approach of this text serves teachers' need to help children meet these state and national standards.

The teacher-instigated approach outlined in this book centers on everyday events and interests of young children. Teachers should present the experiences and extensions in a unified way, continuing for a week or two. The basic experiences are described in detail to provide beginning teachers with a usable, tested model. The Inquiry experiences in each activity chapter are less prescriptive, allowing teachers and children to explore further with greater uncertainty. These activities are denoted with a **?**.

Lasting learning takes place through many encounters with the same ideas in a variety of contexts. A particularly important context is the outdoors, especially because today's children are indoors so much of the time. For this reason, every activity chapter has outdoor activities noted with the clover ♣ symbol. In addition, each chapter contains suggestions for improving the schoolgrounds in ways that support the concepts of the chapter. All such suggestions are easier made than implemented, but in working with others, including parents, all are possible and do exist in some schools.

Science learnings can be referred to and renewed throughout the school year when they relate to other learnings and classroom occurrences. Material reviewed and built onto over a period of time can be retained remarkably longer than isolated fragments of material that have been presented only once. Science knowledge further takes hold when it has utility and when it becomes part of a continuous chain of learning that develops throughout life.

Preparation for Teaching Science to Young Children

There is no question among educators and researchers about the superiority of active discovery over the textbook and lecture method of learning science. Yet it appears that most kindergarten and primary grade teachers continue to use the less-effective methods. The most common reason teachers give for not offering hands-on learning activities is their conviction that they lack enough science background to be able to answer children's questions. The open-endedness of problem solving bothers them. They feel uneasy when more than one solution can be appropriate. When these science anxieties go unchecked, they can be easily transformed into a list of airtight reasons for reading about, instead of "doing," science.

A sense of inadequacy about science can be a real limitation to science teaching because it tends to be communicated nonverbally to children as distaste for the subject matter. However, it is equally possible to do a poor job of teaching science concepts to youngsters because of being overtrained in science! It can be difficult for sophisticated scientists to translate their verbally elaborate concepts to a level of ideas that young children can understand.

Actually, most of us have much more practical science information than we may recognize. We can fill in knowledge gaps as we prepare to teach. A beginning teacher can supplement basic knowledge by carefully reading the *concepts, learning objective statements,* and *activity directions* in this book. We strongly suggest trying out the experiments and recording the results, problems, and personal reactions to the experience before presenting them to children. This will increase one's confidence and also reveal any technical difficulties. Reading some of the starred reference books, written at the young child's level of understanding, will add appropriately to one's knowledge base. Reference books suggested for teachers will provide depth of information to enlarge the teacher's developing interests and to provide answers prompted by a child's urgent curiosity.

The recommended children's reference books and science-based stories for children—especially those by Franklyn Branley, Lynne Cherry, and Gail Gibbons—are written by authors who know both the science concepts and the young learner's capacity to absorb core ideas. Many of these fine writers also know how to incorporate humor and excitement into their work. Other resources were chosen primarily to supplement material in this book with additional activities that children can accomplish easily. Some were included as sources of hard-to-find illustrations of science principles at work or to provide challenges for children who are fascinated by a particular topic.

There is merit in renewing and strengthening our science information, using some of the suggested teacher references, just before we teach. Then the satisfaction gained in becoming reacquainted with the concepts will be fresh and available to spark the interests of children. Finally, it is reassuring to remember these words by Jerome Bruner (1961): "The basic ideas that lie at the heart of all science are as *simple* as they are *powerful*" (p. 12).

Indirect and Direct Teaching

Discovery learning is guided *indirectly* through thoughtful questioning and listening and by sensitive discussion leading. It is guided *directly* by offering conceptual cues and by encouraging effort. Because many of us were not exposed to these kinds of guidelines in our own schooling, it will be helpful to analyze these techniques.

Thoughtful listening to children's ideas is an indirect way to guide and sustain their interest in discovery learning. We do this when we avoid passing judgment on a child's erroneous ideas or private logic that differs from a scientific explanation. A burgeoning research on children's thinking indicates that, from their own experience and as a matter of survival, preschoolers develop personal, workable theories in the "foundational" areas: psychology, biology, and physics (Wellman & Gelman, 1998). When there are gaps in the information they can assemble, children typically fill in those gaps imaginatively to form their personal theories, as did Matthew, whom we met in Chapter 1.

What's more, there is research evidence that hands-on learning alone isn't enough to shift children away from their naïve beliefs. Unless they have some guidance to challenge their comfortable misconceptions, children tend to interpret new experiences in terms of their old convictions. They tend to reject conflicting explanations. There is no conceptual change even after repeated hands-on experiences (Butts, Hofman, & Anderson, 1993).

This process is not unique to children, however. As revealed in a fascinating series of videotapes, *Minds of Our Own* (Schneps, c.1997), adolescent and adult thinking is both idiosyncratic and limited regarding everyday phenomena such as seasons, electrical currents, and mirrors. Teachers of young children thus tend to have a double task: clarify their own understanding of science concepts and help children achieve better understanding. As we struggle with our own misconceptions, it is important to remember that children gain confidence when we respect their naïve attempts to figure things out instead of devaluing them as amusing or quaint, or as serious misconceptions that must be eradicated immediately. Intuitive theories can be gradually clarified and reorganized when discovery experiences reveal the more systematic and complete way of looking at things that we call *science*.

We indirectly guide children's thinking when we show them our own reasoning processes by "thinking out loud." That could occur when we say something like this: "When I found this tiny leaf on the sidewalk, I thought to myself, 'This isn't like any other tiny leaf I've seen before—hmmm. But it has five points, like a star. A big sweet gum tree leaf has that shape, too. I wonder if a new sweet gum leaf starts out as tiny as this?' So, what do you think I did to find out for sure?" Sylvia Farnham-Diggory (1990) describes this important modeling as making invisible thinking processes visible to children.

Learning to Question

Just as the quality of scientific research depends upon asking worthwhile questions, the quality of discovery science learning is indirectly guided by helpful questioning. Open-ended questions are useful for generating several appropriate answers (divergence). *Divergent questions* can serve many purposes:

- *Instigating discovery:* A science activity becomes a discovery challenge when it is initiated as a question to answer. Each activity suggested in the following chapters is headed in bold type by the question the activity can answer. These questions can be used both to introduce the activity and to elicit children's conclusions about their activity. The questions can be printed on index cards and posted in the science area to help reading children stay focused in their work.
- *Eliciting predictions:* Before children experiment, elicit their predictions: "What do you think will happen if . . . ?" Record the responses of preschool and kindergarten children. Older children can write their own predictions, then record their results.
- *Probing for understanding:* "Why do you think that side of the balance went down?"
- *Promoting reasoning:* "Why do you think this arm feels dry and this arm feels wet?"
- *Serving as a catalyst:* Sometimes a question can be a catalyst that sparks renewed interest in a problem, whereas a specific direction from the teacher could make finding out unnecessary. "What could you change to try to make your lever work?" encourages new effort. "If you move the block closer to Robert, you'll be able to lift him with your lever" discourages independent effort.
- *Encouraging creative thinking:* In a group discussion, ask questions such as, "How would our lives be different if there weren't any friction?"
- *Reflecting on feelings:* In a group discussion, ask questions such as, "What was the best part of the dark box experiment?"

There is ample research demonstrating that teachers tend to overuse *convergent questions,* that is, those with a single, correct answer. Convergent questions are less effective in stimulating creative thinking or synthesizing; however, it is useful and suitable to ask certain convergent questions to promote learning. Convergent questions are beneficial for:

- *Directing attention:* By asking a question like, "Does the red cup hold as much water as the blue cup?" we can direct a child's attention to a key part of the activity she has overlooked. The child can then correct her own course of action without feeling criticized.
- *Recalling the temporal order:* "What did you do first? What did you do next?" "When did this happen? What happened afterward?"
- *Recalling prior conditions:* "Does the jar of beans look just the same today as it did yesterday?"

Follow-up questions to convergent questions can be divergent. They can lead to further reflection or to fresh investigation: "How can you find out?"

It is helpful for beginning questioners to role-play with other beginners to improve and feel at ease with new techniques. To overcome habitual closed questioning, it can take concerted effort to change the way we shape our questions. Many of us use the pattern of stating in the form of a question the answers we wish to hear from children. We may say, "So the cup of snow melted into a smaller amount of water, right? Isn't that what you found?" This style of questioning reduces children's need to discover answers for themselves, or tells them that the main discovery is to find out what the teacher wants them to say.

Leading Discussions

Discussions serve different purposes at different points in learning new concepts.

- *Introductory discussions* whet interest in a new topic when children are encouraged to recall events they have encountered personally and to contribute what they already know about the subject. At this time, children's private theories are noted without any challenge to evident flaws. Children are encouraged to raise their own questions about what they would like to find out in the activities.
- *Small-group discussions* follow children's individual activity to process what took place in their investigations and to help clarify their thinking. These discussions can reveal that more than one conclusion can be reached from an activity. They can lead to shifts in naïve theories.
- *Summary discussions* with the whole class pull together the concepts that have been explored in the activities and extensions. They help children get comfortable with new concepts and consolidate associated information. Each of the following chapters offers suggestions appropriate to summary discussions under the heading "Connecting Concepts."

Group discussions allow children to learn from one another if the teacher models respect for the ideas and experiences that children express. To encourage interactive responses among children, quiet children may have to be drawn out in low-risk ways. Recognize a nod of agreement or a responsive smile from such a child as involvement: "It looks like Carrie agrees with your idea." If some children have trouble staying involved in large-group discussions, this concrete illustration can be helpful:

> Ask two children to each get a crayon and then exchange the crayons with each other. Have them verify that each had one crayon *before* sharing with the other, and each still has only one crayon *after* sharing with the other. Next, ask each child to share an idea with the other on a topic such as the day's weather. After each has shared an idea, point out that now each child has two ideas about the day's weather. Add, "We grow in ideas when we share and listen to each other."

It is important not to close off the exchange of ideas as soon as a child offers key information. Keep the discussion open until each willing child has had a chance to be heard, even if the ideas begin to echo one another.

Adults often overlook the fact that it takes a little time for children to produce thoughtful answers to questions. Many people feel they are unsuccessful at teaching if their questions are not answered immediately. The results of Mary Budd Rowe's (1996) seminal research indicate that just the opposite is true. She found that the teachers she observed gave children an average of under one second to answer questions. Teachers who were then trained to wait three seconds or more for responses elicited a greater number of answers, longer answers, and more varied and accurate responses. Furthermore, as the teachers waited longer, children began to listen to and respond to each other's comments. Children other than the "brightest" in the class also began to contribute answers. This suggests that when quick responses by a few children end a group discussion, many untapped ideas may be cut off. This practice leaves many children feeling less confident about themselves as thinkers and learners. Young children especially need time to formulate and express ideas.

A good discussion puts the teacher in the catalyst role by empowering children's ability to think and express their ideas. This seems to be a difficult shift for some teachers to make, especially if they are accustomed to having their voices dominate the classroom. With practice, it becomes easier to support and elicit children's comments by using bridging remarks like, "That was an interesting idea, and others may have different thoughts about it. . . . "

The catalyst teacher underscores what children accurately contribute, adds bits of information to expand those ideas, and clarifies misconceptions that might still linger. The teacher summarizes the various points children make in the discussion. If the contributed ideas do not include certain salient points, the teacher can add, "Scientists also tell us that . . . . " Group discussions are most successful when they are guided with the goal of stimulating children's thinking and reasoning powers.

Organizing Time and Space for Science

The logistics of making exploration time available to small work groups will vary for each classroom. Now that learning centers are more commonly used, teachers are becoming adept at flexible activity scheduling. Problems of managing science activities can be eased with the help of an assistant in the room, whether it is a volunteer parent, a retiree, or an "exchange student" from an upper grade. It is best to delegate overseeing ongoing activities to the helper. In some instances, simple directions printed on index cards or tape-recorded directions can allow children to handle science projects fairly independently.

A good location for science activities facilitates thinking by inviting children to participate and by controlling distractions. Proximity to storage and cleanup aids is important. Varying the setting for activities can build interest. Anticipation is heightened on days when science takes place under a blanket-covered table!

Elaborate bulletin boards aren't needed to attract children's attention to science when a frequently changed PLEASE TOUCH display shelf is available. Many teachers begin the school year with noble intentions of welcoming nature finds and other objects of science interest that children bring from home. Perhaps they initiate the project attractively with a bird's nest propped in the crotch of a small tree branch, some special rocks, and a recently shed snake skin. If the goal of a changing display is forgotten, however, the old things will lose their meaning. Because there is little appeal in a dusty nest or a tattered snakeskin, it is better to retire the too-familiar objects. An easy way to keep the science display pertinent to ongoing activities is to try to display indestructible materials being used in the discovery activities.

Computers capable of accessing the Internet and displaying large graphics are an increasingly rich resource for extending science teaching. Without question, there is no substitute for a live gerbil in an aquarium for learning about its size, shape, smell, habits, bright eyes, and sharp teeth. But it is also valuable to see images of the distant deserts where gerbils are native and wild. (Gerbils are not native to pet stores.) If, because of limited resources, one has to choose between the real and the image, clearly the multisensory real has more power than the merely visual image.

Second and third graders can learn to record and chart data using computer programs. Beginning and more advanced writers can use the simpler word-processing programs. But the ready-made icons that computers provide abundantly should be avoided. Not only are they stereotypical, but more seriously because they also discourage children's own efforts to create informative drawings. Children can produce text on the computer and illustrate their own observations of the phenomenon. The Reggio Emilio centers have demonstrated how well children can draw from life if systematically encouraged.

For further information on using computers with young children, Haugland and Wright (1997) provide a comprehensive guide.

Introducing Science Activities

There are many creative ways to focus children's attention on a new science activity. A physical science activity might be presented as a child-size problem that needs to be solved. "A box of paper clips spilled at the sand table and got mixed into the sand. Perhaps some of you can find a way to get them out." A spur-of-the-moment thinking game could build interest: "There's something that we see in our room every day that we will use in science today. It has a handle on the outside and rollers on the inside." One relaxed teacher intrigues his students as he patiently searches through his pockets for the "something I thought you would like to know about." Opening a brown bag to reveal an unexplained object of science interest can provide enticement to find out more. Any of these attention hooks needs to be followed with, "What do you know about this?"

A topic can be introduced by reading a related story or poem, and then following it with an open-ended question to be answered by the discovery activity. For example, the topic of light could be introduced by reading Russell Hoban's *Bedtime for Frances* and then asking, "Why do you think Frances was confused and scared by her robe on the chair?" A simple description of an occurrence could start the explorations. "Today, when I stood on my porch, a heavy, noisy repair truck rumbled by and I felt the porch shake. Have you ever felt shaking near something noisy? Today you can find out more about shaking and sounds happening together." Although it is not advisable to oversell science as fun and games, placing activities in the context of the child's world sparks interest and adds importance to "doing" science.

Guiding Explorations

Hands-on for children should imply, as much as possible, *hands-off* for teachers. There will be occasions when a tactful offer to steady a screwdriver or to knot a parachute string can help a discouraged child achieve success, but unsolicited help should not be given in the interest of saving time. Butts and Hofman (1993) speak about the difficulty of "unlearning" established ideas. They urge teachers to listen carefully to how children are describing and interpreting their explorations. The authors point out that it is the conversation with children that occurs after a hands-on activity that makes a difference in their thinking.

The consultant role is a delicate one: quietly offering a reasoning cue to highlight the important part of an experiment, or asking a question and allowing the child time to reflect on the answer. (Reasoning cues can be taken from the concept statement headings for activities in this book: "You pushed *down* to lift him *up* with the lever.") Wise consultants resist the temptation to hurry a child along to discover what they, the consultants, already know. They are careful not to smother a child's tender spark of inquiry with a heavy blanket of directions and facts. Experiential learning is weakened when a child is rushed to a premature conclusion or "helped" out of arriving at the child's own solution.

Supporting Interest in Knowing

It would be unrealistic to assume that the spontaneous desire to know will consistently lead all children in a group to take part in every science activity made available to them. It would certainly abuse the developmental goal of encouraging autonomous decision making to require the whole group to engage in each science event that the teacher presents. Knowledge of the uniqueness of individual development should make it clear that each child brings different capacities and motivation into learning situations.

Subtle directives from families can strongly influence the choices children make in school. Direct or indirect messages like, "Be careful with those good clothes . . . Boys don't cook . . . Girls are afraid of spiders and worms," can be powerful inhibitors to children who are unsure of their affection rating with their parents. Such directives may curb a child's interest in trying new experiences.

Children also may have needs that take precedence over the desire to find out. Children who are lonely at home may be very reluctant to pass up any chance to play with special school friends. They may choose a science activity only when friends make that choice. Children who are tired, hungry, or feeling under par may not be able to summon enough interest to observe what is happening at the science table.

If a child consistently spurns science activities, it is advisable to think about possible causes and consider ways to make participation easier. The teacher may simply need to ask for that child's help while organizing materials for the day's science activity. Children usually take a proprietary interest in a project that they have helped to prepare. However, when a science topic becomes a central theme threading through many parts of the school program, even children who do little active exploring will become aware of the concepts being presented.

Teachers positively influence children's involvement in science by valuing efforts to learn and solve problems. Comments that validate children's competence promote a positive disposition toward science. They strengthen children's beliefs of themselves as learners and contribute toward their interest and continued effort to find out more.

Cognitive research shows that when children are praised for their efforts, rather than for their intelligence, they are helped to focus on the process of their work. They stay with the activity because they are trying to understand something new and become more competent. They enjoy what they are doing, and they are more resilient after a setback. On the other hand, praising children for their intelligence tends to undermine both motivation and performance. Such children are likely to avoid challenging projects at which they may not be successful. If they do fail at a task, they are likely to give up, and they perform less well than children who were praised for their efforts (Mueller & Dweck, 1998).

When a child experiences an activity failure, a teacher's encouragement to persist toward mastering the challenge will result in more satisfaction with science than will a teacher's praise for success.

When teachers primarily value and reinforce correct performance, they tend to use automatic, ambiguous praise in a manipulative way to keep children "on task." Unfortunately, excessive, empty praise seems to interfere with children's spontaneous interest in an activity, weakening learning motivation. The children's attention becomes directed toward proper performance to win the teacher's approval, rather than toward what they are learning. They lose interest in the activity for its own sake.

In fact, such needless attention to how well children are working may interrupt the focused concentration needed to attain a satisfying outcome. Eventually such inappropriately motivated youngsters tend to give up on tasks when they encounter obstacles. They may only keep working as long as the teacher is nearby to do the "motivating" for them. In Alfie Kohn's view, overpraising chiefly motivates children to get praise. Unfortunately, praise-seeking diminishes commitment to whatever they were doing that prompted the praise. Instead, Kohn suggests offer-

Table 3–1   Automatic Praise Verses Authentic Encouragement

Situation	Automatic Praise	Vs. Authentic Encouragement
Amelia checks her seed-sprouting jar. She exclaims, "My sprouts have leaves!"	"Aren't you smart?"	"You really looked carefully to find the new growth."
Jake beams with joy when he gets two loads balanced on the scale.	"Good job!"	"It feels great to get both sides balanced."
Nina reports doing yesterday's light-bending experience a new way at home. It worked!	"Superscientist!"	"How exciting to find a new way to do it. Tell us more!"

ing simple, evaluation-free feedback about what the child is accomplishing (2001). Differences between authentic encouragement and artificial, automatic *praise* are illustrated in Table 3–1.

Criticism is mounting against the attempt by schools to raise children's competence by trying to bolster self-esteem. Social scientists are finding unexpected negative outcomes of such attempts. According to Martin Seligman (1995, p. 33), the practice of issuing exaggerated praise to help children feel good, regardless of their actual accomplishments, makes it harder to achieve mastery. This undermines self-esteem. He relates the increasing rates of depression in young people to this misunderstanding of how self-esteem evolves. In reality, self-esteem is a feeling that is a by-product of doing well, not the reverse.

Children need the authentic kind of encouragement that empowers learning and validates accomplishment. Based on outcomes of their early childhood classroom studies, Stipek and Greene (2001) urge us to avoid giving false praise to children to artificially raise their expectations for success. They offer a succinct, research-based principle for supporting learning motivation. "The best way to make children feel competent is to help them be competent" (p. 87).

When children invest their attention deeply in an activity and achieve a meaningful result, or when they go beyond what is expected of them and uncover something new, they grow. They feel the joy of meeting a challenge. These rewarding feelings of increased personal competence are the genuine sources of intrinsic learning motivation (Csikszentmihalyi, 1990).

Dispelling Stereotypes

Gender and minority stereotypes about intellectual capabilities perpetuate self-doubt and create needless limitations to the development of this nation's problem solvers. Teachers' actions and beliefs contribute heavily to the self-attitudes being formed by their students. Self-attitudes, whether negative or positive, are the single most crucial force in shaping what an individual is able to accomplish.

Although we may voice our desire to help each child develop her or his intellectual potential, our actions may belie our words. Our actions are based on our values, some of which we hold unconsciously. We may be acting on buried, leftover prejudices about the thinking capacities and "natural" interests of women and minorities that were passed on to us as schoolchildren. Many people in our society seem to believe that "scientists" are older white males, although this is increasingly less the case. To encourage all children to think of themselves as connected to science, we can take several actions when we teach.

- We give girls and minority children as much verbal and social encouragement as Caucasian boys to answer science questions, contribute to science discussions, and persist at experimenting (Blake, 1993).
- We give the first chance to try new activities to all children equally.
- Science professionals who visit our classes, or whose pictures are posted on our bulletin boards, are as likely to be female and non-Caucasian as they are Caucasian males. When we communicate in these ways our belief that each child can participate effectively in some form of science experiences, we will be making a valid effort to combat crippling stereotypes (Hammrich, 1997).

It might smell yucky, but it still fascinates the girls.

Adapting Experiences for Younger Children

Although the activities in this text's framework were planned for children 4 through 8 years of age, many of the experiences can be adapted for younger preschool children. Two-year-olds can enjoy simple sensory explorations such as feeling air as they move it with paper fans, spinning pinwheels, or swinging streamers on a breezy day; feeling rock textures and weights; touching ice, then touching the water it melts into; watching, then moving like a goldfish; tasting raw fruits and vegetables that have grown from plants; listening to loud and soft sounds; or gazing through transparent color paddles to see surroundings in a new light.

Three-year-olds might be expected to engage in similar activities, taking in greater detail. They will be able to direct deeper attention to activities such as exploring new dimensions with a magnifying glass. This group can enjoy some of the classifying experiences on a beginning level: sorting rocks from objects that are not rocks; things that float from those that do not float; and objects that are attracted by a magnet from objects that are not attracted.

Adapting Experiences for Children with Special Needs

Science is an approach to thinking and behaving that has value for children at any level of motor, behavioral, sensory, communication, or mental functioning. Because discovery science calls for collaboration among children, it fosters the personal interactions that children with special needs often miss. It can help classmates recognize the child with limitations as an individual with ideas and talents to contribute. Nobody laughed at Lori once her worm-scouting skills came to light. Her problems with pencils and numbers and letters didn't interfere with her passion for capturing insects. Her generosity in sharing them improved her social relationships. Scott's "slow" right leg and droopy right arm didn't limit his deep involvement in science. Frequently left behind on the playground, Scott was in his social and intellectual element at the science table. With good-humored inventiveness, Scott found his own way to water our plants. He soaked a clean sponge in the pitcher of water that was too heavy for him to manage. Then he squeezed the sponge for each plant, giving them a simultaneous drink and sponge bath!

Adapting materials to make them more manageable can enable success for a child with special needs. A plastic basting syringe is easier to use than a small medicine dropper for a child who finds it difficult to grasp objects. Bamboo toast tongs may help children with fine motor control problems to pick up small objects.

Changes in approach are important for children with vision and hearing impairments. Advance information about what is going to take place helps the child who has a vision impairment deal with new experiences comfortably. Face-to-face communication is necessary with the child who has a hearing impairment. Because a hearing loss is invisible to others, it is easy to forget that communications are cut off when that child's back is turned.

A child who uses a wheelchair will need to have materials brought into close range. A highlight event might be connecting a child with attention to invest and a grasshopper with a new cage to explore. If obstacles to full participation are too great for a child, assign a record-keeping job or lab assistant role, such as keeping track of materials that might be misplaced.

Potentially disruptive children are often judged by teachers to be risks in science activities but researchers in Anchorage, Alaska disproved this when they offered carefully planned, hands-on science to a class of children with a variety of significant behavioral problems. Videotape analysis showed that these children remained focused on their science activities 90% of the time. They also expressed positive feelings about learning science. The same children were on-task only 25% of the time in a less inviting classroom where other subject matter was presented with heavy emphasis on behavior control (Welton, Smith, Owens, & Adrian, 2000).

An easily distracted child benefits from a simplified, clear arrangement of materials to focus upon. Tangible boundaries, such as individual trays of equipment, can help the child with poor control feel assured of a fair share of things with which to work. The teacher's close presence can help ensure an island of calm around these children to help them pursue their work. Tiny pebbles or seeds that could be inserted into ears or nostrils should not be available without supervision to children who lack safety awareness. Time given to planning for successful activities minimizes the time and attention such vulnerable children demand when frustrating tasks lead to disruptive behavior.

Make use of available professional consultants for specific ways to maximize the potential of a child who has a handicapping condition. Until such help arrives, put yourself imaginatively into the child's situation to think of ways to work around the child's limitations and through the child's strengths. Whatever accommodations you make to provide satisfying science experiences can help children with special needs grow in ability to cope with the challenges that they face. Information about science activities designed for youngsters who are visually impaired or physically disabled is available from the Center for Multisensory Learning, Lawrence Hall of Science, University of California, Berkeley, CA 94720.

Children who face difficulties in mastering developmental tasks deserve every chance to develop confidence and initiative that teachers can provide through science activities. A young teacher, Jane Perkins, did this for her class of children with learning disabilities. She was deeply moved by their responsiveness to the science activities. She said, "It was the first time any of these children ever expressed curiosity. I'll never again deny them the chance to wonder why."

Learning in the Context of Cooperation

Current research on children's thinking and learning regards them as results of both individual development and social interaction. There is also growing recognition in our society that overemphasizing individual accomplishment and competitiveness in the classroom fails to teach children how to work cooperatively. Still other research indicates that acting cooperatively shows up in the brain's pleasure center, indicating that humans are "hard-wired" to cooperate (Rilling et al., 2002). Thus we have an impetus to return to cooperative education. The discovery experiences in this book have always been presented primarily as activities to be shared by small groups, with the introductions, supplements, and follow-ups provided as whole-group experiences. They are readily usable in the cooperative learning context.

Management of discovery activities as cooperative learning tasks will vary according to the nature of the project, the availability of materials in quantity, and the experience of the youngsters in handling independent activities. Certainly, it makes more sense to have only one group of four children working on a particular gravity experience that requires using the one available commercial balance and weights, with other groups working on problems suitable for homemade balance scales. Still other groups could be using that time to make entries in their topic record booklets or to record their earlier findings on a class bar graph. Other children could be working on sections of the class mural of a gravity-free fantasy or creating a skit about being astronauts.

Precisely how cooperative activities are implemented is a matter for the individual teacher to decide. Surely it is wise to make a slow transition to cooperative learning groups from a lockstep approach where each child works independently at the same learning task. Further, the social skills of four- and five-year-olds are better suited to learning groups of two. Seven- and eight-year-olds can, with training, work comfortably in groups of four.

Typically, it is realistic to plan a science period where discovery activities are paired with less structured activities that require little supervision. Teachers can then devote maximum attention to facilitating the discovery activities. There is no particular merit in attempting to simultaneously juggle a number of differing discovery activities.

Time must be allowed before the science period ends for cleanup and for processing with the whole class what has occurred in the cooperative groups. To ensure that all children in the class are given a regular opportunity to report what their group has accomplished, a number-rotation system can be used. Each child in a small group is assigned a number from 1 to 4. Then, instead of asking for a volunteer or choosing a high-visibility child to report for the group, the teacher indicates which number will identify the day's reporters.

Integtared Curriculum Themes

The science themes in Part Two of this book were developed in response to the persistent interests, questions, and concerns of a generation of children in the classroom, at play, and at home. To be precise, many of the themes evolved in response to Michael, the gifted child in my first kindergarten class in a university laboratory school 30 years ago. The retentiveness of his mind was impressive. The range of his curiosity was boundless.

Keeping Michael's curiosity satisfied became a major preoccupation for me, searching for resources that weren't to be found, so had to be improvised. Initially, I fretted about devoting too much preparation energy to meet one child's needs. But something quite unexpected was happening in the classroom. Michael was never alone at the science table; the activities always drew a crowd. Soon, during our group conversations, Michael wasn't the only child sharing interesting information about how things work. Michael wasn't the only one applying those learnings in spontaneous play or in solving practical schoolground problems. Others were chiming in to

"I'm asking questions for our graph."

point out connections between story plots and current science projects. Others were bringing from home various artifacts that related to ongoing science learnings.

By midyear, my weekly planning centered on a single new or continuing science theme. We sang science, we nibbled science, we quantified science activities, we danced science, we took science to the easels and workbench, and we trudged around the school's neighborhood to see science happening. We had a good time, the children and I, learning together.

Happily, Michael and his classmates had inspired a science-oriented kinder-garten program that continued to evolve over the years. It continued to fascinate chil-dren of early childhood ages who represented a wide range of intellectual abilities and family backgrounds. Eventually the pages of weekly plans and observational notes re-sulted in the thematic format of this book. Themes were developed around basic sci-ence concepts that have functional value in the world of young children because they explain how and why familiar events occur. Some topics were developed to modify or replace the naïve, magical explanations that children had formulated for themselves. Topics were selected according to the following criteria:

- relevance to the child's immediate experience
- potential for being understood through simple, hands-on activities
- potential applicability to practical, child-level problem solving
- significance in promoting safety and physical or emotional well-being
- availability of low- or no-cost materials for experimentation and observation

Two topics that interest many youngsters—prehistoric animals and astron-omy—do not meet these criteria for most early childhood settings. They can be more suitably explored by parents and teachers who can provide for children the resources of a natural history museum, a planetarium or observatory, and the night skies.

Early childhood classes may have opportunities to participate in community environmental projects. Every class can incorporate reusing, recycling, and conserving resources into its daily routines (Earthworks Group, 1990). Such involvement allows children to have a valued role in significant matters, but it does not take the place of foundation science experiences. Basic understandings of how matter behaves in the natural and physical worlds give meaning to the more complex interrelationships of environmental issues. In the chapters that follow, many hands-on experiences are suggested that lead to broader understandings. The activities are sequenced to provide foundation concepts for subsequent activities.

Other worthwhile science topics with child appeal can be developed by creative teachers, as long as the conceptual purpose and scientific accuracy are clear. Hands-on activities must lead children to a general truth or law about how matter and living things behave. Related extensions in other curricular areas should be just as enjoyable as the active science experiences, but they, too, must have a conceptual purpose. Shifting children's attention from what has relevance to the attention-catching irrelevant has been shown to interfere with the recall of the significant information (Mayer, Heiser, & Lonn, 2001). Gathering literature resources to extend a topic should be thoughtfully done, as trade books sometimes contain misinformation. Helpful guidelines for selecting good science literature are given by Rice, Dudley, and Williams (2001).

Extensions must not be vaguely connected, aimless "things to do" that trivialize the science learning. Rakow and Vasquez (1998) warn, "At its worst, integrated instruction becomes artificial and superficial."

A teacher's own fascination with an area of knowledge can be the emotional spark for developing a science topic; that interest and enthusiasm communicate a positive disposition toward science. The adult's range of knowledge must then be stepped down to the children's level of thinking development and to the context of the child's immediate world. Activities then can be designed around the "up close and personal" tangible aspects of that topic. A teacher's commitment to aerobic exercise, strength training, and optimal health, for example, can translate into children's beginning experiences with the awareness of air being pulled into their nostrils and filling their lungs, of their own pulses and beating hearts, and of their own moving muscles. Discovery activities could include exploring how breathing rates change and measuring how long it takes to recover normal breath rates after a sprint.

A teacher's strong commitment to protecting the environment can translate into beginning, hands-on explorations with reused plastic bottle terrariums and then expand onto the playground and into the broader community. Bess-Gene Holt (1989) offers excellent leads to exploring the immediate environment and toward understanding the patterns and harmony in the undisturbed natural world.

The activities for the science topics in this book are described as one way of supplying accurate guidance for children's explorations. . The concepts are in accord with those stated in *Benchmarks for Science Literacy* by the American Association for the Advancement of Science (see Appendix C) and the National Science Education Standards, *Content Standards for Grades K-4* (see Appendix D).

Activities illustrating more complex concepts could be made available as options for children who are eager to pursue more challenging ideas. Each teacher is in the best position to make this decision. Children are best served and core concepts are more durably retained when teachers offer only a few topics in depth and with cross-curricular reinforcement each school year than when many topics are touched on lightly.

Objectives and Assessment

The broad objectives underlying the learning experiences in this book focus as much upon the individual's feelings and approach to learning as they do upon the acquisition of information. Observations of the basic harmony in physical and natural world relationships build feelings of security and confidence in children. Reducing fear of the unknown leads to feelings of mastery and strength. Support for curiosity promotes problem-solving ability and offers an avenue for learning how to learn.

In order to quantify certain learning outcomes, behavioral objectives are still used in many schools. However, what a child really learns from an activity might not immediately be evident in the classroom. Instead, that feedback may spill out to a parent at home during a sleepy bedtime conversation. The learnings may be fragmentary until they are consolidated through participation in the integrating activities. Or, perhaps the learning is applied nonverbally weeks after the classroom experience has taken place. The real nature of the teaching/learning process is obscured if we assume that children learn only and precisely what a narrow behavioral objective decrees.

Formal evaluation of children's accomplishments in discovery science is required in many schools. It marks our maturity in science education that the difficulty of valid, comprehensive evaluation is widely acknowledged (Hein, 1990). One form of assessment most consistent with discovery science and most useful for identifying misunderstandings that need further clarification is observation of children's verbalizations. Listening to children's comments and asking questions as they work with science materials can reveal a great deal. Such questions include, "What did you find out about . . . ?" and "Can you show me what happens when . . . ?" For longer plant, animal, or weather observations, the question "What did you find out about . . . ?" asked at a natural closure point provides a gauge for conceptual learning. Children's responses can be recorded most conveniently on a simple checklist. Ideally, the check sheet items should center on the grasp of basic concepts, activities completed, and evidence of interest and satisfaction expressed by the child. Such data also serve as self-evaluation for the teacher about the success and value of the learning experiences.

As we increasingly appreciate how the child builds knowledge, partnering with a child in assessing that learning becomes desirable. We may, for example, invite the child to represent knowledge: "How can you show what you learned about . . . ?" A journal entry, a drawing, a story, or a dance may result, as well as a verbal explanation. A work folder or a portfolio would include that child's representation or a description of it. "What else do you wonder about . . . ?" is a question that further assesses the distance the child has traveled.

The word *assess* originates in the Latin *assidere,* meaning "sit by." When we ask children to tell us, in their own way, what they know and what else they would like to know, we do sit by them, facilitating, rather than prescribing, what they learn. Nor should we think that individual assessments are the only way of seeing what children have learned. Just as children work in small groups to develop knowledge, they can present their work jointly. Older children may paint a mural or dramatize a concept. Younger children might engage in creative movement together. Teachers can jot down notes on such activities, as well as photograph or sketch them.

In addition, group conversations about a science topic can both reveal and help develop children's understanding, as Rhoda Kanevsky (1995) has demonstrated. With her first-grade children seated in a circle around her, she introduces a topic and offers each child a chance to comment or ask a question. Writing rapidly, she preserves their words. By the next day, she has their remarks typed and posted by the door for all to notice. Meanwhile, interesting topics have spurred children's research, such as talking to their parents or reading books about the topic. This leads to further group conversations, journal writing, and drawing. The rules of the conversations are simple: no shouting out, no telling others that they are wrong, and no arguing. Reviewing several conversation transcripts shows how individual children come to correct and refine their thinking and how they help one another with new ideas and questions. This kind of documentation of children's thinking also helps the teacher decide what to teach next, tightly linking curriculum and assessment (Chittenden, 1990).

Paper-and-pencil tests of factual knowledge for older primary grade children can be a barrier to adequate responses because the flow of ideas can be blocked by the need to correctly write, spell, and punctuate the written answer. This problem can be avoided to a certain degree if questions can be asked and answered using simple sketches as well as words.

Assessing science learning is complex. Not only is there much to assess, including concepts, skills, and attitudes, but there is also much uncertainty about how science education should be evaluated. Price and Hein (1994) advise:

> Remember, there is no universally accepted, absolute standard for judging the science activities of children. We simply don't have enough information or research evidence to determine what is an "appropriate" or "outstanding" observation for a 6-year-old, or what level of experimental design can be expected from a 10-year-old. (p.27)

Current best practice includes making multiple observations over time; having a variety of things observed, for example, conversation, projects, and drawings; and collecting a variety of artifacts, both of individual and small group work (Jones & Courtney, 2002).

Teachers make assessments of the whole group as well. How engaged are the children? How well do they keep track of the science materials? How much investigation of the library books occurs? What gets brought in from home or elsewhere outside the classroom? Judgments of these kinds help teachers evaluate their own effectiveness and monitor their own work.

The assessment method most appreciated by parents at conference time, however, does not involve convenient check marks on a rating scale. Rather, it consists of sharing your casual, on-the-spot jottings on Post-its® filed in the child's work folder. Use a digital camera to record the constructions, projects, and drawings to create electronic folders on individual children or the class, or print photos to store in traditional paper folders. Some teachers, following the Reggio Emilio model, prepare "documentations" of children's learning that are displayed in the classroom (Curtis & Custer, 2000). One of us has several years of digital science class photos in her computer. Viewed as a whole, they document the themes of her work with students. Such documentations are tangible evidence of having passed along life-enriching awareness of the world we know and appreciate through science knowledge.

Gaining From Our Mistakes

Many of the materials and activities in this text have been revised as a result of trial-and-error encounters with the logic of young minds. On one occasion, the children in my class were given matching plastic vials—some capped, some uncapped—to use in a buoyancy experiment. Then five-year-old Greg explained why his capped, empty vial floated on the water while his uncapped vial sank. According to Greg, the cap held up the first vial! To my dismay, he verified his conclusion by removing the plastic cap and floating it on the water. How confusing! According to my plan, he should have noticed that the capped vial was filled with air, hence, it was lightweight; the uncapped vial filled with water, hence, it became heavy. It took a while for my supposedly flexible, adult thinking to find a way back to the objective of the experiment. "Greg, you had a good idea about the cap. It does float by itself. Let's see what happens if we put the cap on the container full of water. Now let's put the same kind of cap on the empty-looking container and watch them again." Tuning in to a child's logic makes teaching an exciting learning process for the teacher.

If children have difficulties with an activity, it may be possible that further modifications are needed. It is important not to give up on science activities because of an occasional unexpected outcome. Keep in mind Thomas Edison's observation that a mistake is not a failure if we learn how not to do it next time.

Professional Growth

Teaching can be an endlessly challenging profession when we consider ourselves learners along with the children. Taking time to investigate questions we are interested in, talking with other teachers about common concerns in science teaching, and refreshing ourselves by attending lectures, visiting museums, and reading can all help to keep us open to new ideas. We can enliven our interest in teaching science by acquainting ourselves with these resources for children and for teachers.

- *Connect K–8 Hands-On Science and Math Across the Curriculum* (bimonthly). Teachers' Laboratory, P.O. Box 6480, Brattleboro, VT 05302.

- *Grapevine.* On-line newsletter from the Center for Environmental Education, Antioch New England Institute. At *www.cee.ane.org.*
- *Science & Children.* A journal of the National Science Teachers Association, 1840 Wilson Blvd., Arlington, VA 22201-3000. The Web site for NSTA is lively and informative (*www.nsta.org*).
- *Your Big Backyard*, for preschool children; *Ranger Rick*, for primary/elementary grade children; *Ranger Rick's NatureScope*, for teachers (includes activities, extensions, and outdoor projects). These are all publications of the National Wildlife Federation, 11100 Wildlife Center Drive. Reston, VA 21090. NWF's Web site is worth visiting (*www.nwf.org*).

For your own interest in science discoveries, not necessarily to teach to young children, use these Internet resources.

The *New York Times* Science Section is published on Tuesdays. *www.nytimes. com.*

Scientific American is published monthly and maintains an active Web site. *www.sciam.com.*

The teaching framework will achieve its greatest effectiveness when it stimulates teachers to continue growing and generating their own ideas for presenting science experiences to the children they know best.

REFERENCES

AMERICAN ASSOCIATION FOR THE ADVANCEMENT OF SCIENCE. (1993). *Benchmarks for science literacy.* New York: Oxford University Press.

BLAKE, S. (1993). Are you turning female and minority students away from science? *Science and Children, 30,* 32–35.

BRUNER, J. (1961). *The process of education.* Cambridge, MA: Harvard University Press.

BUTTS, D. P., & HOFMAN, H. (1993). Hands-on, brains-on. *Science and Children, 30,* 15–16.

BUTTS, D. HOFMAN, H., & ANDERSON, M. (1993). Is hands-on experience enough? A study of young children's views of sinking and floating objects. *Journal of Elementary Science Education, 5* (1), 50–64.

CASE, R. (1986). *Intellectual development: Birth to adulthood.* New York: Academic Press.

CHITTENDEN, E. (1990). Young children's discussion of science topics. In G. Hein (Ed.), *The assessment of hands-on elementary science programs* (pp. 220–247). Grand Forks, ND: North Dakota Study Group on Evaluation.

CSIKSZENTMIHALYI, M. (1990). *Flow: The psychology of optimal experience.* New York: Harper & Row.

CURTIS, D., & CUSTER, M. (2000). *The art of awareness: How observation can transform your teaching.* St. Paul, MN: Redleaf Press.

EARTHWORKS GROUP. (1990). *50 simple things kids can do to save the earth.* Kansas City: Andrews & McMeel.

FARNHAM-DIGGORY, S. (1990). *Schooling.* Cambridge, MA: Harvard University Press.

HAMMRICH, P. (1997). Yes, daughter, you can. *Science and Children, 34*(4), 20–23.

HAUGLAND, S. W., & WRIGHT, J. L. (1997). *Young children and technology: A world of discovery.* Boston: Allyn & Bacon.

HEIN, G. (ED.). (1990). *The assessment of hands-on elementary science programs.* Grand Forks, ND: North Dakota Study Group on Evaluation.

HOLT, B. G. (1989). *Science with young children.* Washington, DC: National Association for the Education of Young Children.

JONES, J., & COURTNEY, R. (2002). Documenting early science learning. *Young Children, 57*(5), 34–40.

KANEVSKY, R. (1995, March). *Alternative assessment: A developmental perspective toward understanding children's work.* Workshop presented at the National Science Teachers Association National Convention, Philadelphia, PA.

KOHN, A. (2001). Five reasons to stop saying "good job." *Young Children, 56*(5), 24–28.

MAYER, R., HEISER, J., & LONN, S. (2001). Cognitive constraints on multimedia learning: When presenting more material results in less understanding. *Journal of Educational Psychology, 93*(1), 187–198.

MUELLER, C., & DWECK, C. (1998). Praise for intelligence can undermine children's motivation and performance. *Journal of Personality and Social Psychology, 75,* 33–52.

NATIONAL ASSOCIATION FOR THE EDUCATION OF YOUNG CHILDREN (2001). *2001 standards for the baccalaureate or initial level.* Washington, DC: Author.

NATIONAL COMMITTEE ON SCIENCE EDUCATION STANDARDS AND ASSESSMENT. (1996). *National science education standards.* Washington, DC: National Research Council.

PRICE, S., & HEIN, G. (1994). Scoring active assessments. *Science and Children, 32*(2), 27.

RAKOW, S., & VASQUEZ, J. (1998). Integrated instruction: A trio of strategies. *Science and Children, 35*(6), 18–22.

RICE, D., DUDLEY, A., & WILLIAMS, C. (2001). How do you choose science trade books? *Science and Children, 38*(6), 18–22.

RILLING, J. K., et al (2002). A neural basis for social cooperation. *Neuron, 35,* 395–405.

ROWE, M. B. (1996). Reprint: Science, silence and sanctions. *Science and Children, 34*(1), 35–37.

SCHNEPS, M. H. (c. 1997). *Minds of our own.* Videotape series. Cambridge, MA: The Private Universe Project at Harvard-Smithsonian Center for Astrophysics.

SELIGMAN, M. (1995). *The optimistic child.* Boston: Houghton Mifflin.

STIPEK, D., & GREENE, J. (2001). Achievement motivation in early childhood: Cause for concern or celebration? In S. Golbeck (Ed.), *Psychological perspectives on early childhood education.* Mahwah, NJ: Erlbaum.

WELLMAN, H. M., & GELMAN, S. A. (1998). Knowledge acquisition in foundational domains. In W. Damon, D. Kuhn, & R. S. Siegler (Eds.), *Handbook of child psychology (5th ed.): Vol. 2. Cognition, perception, and language.* New York: John Wiley.

WELTON, N., SMITH, W., OWENS, K., & ADRIAN, M. (2000). Hands-on science as a motivator for children with emotional/behavioral disabilities. *Journal of Elementary Science Education, 12*(2), 33–37.

PART TWO

CONCEPTS, EXPERIENCES, AND INTEGRATING ACTIVITIES

Plants

Do you remember drawing pictures with a strip of green at the bottom, a brown column with a green ball on the top, and a row of brightly colored flowers? Were you, like most children, interested in grass, trees, and flowers? Did you pick bouquets of dandelions or other blossoms? Starting from this interest and experience, you know more about plants than you may realize. You can build on young children's innate interest in growing things.

They feed us, clothe us, shelter us, purify the air we breathe, and fill our visual world with beauty: the living things called plants. Children may be captivated by towering giant plants or the tiniest weed blossoms underfoot. When we share their delight, we renew our own appreciation of nature's exquisite order. The following concepts will be explored in this chapter:

- There are many kinds of plants; each has its own form.
- Most plants make seeds for new plants.
- Seeds grow into plants with roots, stems, leaves, and flowers.
- Most plants need water, light, minerals, warmth, and air.
- Some plants grow from roots.
- Some plantlike forms do not have seeds or roots.
- Many foods we eat are seeds.

The first suggested experience will be limited by climate to areas where deciduous trees grow. The next group of activities calls for gathering natural materials. This may require the ingenuity of teachers in urban schools. The concluding experiences with seeds and plant growing should be possible anywhere. Suggestions for seedling care and for transplanting are included.

CONCEPT: There are many kinds of plants; each has its own form.

1. ♣ *How do the parts of different plants look?*

LEARNING OBJECTIVE: To enjoy finding similarities and differences in plants and trees.

MATERIALS:

Large collecting bag full of found items such as:

    leaves (2 or 3 of each kind)

    tall grasses (include seeds or blossoms)

    flowers

    twigs

    bark

    seed pods, nuts

    mosses, lichens

Paper lunch bags

GETTING READY:

Sort the found materials.

Fill a teacher's bag with one of each kind of item.

Distribute an assortment of materials into small bags for the children.

Place a closed bag at each place at the science table.

SMALL-GROUP ACTIVITY:

(Complete this activity after taking a walk to collect nature materials.)

1. Take one object from your bag. "Look into your bags to see if you can find a leaf that matches this one."
2. As children find similar items to compare, encourage them to notice details: "Is it just like mine? Are the tips of your leaf rounded like this one? It almost matches. Who found one with rounded tips?" (Children may have lots of information about plants already. Listen.)
3. Point out that all leaves from the same kind of tree have the same general shape. (Size and fall coloration may vary.) For example, "When they have finished growing, all sweet gum tree leaves have five points. That's one way to know that the tree is a sweet gum tree."

Note: Specimens can survive close inspection by enclosing them in a no-cost display cover. Use a drop of glue to attach a well-dried specimen to the inside of a clear plastic deli carton or yogurt container. Cover with a matching lid. Join rim edges to form a case and seal with tape (Figure 4–1). (Remove dating ink by warming the lid over a cup of steaming liquid, then wiping with nail polish remover.)

2. ♣ *How do some plants rest for winter?*

LEARNING OBJECTIVE: To make a satisfying connection with nature's seasonal changes.

FIGURE 4–1

MATERIALS:

Shopping bag

Old, thick phone book

Newspaper

Waxed paper

Electric iron or bricks

GETTING READY:

Try to do this a week in advance. Save waxed leaves for another year.

Get a good specimen leaf from each tree you plan to visit with the class.

Press leaves for several days between pages of newspaper inserted into the phone book. Weight with the iron or bricks.

Fold waxed paper over each dried leaf. Press warm iron on paper to coat leaves with wax.

Tape the leaves to a low bulletin board and label.[*]

SMALL-GROUP ACTIVITY:

1. When deciduous trees start to change color, take a tree trip. Have children circle a tree, holding hands. "What can you see above you? Below?" Repeat with an evergreen tree. (Old needles on the ground have been replaced by new ones, but not all at once.) Visit shrubs if trees are not within walking distance.

2. Supply these ideas, as needed: Leaves make food for trees to grow; green color (chlorophyll) in leaves uses the energy from sunlight to help turn water, minerals, and air into food; this work is finished for leaves on some trees when summer ends.

3. Gather leaves from the ground.

4. Let children put like kinds of leaves together when you get back. Ask them to try to match their finds with the mounted specimens. Encourage them to bring leaves from home to try to match them.

5. Save the surplus leaves for art activities or for compost.

[*]Other methods of preserving leaves are detailed in *Science and Children,* September, 1994, 32.

Group Discussion: Recall the fun of collecting leaves. Ask what happens to the leaves from deciduous trees and shrubs that rest for winter. Introduce the idea that when chlorophyll goes out of these leaves, other colors that are also in the leaves show instead of only the green chlorophyll. (You might be able to find mottled leaves that fell before all the chlorophyll left.) Talk about how the leaves can still be valuable after they fall. If possible, start a compost bag or heap (see p. 78).

CONCEPT: Most plants make seeds for new plants.

1. What can we find out about fruit seeds?

LEARNING OBJECTIVE: To be reassured by discovering that most plants form seeds to create more plants of the same kind.

Introduction: Show a large seed pod (e.g., daylily, iris, milkweed), preferably still attached to its stalk. Ask for children's ideas about it. Summarize that each kind of plant has a job to do: make seeds for new plants just like it. Each plant forms seeds when its flowers stop blooming. "Some seeds are protected by covers we like to eat. Let's explore some fruits and vegetables to see if they are seed covers."

MATERIALS:

Any seed pods like:

   flower, tree, shrub, tall grass
   seed head

As many of these as can be
   brought in:

   apple, tomato,* pomegranate,
   peach, ear of corn in husk,
   orange, nuts in shells, melon,
   squash,* green beans, apri-
   cot, cucumber*

Foam produce trays

Paring knife *(adult use only)*

Smocks

Newspapers

GETTING READY:

Wash fruits and vegetables.

Cover table with papers.

Have all children wash their
   hands.

Put out plants with seed pods to
   examine first.

SMALL-GROUP ACTIVITY:

1. Let children predict if seeds will be inside each item. Find out. Carefully cut the fruits open. Share tastes and sniffs with everyone.

2. Save melon and squash seeds. Later let children wash them, and dry on trays. Save seeds for bird-feeders. If corn is fresh, pull back husks, hang to dry. Let children shell dried corn for the birds and for a later sprouting project. Tack one dried husk and ear of corn to a tree for the birds, if possible.

3. Ask older children to figure out a way, such as grouping, to count the large number of seeds in a pumpkin.

*The edible part of a plant that develops from a flower is a fruit, but some are commonly called vegetables. Children can make the botanical distinction in more advanced science classes.

Group Discussion: When discussing this experience, consider how many seeds each fruit or vegetable has, and that a new plant could grow from each one. Comment on the abundance of nature: a welcome thought for children who hear frequently and worry about endangered species.

Read: One Bean by Anne Rockwell.

2. How are seeds scattered?

LEARNING OBJECTIVE: To be intrigued by the ways different seeds are scattered.

MATERIALS:

Locally available seeds from garden plants; weeds (teasel, milkweed, burdock); grasses (wheat, oats); and trees (ailanthus, locust, oak, pine,* chestnut)

Magnifying glasses

Old fuzzy mittens and socks

Trays

GETTING READY:

Gather ripe seed stalks in advance.

Store in open containers or hang in tied bunches to dry.

Preserve husks and pods intact.

Find weeds in vacant lots or in roadside ditches.

SMALL-GROUP ACTIVITY:

1. Arrange materials on trays. Let children shake seeds from pods, brush hairy seeds against the mitten, beat grass seed spikes against trays to release grains.
2. Examine burrs and hairy seeds with magnifiers to see tiny hooks on the tips.
3. Take winged seeds and a few heavier nuts to the playground. Let children launch them from a high place. Compare what happens to each kind of seed.

Group Discussion: Ask if children have seen plants growing in places where people couldn't plant them—in sidewalk cracks or rock crevices. How could seeds get there? How many ways can children think of?

*Seeds lie beneath separate cone scales. Old cones on trees may no longer contain seeds. Tightly closed new cones can be dried in a warm oven with the heat turned off. Seeds can then be found in the open cones.

CONCEPT: **Seeds grow into plants with roots, stems, leaves, and flowers.**

1. What is inside a seed?

LEARNING OBJECTIVE: To delight in finding a beginning plant in seeds.

Introduction: "There is a surprise inside a seed. Let's find it."

MATERIALS:

Dried beans, several for each
child.

Desirable if available: maple
tree seeds, avocados, fresh
green beans or peas

Magnifying glasses

GETTING READY:

Soak beans overnight in enough
water to cover.

Keep a few beans dry for
comparison.

SMALL-GROUP ACTIVITY:

1. Demonstrate by carefully slipping off a
   seed coat. Pull apart the two parts (cotyle-
   dons, the food source for starting a new
   plant). Find the "surprise": the tiny new
   plant (embryo) ready to start growing.
2. Let children continue to open seeds to find
   new plants, and examine with magnifying
   glasses.
3. If a very ripe avocado is available, slice the
   fleshy part in half. Twist slightly to pull
   apart. Examine the seed. Peel the seed coat
   at the base. A ripe fruit seed may already
   be splitting, revealing a root tip. Do not
   split it open if you want to plant it.

To Start an Avocado Tree: Slice away about 1/4 inch (1 cm) from the base of
the avocado seed. Insert three round toothpicks midway through the seed to suspend the seed in a jar of water. Keep in a warm place away from direct sunlight.
Change the water weekly. (If a seed fits in a water-filled carafe, toothpicks aren't
needed, see Figure 4–3 on page 65.) After the root appears, move the jar to a
sunny location. When leaves appear on the stem, gently plant in a pot at a depth
of approximately 5 inches (13 cm). Leave the top quarter of the seed exposed
above the soil. Water at least every other day. Spray or wash leaves frequently.

2. How do seeds start to grow?

LEARNING OBJECTIVE: To focus on the wonder of new plant life beginning.

MATERIALS:

Method 1

Matching disposable plastic
tumblers

Transparent tape

Cotton balls or sand

Dried legumes: navy or lima
beans, lentils (fresh stock)*

Water

Plastic prescription vial

Desirable: mung beans (natural
food store)

SMALL-GROUP ACTIVITY:

Method 1

1. Make a sprouting dome: Wet four or five
   cotton balls, press out excess water, and
   flatten (or dampen sand). Line the bottom
   and sides of one tumbler with wet cotton
   or sand.
2. Let children see and feel the beans. As the
   children help place 4 beans between the
   cotton and the tumbler side, recall the surprise inside the seeds. (Try to use more
   than one kind of legume to see which
   sprouts first, which gets tallest, and which
   grows for the longest time.)
3. Upend the matching tumbler on the rim of
   the prepared tumbler. Tape the rims to
   make a dome enclosure (Figure 4–2).

4. Place it away from direct sunlight where temperature will be even.
5. Put one of each kind of seed in the vial for later comparison. Start a calendar record of starting date, first root, first stem, and first leaf appearance. Crayon-mark daily growth level on the tumbler.

Method 2

Plastic sandwich bags
White paper toweling
Stapler
Masking tape

Method 2

1. Each child makes a sprouting bag. Fold toweling to fit bag and dampen the toweling. Place 5 lentils on damp toweling; staple bag shut. Label with child's name on a piece of tape.
2. Children keep daily sprout growth logs by sketching or writing descriptions, and by measuring root and stem length.

*Two common causes of germination failure are old seeds and an overheated, dry room. Don't expect good results with seeds of unknown vintage, nor with uncovered sprouting containers.

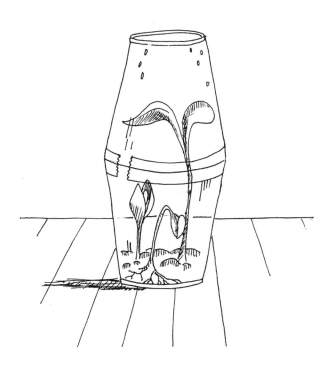

FIGURE 4–2

Note: It's a good idea to start two germinating domes. Keep one available for children to pick up for a close look. If sprouts don't survive the inspection, the other dome will be available. It's hard to only look and not touch when leaves are showing beneath a rakish seed cover cap.

3. *How do roots and stems grow?*

LEARNING OBJECTIVE: To verify the surprising tendency of roots to grow downward toward water and of stems to grow upward toward light.

MATERIALS:

Same as for the seed-sprouting experience

SMALL-GROUP ACTIVITY:

1. "Notice which direction the seedling roots and stems take. Is it the same for each seedling?"
2. Gently turn one seedling so that the stem points down and the root reaches up. Mark an *X* on the glass beneath it.
3. Draw picture records each day of changes in root and stem growth. Check the cotton behind the seeds. Roots may poke down into it toward water.

Group Discussion: Ask children if trees grow with their branches and leaves in the soil and their roots in the air, if flowers blossom underground, or if plants send roots into the ground and other parts into the light. Why is this so? Help the children recall that leaves need light and air to perform their food-making job. Roots have the job of getting water and minerals from the soil so that the plant can live and grow. The upended seedling root and stem twisted and turned to grow in the directions where each could get what it needed.

CONCEPT: Most plants need water, light, minerals, warmth, and air.

1. *What do seeds need to start growing?*

LEARNING OBJECTIVE: To experience the joy of nurturing plant growth.

MATERIALS:

Zinnia or marigold seeds, package-dated for current year
Dried corn seeds, if available
Small package of commercial potting soil (sterilized)
Teaspoons
Empty yogurt cups

SMALL-GROUP ACTIVITY:

Let the children:

1. Fill cups almost to the top with soil.
2. Use spray bottle to dampen soil well.
3. Place one seed on soil, then cover lightly with soil, press firmly, water again. Plant some seeds in extra cups to replace possible failures. (If dried corn seeds have been saved from a fall seed activity, plant them as well.)

Masking tape

Water

Trays

Water spray bottle

GETTING READY:

Collect empty yogurt cups well
  in advance, more than enough
  for each child.

Cover table with newspapers.

Make masking tape name tags
  for each child's cup.

4. Place trays of cups in a spot away from
   drafts, radiators, and direct sunlight. Cover
   loosely with plastic sheet.

5. As soon as tiny shoots appear, remove
   plastic cover. Move trays to sunny spot.
   Keep soil damp with sprayer.

6. Draw pictorial records of seedling growth
   stages.

7. Set aside a seedling dampening time
   every other day. Ask, "If you were a tiny
   new plant, how would you want to be
   cared for?"

Group Discussion: Compare the calendar records of the germination dome
and the plant-raising experiences. "Were seeds treated alike in both experiences?
Which seedlings stopped growing and withered? Which ones kept growing?"
Moist seeds can grow only until their built-in food supply is used up. Plants
rooted in soil can use minerals and moisture from the soil to help the leaves make
their food for growth. Would the seeds grow in a freezer? Find out.

Additional Experiences: Keep some soil on hand all year to be ready for
planting opportunities. Plant seeds used in the earliest seed investigation activities. Fresh peas or beans can be planted directly into the soil. Corn must be dry
enough to be pried off the cob without breaking open before it should be planted.
Plant some dried pumpkin seeds after Halloween. Try growing plants from
grapefruit seeds. Late season, tree-ripened grapefruit seeds seem to respond
most promptly. Soak them in a small amount of water until the seeds sink to the
bottom of the container (about three days) before planting. Try planting fresh
date pits. A general rule for planting is that seeds should be planted at a depth
twice the width of the seeds.

Seedling Care: After leaves appear, provide moderate light, such as a northern exposure. Cover only at night to retain moisture. Allow children to water
their own plants with the sprayer. It's hard to over-water this way, but if it happens, blot up standing water with absorbent materials. Check each cup before
covering trays at night in case someone forgets to water a plant.

About Soil: To control one possible source of failure, commercially prepared potting soil is recommended for germinating seeds. For other classroom
use, let children enjoy mixing their own potting soil: 1/3 ordinary soil, 1/3 sand,
and 1/3 peat moss. Talk about how soil is made of crumbled rocks, dead plants,
and insect matter.

Transplanting: For several days after the second pair of leaves appears, give
seedlings a few hours of direct sunlight, preferably outdoors in a sheltered spot.
Tell parents that if the bottoms of the cups are torn off, the cups can be planted
directly into the ground when the soil is warm.

If many children in the class are apartment dwellers, you may want to grow
dwarf plant varieties. Transplant the seedlings before sending them home. Use any

container large enough to hold about three cups of soil. Punch a drainage hole in the bottom of cartons or cans, add a layer of small rocks, and fill 1/3 full with soil. Cut away the lower half of the cup, plant firmly, cover with more soil, and water it.

2. How do plants take up water?

LEARNING OBJECTIVE: To watch the fascinating way water moves up a stem.

MATERIALS:

2 stalks of celery, with leaves

2 jars ·

Food coloring, blue or red
  (enough to make dark color)

Water

SMALL-GROUP ACTIVITY:

1. "How does water get into the leaves of a plant?"
2. "Let's see if we can figure out how water moves up these stalks of celery." Let children stir food coloring into one jar of water.
3. Check within an hour for signs of color in leaf tips. Separate a dyed tube from the stalk so the dye can be seen in the whole length. Slice a cross section from the bottom of the stalk to examine.
4. "What do you think would happen to a stalk of celery if it had no water for a while? Let's find out." Leave the other stalk in the empty jar overnight. Check its condition the next day.
5. "Do you think water will change this stalk? Let's try it." Trim 1/4 inch from the stem bottom and add water to the jar. Check it the next day. Has it revived? Clarify that celery plants have roots in the ground when they are growing. Roots take up water from the soil and the water travels up through the stalk tubes.

CONCEPT: Some plants grow from roots.

1. What can we find out about growing potatoes?

LEARNING OBJECTIVE: To observe the satisfying ways tubers and bulbs produce new plants.

MATERIALS:

Potatoes, some sprouting,
  some not

Potting soil

Pots

Knife

GETTING READY:

To avoid disappointing the class, first try at home to sprout a potato from the same source.

? *Inquiry Activity:* Ask the class their ideas about whether or not new plants can start from parts of plants other than seeds. Take suggestions and help children experiment by setting up various growing situations with the potatoes. Keep a written calendar or a series of observational drawings and measurements to record the plants' growth.

Follow-Up Observation: If you can find a homegrown sweet potato (not commercially treated to retard sprouting), suspend it in a jar of water. (See Figure 4–3.) Ask for predictions about what will happen to it. Keep it out of direct sunlight until first sprouts appear. Add to or change water as needed. A successful sweet potato vine will flourish for months before its food supply is depleted. It may be planted in the ground when the old potato starts to cave in. It can still produce a new crop of potatoes.

Plant some daffodil bulbs outdoors in fall. Later, if you should find a sprouting onion in your kitchen, slice it open vertically so the children can see the new plant tucked inside its food supply bulb. Talk about the bulbs outdoors waiting for the spring sunshine to warm the earth and for the rain to start them growing. Start a few paperwhite narcissus bulbs or an amaryllis bulb in the room. Follow package

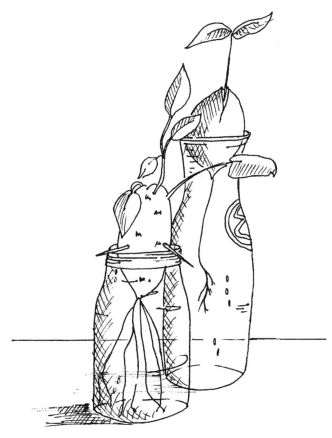

FIGURE 4–3

Tanisha studies the sweet potato roots, leaves, and stems.

directions for growing conditions. The amaryllis bulb is huge, grows dramatically, and produces spectacular flowers. Children can readily see the flower's pistils and stamen without a magnifying glass. A large seedpod forms as the blossom dies away which can be opened when dry to provide more seeds for experimenting.

Read: Paperwhite, by Nancy Wallace. Try to locate a library copy of an amaryllis story, now out of print: *A Flower Grows,* by Ken Robbins.

CONCEPT: Some plantlike forms do not have seeds or roots.

1. ♣ *What is mold?*

LEARNING OBJECTIVE: To notice the amazing ways simple plantlike forms grow and develop.

Group Discussion: Bring a piece of bread, two screw-top jars, and a drop-top bottle (like a soy sauce bottle) of water to a group gathering. Recall with the children that most plants make new plants from seeds or from root and stem parts. Say that a few kinds of plants grow from tiny, dust-speck bits called *spores.* Millions of spores blow about in the air, but they are too small to see. When spores land on a warm, moist food source they grow into plants that we can see.

"Perhaps we can grow a plant like that on a bit of bread." Put half of the bread in each jar. Cover one jar. Let the children sprinkle water on the piece of bread in the second jar. Leave this jar uncovered for an hour. Then cover it and store it in a warm, dark place for a few days. Compare the two pieces of bread. Do they look the same? Leave the moldy bread in the jar to develop a luxuriant fur coat. (Perhaps the black spore clumps will be visible as specks on the mold.)

JEUNESSE, G., DELAFOSSE, C., & METTLER, R. (1999). *Flowers.* New York: Scholastic. Excellent acetate overlay pages add depth by uncovering the inner working parts of the blossom to intrigue preschool/primary children. Also in this First Discovery series is *Trees,* by the same authors.

KILE, PATRICIA. (1998). *Dandelion adventures.* Brookfield, CT: Millbrook. Soft watercolors trace the course of seven dandelion seeds carried aloft by silken parachutes. Endnotes caution us to eat only those dandelion blossoms and new leaves untouched by toxic sprays.

LERNER, CAROL. (1999). *My indoor garden.* New York: Morrow. This attractive, well-organized primer on houseplants will answer many questions about classroom gardening projects.

LEVENSON, GEORGE. (1999). *Pumpkin circle.* Berkeley, CA: Tricycle Press. Photographs taken with a filmmaker's eye for impact, and a simple, lyrical text about the seed-to-seed lifecycle of pumpkins explain the awards won by this book. A companion video is available also.

LIN, GRACE. (1999). *The ugly vegetables.* Watertown, MA: Talewinds. A young girl thinks her mother's garden is the ugliest in the neighborhood until she finds that flowers look and smell pretty, but the soup mother makes from the vegetables grown in her garden smells best of all. Delighted neighbors think so, too.

LOBEL, ANITA. (1996). *Alison's zinnia.* New York: Morrow. Striking flower paintings are the focus of this clever, alphabet-sequenced story line. Its alliterations are fun to read and hear.

LOBEL, ARNOLD. (1972). *Frog and toad together.* New York: Harper & Row. Toad has some funny ideas about coaxing seeds to grow in this classic story. Paperback.

LOBEL, ARNOLD. (1993). *The rose in my garden.* New York: Morrow. This cumulative tale in lovely prose takes place among garden flowers. Charming illustrations by Anita Lobel. Paperback.

LOCKER, THOMAS. (1995). *Sky tree.* New York: HarperCollins. This remarkable book layers appreciation of nature, science, and art with deliberately evoked emotional responsiveness and lucid watercolors into a pleasant narrative of the seasons of a tree's life. It is a treasure.

MACDONALD, MARGARET. (1998). *Pickin' peas.* New York: HarperCollins. A pesky rabbit likes to eat the peas a young girl plants. Children will enjoy this battle of wits. Vibrant illustrations.

MAESTRO, BETSY. (1994). *Why do leaves change color?* New York: HarperCollins. This book presents an attractively illustrated, careful explanation of chlorophyll functioning and seasonal changes of leaves.

MCCULLY, EMILY. (1997). *Popcorn at the palace.* San Diego, CA: Harcourt Brace. Based on an actual presentation of American popcorn to Queen Victoria's court, this story can link with social studies.

OPPENHEIM, JOANNE. (1995). *Have you seen trees?* New York: Scholastic. Gorgeous watercolors add to the delight of this sparkling poem of trees in all seasons. The tree facts afterword will also interest young children.

POSADA, MIA. (2000). *Dandelions: Stars in the grass.* Minneapolis: Carolrhoda. Pleasant art and interesting activities comprise this simple book about the lifecycle of the dandelion plant. NSTA[*] Outstanding Trade Book.

ROBBINS, KEN. (1999). *Autumn leaves.* New York: Scholastic. The author's elegant photographs and concise text make tree identification easy, and changing leaf colors intriguing. NSTA[*] Outstanding Trade Book.

ROCKWELL, ANNE. (1998). *One bean.* New York: Walker. Two youngsters delight in discovering how a single bean seed can grow into many. Have some fresh green beans on hand to share with listeners, as well as seeds to plant. Paperback.

SCHAEFER, LOLA. (2000). *This is the sunflower.* New York: Greenwillow. Splashy illustrations and a catchy cumulative rhyme convey the life cycle of a sunflower plant to young listeners.

SCHORIES, PAT. (1996). *Over under in the garden.* New York: Farrar, Strauss, & Giroux. This beautiful alphabet book of plants and flowers is an NSTA[*] Outstanding Trade Book.

SILVERSTEIN, SHEL. (1986). *The giving tree.* New York: Harper & Row. A boy grows up with a tree that gives him shade, apples, shelter, and finally, a resting stump.

STEVENS, JANET. (1995). *Tops and bottoms.* New York: Harcourt Brace. In this adapted folktale, an enterprising rabbit outwits a dozing farmer to feed his family. The lush vegetable paintings won Caldecott Honors.

STEWART, SARAH. (1997). *The gardener.* New York: Farrar, Strauss, & Giroux. A Caldecott Honor Book. This story, told as letters home, reveals how a spunky girl transforms a drab city roof into a blooming garden.

VANDERLINDEN, KATHERINE & GOLD, CAROL (ONTARIO SCIENCE CENTRE). (1998). *Plants.* Toronto, ON: Kids Can Press. Lively photographs add life to this book of clearly communicated plant experiments. Directions are given for making a hydroponic garden.

WALLACE, NANCY. (2000). *Paperwhite.* Boston: Houghton Mifflin. A youngster helps her neighbor coax paper white narcissus bulbs into bloom in this simple story, illustrated by the author's delightful collages.

*National Science Teachers Association

Poems (Resources in Appendix A)

The collection *Poems to Grow On*, compiled by Jean McKee Thompson, has four poems about seeds appropriate to read during the seed investigations:

> "The Little Plant" by Kate Louise Brown
>
> "The Seed" and "Carrot Seeds" by Aileen Fisher
>
> "Seeds" by Walter de la Mare
>
> X. J. Kennedy's poem, "Art Class," in *I Thought I'd Take My Rat to School* by Dorothy Kennedy (Ed.), describes a child's speculations about drawing a tree.
>
> Nancy Turner's poem, "A Popcorn Song," is in the collection *Sing a Song of Popcorn*, compiled by DeRegniers, et al.

Fingerplays

This traditional fingerplay fits well with the concept that living things reproduce in their own special form.

The Apple Tree	
Way up high in the apple tree	(Stretch arms up.)
Two red apples, I did see.	(Make circles with hands.)
I shook that tree as hard as I could.	(Shake "trunk.")
Mmmmm, those apples tasted good!	(Pat tummy.)

—AUTHOR UNKNOWN

Substitute "orange carrots, green pears, two bananas," and so on for "two red apples, I did see." The children will enjoy catching and correcting your mistake. Ask them why it must be apples growing on the apple tree. "Really? Don't carrots grow on apple trees? Then, where do they grow? Do they grow in the ground from apple seeds?"

My Garden

This is my garden	(Hold one hand palm upward.)
I'll rake it with care.	("Rake" with curled fingers of other hand.)
Here are the seeds	(Pantomime planting, seed by seed.)
I'll plant in there	
The sun will shine	(With arms, make circle above head.)
The rain will fall	(Fingers flutter down.)
The seeds will sprout	(Spread fingers of one hand. Push up other fingers between them.)
And grow up tall	(Bring hands and forearms together. Move up, spreading palms outward as arms move up.)

—AUTHOR UNKNOWN

Art Activities

Collage. Dried grasses, leaves, pressed flowers, flat seeds, and small twigs make lovely collage materials. Tape may be needed when younger children include twigs and long grasses in their work. Vary the background colors to bring out the hues of the dried materials.

Rubbings. Tape a single fresh leaf or a pattern of small leaves to the table in front of each child. Cover with a sheet of heavy paper. Let children rub a crayon over the paper to bring out the relief design of the leaf veins.

Translucents. Fresh leaves, flower petals, and grasses can be sealed between two sheets of waxed paper to make translucent window hangings. Do not use an electric iron in the classroom to seal the paper. For safety, and for maximum child participation, use a newspaper-covered electric food-warming tray as a heat source. Give children a pizza roller or a child-size rolling pin to apply light strokes of pressure to the waxed paper.

Cut-Paper Mural. Flower inventions: Offer strips of green paper for stems and leaves and assorted sizes of circles in blossom colors. Indicate ways to change the texture and shape of the rounds such as notching, slashing for fringes, scoring with a ruler edge and pinching into cup shapes, cutting into spirals, and curling edges around a pencil. Put out scissors and white glue or paste. Assemble the children's fantasy flowers into a beautiful mural for your classroom door.

Leaf Mobile. Let children cut out freehand leaf shapes (or whatever satisfies them as appearing leaflike). In spring, use green paper; in fall, use orange, brown, and red. Use 5-inch squares of paper. Suggest making the job easier by folding the paper in half. Let them punch a hole in each leaf and thread it with a small bit of yarn. Help them tie or tape their leaves to an interestingly shaped branch. Hang the branch from a ceiling beam, or staple it to a bulletin board with some of the twigs extending into the room.

For more nature art ideas, consult *Good Earth Art: Environmental Art for Kids* by Mary Ann Kohl and Cindy Gainer.

Play

Farming. Playgrounds that offer a bit of shady ground for digging are natural settings for spontaneous farm play. Provide children with small, sturdy rakes, hoes, shovels, buckets, and a wheelbarrow. They will find rocks or cones to plant, and leaves, grasses, or pine needles to harvest without further suggestion. Children will need to know the boundaries of the permissible digging area. Listen to their planting ideas.

Sand Table Indoor Gardens. A collection of twigs, pinecones of several sizes, dried grasses and pods, or perhaps blossoms can be arranged by the children to create small landscapes in the sand table. (Dampened sand will hold better than dry sand.) Rubber toy animals and people can be added.

Blossom Fun. If you can find an abundance of grassflowers for children to gather, use the small blossoms to make beautiful (though short-lived) decorations. Show children how to make a split midway in a dandelion stem in which to insert another dandelion stem, and so on. The resulting rope can be looped into necklaces or crowns, or be allowed to get as long as possible. Leaves and sturdy blossoms can be threaded on soft, covered wires from a telephone cable to make bracelets. Large leaves strung together can become headdresses. Two hollyhock blossoms can be stacked and joined through the center with a toothpick to make dolls with hollyhock-bud heads and daisy hats.

Children can place small sprigs of evergreen in a water-filled ring mold to make a tabletop Christmas wreath. Use small pinecones for turkey bodies; tiny hemlock cones, painted red, for heads; and bird feathers for tails.

Creative Movement

Curl up on the floor with the children, pretending to be seeds that have been planted in spring (or bulbs planted in fall if this was a class project). Move with the children to enact the growing story as you softly tell it. "Here we are waiting under the ground. The sunshine makes the soil warm; rain falls, and we begin to expand. The tiny plant inside grows bigger and pokes out of the seed cover. We send a root down to get water. Now our stem starts to push its way up . . . up . . . up to find the sunlight." Slowly describe the growth of the plant above the ground: leafing, budding, blooming, swaying in the breeze, feeling the sun and rain, losing petals, forming seeds, then slowly withering and scattering seeds for next year's plants.

Creative Thinking

What If? What if you were as tiny as your thumb? Which plants would you want to live near? To sleep in? To use for food? To hide under when it rains? To climb for fun? Would you enjoy curling up inside a tulip blossom for a nap? For inspiration, read "The Little Land" by Robert Louis Stevenson in *A Child's Garden of Verses,* or "Oak Leaf Plate" by Mary Ann Hoberman in *The Llama Who Had No Pajama* (Appendix A).

Ask children to listen with eyes closed, imagining a special tree to enjoy, as you read aloud Joanne Ryder's *Hello Tree!* Afterward let children draw the trees they imagined.

Food Experiences

Make applesauce when apples are in season. Try drying raisins if grapes are abundant in your area. Children can learn to scrub and peel raw fruit or vegetables for snacks and prepare vegetables for soup. Any time flour or sugar is used in classroom cooking projects, mention its plant source.

Discuss the parts of plants that are being served for lunch. "Are we eating the leaf, the root, or the stem of the celery plant (the potato, the carrot)?" Talk about the wheat seeds and the stems of sugar cane plants or the roots of sugar beet plants that went into the snack-time graham crackers.

Field Trips

We usually think of pleasant woods and meadows as ideal sites for plant life field trips, but the closest grocery store also has important plant learnings for children. Go there to see how much we depend on plants for food. Visit the produce section, the shelves of dry staple foods (flour, pasta, sugar, legumes, cereals, and all the packaged mixes), the canned and frozen fruits and vegetables, and the baked goods. A natural foods shop (not a health food store that features vitamin preparations) is a fine place to see what whole grains look like and to watch a small flour mill in operation. Flower shops and greenhouses can be fascinating, but make sure children are welcomed by the owners.

Indoor/Outdoor Tree Walks. ♣ How many different kinds of trees grow within walking distance of your school? How can children tell that they are different? If leaves are too high to be examined closely before they fall, bark characteristics can provide identification clues. Let children make bark rubbings with old crayons on thick, flexible paper. The backs of vinyl-coated wallpaper samples are good for this. Compare the differences in bark textures for different species.

Now move indoors to complete your tree walk. Ask the children to tour the classroom looking for all the wood they can find in use there. Old buildings may have ceiling moldings and window and door frames of wood, so suggest looking up to find wood. Make a list of the found items. Pencils and paper should be on the list, too.

Having a Quiet Look Outdoors. ♣ When the weather is good, explore a nearby weedy patch. Minimize the scatter tendency of unconfined children by defining small observation spaces with 6-foot loops of yarn. Before going outdoors, decide on groups of three or four children to share a looking loop. Children can stretch out on the ground, radiating from the loop like the spokes of the wheel. Ask children to report what they see in their space. Later make a summary chart of the observations, including soil, rocks, and small creatures, as well as plants. Tape samples to the chart.

Grassflower Gathering. ♣ Check grassy areas near your school in early spring for the presence of tiny flowers. Try to obtain permission for your children to pick tiny bouquets to take home. (Small groups make it a happier occasion.) Show the children where they may hunt, then let them take their time to find spring beauties, chickweed, violets, or whatever the lawnmower spares. Put the flowers in capsule vials of water. Label each with the child's name. Use them for table decorations, then wrap each child's flowers in a twist of waxed paper when it is time to go home.

PROMOTING CONCEPT CONNECTIONS

Maintaining Concepts

A row of potted plants on the classroom windowsill guarantees year-round attention to plant growth needs. Plant tending can occupy an honored position on the children's daily job chart. Younger children may need some help carrying the pitcher and deciding how much water to use. Older children can handle the task independently if pots are labeled with suitable watering advice. Comment on changes taking place, such as new buds, fading leaves, and unwanted insect tenants.

Classes in session during the regional growing season might be able to keep plant life concepts in focus by planting and maintaining a garden. Other classes could try portable gardens: plants started at school in the spring, moved to the home of a child or teacher for summer care, and returned to school for a fall harvest-with luck. Start pumpkin and sunflower seeds in good soil, using 2-gallon plastic buckets with drainage holes cut in the bottom. Thin out all but one vigorous seedling. Give it full sunshine and plenty of water. The plants won't attain full growth, but the pumpkin can produce a vine with leaves, tendrils, blossoms, and possibly a fledgling pumpkin. The sunflower will develop a seed head and may grow taller than a five- or six-year-old. Slip a section of old hosiery or netting over the fading blossom to keep the birds from feasting on the seeds too soon.

If long-term growing projects cannot be worked out, perhaps you can duplicate the efforts of one very fine teacher of three-year-olds. Each fall she scouts the countryside to find a whole, dried cornstalk complete with ears of corn. It creates a fall harvest mood in her room and provides an awesome lesson for the children who seem dwarfed by the giant that grew from a single kernel of corn. Later, shelling the corn becomes an absorbing task for the children. They feed some kernels to the birds and save some to germinate in spring. Other plant life experiences sometimes come about inadvertently. Capitalize on them. For example, an aging jack-o-lantern might develop a moldy spot. Instead of quietly discarding it, keep it in a sheltered outdoor spot to observe the changes. Then add it to a compost pile

Plant tending can occupy an honored position on the children's daily job chart.

so that it can contribute soil enrichment for next year's plants. Read excerpts from *What Rot! Nature's Mighty Recycler* by Elizabeth Ring.

Improving Schoolgrounds

In a protected place, begin a small orchard (apples, pears, plums) and berry patch (blueberry, raspberry, gooseberry). Children delight in growing real food. Add a few trees each year.

Connecting Concepts

Soil Composition Relationships. The natural cycle of renewing limited materials in the ecosystem is well illustrated in the creation of fertile soil. Pulverize shale to form powdery clay (see Chapter 10), or use sand or clay if shale isn't available. Try growing an extra seedling in it. Compare its growth with seedlings growing in true soil that also contains bits of decayed plant and animal matter. This idea could lead to starting a compost pile or bag in the fall. Let the children rake available leaves and grass clippings into a large plastic trash bag. When it is approximately half full, add a soup can full of fertilizer or powdered lime, a can of water, and a few shovels of dirt. Close the bag and leave it outdoors where it won't be forgotten during the winter. It will need to be turned, shaken, and opened several times for air. Although the completeness of the change that will occur by spring is not predictable, bacterial growth within the bag environment will have interacted with the materials to promote decay into compost (humus) to enrich the soil.

If molds appear on some of the decaying materials, examine them with magnifiers. Talk about how molds use other materials as food.

Discuss how completely rotted natural materials improve the soil and make it possible for strong, new plants to grow and produce food. Talk about renewing the soil this way as one of the wonderful cycles of nature: from living plants to decomposition . . . from enriched soil to healthy living plants again . . . and again . . . and again. It is comforting to understand the concept that once-living things continue to have a function after they die (see Furman, 1990, in Resources).

Plants That Help Crumble Rocks. Look in shady areas for greenish-gray patches of lichen growing on rocks. Lichen are fungi and algae that live together as a single unit. Together they make acids that slowly dissolve the rock surface.

Other plants sometimes grow in rock crevices, and their roots may break off pieces of rock. Perhaps there is a section of concrete sidewalk near your school that has been cracked or pushed up by strong tree roots. Watch for them as you take walks with children. Stop to look at them. Recall with the children that slowly crumbling rocks become part of the soil that plants grow in. (See Resources, Chapter 10.)

Air. The wind helps ripe dandelion and milkweed seeds float long distances under silky parachutes, and helps maple and ash tree seeds spin down and away to germinate. Try germinating a ripe, winged seed, if you have a maple tree nearby. A ripe seed splits in half. Plant it seed deep in a plastic tumbler. Leave the wing part out as a reminder of how it spun down on a breeze from the tree. It can produce a sturdy sprout and tiny leaf in about a month.

Air/Water Cycle. Use the term *evaporation* when plants are being watered. Some of the water will be taken up by the roots of the plants; the rest will evaporate. (See Resources, Chapter 8.)

If you make a terrarium, talk about how rarely it will need to be watered. Bring out the idea that the water taken up by the air in the closed terrarium will change into large drops on the cool glass sides. If you make the terrarium before the children have tried the evaporation and condensation experiences, postpone the discussion.

To make a small terrarium from a 2-liter plastic soda bottle, cut the bottle through about one-third of the way from the bottom, making two sections. (Do away from children.) Put a layer of gravel and some charcoal bits in the bottom third. Add a layer of potting soil. Arrange small plants in the soil. Dampen the soil; do not saturate. Replace the upper two-thirds and tape to seal. Cap the terrarium.

Family and Community Support

Children may take care of keeping their parents well informed as to the progress of their seedling experiences. Family help will be needed in providing a good growing location and in overseeing the care of the seedling that is sent home. Printed plant care tips could be fastened to the container. Include a few lines about other aspects of the projects that can help parents become informed listeners to their children. Encourage gardening families to set aside a small space for their child to plant and tend.

Share information with parents about nearby nature center or natural history museum programs for children. Inquire about naturalist-led walks through the nature center for families. A community gardening program may sponsor family gardening activities. There may be special seasonal displays of gardening and plant books in both children's and adult libraries.

RESOURCES

BERGER, T. (1992). *The harvest craft book.* Edinburgh: Floris Books. This book includes directions for making the cornhusk dolls and wheatstraw figures that older children could make as a craft for related studies of pioneering life. (Available through *Hearthsong: A Catalog for Families,* P. O. Box B, Sebastopol, CA 95473.)

FURMAN, E. (1990, November). Plant a potato—learn about life (and death). *Young Children, 46,* 15–20.

GEORGE, J. (1995). *Acorn pancakes, dandelion salad, & 38 other wild recipes.* New York: HarperCollins. This charmingly presented book on eating from the wild is written by a respected naturalist/author. She does, however, fail to caution against eating weeds that may have been sprayed with toxic chemicals.

GROWING IDEAS. This great journal of garden-based learning activities is published three times a year by the National Gardening Association, 180 Flynn Ave., Burlington, VT 05401. Write for a complimentary issue and subscription form.

HAMPTON, C., & KRAMER, D. (1994). *Classroom creature culture: Algae to anoles.* Washington, DC: National Science Teachers Association. This anthology of articles from *Science and Children* on the care of plants and animals brought in to school from the wild is an important resource for teachers.

KEPLER, L. (1996). *Windowsill science centers.* New York: Scholastic. Activities headed "Evergreen Explorations" develop understanding of how these trees survive winter weather.

KOHL, M., & GAINER, C. (1991). *Good earth art.* Bellingham, WA: Bright Ring Press. This book contains many good art extensions of plant life.

LERNER, C. (1988). *Moonseed and mistletoe: A book of poisonous wild plants.* New York: Morrow.

LERNER, C. (1990). *Dumb cane and daffodils: Poisonous plants in the house and garden.* New York: Morrow. It is important to bring this information to the attention of children.

LOVEJOY, S. (1991). *Sunflower houses.* Loveland, CO: Interweave Press. Directions for planting a sunflower and morning glory summer playhouse alone would make this charming book worth searching out. It also suggests making flower dolls, grass whistles, and pumpkin and bean tepees. (Reprint 2001 by Workman Press.)

LOVEJOY, S. (1994). *Hollyhock days.* Loveland, CO: Interweave Press. This pleasant book on gardening with children details how to grow a hollyhock tent, if playground space is available.

PETRASH, C. (1992). *Earthways.* Mt. Rainier, MD: Gryphon. This gentle book includes directions for braiding wheatstalk wreaths and making simple cornhusk dolls, time-honored crafts from pioneer days.

RICHARDSON, B. (1998). *Gardening with children.* Newtown, CT: Taunton Books. This complete gardening handbook includes intriguing ways to start seedlings, and directions for making seedling pots from newspaper.

RING, E. (1996). *What rot! Nature's mighty recycler.* Brookfield, CT: Millbrook Press. Excellent photographs and clear text about molds, fungi, mosses, insects, and other animals that help in decomposition.

RUSSELL, H. R. (2001). *Ten-minute field trips: Using the school grounds for environmental studies* (2nd ed.). Washington, DC: National Science Teachers Association. Every city-bound teacher should know this book. Nature's ability to triumph over asphalt and concrete permeates the text.

VANCLEAVE, J. (1989). *Basic biology for every kid.* New York: Wiley. Basic plant phenomena are illustrated by the 20 experiments for older children, but some are referenced for younger children.

Animals

How do you feel about animals? Have your feelings changed since you were a child? Most children are interested in animals, so it's fun to help them develop some basic concepts.

Animals of all sizes and conditions fascinate many children who are eager to watch, touch, and care for creatures. Other children have limited tolerance for anything that creeps, crawls, or nips. The experiences suggested in this chapter can both expand the knowledge of the creature lovers and soften the feelings of anxious children into moderate respect for the useful and beautiful small animals around us. These concepts will be explored:

- There are many kinds of animals.
- Animals move in different ways.
- Each animal needs its own kind of food.
- Many animals make shelters to rear their young.
- Humans and animals often live together.

The feasibility of this chapter's experiences will depend upon having specimens for observation. Flexible planning is necessary. It would be sheer luck for a spider and a teacher to meet precisely on the day set aside for spider study.

Buying, housing, and maintaining classroom pets can be expensive. However, earthworms, spiders, and insects exist everywhere and can be easily obtained. The experiences that follow use insects, worms, fish, wild birds, and pictures to illustrate concepts. Suggestions for acquiring and understanding insects, as well as ideas pertaining to borrowed pets, are included.

CONCEPT: There are many kinds of animals.

Introduce this topic with a question for children to think about: "What is an animal?" Responses about specific animals will flow easily. Then suggest that there are so many kinds of animals in the world that it would take days just to say their names. "Here is a shorter way to say what an animal is: An animal is a living thing, but it is not a plant." How many animals can the children think of now? Their list can include people, spiders, earthworms, and insects. There are more than a million species of insects alone! All insects—indeed, all animals—have some features in common.

1. What is an insect?

LEARNING OBJECTIVE: To develop interest in insect features.

MATERIALS:

Temporary cages (see p. 83)
Live insects
Leafy plant sprigs
Water spray bottle
Magnifying glasses
Drawing materials

GETTING READY:

Use capture techniques that follow.
Keep live insect cages out of direct sunlight.

SMALL-GROUP ACTIVITY:

1. Ground rules for observation should be set: (a) Insects or other small animals stay in the cages and (b) cages must be handled gently.
2. Suggest looking for things that identify members of the insect family: three body parts (head, thorax, abdomen); six legs; two feelers (antennae). Spiders are *not* insects (they have eight legs); caterpillars *are* (only six legs are true, jointed legs).
3. Have children draw pictures of the insects they are watching.
4. Mention: (a) These are adult insects. First they were eggs, then larvae (wingless, wormlike) before changing to adult form. (b) Insects have no bones. They have stiff coverings protecting their soft bodies.
5. Release insects outdoors at the end of the day.

Further observation suggestions are found in Sally Kneidel's *Pet Bugs* books. (See Resources.)

Capture Techniques

Locating Creatures. ♣ Start looking for specimens near your own doorstep. On warm nights, check screen doors for insects that are attracted by light. Hunt for web-building spiders on window frames and shrubs. Turn over rocks on the ground to find crickets, beetles, and such. Look in flower borders for ladybugs, bumble-bees, grasshoppers, ants, and wandering spiders that chase their prey instead of catching them on webs. Examine weed clumps like Queen Anne's lace and milk-weed for caterpillars.

Catching Creatures. Cold-blooded animals do not move rapidly in cool parts of the day. A bumblebee is groggy and easy to catch early on a crisp fall morning. Scoop it up with an open jar, then quickly clap on the lid. Slip in a dewy sprig of the plant that the bee rested on and re-cover the jar with a piece of nylon hosiery or netting, held with a rubber band. Bees may be easier to locate during warmer parts of the day *but are quicker to defend themselves.* Try using bamboo toast tongs to catch an alert bee. Use tongs to pick up very spiky-looking caterpillars. Some cause skin rashes if touched.

Wandering ground spiders and grasshoppers may be caught by clapping an open jar over them. Both species seem to hop straight up inside the jar, making it easy to slip the lid under it. Nets are preferred for the safe capture of butterflies and moths. Sweep the net over the insect; flip the bag to fold it over the catch. Remove the butterfly by gently holding two wings folded back together. Slip it into a sandwich bag. Keep the insect out of the sun until it can be transferred to an observation terrarium or box.

Only two small spiders have a dangerous bite. **Avoid:**

- *The black widow:* Shiny black body with a bright red hourglass mark beneath the abdomen (back section). Young may have three red dots on top of the abdomen.
- *The brown recluse:* Rare. Lives indoors in attics, closets, or other dark corners. Yellow to brownish color. Fiddle-shaped mark on top of front section (cephalothorax) is dark brown. The base of the fiddle is between the feelers; the neck of the fiddle runs toward the spider's abdomen.

More specific advice on capturing and caring for insects is given in Sally Kneidel's fine books, *Pet Bugs: A Kid's Guide to Catching and Keeping Touchable Insects,* and *More Pet Bugs.*

Temporary Housing

There are several ways to make inexpensive cages for small creatures; however, releasing a specimen after a day in the classroom teaches responsible stewardship. Comment that the insect is needed outside for cleanup work or pest control, or to help flowers make seeds (see p. 85). This also skirts the problem of providing live food for some small animals.

A simple temporary cage for small insects can be made by covering a clean plastic tumbler with a piece of nylon hosiery, stretched and held in place with a strip of tape. For larger insects, cut large windows in the sides of a plastic deli container, as shown in Figure 5–1. Add a dampened piece of sponge and a sprig of a plant from near the insect catching location. Pull the foot half of an old nylon stocking over the container, gathering the top tightly with a rubber band. Snap the carton lid over the gathering.

If a small terrarium is available, use it to house active grasshoppers. Put a layer of sand on the bottom along with small branches or plant sprigs for the grasshopper to climb.

Some reusable, clear containers for fragile berries have ventilation holes and snap-on lids. If available, they make perfect cages without any further preparation.

FIGURE 5–1

Keep cages on hand to use whenever children bring small creatures to share. (It can be difficult to sell some children on the cage idea. Joey, for one, was in favor of keeping his caterpillar on a leash of "gotch tape.") More specific ideas on housing and care for visiting insects are offered in *Classroom Creature Culture: Algae to Anoles,* edited by Hampton and Kramer.

One fascinating exception to the same-day-release rule is a mother spider. She does not feed during the period of egg sac construction, nor during the weeks before the spiderlings emerge from the sac. The spiderlings also have a stored food supply for use after their birth.

Wolf spiders fasten egg sacs to their undersides. The babies migrate to the mother's back after emerging. There, they cling as passengers to knob-tipped hairs. A wolf spider and her young can survive for a week of observation in a plastic playing-card box if moisture is provided.

A potential disappointment with spider watching is that the mother spider spins an egg sac whether the eggs have been fertilized by a male spider or not. If the eggs are infertile, the mother does not tear the sac open.

Insect Pests

Some insects do more harm than good to humans and plants. Among them are flies, mosquitoes, cockroaches, black widow and brown recluse spiders, miller moths, and clothes moths. Many insects that sting to defend themselves will not bother people if they are not disturbed. Among them are wasps, hornets, bees, and spiders (Table 5–1).

2. *How do insects' bodies change as they grow?*
LEARNING OBJECTIVE: To observe the fascinating process of insect metamorphosis.

Introduction: Elicit children's information about the special way that most insects grow. Clarify that insects' bodies change in surprising ways as they grow

Table 5–1   Facts About Common Insects

Insect	Function	Interesting Features
Ants	Scavengers who clean their surroundings. Pollinators of flowers.	Social insects who live in colonies with separate jobs to perform: some nurse young, some gather food.
Bees	Highly valued pollinators of plants. Producers of honey and beeswax.	Social insects who live in colonies with specialized jobs to perform.
Butterflies	Pollinators of plants. (Explain to children that they help plants make seeds.)	Slender bodies. Antennae have ball tips. Fly by day. Fold wings straight up when resting. Usually form a chrysalis.
Moths	Some are pollinators. Silk moths spin strong, lustrous fibers that are made into fabric.	Fat, furry bodies. Feathery antennae. Wings spread flat when resting. Usually spin cocoons. Fly at night.
Beetles	Some kinds are scavengers who tidy up. Ladybug beetles are valued by gardeners for pest control. Some beetles destroy crops.	Many handsome varieties: striped, spotted, iridescent.
Crickets	Serve as food for other animals. They are destructive to some crops.	Only male crickets chirp. They raise and rub their hard wing covers to make vibrations.
Fireflies (soft-bodied beetles)	Appreciated for adding charm to summer nights.	Fireflies signal to one another with flashes of light.
Grasshoppers, Locusts	Destroy some crops but serve as food for other animals.	Wings barely visible when flying. Use hind pair of legs to jump. Hearing area is in the abdomen.
Praying Mantis	So valuable for pest control that egg cases are sold to gardeners.	Almost 4" (10 cm) long, so body parts easily seen. Frightening to see them tearing other insects apart.
Wasps and Hornets	Some wasps pollinate fruit trees. Some eat destructive larvae.	Hornets and some wasps chew dead wood into paper to make nests for their young. Some wasps make nests from mud. Beautiful engineering.

from tiny eggs to adults. The change process is called *metamorphosis*, (the transforming stages of the lifecycle). "We can see how some of the changes happen with one kind of insect, here in our classroom. For many weeks we will watch mealworms change forms, and also discover what they can do and like." Explain that mealworms and the adult beetles they become are harmless. They can't crawl out of their containers. Because the eggs are too small to be seen without a microscope, these observations will begin with the *larva*, mealworm, stage.

MATERIALS:

Mealworms, two for each child (buy at pet store)

Pint freezer storage boxes, one for each group of 4-5 children*

Produce trays

Marking pen

Hammer, nail

Pound of bran meal (not break-fast cereal; buy at health food store)

Apple or potato

Paring knife

Magnifiers

GETTING READY:

Mark a group number on each box.

Punch a few air holes in box tops with hammer and nail

Pour 3" (7.5 cm) bran into each box.

Add slice of apple or potato

Gently place mealworms on the bran.

Cover with boxtops after obser-vations.

SMALL-GROUP ACTIVITY:

1. Hold a mealworm in your hand. "How would you feel if you were being held softly in a big person's hand?" Establish ground rules for studying mealworms: (a) They should be held softly; (b) they should be looked at with magnifiers; (c) they should be put on different places on the tray; (d) children wash their hands after handling mealworms.

2. Gently lift a mealworm onto each tray for children to observe with magnifiers. Watch reassuringly slow movements. Look for eyes, mouth, legs, antennae, and body seg-ments. Have children draw their observa-tions. Return mealworms to boxes in the science center. Add fresh apple/potato slices if mold appears, or when withered and dry. Mealworms also enjoy citrus peel, such as a grapefruit half.

3. Encourage independent daily observations for signs of activity or change, i.e., collecting on apple/potato to suck moisture; shedding skins as worms (larva) grow; changing to in-ert pupa, changing to adult beetles (eggs are too small to be seen without a microscope).

4. Experiment each week with a different envi-ronmental condition to learn how meal-worms prefer to live: (a) put wet paper toweling on half the tray; (b) cover half the box with dark paper to create half shade, half light; (c) put mealworms on tray with small piles of bran, grass, shredded paper; (d) put mealworms on tray with a cotton ball dipped in vinegar. Allow an hour for mealworms to make choices. Chart children's observations.

5. You can keep a mealworm colony going in-definitely. Or you can put them outside in the grass to become bird food and to help decompose waste products.

*Mealworms can be kept in a terrarium, but children can feel more connected to those "owned" by their small group. Each small study group is given a number.

The practice of close observation can provide lasting satisfaction.

Group Discussion: As transformations occur, point out the persistence of characteristic body parts such as six legs, head, and antennae, in all three stages. Note that the larva sheds its skin when it outgrows the old one. The larval stage can take up to 10 weeks. The pupa rarely moves for 2 or 3 weeks, but it's changing inside. Record the children's observations and insights into this basic life process. This activity challenges children's expectations, but if the mealworms can be kept for two or more months, the repeated transformations will be persuasive.

Read: Mealworms: Raise Them, Watch Them, See Them Change, by Adrienne Mason. Online resources for more information are the Web pages for the North American Bluebird Society and for the Center for Insect Science Education Outreach.

CONCEPT: **Animals move in different ways.**

1. How does an earthworm move?
LEARNING OBJECTIVE: To be intrigued by legless animal movement.

Introduction: Ask children, "Do you need six legs to walk? If your body were bent over and close to the ground, would more legs help keep you balanced? What helps some insects and birds move through the air? Can you think of a very small animal that has no legs—one that only has muscles and tiny bristles to help it move? Perhaps we'll find some worms to watch when we go outdoors."

MATERIALS:

Shovels, if a digging place is
available

Bucket

Scoop

Produce trays

Magnifiers

Light-colored sand

Potting soil

1 qt.(1L) clear deli container

Small Dixie cup

Nylon stocking

Rubber band

Crumbled dry leaves (not oak
leaves)

Black paper

Tape

GETTING READY:

Before taking children to the
digging spot, check for presence of earthworms.

If digging isn't possible, buy
worms locally or from science
supply catalog.

SMALL-GROUP ACTIVITY:

1. ♣ Let children help dig earthworms, if
permitted, in light soil.
2. Let children help make a worm farm.
Spread a layer of sand on the bottom of the
deli container. Invert the cup. Center it on
the sand. Surround the cup with a 2-inch
(5 cm) layer of soil. Top with 2-inchs (5 cm)
of sand. Add a final layer of soil. Moisten
with a small amount of water.
3. Cover with bits of crushed leaves. Put *all
but two* earthworms *on* the leaves. Do not
cover with soil. Stretch stocking over the
top. Secure with a rubber band.
4. Put two worms on trays to observe movement with magnifiers. (Bristles are re-
tractable and hard to see.) A wide, light
band at the midsection is the egg case. The
tail end is tapered; the head end is
rounded. "Do they have eyes?" Have children record their observations as drawings, written descriptions, or creative
movement.

Care of Earthworms

Earthworm Farm Care. Wrap black paper around the worm farm to encourage tunneling where it can easily be seen. It will take about a week for the earthworms to get used to the new soil before they start tunneling. Remove the paper
for short periods of time to check for signs of activity.

Earthworms will not survive long in dry soil. Keep the farm away from a heat
source. Sprinkle the soil frequently to keep it damp.

Dark soil streaks in the light sand show how earthworms mix soils as they
make tunnels. Bits of leaf will be pulled into the tunnels. Let children investigate
what worms will eat, putting out a different small bit of food each day, such as celery leaves or dry oatmeal. Observe and record what disappears into worm tunnels.

Tiny balls surrounding tunnel holes on the surface of the soil are the castings
of soil digested by the earthworms. This is one way that worms enrich the soil.
They also help water and air reach plant roots as they make their tunnels. (See
Edwards, Nabors, and Camacho, *The Dirt on Worms*.)

How to Hold an Earthworm. Youngsters credit adults with unlimited ability and courage. Measuring up to this idealism can be hard for some of us when it means holding a child's cherished earthworm. Bolster your courage for this eventuality by understanding your tactile senses: Compare the sensation of holding a slippery object in the palm of your hand with that of holding the same object between your thumb and forefinger. The palm of the hand has fewer nerve endings to convey tactile sensations. Therefore, a placid worm that is loosely cupped in the palm of your hand will scarcely be felt. Hand washing is required after holding earthworms.

2. *How does a fish move?*

LEARNING OBJECTIVE: To enjoy noticing the working parts of fish movement.

MATERIALS:

1 wide-mouthed gallon jar

Aquarium gravel or lake sand

Rocks

Water plant—purchased or from lake or stream

1 small goldfish

Black paper

Newspaper

Water

GETTING READY:

Involve children in preparations.

Let a gallon of water stand overnight in open containers so chlorine can escape.

Wash local water plants carefully. Wash lake sand in a deep pan by letting a slow stream of *hot* water fill pan. (Plants and gravel from a good pet store need not be washed.)

Put an inch of sand or gravel in jar. Put plant roots in sand and anchor with a rock.

Cover sand with folded newspaper while pouring in water.

Remove paper.

Put fish in water.

SMALL-GROUP ACTIVITY:

1. Look at the body of the fish. Discuss how it is different from the earthworm's body.
2. Recall the looping, sliding movements of worms. Compare with varied movements of the fish as it darts up, down, forward, backward, or rests.
3. Find seven fins: two pairs approximately where our arms and legs grow, topside, underside, and tail fins. (Arm and leg position fins work fast to move fish forward and back; top and bottom fins give balance; tail fins steer fish as it swings from side to side. Some fins look like fancy decorations; although they have delicate bones, they work hard.)
4. Tap the tank lightly. Does the fish go faster? Does it move differently to speed up? Watch closely.
5. To keep the fish as a class pet, put fish feeding on a rotating routine chart. Each day a different child can feed it a *pinch* of tropical fish food.* No weekend feeding is needed. Keep the aquarium away from direct sunlight. Tape dark-colored paper around the side closest to the window to reduce algae growth. Some light is needed, however. Siphon or dip out one third of the water and replace with aerated water as needed.

*Try training the fish by always dropping the pinch of food in the same corner of the tank. Children will be interested to find that fish can learn, just as they can.

CONCEPT: Each animal needs its own kind of food.

Introduction: Ask children, "Did you have a nice bowl of acorns and a plate-ful of grass with ladybugs for breakfast today? Why not? What did you have?" Help children recognize that each kind of animal needs its own kind of food in order to live. Discuss making a feeder to help winter birds get the kind of food they need. Plan to maintain the feeder until spring. Some birds may come to depend on that food supply and starve without it.

1. How can we feed winter birds?

LEARNING OBJECTIVE: To enjoy nurturing wild animals with food.

MATERIALS:

Half-gallon (2 L) milk carton

12-inch (30 cm) stick

Scissors

Twine or monofilament fishing line*

Commercial wild birdseed plus seeds saved from plant experiences

Dried pinecones

String

Peanut butter

Plastic pint berry baskets

Suet

SMALL-GROUP ACTIVITY:

Let children help make and supply feeders.

A. *For chickadees, cardinals, and others:* Cut out long windows on two sides of the carton, two inches above the bottom. Push the stick through the feeder near the bottom to form two outside perches. Pierce holes through the carton top. Thread with twine or fishing line. Tie to a tree branch low enough to reach easily for refilling with wild birdseed.

B. *For nuthatches, woodpeckers, others:* Wind string around top scales of cones to form a hanging loop. Let children use spoon handles to stuff peanut butter between scales. Roll filled cones in birdseed. Hang on branches.

C. *For flickers, jays, mockingbirds, others:* Let children lace two baskets together with twine to form a closed container. Add chunks of suet before last side is lashed together. Fasten to tree.

Keep a record of visitors observed at feeders.

See: Birdhouses and Feeders, by Robyn Haus.

*Monofilament fishing line is too smooth for squirrels to grip, so they won't gobble all the bird food. Position feeders out of reach of squirrels or cats. Sprinkle seeds on the ground beneath feeders for a few days to attract birds.

CONCEPT: Many animals make shelters to rear their young.

1. How can we help nest-building birds?

LEARNING OBJECTIVE: To enjoy supporting wild birds with nest-building materials.

Introduction: Ask children, "Do you think that a mother bird lays eggs on tree branches and leaves them to hatch by themselves? Of course not! She works hard, sometimes with the father bird, to build a nest where she can keep the eggs warm and keep the hatched babies safe and fed. When the babies are big enough to take care of themselves, usually the whole family leaves the nest. Some kinds of birds return to old nests each year; others do not. We can help birds build new nests."

MATERIALS:

Plastic berry baskets or mesh
  onion bags
6-inch (15 cm) pieces of yarn
Spanish moss, if available
Dried tall grass
Dryer lint
Desirable: Bird nest, legiti-
  mately salvaged* or loaned by
  a nature center, or existing nest
  to visit on site near your school
Magnifiers

SMALL-GROUP ACTIVITY:

1. If a nest can be brought in or visited, let children examine the structure. "Is it lined with special material? Why?"
2. Let children prepare nest materials for birds that come to school feeders. Pull apart clumps of Spanish moss. Place loosely in berry baskets. Work strands of yarn, dryer lint, short twigs, long grass through mesh bags.
3. Hang baskets outdoors near feeders.

* The Migratory Bird Treaty Act of 1918 forbids the collection of most *migratory* bird nests, eggs, or feathers without a Federal Migratory Bird Permit. For information about applying for a salvage permit for educational purposes, contact your State Fish and Wildlife Service. **Health precaution:** Children should not be allowed to touch a nest, since it may harbor mites or other allergens.

CONCEPT: Humans and animals often live together.

1. Why do people have pets?

LEARNING OBJECTIVE: To enjoy learning personal information about pets.

? *Inquiry Activity:* Ask children, "Do you know people who have pets in their homes? Why do you think people have pets? How do they take care of their pets? Would you like to find out about pets belonging to children in our class? In our school?" Discuss how the group could conduct an inquiry about pets. Consider questions to ask and ways to keep track of and organize information. Decide on how the information could be shared with others. Children could vote on the questions and survey methods suggested. This could be a large- or small-group inquiry, depending on the children's interests. Read *Measuring Penny* by Loreen Leedy.

Animals in the Classroom

The Borrowed Pet. Much can be learned by children who help provide for the daily life requirements of a classroom pet. Many of those learnings can also be sampled during a short visit by a borrowed pet.

Before the pet arrives, discuss with the children safe ways to watch and care for it. For small pets accustomed to pens, make an observation box from a large carton. Cut windows in the sides and cover them with plastic wrap, if needed. Some pets are better off being held by their owners during the visit. Try to let children see the animals eating and drinking water. Help children find answers to questions about how the animal moves, gets its food, and protects itself. Does the pet have bones inside, or a hard outside covering? Does it have hair or fur, smooth skin or feather-covered skin? Does it nurse its young? Does it build a shelter for its young?

Recent animal visitors to our school included a pet boa constrictor, which laced itself through the rungs of a chair, and a small pony that was unexpectedly led into the building by a mischievous owner.

Animal Rearing. Rearing butterflies or moths from the caterpillar, chrysalis, or cocoon stage can be enthralling or disappointing. Strong interest and luck are required for success. Using commercial butterfly kits may have the unfortunate effect of introducing non-native species to your area, and may release butterflies into an environment lacking appropriate food. If you can find caterpillars or cocoons in your local environment, rearing them is environmentally more sensible. Follow the procedures described in *Monarch Magic,* by Lynn Rosenblatt.

The same mixture of dedication and luck also contributes to a good outcome with an egg-incubating project. A commercial incubator is probably a better choice than improvised equipment for classroom use. Follow the instructions included with

Animals elicit a range of responses from children.

the incubator. Be sure the fertile eggs have not been allowed to cool after being laid. Plan to find a home for the chick or duckling after it has hatched. Read Mary Ann Hoberman's poem "Eggs" from *The Llama Who Had No Pajama*. (See Appendix A.)

Are Classroom Pets Necessary? Good teachers allow for individual differences in children's responses to animals. They do not assume that all children adore animals. They do not insist that a fearful child make physical contact with animals. Although they should avoid expressing negative attitudes about animals to children, teachers should extend the same consideration to their own feelings about animals.

They need not feel obligated to undertake year-long care if they cannot manage the responsibility. The teacher's primary affective focus and primary responsibility are caring about children. Feeling similar warmth toward animals is an asset, but not a requirement. It should be a consideration, however, that many urban children have no other opportunity than classroom pets to interact positively with animals.

INTEGRATING ACTIVITIES

Math Experiences

Animal Math Materials. Many commercial math materials incorporate animals. These include:

1. Animal match-ups puzzle cards that link numerals with sets of animals
2. Magnet and flannel board counting sets
3. Sequence puzzles showing the development from egg to butterfly, from egg to frog, from nest building to robin egg hatching
4. Animal rummy puts set-making into a game context; the cards can also be used for playing Memory (Concentration)

Record Keeping. Keep a flannel-board tally of small animals brought into your classroom or observed outdoors. Mount pictures of the animals, cut from magazines, on flock-backed adhesive paper backing. Bring out the pictures for children to count when new observations are reported.

If your class tries a chick-incubating project, make a chain of 21 large paper clips to represent the days of the incubation period. Remove a clip each day and count the days left in the waiting period.

Measuring. Read *Measuring Penny*, by Loreen Leedy, to introduce standard and nonstandard measuring activities. Read *Room for Ripley*, by Stuart Murphy, which illustrates liquid measurement.

Graphing. Read *Tiger Math* by Ann Magda.

Set Making. Enjoyable set-making and probability games spinning off from Arnold Lobel's *Toad and Frog* books are offered in *Frog Math*. It is obtainable from Great Explorations in Math and Sciences (GEMS), Lawrence Hall of Science, Berkeley, CA. (See Appendix A.)

Fractions: Read *Inchworm and a Half*, by Eleanor Pinczes, for beginning ideas about fractions.

Music (Resources in Appendix A)

Sing along with "You Can't Make a Turtle Come Out" on Mary Miche's cassette, *Earthy Tunes*. It reminds children that, to observe animals, . . . "you'll have to patiently wait." Also on that cassette is "Snakes and Spiders."

Listen to songs about raccoons, ants, otters, fish, moose, and more on *Penguin Parade*, a CD by the American Library Association award-winning environmental musicians group, the Banana Slug String Band.

Listen to *Birds, Beasts, Bugs, and Little Fishes*, sung by Pete Seeger. The songs were written by Ruth Seeger in *Animal Folk Songs for Children*.

Younger children enjoy "I Like the Animals in the Zoo," sung by Ella Jenkins on *Seasons for Singing*. The song provides a good pattern for improvising about the animals that visit your room:

> *I like the grasshopper, in the jar.*
> *I like the grasshopper, it jumps far.*

Listen to *I'd Like to Be a Marine Biologist* by Kim Thompson and Karen Hilderbrand for songs about large and small sea creatures.

Also note that animal horns were among the earliest forms of musical instruments. Conch shells are still used as horns in some parts of the world. A ram's horn, the *shofer*, is blown through in Jewish High Holiday ceremonies. One of the percussion instruments on our classroom music shelf is an unoccupied box turtle shell. The children enjoy tapping rhythms on it.

Literature Links: Animal Characteristics

BANCROFT, H., & VAN GELDER, R. (1997). *Animals in winter*. New York: HarperCollins. This simple look at hibernating and nonhibernating North American animals will absorb young listeners and independent readers. Endearingly illustrated, it gives winter feeding suggestions. Paperback.

BONSIGNORE, JOAN. (2001). *Stick out your tongue*. Atlanta: Peachtree. The amazing functions of various animals' tongues are compared to children's tongue functions in this captivating book.

EMORY, JERRY. (1994). *Nightprowlers*. San Diego, CA: Harcourt Brace. This book for older children makes a good general reference about nocturnal creatures both for the classroom and for parents, who are the available night nature guides. Paperback.

HICKMAN, PAMELA. (2001). *Animals eating: How animals chomp, chew, slurp, and swallow*. Buffalo, NY: Kids Can Press. This blend of superb illustrations by Pat Stephens with facts, activities, and model-making comparing animal and human abilities makes an intriguing reference for youngsters. Also in this series: *Animal senses* (1998), and *Animals in motion* (2000). NSTA* recommended.

JENKINS, STEVE. (1997). *What do you do when something wants to eat you?* Boston: Houghton Mifflin. Elegant collage illustrations are as fascinating as the descriptions of defenses animals use to escape hungry predators.

JENKINS, STEVE. (2001). *Slap, squeak, and scatter: How animals communicate*. Boston: Houghton Mifflin. Surprising facts are revealed in this clearly focused picture book about the ways 25 different animals communicate.

KANER, ETTA. (2001). *Animal defenses.* Buffalo, NY: Kids Can Press. Wonderful textural renderings by Pat Stephens add lifelike dimension to the fascinating reports of some unique survival mechanisms in the animal world.

KANER, ETTA. (2001). *Animals at work: How animals build, dig, fish, and trap.* Tonawanda, NY: Kids Can Press. An excellent text, awesome Pat Stephens illustrations, informative activities, and imagination stretchers combine to increase respect for diversity in animal life.

LLEWELLYN, CLAIRE. (1996). *Disguises and surprises.* Cambridge, MA: Candlewick. This book emphasizes some of the weird camouflages and grim survival tactics of animal life that fascinate many older primary children.

PANDELL, KAREN. (1996). *Animal action ABC.* New York: Dutton. Striking photographs and rhyming facts identify various animal movements, as lively children mimic them. This book provides inspiration for animal creative movement activities.

RYDER, JOANNE. (1996). *Night gliders.* Mahwah, NJ: Bridgewater. A simple, lyrical text, suitable for beginning readers, trails four flying squirrels through a night of hunting, leaping, and playing in the moonlight.

SINGER, MARILYN. (2001). *A pair of wings.* New York: Holiday House. This book explores the advantages wings provide to birds, bats and insects. The illustrations soar and lift the spirits.

WALLACE, KAREN. (1996). *Imagine you are a tiger.* New York: Henry Holt. It would be hard to sit still while listening to these vivid descriptions of tiger actions from infancy to maturity.

ZOLOTOW, CHARLOTTE. (1993). *Peter and the pigeons.* New York: Greenwillow. Peter's first visit to the zoo introduces him to new animals, but his favorite animals are the familiar pigeons.

Literature Links: Insects, Spiders, and Earthworms

BOOTH, JERRY. (1994). *Big bugs.* San Diego, CA: Harcourt Brace. *Big* refers to the size of this book, not the bugs. Written for older children to "take the *ug* out of bug," the facts are accurate and activities lively. Paperback.

BRENNER, BARBARA. (1997). *Thinking about ants.* Greenvale, NY: Mondo Publishing. Larger-than-life illustrations help listeners understand what it's like to be an ant. The rhythmic, question/answer prose will hold youngsters' attention.

BUNTING, EVE. (1999). *Butterfly house.* New York: Scholastic. A child and her grandfather make a beautiful house to protect her caterpillar as it forms a chrysalis and evolves into a painted lady butterfly. Directions for butterfly raising are included.

CARLE, ERIC. (1985). *The very busy spider.* Other engaging Carle classics for preschoolers include: (1990) *The very quiet cricket,* and (1998) *The very clumsy click beetle.* New York: Philomel Books.

CHRUSTOWSKI, RICK. (2000). *Bright beetle.* New York: Holt. Listeners will be wide-eyed as the life cycle and survival tactics of a ladybug unfold in this book. Excellent illustrations add to the drama.

COLE, JOANNA. (1996). *The magic schoolbus inside a beehive.* New York: Scholastic. The schoolbus accidentally turns into a beehive, and the children into bees. They learn what it means to be a hard-working social insect.

EHLERT, LOIS. (2001). *Waiting for wings.* San Diego: Harcourt. The butterfly lifecycle is told to preschoolers against a background of Ehlert's acclaimed bold, splashy illustrations. Cut pages add interest. Accurate butterfly information is given in endpages.

FARENDON, JOHN. (2002). *Butterflies in the garden.* New York: HarperCollins. Beautiful illustrations identify four families of butterflies, the flowering plants they are attracted to, and other butterfly needs.

FELTWELL, JOHN. (1997). *Butterflies and moths:* Eyewitness explorers. New York: Dorling Kindersley. Great color photographs enlarge children's understanding of these creatures.

FLACKLAM, MARGERY. (1999). *Creepy, crawly caterpillars*. Boston: Little Brown. Mature readers and younger browsers will enjoy the striking illustrations and fascinating details about the habits and metamorphosis stages of common caterpillars. Paperback.

FLACKLAM, MARGERY. (2001). *Spiders and their web sites*. Boston: Little, Brown. This lucidly written, strikingly illustrated book invites advanced readers to learn about 12 interesting spiders.

GALVIN, LAURA. (2000). *Bumblebee at apple tree lane*. Smithsonian backyard series. Norwalk, CT: Soundprints. A bumblebee's life is followed from spring through fall. Illustrations often take the bumblebee's perspective of its territory. End pages add scientific information about bees.

GIBBONS, GAIL. (2000). *The honey makers*. New York: HarperCollins. Watch an organized colony of bees build their honeycomb, breed, nurse their young, and gather nectar. Cheerfully illustrated by the author.

GROSSMAN, PATRICIA. (1997). *Very first things to know about ants*. New York: Workman. At last! This interactive, reusable sticker book engages children in meaningful activity as they absorb accurate, interesting information. This well-designed book is a project of the American Museum of Natural History.

HAMILTON, KERSTEN. (1997). *The butterfly book*. Santa Fe, NM: John Muir Publications. Careful directions and clear illustrations take the guesswork out of attracting, raising, and housing butterflies in the classroom. Paperback.

HEILIGMAN, DEBORAH. (1996). *From caterpillar to butterfly*. New York: HarperCollins. Lively illustrations and clever graphics pull listeners and beginning readers into a classroom observation of metamorphosis, from caterpillar to painted lady butterfly. An NSTA Outstanding Trade Book.

HELLER, RUTH. (1992). *How to hide a butterfly*. New York: Platt & Munk. The clever, accurate rhyming text is minimal. Combined with the author's fascinating, precise illustrations, this book about protective camouflage in nature makes an unforgettable impact. Paperback.

HICKMAN, PAMELA. (1996). *The bug book*. Buffalo, NY: Kids Can Press. Appealingly written and illustrated, this introductory overview of insect characteristics includes directions to make a fine soda bottle insect feeder, and ways to help endangered insects. NSTA* recommended.

HICKMAN, PAMELA. (1997). *A new butterfly*. Toronto, ON: Kids Can Press. This simple, cumulative story is matched by cheerful illustrations. Excellent additional facts in fold-out sections don't have to interrupt the flow of the story.

HOROWITZ, RUTH. (2001). *Breakout at the bug lab*. New York: Dial. Two boys scramble to find the exotic insect that escaped from their mom's lab during dedication ceremonies at the entomology research center. Independent readers will enjoy this amusing and reassuring story.

JOOSSE, BARBARA. (2001). *Ghost wings*. San Francisco: Chronicle Books. A Mexican girl and her grandma love the monarch butterflies' wintering forest. Grandma's death is linked symbolically to the northern migration of the monarchs. Endnotes give accurate migration information.

LONDON, JONATHAN. (1998). *Dream weaver*. San Diego, CA: Harcourt Brace. This simple, evocative picture book lets a young child see the world from a small spider's perspective.

MASON, ADRIENNE. (1998). *Mealworms: Raise them, watch them, see them change*. Buffalo, NY: Kids Can Press. This book provides good information and lots of ideas for experiments with these cheap, easy-to-obtain classroom animals that stay in their cages!

MCDONALD, MARY ANN. (1999). *Grasshoppers*. Chanhassen, MN: Child's World. Larger-than-life photographs amplify the descriptions in this well-organized, interesting text.

MCDONALD, MEGAN. (1995). *Insects are my life*. New York: Orchard Books. Amanda is a passionate collector and protector of bugs. Her fascination with insects creates friction at school, but leads her to a new friend who understands. This exuberant story will also inspire creative movement ideas.

MOUND, LAURENCE. (1993). *Amazing insects*. New York: Alfred A. Knopf. Insects are looked at with the fresh perspectives, striking color enlargements, amusing cartoons, and intriguing facts usually found in the Eyewitness Juniors series. Paperback.

OPPENHEIMER, JOANNE. (1996). *Have you seen bugs?* New York: Scholastic. A lilting, needs-to-be-read-aloud text, matched with beautiful paper sculpture art, makes this a book children will treasure.

PANDELL, KAREN. (1996). *Animal action ABC.* New York: Dutton. Striking photographs and rhyming facts identify various animal movements as lively children mimic them.

PARKER, STEVE. (1996). *Insects.* Eyewitness Explorers. New York: Dorling Kindersley. This book provides interesting perspectives for understanding insects. It describes making and maintaining an insect aquarium. Paperback.

PASCOE, ELAINE. (1997). *Earthworms.* Woodbridge, CT: Blackbirch Press. This book contains good photographs, information, and activity suggestions.

PERRY, PHYLLIS. (1995). *The fiddlehoppers: Crickets, katydids, and locusts.* New York: Grolier/Watts. Lots of information about these omnipresent species can be found in this book.

PHILPOT, LORNA, & PHILPOT, GRAHAM. (1994). *Amazing Anthony Ant.* New York: Random House. Follow a jaunty ant through pages of clever mazes while singing endless verses of "The Ants Came Marching in a Line." A flip-tab feature provides clues and lures for language acquisition. Information about ant predators is imaginatively incorporated into the illustrations.

PLACCO, PATRICIA. (1993). *The bee tree.* New York: Philomel. Grandfather uses a bee tree search, and the prize of honey, to encourage Mary Ellen to search for the sweetness of knowledge in books. Paperback.

PRINGLE, LAURENCE. (1997). *An extraordinary life. The story of a monarch butterfly.* New York: Orchard Books. Share the courageous life of Danaus, the monarch butterfly, from caterpillar days to her harrowing 2,500-mile journey to her winter home in Mexico. Older children can absorb information from this long book about a fascinating endangered creature.

ROBERTSON, MATTHEW. (2000). *Insects and spiders.* Pleasantville, NY: Readers' Digest. This compendium of inside information on insects will suit older children who are used to computer screens crammed with sidebars. Hands-on activities are woven through the pages.

ROCKWELL, ANNE. (2001). *Bugs are insects.* New York: HarperCollins. This easy reader introduces the characteristics of insects and defines the subspecies called *bugs.* Now we know: the ladybug isn't really a bug. Cut paper illustrations add fascination. Activity ideas are included. NSTA* recommended.

ROCKWELL, ANNE. (2002). *Becoming butterflies.* New York: Walker. A class waits and watches the metamorphosis of monarch caterpillars. They keep careful records of what they observe. The story is supplemented with informative sidebars. End notes include Web sites for further information. NSTA* recommended.

SPINELLI, EILEEN. (2001). *Sophie's masterpiece: A spider's tale.* New York: Simon & Schuster. Most boarders at Beekman's boarding house don't appreciate Sophie's artistic webs until her final effort is complete: spinning moonbeam strands into a special baby's blanket.

STURGES, PHILEMON. (1996). *What's that sound, woolly bear?* Boston: Little Brown. Young children will join the chorus of 14 chirping, buzzing, and whining insect sounds as they listen to this simple story. Endnotes provide information about the insect species.

SWOPE, SAM. (2000). *Gotta go! Gotta go!* New York: Farrar, Strauss. Young children will enjoy this simple, cumulative tale of a monarch caterpillar's metamorphosis and miraculous flight to Mexico, where its life cycle is renewed.

WALKER, SALLY. (2001). *Fireflies.* Minneapolis: Lerner. This is a fine resource for independent readers who want detailed information about the characteristics of this fascinating insect. NSTA* recommended.

WALLACE, KAREN. (2000). *Born to be a butterfly.* New York: Dorling Kindersley. Beginning readers will enjoy the simply told story of the butterfly life cycle. Close-up photographs add to the drama.

WALLACE, NANCY. (2001). *A taste of honey.* New York: Winslow. Lily's persistent questioning and Poppy's patient answers trace honey production from flowers to the jar.

WINER, YVONNE. (2001). *Butterflies fly.* Watertown, MA: Charlesbridge. While the imagery of the text is more poetic than informative, the glorious Lloyd-Jones illustrations of 15 species and their habitats make this book fascinating. Clear end notes identify and describe each illustrated butterfly.

ZUCHORA-WALSKE, CHRISTINE. (2000). *Leaping grasshoppers*. Minneapolis: Lerner. Great photographs and a crisp, revealing text will fascinate independent readers. NSTA* Outstanding Trade Book.

Literature Links: Fish, Mollusks, Amphibians, and Reptiles

ABBOT, R. TUCKER. (1994). *Seashells*. Science Nature Guides. San Diego, CA: Thunder Bay Press. 175 color photographs identify shells from four shore areas in the United States and Canada.

ALIKI. (1993). *My visit to the aquarium*. New York: HarperCollins. Fascinated children are caught up in the sea life exhibits surrounding them. Facts about marine life are easy to absorb in this good story.

ARNOSKY, JIM. (1997). *All about rattlesnakes*. New York: Scholastic. A life-size portrait of a rattlesnake takes up the first four pages of this detailed reptile account for independent readers.

ARNOSKY, JIM. (2000). *All about turtles*. New York: Scholastic. The naturalist-artist author provides experienced information about these shell-covered reptiles for independent readers.

BARRISH, WENDY. (1998). *Fish*. New York: Scholastic. Basic information, bright drawings, and fun overlays are presented in this small format book for preschool hands.

BELL, SIMON, (Ed.). (1994). *What's inside shells?* New York: Dorling Kindersley. Vivid color photographs of shelled creatures are paired with cross-sectional drawings of the snails, oysters, tortoises, crabs, and other mollusks living within. Eyewitness Explorers series. Paperback.

BROWN, RUTH. (1997). *Toad*. New York: Dutton. Author/artist Brown spins a humorous tale about an untidy toad's unexpected salvation. All ages are likely to laugh at his plight.

CANNON, JANELL. (1997). *Verdi*. San Diego, CA: Harcourt Brace. An independent young green tree python seeks a more venturesome life than his elders choose. Lavishly illustrated by the author, it includes snake facts endnotes. A *Reading Rainbow* book.

COLDREY, JENNIFER. (1998). *Shells*. New York: Dorling Kindersley. Details about how shellfish are born, grow, and travel mingle with advice on how to record projects, things to make, and things to do with shells.

COWLEY, JOY. (1999). *Red-eyed tree frog*. New York: Scholastic. Striking color close-up photos follow this frog's encounters with other rain-forest creatures. It's sure to fascinate listeners. The simple story has detailed frog-fact end notes. NSTA* recommended.

CUTLER, JANE. (1996). *Mr. Carey's garden*. Boston: Houghton Mifflin. We learn to appreciate a snail's effect upon a garden at night, and learn that a problem can have many solutions.

DAVIS, NICOLA. (2001). *One tiny turtle*. Cambridge, MA: Candlewick. A flowing, watery layout enhances the metaphoric telling of a sea turtle's life cycle. Thirty years of growth and wandering lead to an amazing return to the beach where she hatched to lay eggs for new life.

DEWEY, JENNIFER. (1997). *Rattlesnake dance*. Honesdale, PA: Boyds Mill. A gripping story of the author's girlhood recovery from a rattlesnake bite opens this collection of snake lore written for older primary students.

HOROWITZ, RUTH. (2000). *Crab moon*. Cambridge: Candlewick Press. Daniel's moonlit observation of masses of horseshoe crabs crawling ashore to lay their eggs is told and illustrated with warmth and awe. End pages give scientific facts about horseshoe crabs. NSTA* Outstanding Science Trade Book.

JAMES, BETSY. (1999). *Tadpoles*. New York: Dutton. A charming story and lively illustrations blend tadpole growth progression with the evolving (and frustrating) motor skills of Molly's baby brother. Tadpole-raising tips are given for areas where frog egg collection is permitted.

KORMAN, SUSAN. (2000). *Box turtle at silver pond lane*. Norwalk, CE: Soundprints. Smithsonian. The quiet saga of an Eastern box turtle is photographed as she finds a spot to dig a nest and lay her eggs.

JEUNESSE, GUILLIMARD. (1994). *Fish*. New York: Scholastic. Attractive laminated pages with acetate overlays add appeal to this simple book for young children.

JOHNSON, ANGELA. (1993). *The girl who wore snakes*. New York: Orchard Books. The lively illustrations enrich this simple story of Ali, whose pet snakes wind through her home and school life.

MAZER, ANNE. (1991). *The salamander room*. New York: Alfred A. Knopf. A conversation between a child and his mother is captured in lovely prose and illustrations to imaginatively inform us about the life requirements of a salamander.

MCDONALD MEGAN. (2001). *Reptiles are my life*. New York: Orchard. Amanda, the insect lover, and Maggie, the reptile fan, lose and regain their friendship, dispensing interesting animal facts as they argue.

PASCOE, ELAINE. (1997). *Tadpoles*. Woodbridge, CT: Blackbirch. Well-illustrated information is presented with many suggestions for noninvasive experiments and observations.

PASCOE, ELAINE. (2001). *Pill bugs and sow bugs and other crustaceans*. Woodbridge, CT: Blackbirch Press. These familiar garden dwellers have surprising, hard-shelled relatives in the sea: lobsters, crabs, and shrimp. Many are photographed in this book for advanced readers.

PATENT, DOROTHY. (2000). *Slinky, slithery snakes*. New York: Walker. Bold illustrations draw readers into intriguing aspects of many species of snakes. NSTA* Outstanding Trade Book.

REISER, LYNN. (1996). *Beach feet*. New York: Greenwillow. An imaginative look at shells from the perspective of barefooted beach visitors. The beach sand and shell art could inspire creativity at the sand table. Background information on shells is given in the end pages.

RYDER, JOANNE. (1993). *One small fish*. New York: Morrow. Imagination turns a dull moment in the science room into an undersea adventure for a girl. Wonderful sea creatures swim out of the pages and crawl through backpacks as readers explore marine life with the girl.

SAYRE, APRIL. (2001). *Dig, wait, listen: A desert toad's tale*. New York: Greenwillow. Other desert dwellers pass overhead as a patient spadefoot toad listens underground. She's waiting to hear the rainfall she needs to lay her eggs. The graceful text begs to be read aloud. NSTA* Outstanding Trade Book.

SIMON, SEYMOUR. (1995). *Sharks*. New York: HarperCollins. Fascinating text and color photographs provide about as much as you need to know, including how to avoid being shark bait.

WINNER, CHERIE. (1993). *Salamanders*. Minneapolis, MN: Carolrhoda Books. The detailed information offered on these fascinating amphibians can be summarized for young children. Excellent color photographs. An NSTA* Outstanding Trade Book. Paperback.

Literature Links: Birds

BAILEY, JILL, & BURNIE, DAVID. (1997). *Birds*. New York: Dorling Kindersley. This fine resource for children covers the way birds fly, mate, hatch, and care for fledglings, tells how they build nests, and explores their feeding habits and habitats.

BAKER, KEITH. (2001). *Little Green*. San Diego: Harcourt. Young listeners will reach for paintbrushes after seeing the bold colors and swirling movement illustrating this simple story of a boy watching a hummingbird. NSTA* recommended.

GIBBONS, GAIL. (2001). *Gulls . . . gulls . . . gulls*. New York: Holiday. Colorful, informative drawings enliven the basic facts about the herring gull, familiar to many children.

GOLDIN, AUGUSTA. (1999). *Ducks don't get wet*. New York: HarperCollins. This is a beautiful introduction to wild ducks: what they eat, how they migrate, and more. An experiment reveals how ducks can swim and dive without getting wet. Paperback.

HAUS, ROBYN. (2001). *Make your own bird houses and feeders*. Charlotte, VT: Williamson. An inviting, kid-friendly style leads to practical construction tips and species-appropriate feeding. A helpful chart summarizes species and their locale, food preferences, and correct feeder type and placement.

HICKMAN, PAMELA. (2000). *Starting with nature bird book.* Niagara Falls, NY: Kids Can Press. This slim book offers a broad sweep of basic bird facts, even including bird song identification.

HOPKINSON, DEBORAH. (2001). *Bluebird summer.* New York: Greenwillow. Two children help restore an abandoned garden to encourage bluebirds to return and nest there.

JAMES, SIMON. (2002). *The birdwatcher.* Cambridge, MA: Candlewick. Granddad's tales about his birdwatching adventures draw a child into sharing his fascination. Lighthearted illustrations by the author.

JENKINS, MARTIN. (1999). *The emperor's egg.* Cambridge, MA: Candlewick. Here's a delightful look at what father penguins endure to incubate a chick, and mother's supporting role. NSTA* recommended.

PRELLER, JAMES. (1998). *Cardinal and sunflower.* New York: Farrar, Strauss, & Giroux. This informative book describes how both species develop through the seasons.

ROYSTON, ANGELA. (1994). *Birds.* Science Nature Guides. San Diego, CA: Thunder Bay Press. Birding activities are included with colorful illustrations and brief identifying characteristics of 150 common birds of North America from seven habitats.

WARD, HELEN. (1997). *The king of the birds.* Brookfield, CT: Millbrook. Children will enjoy this story about choosing the king of the birds because the smallest and cleverest is chosen, not the biggest or most spectacular. Elegant watercolor illustrations.

WEBB, SOPHIE. (2000). *My season with penguins: An Antarctic journal.* Boston: Houghton Mifflin. The biologist/author's field notes and sketches delightfully recapture her penguin study trip. Intended for older grade levels, others also will be drawn to it. NSTA* Outstanding Trade Book.

WINER, YVONNE. (2002). *Birds build nests.* Watertown, MA: Charlesbridge. Unique nest construction techniques of 16 birds from around the world are described. Web sites are listed for more information.

WOOD, AUDREY. (2001). *Birdsong.* San Diego, CA: Harcourt Brace. Familiar birds flit through richly illustrated pages, while children in many different settings hear their distinctive calls. Paperback.

Literature Links: Mammals

ARNOSKY, JIM. (1996). *All about deer.* New York: Scholastic. Did you know that deer shed their antlers in winter? The author/artist shares fascinating information about these appealing, increasingly common animals. An NSTA* Outstanding Trade Book.

BLAKE, ROBERT. (2000). *Fledgling.* New York: Philomel. Four fledgling kestrels prepare for their first day of flight in their urban setting. The author's detailed drawings show New York City from the dizzying, fearsome perspectives of the fledglings. They end their exciting, successful day back on their rooftop home.

BURNIE, DAVID. (1998). *Mammals.* New York: Dorling Kindersley. A broad spectrum of mammals' characteristics are considered in this well-organized resource, such as newborns, growth, movements, feeding, play, defenses, and group living.

CHERRY, LYNNE. (1994). *The armadillo from amarillo.* San Diego: Harcourt Brace. Written as a whimsical rhymed fantasy, much of the natural history and geographic information was researched on-site under a Smithsonian Institution grant. The author's illustrations add rich detail and interesting perspectives to the curious armadillo's odyssey.

CYRUS, KURT. (2001). *Oddhoppers opera: A bug's garden of verses.* San Diego: Harcourt. The hilarious odyssey of seven snails trekking through their vegetable garden habitat, passing other small creatures stuggling to grow and survive. The author's clever verse, as well as his accurate paintings of this busy scene, combine to make this a not-to-be-missed book. NSTA* Outstanding Trade Book.

DAVIES, NICOLA. (1997). *Big blue whale.* Cambridge, MA: Candlewick. Playful graphics and comfortable language make this a broadly appealing book. Factual information is separated from the flow of the larger-type text. NSTA* Outstanding Trade Book.

DAVIES, NICOLA. (2001). *Bat loves the night.* Cambridge MA: Candlewick. Tender illustrations blend well with the lyrical text detailing feeding, flight, and nurturing patterns of bats. Baby batlings are described as "tiny velvet scraps."

DAVIES, NICOLA. (2001). *Wild about dolphins.* Cambridge, MA: Candlewick. The zoologist-author recalls the excitement of a scientific expedition in Newfoundland waters, and of swimming with dolphins in the Indian Ocean. NSTA* recommended.

DRAGONWAGON, CRESCENT. (1997). *Bat in the dining room.* New York: Marshall Cavendish. Only Melissa considers how the bat must feel when its arrival upsets a restaurant full of guests. The poetic text and expressive illustrations reveal how she saved the day for both bat and diners.

GIBBONS, GAIL. (1999). *Bats.* New York: Holiday. Friendly illustrations debunk myths and clarify the interesting features of these valuable animals. The bat's sound system, echolocation, for locating flying meals is carefully described.

HANSARD, PETER. (2001). *A field full of horses.* Cambridge, MA: Candlewick. Together with careful renderings, this simple story fondly captures the appealing characteristics of horses and introduces several breeds. Paperback.

HODGE, DEBORAH. (1998). *Beavers.* Buffalo, NY: Kids Can Press. Readers can almost feel the fur in Pat Stephens's illustrations as they learn the usefulness of these fascinating animals. Also in this wildlife series: *Deer, Moose, Elk & Caribou; Bears; Wild Cats;* and *Wild Dogs.*

LESSER, CAROLYN. (1996). *Great crystal bear.* San Diego: Harcourt Brace. Poetic language combines myth and fact about this intrepid hunter of the North.

MARKLE, SANDRA. (1999). *Down, down, down in the ocean.* New York: Walker. Capable readers can follow the food chain from the warm surface waters, gradually descending to the sea floor.

RYDER, JOANNE. (1996). *Jaguar in the rain forest.* New York: Morrow. A child climbs a tree, imagining himself as a jaguar. The lyrical text follows his day searching for prey. Richly detailed paintings of varied rain forest life add fascination. Read aloud to stimulate creative thinking and creative movement.

SCHUCH, STEVE. (1999). *A symphony of whales.* San Diego: Harcourt. The naturalist-musician author tells, through a child protagonist, of the amazing actual musical rescue of whales trapped near an Arctic village. The winter landscape art adds to the drama. NSTA* Outstanding Trade Book.

STUART, DEE. (1993). *The astonishing armadillo.* Minneapolis, MN: Carolrhoda Books. This careful description of these armor-coated mammals includes fascinating photographs of newborns.

WALLACE, KAREN. (1996). *Imagine you are a tiger.* New York: Henry Holt. Follow the life of a tiger cub from infancy to maturity in this simple text. It would be hard to listen to the action language without moving to it.

WOOD, TED. (2001). *Bear dogs: Canines with a mission.* New York: Walker. Follow a bear biologist and the dogs she has trained to teach bears to stay safely away from humans, and vice versa.

Literature Links: Habitats

ARNOSKY, JIM. (1997). *Rabbits and raindrops.* New York: Putnam. This charming, large-type picture book portrays a rabbit's eye view of the world at beneath-the-hedge level. Other small creatures share this space to get out of a rain shower.

BERNHARD, EMERY. (1997). *Prairie dogs.* San Diego: Harcourt Brace. This fascinating description of prairie dog characteristics and life in their complex burrows includes a plea to value their contribution to prairie life, instead of trying to extinguish it. Appealingly illustrated by Durga Bernhard.

EARLE, SYLVIA. (2000). *Hello fish! Visiting the coral reef.* Washington, DC: National Geographic. The world-renowned marine biologist writes invitingly to a child audience.

The dramatic, full-page color photographs draw immediate attention. NSTA* Outstanding Science Trade Book.

GEORGE, LINDSAY. (1995). *In the snow: Who's been here?* New York: Greenwillow. Listeners and beginning readers will want to join Cammy and William as they search for signs of animal life in the snowy woods. In this beautiful book, they spot evidence of wintering birds, a chipmunk, a squirrel, and a deer.

GEORGE, LINDSAY. (1995). *In the woods: Who's been here?* New York: Greenwillow. Outstanding lifelike illustrations by the author invite close attention to the signs of wildlife followed by two observant children.

GEORGE, LINDSAY. (1996). *Around the pond: Who's been here?* New York: Greenwillow. The two keen-eyed children on a blueberry-picking expedition carefully observe signs of wildlife. They see evidence of ducks, a raccoon, a turtle, and a snake. Warm, precise illustrations by the author.

HELLER, RUTH. (1999). *How to hide a butterfly and other insects.* New York: Penguin. The clever, accurate rhyming text combines with the author's stunning illustrations to make an unforgettable book about how camouflage helps animals hide safety in their habitats. Paperback.

HOCKMAN, HILLARY (Ed.). (1993). *Animal homes.* New York: Dorling Kindersley. Vivid exterior photographs pair with cutaway drawings to peek inside a beehive, beaver lodge, squirrel nest, and rabbit warren, in this *What's Inside?* series book. Paperback.

KITCHEN, BERT. (1995). *And so they build.* Cambridge, MA: Candlewick Press. A lovely text and striking, detailed paintings provide a respectful look at the intricate shelters built by animals. Paperback.

LESSER, CAROLYN. (1996). *Dig hole, soft mole.* San Diego, CA: Harcourt Brace. A simple, lyrical text and gentle illustrations inform young children about the dim world and friendly neighbors of the common mole.

RILEY, PETER. (1998). *Our mysterious ocean.* Westport, CT: Joshua Morris Publishing. Well-designed diecut pages and acetate inserts effectively convey that different ocean depth zones form specific habitats. Older children will appreciate the information, though the reading may be hard.

RYDER, JOANNE. (1996). *Jaguar in the rain forest.* New York: Morrow. A boy climbs a tree, imagining himself to be a jaguar. He spends a sun-dappled day in the jaguar's life, listening, watching, and searching for food. Detailed paintings of the myriad animal life are a feast for the eyes. A good trigger for creative thinking and creative movement.

SILVER, DONALD. (1993). *One small square: Backyard.* New York: Freeman. This richly detailed look at the awesome complexity of what lives in your own backyard is beautifully laid out and illustrated.

TAGHOLM, SALLY. (2000). *Animal lives: The rabbit.* New York: Kingfisher. This is a warm, accurate protrayal of a rabbit colony, both in and beyond their warren. NSTA* Outstanding Trade Book.

YOLEN, JANE. (1997). *Welcome to the green house.* New York: Putnam & Grosset. Laura Regan's opulent art captures the complexity of the rain forest, enhancing the patterned text that describes dwellers in this exotic habitat. Paperback.

Literature Links: Baby Animals, Hatching, and Pets

BAUER, MARION. (1997). *If you were born a kitten.* New York: Simon & Schuster. Clear, large-type text and lovely chalk art focus attention on the birth stories of 12 different animal babies.

BURTON, ROBERT, (1998). *Egg.* New York: Dorling Kindersley. Wonderful color photographs show the incubation and hatching processes of 28 birds, insects, mollusks, reptiles, and fish.

COHEN, MIRIAM. (1989). *Best friends.* New York: Aladdin. The friendship of Jim and Paul is cemented by their mutual rescue of the classroom incubation project in this classic story.

DARLING, KATHY. (1996). *Rain forest babies.* New York: Walker. This book contains endearing photographs and minimal text about the young of 14 species.

DEWEY, JENNIFER. (1996). *Faces only a mother could love.* Honesdale, PA: Boyds Mills Press. Tender drawings by the author enrich the descriptions of bizarre-appearing animal babies bonding with their mothers. Characteristic behaviors are also presented.

FRENCH, VIVIAN. (2000). *Growing frogs.* Cambridge, MA: Candlewick. A mother helps her daughter collect frog eggs to observe the metamorphosis at home.

GRAHAM, BOB. (1997). *Queenie, one of the family.* Cambridge, MA: Candlewick. Good story-telling and cartoon art by the author will keep children intrigued with this egg-hatching situation.

GRAHAM, BOB. (2001). *"Let's get a pup!" said Kate.* Cambridge, MA: Candlewick. Another warm story, humorously illustrated by the author, portraying a family's indecision about replacing a family pet.

HELLER, RUTH. (1999). *Chickens aren't the only ones.* New York: Penguin. The simple and direct information in the text is vividly reinforced with the author's striking illustrations. NSTA[*] Outstanding Trade Book.

HICKMAN, PAMELA. (1999). *A new frog.* Buffalo, NY: Kids Can Press. This small book is designed for leisurely adult/child sharing: a charming cumulative story about a frog's life cycle for the child; fold-outs of facts for the adult to enrich the discussion. Endnotes give directions for making a water scope. Also in this series: *A New Duck.*

JENKINS, PRISCILLA. (1995). *A nest full of eggs.* New York: HarperCollins. Two children watch and help a pair of robins nest, hatch, and raise their brood. Good bird information is woven into this simple story.

LIERSCH, ANNE. (2001). *Nell and Fluffy.* New York: North-South Books. Appealing drawings capture Nell's emotions as she learns the true meaning and responsibility of pet ownership.

MACMILLAN, BRUCE. (1993). *A beach for the birds.* Boston: Houghton Mifflin. Romping children share a beach in Maine with least terns (water birds) that court, set up housekeeping, raise young, and prepare to migrate. Older children will appreciate this detailed account of an endangered species.

MCCLOSKEY, ROBERT. (1976). *Blueberries for Sal.* New York: Puffin. Four sets of mothers and their offspring are part of this classic story: Sal and her mother, plus bear, quail, and crow families.

MCCLOSKEY, ROBERT. (1979). *Make way for ducklings.* New York: Viking Press. Finding a suitable home and raising a brood of ducklings occupy Mrs. Mallard's time in this timeless book.

YOLEN, JANE. (1993). *Honkers.* Boston: Little Brown. Watching over three newly hatched goslings softens loneliness for Betsy in this story of her summer away from home.

Literature Links: Animal Math

LEEDY, LOREEN. (2001). *Measuring Penny.* New York: Henry Holt. Lisa chooses her pet terrier, Penny, as her homework assignment to measure something. Lisa quantifies Penny's anatomy, as well as the time requirements and cost of her upkeep. NSTA[*] recommended.

MAGDA, ANN. (2000). *Tiger math.* New York: Holt. The engaging story of raising an orphaned tiger cub occupies one side of this clever book. Learning to graph his growth in various ways occupies the other side. NSTA[*] Outstanding Trade Book.

MURPHY, STUART. (1999). *Room for Ripley.* The math of measuring capacity is central to this pleasant tale of preparing a home for Carlo's new pet guppy. Activities involving liquid measurements are included.

PINCZES, ELINOR. (2001). *Inchworm and a half.* Boston: Houghton Mifflin. A sprightly inchworm nibbles as she measures vegetables in the garden. Smaller worms introduce the concept of fractions.

SCHWARTZ, DAVID. (1999). *If you hopped like a frog.* New York: Scholastic. This book introduces the concepts of ratio and proportion by imagining comparisons of what kids could do if they shared different animals physical capabilities. This is good inspiration for creative thinking and creative movement.

Literature Links: The Death of Pets

BROWN, LAURIE, & BROWN, MARC. (1996). *When dinosaurs die: A guide to understanding death.* Boston: Little Brown. The author of the beloved public television series *Arthur* addresses this topic well.

HARRIS, ROBIE. (2001). *Goodbye mousie.* New York: Simon & Schuster. This tender, satisfying story of a pet mouse's death expresses the full range of a child's emotions as he comes to terms with his loss.

KING-SMITH, DICK. (1995). *I love guinea pigs.* Cambridge, MA: Candlewick. This appealing book introducing the nature and care of these pets closes with a gentle farewell to favorites who died.

ROGERS, FRED. (1988). *Mister Rogers's first experience book: When a pet dies.* New York: Putnam. Mister Rogers helps children manage their feelings of loss, loneliness, and frustration after a pet dies. Highly recommended.

VIORST, JUDITH. (1971). *The tenth good thing about Barney.* New York: Atheneum. A family marks the loss of their loved pet by composing memorial lists of his best qualities.

* National Science Teachers Association

Poems (Resources in Appendix A)

There is an abundance of evocative and amusing poems about animals for children. Some are found in these collections:

> Paul Fleischman, *Joyful Noise: Poems for Two Voices.* Newberry Medal award poems evoke the delicate sounds of insects as they move.
>
> Douglas Florian has written six books of amusing animal poems: *Insectlopedia, In the Swim, On the Wing, Mammalabilia, Beast Feasts,* and *Lizards, Frogs, and Polliwogs.* He has collected several notable awards along the way. His childlike illustrations will inspire young painters.
>
> Dorothy Kennedy (Ed.). *I Thought I'd Take My Rat to School.* In X. J. Kennedy's poem, "Science Lesson," children tickle tadpoles.
>
> Pat Moon, *Earth Lines.* In "The Bird's Nest," children compete with a bird to build the best nest. They lose.
>
> Robert Louis Stevenson's "The Little Land," from *A Child's Garden of Verses,* records a charming perspective of insects projected by a diminutive sailor on a leaf boat.

Fingerplays

Add to this fingerplay to include the movement of small animals observed by children in your classroom:

> *Small Animal Parade*
>
> *A slow, slow snail*
>
> *Drags down the trail*   (Stretch and contract right hand, dragging along left arm)
>
> *A looping earthworm*
>
> *Moves along with a squirm*   (Loop and wiggle one finger)

A spider runs past
With eight legs so fast   (Hands one on top of the other, tuck thumbs under, wiggle eight fingers)

The grasshopper springs
With six legs and wings   (One hand crossed on top of other, thumbs and little fingers held under. Leap up and down)

The green and white frog
Leaps over a log   (Right fist leaps over left arm)
A seven-fin fish
Swims by with a swish   (Palms together, hands twist and turn, moving forward)

Art Activities

Easel Painting. One of the early shapes many children paint spontaneously is a loop with many strokes radiating from it. Often these are called "spiders" or "bugs" by the painter. Provide green and brown paint on insect-watching day and casually suggest that some children could have fun making paintings of the spider, grasshopper, caterpillar, or whatever creature is of current interest. Newsprint sheets may also be cut into large butterflies or bird shapes for children to paint at the easel.

Crayon and Picture Collage. Provide pictures of animals (for children to cut out, or have some precut for those new at cutting), paste, construction paper, and crayons for crayon-enhanced collages. Animal pictures are not easy to locate in the typical household magazines. Old children's magazines, free nature publications from your state natural resources department, or animal stamps from the National Wildlife Federation are good sources.

Leather and Feather Collage. Scraps of leather from a crafts shop and domestic bird feathers make interesting collage material. Use durable paper and white glue for best adhesion. Before using untreated feathers, seal them in plastic zip closure bags and microwave for a few minutes, watching closely, to kill any mites or other allergens they may carry.

Additive Sculpture Animals. Pinecones are good bases for making animal forms. Turkeys can have rounded Scotch pinecone bodies, red painted balsam cone heads, and feather tails. Use strips of molded paper egg cartons as caterpillar bodies. Offer tempera paint, fabric, paste, feathers, and snips of pipe cleaners for fanciful decorations.

Eggshell Mosaics. Broken, dyed eggshells can be glued to paper for egg-hatching project extensions. The younger the age group, the larger the shell bits should be for best management of materials.

Play

Animal Puppet Play. Put out animal hand puppets for children to animate. A small table turned on its side makes a good improvised stage.

Dramatize Animal Stories. When a group of children is familiar with an animal story that involves "a cast of thousands," they enjoy acting out the story in an informal, simplified way. Assign roles to all the children so that no one is left out, even if someone has to play the part of a tree in the forest. Some children will accept multiple actors in the same role–acting is the point rather than the audience view. Good animal stories that meet the casting requirements include *Make Way for Ducklings* and *The Tortoise and the Hare.* Help move the story along informally as needed. Assign areas in the room for different scenes: "Here's the island on the river where the Mallards build their nest, and the block area is the Public Garden where they swim." Use simple props if they help carry out the story.

Creative Movement

It's easy to draw children into the fun of acting out animal characteristics. Creative movement suggestions may also strengthen children's recall of the life cycles of animals that undergo metamorphosis. Slowly and dramatically, read animal poems aloud for children to interpret with you.

Poems about inchworms, treehoppers, and whirligig beetles, found in *Insectlopedia* by Douglas Florian (see Appendix A), irresistibly inspire children to action.

Eve Merriam's poem, "On Our Way," describes movement patterns of many animals. It's found in *Sing a Song of Popcorn,* compiled by DeRegniers, Schenk, et al.

Clare Cherry suggests many animal movement stimuli in her book, *Creative Movement for the Developing Child.* Karen Pandell's book, *Animal Action,* will inspire animal creative movement activity. The Nature Company offers an imaginative sing-and-dance-along videotape, *Baboons, Butterflies, and Me,* blending African wildlife footage with children imitating those movements. It is appropriate for two- to six-year-olds (see Appendix A).

Children can be invited, one by one, to travel across the floor like the animal of their choice. (Groups of young children wait turns more patiently if they are sitting on the floor before and after their turn to travel.) One quick-thinking pair of five-year-olds brightened our day when they piggybacked to crawl together as an eight-legged spider. (For further animal movement ideas, see Smith, K., 2002.)

Creative Thinking

What If? Read aloud Mary Anne Hoberman's poem, "Cricket," from *The Llama Who Had No Pajama.* Ask, "Imagine what it would be like if your leg could hear and your ear could walk. Imagine how the world would seem to you." Offer this as a group discussion, or let older children draw and write their responses.

Ask, "What if we had six legs to travel on? How would our lives be different? What could we do that we can't do with two legs? What couldn't we do? What if we had to spend most of our day gathering food for ourselves? What if we had working wings? How would our lives be different? What if we had to build places to live without using tools?" Encourage as many imaginative responses as possible. Let children generate their own "what if" questions to explore.

Animal Inventions. Encourage children to invent new animals, name them, draw what they would look like, and describe them.

Food Experiences

Children accept the idea that people eat fish and chicken, as the terms are customarily used at mealtimes. There seems little to be gained, however, from pressing the point that the hamburgers being served for lunch were once a steer or that the ham in the casserole was once a pig. Concentrate instead on ideas that foster positive emotions: cows giving milk, hens giving eggs, or bees making honey for people to enjoy. To confirm human dependence on other forms of animals for food, many cooking experiences are possible in the classroom: making butter (use fresh, not sterilized, whipping cream), instant puddings, ice cream, or custard. Read aloud "The Friendly Cow," by Robert Lewis Stevenson, in *A Child's Garden of Verses*.

Field Trips

♣ The list of potential problems and hazards that might be part of an outdoor animal observation hike could rule out this kind of field trip for a large group of young children. It can also be very disappointing when the objects of the trip do not display themselves. Try instead to pause for watching time whenever you encounter small animals while in the schoolyard with your children: ants at work in a sidewalk crack nest, limp worms washed out of their tunnels after a hard rain, or squirrels and birds gathering food.

Other field trip possibilities are to a farm, zoo, pet shop, or animal shelter. The state conservation department will have information about the location of animal preserves, hatcheries, or parks with programs by naturalists. They may also have free or inexpensive leaflets about animals.

Do not forget the grocery store as an animal study resource. Animals provide, indirectly, many dairy products, eggs, and honey.

PROMOTING CONCEPT CONNECTIONS

Maintaining Concepts

A teacher vividly reinforces concepts about the usefulness of insects by reacting calmly to an intruding bee or wasp. Remind children that insects of this sort sting only when disturbed. Open the windows from the top so that the insect can eventually fly out. Offer an observation jar to a shrieking child who is about to squash an uninvited spider. Do not undo what you have previously taught about the creature's place in the web of life by joining the chase with a can of insecticide. (The use of insecticides is highly discouraged in schools.) On the other hand, there is no need to be solicitous toward roaches, flies, or mosquitoes. If you must eliminate them in front of children, mention that they are pests to people, but good food for birds and toads.

Another reinforcement of respect for living creatures may occur if a classroom pet dies or if a dead bird is found on the playground. Let the children be aware of the death and take part in a gentle burial. Say that the animal's useful life has ended. Try to read one of the stories about the death of animals that coincides with your views of death (see Literature Links: The Death of Pets earlier in this chapter).

Improving Schoolgrounds

Consider a "minibeast" pit like those found in many British schools, which can supply numerous insects and other crawlies as needed. In a corner of the asphalt or field, dig a hole 15-18 inches deep and about 2 × 3 feet wide and long. Fill with logs laid on their sides. A range of bugs can congregate and breed there. A simpler method is to lay down pieces of old carpet in a low-traffic setting; bugs appreciate the dark and wet environment.

A butterfly garden stocked with native perennials will last for many years without heavy maintenance. Numerous resources exist to help, including the Schoolyard Habitat Program at the National Wildlife Federation, state departments of natural resources, and cooperative extension agents. See *Greening Schoolgrounds* by Grant and Littlejohn.

Connecting Concepts

The broad ecological relationships between plants, animals, soil, water, air, and temperature are awesome and complex. Preschool and early elementary-age children can take beginning steps toward understanding ecological relationships through small, concrete instances. For example, a child may observe a bird pecking at tree bark and wonder aloud if the bird is hurting the tree. An adult can clarify the bird's immediate purpose and expand the idea of mutual dependency. "Yes, it does look a bit like the bird is hurting the tree. Really, it is getting its food and helping the tree at the same time. The bird is catching tiny insects that are eating the tree. Can you think of a way that the tree helps the bird?" Emphasize that plants and animals need each other.

A child may question the fitness of animals eating other animals, plants, and seeds for sustenance. One can appreciate the child's concern. Then suggest that each living thing can make many more seeds or eggs than are needed to make a young plant or animal like itself. If all the seeds grew into plants and all the eggs became animals, there would not be enough room in the world for all the living things. Some of the plants and animals need to be used in this way to keep the proper amount of each kind growing well to maintain the balance of nature. Young children can be upset by the recognition of our human role in the food chain. The fact that humans are animals that eat other animals may be better tolerated after the primary grade years.

Sound concepts can be linked to the study of animal life. Compare the high pitch of the wren's song with the low pitch of the dove's coo. Feel the vibrations of a purring cat. Think of the swelling air pockets that make a frog's loud croak possible. Recall the vibrating wing covers that can be seen when the male cricket sings. Relate air concepts to the life requirements of animals. (See Chapter 7, Air.)

Family and Community Support

Inform families early in the school year that children are encouraged to bring in captured insects. After the first few planned experiences, you may never have to track down a specimen by yourself.

Knowledgeable parents might be willing to set up a classroom aquarium, make a pet cage, or arrange to bring in and show a family pet. Their children's social standing with the group usually blossoms as a secondary benefit.

Alert families to special programs being offered by the children's library or by a nearby nature center, zoo, or aquarium. Find out about interactive exhibits and events for children in the nearest natural history museum. Watch for announcements of bird-watching hikes or moonlight animal hikes offered to families by state park naturalists or national forest rangers.

RESOURCES

BURNETT, R. (1994). *The pillbug project.* Washington, DC: National Science Teachers Association. This book provides science and math activities using these extremely accessible insects for observation. Paperback.

BURTON, R. (1997). *National Audubon Society birdfeeder handbook.* New York: Dorling Kindersley. This authoritative guidebook provides tips for attracting and feeding birds in varied locations. It also illustrates common birds. Paperback.

DUNN, G. (1994). *Caring for insect livestock.* Lansing, MI: Young Entomologist's Society.

ECHOLS, J. (1990). *Animal defenses.* Berkeley, CA: Lawrence Hall of Science. The creative activity plans are useful for exploring animal defenses.

ECHOLS, J. (1990). *Buzzing a hive.* Berkeley, CA: Lawrence Hall of Science. The art and drama activities are helpful for exploring behavior of bees.

ECHOLS, J., HOUSOUME, K., & KOPP J. (1996). *Ant homes under the ground.* Berkeley, CA: GEMS, Lawrence Hall of Science. This outstanding unit for preschool-K classes provides background information for teachers and a multifaceted curriculum for children, including games.

EDWARDS, L., NABORS, M., & CAMACHO, C. (2002). "The dirt on worms." *Science and Children, 10*(1), p. 42–46. Details a successful classroom project with earthworms.

Environmental discovery units. These inexpensive teaching guides for ecology study can be obtained from the National Wildlife Federation, 11100 Wildlife Center Dr., Reston, VA 21090.

GLASER, L. (1992). *Wonderful worms.* Brookfield, CT: Millbrook. Comprehensive, respectful treatment of this creature's ecological significance is found in this NSTA Outstanding Trade Book for 1992.

GRANT, T., & LITTLEJOHN, G. (2001). *Greening school grounds: Creating habitats for learning.* Toronto, CA: Green Teacher.

HAMPTON, C., & KRAMER, D. (1994). *Classroom creature culture: Algae to anoles.* Washington, DC: National Science Teachers Association. This collection of articles from *Science and Children* emphasizes respect for the needs of living things and is the resource to reach for when a new small creature joins the classroom.

IMES, R. (1997). *Incredible bugs.* New York: Barnes & Noble. Splendid drawings, great color photographs, and well-organized information make this a valuable resource.

KEPLER, L. (1996). *Windowsill science centers.* New York: Scholastic. Clear, simple directions are given to make a 2-liter plastic bottle bird feeder. Bird observation tips and related activities are offered.

KNEIDEL, S. (1993). *Creepy crawlies and the scientific method.* Golden, CO: Fulcrum Publishing. This book provides guidance with finding, housing, and setting up experimental conditions for insects to respond to. The writing respects both the creatures and the learning children.

KNEIDEL, S. (1994). *Pet bugs: A kid's guide to catching and keeping touchable insects.* New York: Wiley. This is a wonderful classroom resource for learning how to catch and keep 26 species of insects, with additional information about how they behave. Paperback.

KNEIDEL, S. (1999). *More pet bugs: A kid's guide to catching and keeping insects and other small creatures.* New York: Wiley. From ants to wooly bears to crayfish: 23 creatures are considered in Kriedel's comfortable approach to gathering, housing, and observing these interesting animals.

KNEIDEL, S. (2000). *Stinkbugs, stick insects, and stag beetles, and 18 more of the strangest insects on earth.* New York: Wiley. Three groups of strange insects are inspected: those you can probably find; those you might find; and those you probably won't find.

KNOTT, R., HOSOUME, K., & BERGMAN, L. (1989). *Earthworms: Teacher's guide.* Berkeley, CA: Great Explorations in Math and Science (GEMS).

KOPP, J. (1998). *Frog math: Predict, ponder, play.* Teacher's Guide. Berkeley, CA: Lawrence Hall of Science. Directions are given for lively, carefully developed set-building and probability activities plus extending ideas. Paperback.

KRAMER, D. (1989). *Animals in the classroom.* New York: Addison-Wesley. This is a good source of information on housing and caring for classroom animals.

LEVI, H., & LEVI, L. (1990). *Spiders and their kin.* New York: Golden Books. Pocket-size paperback. Comprehensive information is easy to find in this book.

MIKULA, R. (2000). *The family butterfly book.* Pownel, VT: Storey Books. All aspects of butterfly raising are covered, from how to lift a caterpillar to housing and hatching conditions.

PARKER, S. (1992). *How nature works.* New York: Random House. This book presents excellent background information on how animals meet their needs for food and air, and how they grow, move, and protect themselves. Detailed illustrations. Paperback.

PYLE, R. (1994). *National Audubon Society field guide to North American butterflies.* New York: Knopf. Color photographs identify common eggs, caterpillars, and chrysalises. This is good information for those wishing to offer a butterfly-hatching experience in the classroom.

ROSENBLATT, L. (1998). *Monarch magic: Butterfly activities and nature discoveries.* Charlotte, VT: Williamson. Concise explanations and detailed photographs describe monarch life stages. Suggestions are given to enable kids across the country to help save the Monarch habitat. NSTA-recommended.

ROSNER, M. (2000). *Scientific American great science fair projects.* New York: Wiley. Good directions for breeding butterflies are given.

RUSSELL, H. (2001). *Ten-minute field trips: Using the school grounds for environmental studies* (2nd ed.). Washington, DC: National Science Teachers Association.

SMITH, K. (2002). "Dancing in the forest: Narrative writing through dance." *Young Children,* 57, 90–94.

VAN CLEVE, J. (1999). *Play and find out about bugs.* New York: Wiley. Simulation projects will help preschoolers recall insect features, such as learning how six-legged creatures walk.

WANGBERG, J. (1997). *Do bees sneeze?* Golden, CO: Fulcrum Press. The best of "questions-kids-ask" books is well-organized to be a handy classroom resource. Written by an entomologist, it includes interesting projects for insect enthusiasts.

ONLINE RESOURCES

Children's butterfly site:
www.mesc.usgs.gov/butterfly/butterfly.html

Monarch Watch:
www.MonarchWatch.org/

The Human Body:
Care and Nourishment

Do you ever wonder what you can do to encourage a healthy lifetime for children in your classes? Do you remember learning to eat your veggies and brush your teeth? Did you feel proud about growing? This chapter will help you re-create important health-care experiences for your children.

Young children yearn to grow and become strong. They are eager to know what is inside their bodies. The experiences suggested in this chapter contribute to clarifying misconceptions and overcoming worries that children may have about their bodies. They help children take the beginning steps toward a lifelong responsibility for their own physical well-being. The following concepts are explored:

- Each person is unique.
- We learn through our senses.
- Bones help support our bodies.
- Muscles keep us moving, living, and breathing.
- We help ourselves stay healthy and grow strong.
- Strong, growing bodies need nourishing food.

The goal of this chapter is to help children learn to value themselves as unique individuals, respect differences among individuals, and care for their own bodies. Mere knowledge of these concepts and health-care rules may not lead children into healthy practices. Positive attitudes about health lead to positive actions. Such attitudes grow through identification with a trusted person or symbol. With this in mind, a teacher might choose to introduce activities by using a puppet with whom young children can identify.

Within this chapter, specific experiences lead to ideas about individuality, the senses, bones, muscles, and the heart. Simple health care and nutrition concepts follow from these activities.

CONCEPT: Each person is unique.

1. What do I look like?

LEARNING OBJECTIVE: To take pride in our growing bodies.

MATERIALS:

Manila folder or construction-
  paper cover for each child

Paper punch, fasteners

Crayons

Paper

Yardstick or meterstick

Scale

Full-length mirror or several
  smaller mirrors

GETTING READY:

Prepare book covers; label
  "About Me, (child's name)".

Label page 1, "I am ____ tall, I
  weigh ____, on (date)."

Label page 2, "I look like this."

Fasten tape measure to wall securely, if used.

Play the tape "Everybody's
  Fancy," sung by Fred Rogers
  on *Won't You Be My Neighbor?*

SMALL-GROUP ACTIVITY:

1. Measure and weigh each child. Let child record the data on page 1. (Teasing about size differences hurts and must not be allowed.)

2. Encourage children to tell what they see in the mirror, then on page 2, draw what they see. Record each child's self-description on the page. (Withdrawn children may be unable to describe or draw themselves. You can help build a withdrawn child's self-confidence by describing what the child's face looks like to you.)

3. Fasten completed pages in covers and tack to bulletin board until the next book entry is made.

2. What do my fingertips show?

LEARNING OBJECTIVE: To appreciate our uniqueness.

MATERIALS:

Two *About Me* pages

Extra paper

Marker or crayon

Soft paper towels

Meat trays

Dry or premixed tempera paint,
  dark color

Water

SMALL-GROUP ACTIVITY:

1. Invite children to use marker or crayon to trace around their hands, fingers spread wide, on the appropriately marked pages. (Offer help if needed.)

2. Compare hand tracings for similarities and differences. Suggest looking at palms and fingertips through magnifying glass. How do they look?

Numbers are significant when they tell a boy how much he has grown.

Magnifying glasses

Scissors

Paste

GETTING READY:

Make paint pads for fingerprint-
ing by folding damp towels to
fit trays. Sprinkle dry tempera
or pour thick, mixed tempera
onto damp pad.

3. Show children how to lightly stamp fingertips on paint pads, then press their fingers
firmly on extra paper. Encourage examining the prints with magnifiers to compare
patterns of each fingertip. Discuss the
uniqueness of prints and the use of fingerprints or footprints when babies are born
in hospitals. Mention that the patterns children are printing are theirs alone.

4. After children have enjoyed making many
prints, suggest making a careful print in
the corresponding fingers of the hand tracings. Children with mature cutting skills
may wish to cut out the completed hands
to paste in their *About Me* books.

5. Mark book pages "Mine Alone, Right" and "Mine Alone, Left." (Children's names should be put on pages promptly to avoid confusion.)
6. Handprints of the class members make a meaningful bulletin board display for a parent meeting, stressing that individuality is to be celebrated.

CONCEPT: We learn through our senses.

Appreciation for the perceptual functions of our senses can be vividly experienced through their temporary absence. The following experiences make use of this principle.

1. What can we learn by hearing?

LEARNING OBJECTIVE: To appreciate hearing and develop empathy for hearing impaired people.

Group Experience: Introduce this experience by asking what children already know about hearing loss. Read aloud *Moses Goes to School,* by Isaac Millman, to provide insights on hearing impairments. Demonstrate what it would be like for a child who could not hear by silently mouthing the words in the book while holding it up to share the pictures. If a television set is available, watch a program with the sound turned off. Would a hearing loss make it hard to learn and to play with friends at school? Without specific guidance, children find it hard to empathize with the limitations of a classmate whose hearing loss has no external signs.

Discuss how our ears function (see Chapter 14, Sound). Discuss ear safety hazards. Try to arrange a visit from the public health nurses who conduct audiology screenings or from a hearing impaired person who is willing to show children a hearing aid or demonstrate sign language. Talk about how much we learn about the world through our hearing. Take a listening walk to encourage children to appreciate their ears.

2. What can we learn by seeing?

LEARNING OBJECTIVE: To appreciate vision and develop empathy for visually impaired people.

Introduction: Invite children to find out what it is like to identify objects and to move about without help from their eyes.

MATERIALS:

Lengths of soft paper toweling, long enough to fold into thick blindfolds for each child (To avoid spreading eye infections, do not share blindfolds.)

SMALL-GROUP ACTIVITY:

1. Fasten blindfolds. Because it is hard for children to stay blindfolded for more than a few minutes, pass only a few items from child to child for them to identify.
2. Loosen blindfolds. What did the children find out?

Paper clips to secure blindfolds

Small objects to identify by touch. Mix easily identified items (brush, Lego) with harder items (penny, nickel, 2 different books)

Small mirrors

Collection of objects to identify by sound: bell, clock, pieces of sandpaper to rub together, rubber band to snap

3. Fasten blindfolds. Encourage children to identify sounds. Remove blindfolds to let children use both eyes and ears to identify the sounds.

4. Let children examine their eyes in the mirrors and report what they see. Are the eyes still or moving? What do the lids do? How do their eyes feel when the children gently hold lids open without blinking for a minute? Is someone in the group wearing glasses? Why?

5. Offer to lead a blindfolded walk in the room. Fasten blindfolds for those willing to participate. Put children's hands on the shoulders of the child ahead. Slowly walk through the room, stopping to ask children where they are and how they know.

3. What can we learn by smelling and tasting?

LEARNING OBJECTIVE: To discover the surprising way some senses work together.

Introduction: Let children tell you what they already know about how food tastes when a head cold dulls the sense of smell. Suggest that children find out more about tasting and smelling at the science table.

MATERIALS:

Apple

Potato

Two bowls

Water

Lemon juice

Paring knife

Salt

Sugar

Fruit gelatin granules

Paper towel for each child

GETTING READY:

Peel apple and potato.

Slice thinly and drop into separate bowls of water.

Add a few drops of lemon juice to prevent darkening of the slices.

SMALL-GROUP ACTIVITY:

1. Ask children to hold their noses closed. "Let's use our tongues to find out what we are eating. Taste these slices and decide what they are." (If the two foods look very different, have children take turns to help each other taste with eyes and nostrils closed.)[*]

2. "Now taste your slices without holding your nose. How do they taste now?" Encourage more experimentation with tiny amounts of salt, sugar, and gelatin granules to find out if tongues alone tell us how food tastes.

[*]See *Sense-abilities* by Michelle O'Brien-Palmer, for additional smell/taste activities.

Read: Animal Senses, by Pamela Hickman (p. 26) about animals' dependence on discerning scents for survival.

4. What does our skin tell us?

LEARNING OBJECTIVE: To admire how the sense of touch informs us.

Introduction: Ask the children to find out one thing about the contents of two containers that are on the science table without lifting or opening the containers.

MATERIALS:

Ice cubes or very cold water

Hot water

Two small containers with tight lids

Feathers

Chalk

GETTING READY:

Fill one container with ice water and the other with hot water.

Cover with layers of paper toweling to retain temperature differences until children can use them.

SMALL-GROUP ACTIVITY:

1. "What can you learn about what is inside the containers without opening them? How can you find out?" Which part of their bodies did they use? Could they find out the same thing by using their elbows? Foreheads? Backs of their hands? What covers each of these body parts?
2. Suggest finding out if it is easy for our skin to inform us about what it touches. "Try stroking your skin so gently with a feather that you can't feel it. Is it possible?"
3. Ask whether skin on some parts of the body gives better information about how things feel. "Does chalk feel the same when stroked across an arm; when rubbed by the fingertips?"*
4. Encourage children to bring in an object with a special texture to put on a "Please Touch" tray.

* See *Feeling Your Way,* by Vicki Cobb

CONCEPT: Bones help support our bodies.

1. What do our bones feel like?

LEARNING OBJECTIVE: To be reassured that bones hold us up and help us move.

Introduction: Ask what children can feel deep inside their arms and legs when they gently press on them with a hand. Can they feel something in the middle of another child's back? Encourage them to investigate. The children could find out more about bones at the science table.

MATERIALS:

Chicken bones with rib section intact (mealtime leftover)

Illustration of the human skeletal system

Desirable: plastic model of the skeleton

GETTING READY:

Remove bits of breast meat from chicken rib section, leaving connective tissue and ribs intact.

SMALL-GROUP ACTIVITY:

1. Examine straight and curved chicken bones, long and short bones. Look at the connective tissue joining ribs. Help children feel their own ribs, tracing the curve of ribs from front to back. Are children's bones harder? Longer? (Bring out the idea that children grow bigger as their bones grow longer.)
2. Encourage children to curve their backs and curl up tight. Have them feel small bones in the spine and compare them with long bones in arms and legs. "Why do arms and legs bend differently than backs?" Have children feel joints that connect the long bones in arms and legs.
3. Encourage discussion of the bones children recognize in the model or illustration of the skeleton.

Read portions of *The Skeletal System* by Helen Frost.

CONCEPT: **Muscles keep us moving, living, and breathing.**

1. What do our muscles do?

LEARNING OBJECTIVE: To take pride in voluntary muscle control.

Introduction: Begin the focus on muscles by guiding some seated stretches of the upper body. Let the children tell you what they already know about muscles. Point out that muscles move in two ways: by tightening and by loosening. For most of us, our brains automatically choose how tight or loose our muscles need to be to do their work correctly. Other people have to think and work hard to use their muscles. They may need to have help from special braces, crutches, or chairs.

"We have hundreds of muscles in our bodies. Let's find out if we can feel some of them working to move our bodies."

Large-Group Experience: This pattern for exploring the use and feeling of muscle groups is best done together, lying on the floor, but can be adapted to seated groups.

1. "Lift your fingers off the floor. Move just your fingers while the rest of your body is still and relaxed. Stretch your fingers high. Do you feel pulls in your hands and your wrists?"

2. "Now lift your whole hand off the floor. Lift just your hands while the rest of your body is still and relaxed. Turn your hands in circles. Do you feel pulls in your wrist and your arms?" Continue this way with lower arms and then with whole arms. Explore the pulls felt when the extended arm is slowly moved back and forth.

3. Continue the quiet, relaxed investigation of toe, foot, and ankle movements, asking children what they feel as they slowly lift, twist, and turn these body parts. When lying on their backs, can they lift their lower legs only? Why not?

4. Explore the muscles involved in curling up tightly, then slowly unfolding, sitting up, and twisting and turning the trunk.

5. Stretch the shoulder, neck, and jaw muscles. Appreciate smoothly working muscles. Conclude by using the facial muscles to make a smile.

6. Provide each child with a paper clip. "Let's find out if making our muscles tight is always helpful. Make your arm and hand and spread-out fingers as tight and stiff as you possibly can. Now try using those tight muscles to pick up the paperclip. . . is it easy or hard to do? Now loosen all of those muscles and see if the fingers can pick up the paper clip. What does that tell you about holding pencils and crayons when we use them?"

2. How does our heart help us?

LEARNING OBJECTIVE: To appreciate our heart as a powerful muscle.

Introduction: Ask the class to try for a moment to be perfectly still without moving a single muscle. Is it possible? No, fortunately! Can children feel some muscles continuously moving, even when their arms and legs are still? "Some muscles must continuously move to keep us breathing. We couldn't live if the mightiest muscle of all stopped moving; it is our blood-pumping muscle, the heart. The heart pushes blood through thin tubes to send energy and oxygen to all parts of the body. We can't see our heart working because it is safe inside our rib cage, but we can feel it working (demonstrate location)."

Show the children how to fold their hands together, then squeeze and release the grasp rhythmically. "Your heart works something like this, pumping and pushing day and night. Let's see how long we can do this with our hands. We can stop pushing our hands together when we get tired, but our hearts can never stop pumping."

MATERIALS:

Paper towel tubes

16-inch (40 cm) lengths of garden hose

Watch with second hand

Stethoscope (desirable)

SMALL-GROUP ACTIVITY:

1. Ask children to fold their clasped hands next to their ears to listen as they squeeze their hands together. "Your heart makes a soft thumping sound like that each time it pumps and relaxes."

2. Children can listen through paper towel tubes to hear one another's heartbeats. One ear rests on the tube end; the other is

covered with a hand. Children can curve the hose to listen to their own beating hearts. (If a stethoscope is used, wipe earpieces with alcohol after each child's use.)

3. Try counting heartbeats for half a minute when children are quiet. ♣ Move outdoors, if possible, to let children run fiercely for a few minutes. Count heartbeats immediately after exercising. Compare with the resting heartbeat. What happens during exercise?

Read *Hear Your Heart,* by Paul Showers.

Note: If a child seems worried about the increase in heart rate during exercise, reassure the child with more information: "Heart muscles grow stronger and work even better when they are well-exercised." Children may have much to contribute to a discussion about muscle-building exercises.

3. Where does air go in our bodies?

LEARNING OBJECTIVE: To take pleasure in feeling our muscles pull in air.

Group Experience: Discuss children's recollections about changes in the heart rate after exercising. Ask whether they have noticed another change in their bodies when they run hard. Do they ever pant after exercising hard? "Our breathing gets faster, just as the heart rate gets faster. Breathing and heart rates change together to meet the changing needs of the body. Hard-working muscles need a fast supply of blood and oxygen to get energy. The heart works hard to pump blood faster and other muscles speed up to pull oxygen from the air into the lungs." In the following activity, children can find out more about how these muscles lift the rib cage to let new air come into the lungs.

MATERIALS:

Yardstick (or meterstick)

Large mirror

Card or stiff paper for each child

Skeleton model or illustration

SMALL-GROUP ACTIVITY:

1. Look at the curved rib cage on the skeleton model or illustration. The rib cage protects important parts inside our bodies like the heart and lungs.
2. Have each child find his or her lower rib, then hold a card at right angles to the rib. What can be seen in the mirror? Is the card moving? How? Hold the yardstick next to a child as he or she watches the card rising and falling. How far does the card move? Special muscles near our midsections move our rib cages up and down. Why?

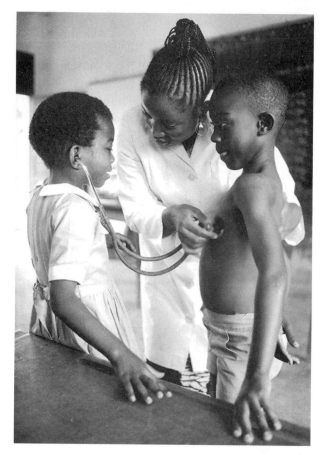

Robert's heart pumps, the visiting nurse facilitates, and Regina listens to life.

Note: An excellent guide for further meaningful activities to understand the body systems is described in Helen H. Johnson's book, *The Growing Edge.* (See Resources, p. 140.)

CONCEPT: **We help ourselves stay healthy and grow strong.**

1. Why do our bodies need rest and exercise?

LEARNING OBJECTIVE: To thaw resistance to resting and to relish exercise.

Introduction: Our bodies get tired from working hard. When we are very active, our muscles can use up the nourishment and oxygen they get from the bloodstream. Then the muscles lack energy to keep working. They are tired. They need to relax and rest before they can go on working hard. Other things happen to all of us when we are tired at the end of the day. Our eyes get sleepy, our minds don't think as well, or we may feel cross. We need rest. Children have another important reason for slowing down to rest. Their bodies need extra energy to grow. When they rest and sleep at night (about 10 hours), their bodies can get ready for another day of working, playing, and growing. Children can draw or cut out and paste pictures of these two things their bodies need for health and growth: exercise and rest.

MATERIALS:

Scissors

Paste

Crayons

Magazine or catalog pictures of active and resting people

About Me pages

SMALL-GROUP ACTIVITY:

1. Encourage children to draw themselves enjoying exercise, or to cut and paste pictures that remind them to exercise and rest.
2. Help children write a realistic statement about how much sleep they need to stay healthy.

Read: Sleep Is for Everyone, by Paul Showers.

2. Why do we wash with soap?

LEARNING OBJECTIVE: To spark interest in the importance of washing with soap and water.

Introduction: Share some surprising information about hand washing with the class. "One of the greatest health inventions of all time is soap! Bars, liquid, powder—whatever you use to wash your hands helps loosen and wash away illness-causing germs on our skin." Find out what children know about germs. Supplement their responses, if necessary, with the fact that the germs that cause illness are too small to see. Unless soap helps to wash them off, germs may still be on the hands when children eat. Then the germs can spread onto their food. Children could experiment to find out more about the effects of washing with soap and water.

MATERIALS:

Old white fabric

Two dishpans

Bar of soap

Water

Paper towels

Two trays

Paper and paste

Scissors

Potting soil

Oil

SMALL-GROUP ACTIVITY:

1. Let children wash one sample of dirty fabric in a dishpan of water and a second sample of dirty fabric in a separate dishpan of water, scrubbing it with a bar of soap.
2. Line two trays with paper towels. Put the water-washed samples on tray 1 and the soap-and-water-washed samples on tray 2. Mark children's initials next to damp samples.
3. Compare dried fabric samples to see which ones are cleaner. Paste samples on booklet page next to a sample of the control fabric for comparison. Label.

GETTING READY:

Experiment with water, soil, and
small amounts of oil to make
thin solution.

Cut off pieces of the fabric to
save as control samples.

Dip remaining fabric into soil
solution. Let dry and cut into
pieces, allowing two for each
child.

Collect pictures of soap and of
people washing.

Mark *About Me* pages: "I wash
myself with soap."

? *Inquiry Activity:* In small groups, wipe the palms of children's hands with petroleum jelly. Rub with potting soil. Let each child choose a cleaning method: wiping with a dry towel, rinsing with water, washing with soap, scrubbing with soap and a small brush, or other methods they might devise. Which did they decide was most effective? Record each group's findings. Discuss how they will apply this information.

3. How does immunization help us?

LEARNING OBJECTIVE: To help children cope with immunization.

Large-Group Experience: Encourage children to share what they know about measles, mumps, and other childhood illnesses caused by viruses. Read aloud selectively from *Germs Make Me Sick!* by Melvin Berger. Place special emphasis on page 27, which deals with giving shots to prevent viral diseases that can't be cured with drugs. Support children who express fear of getting shots.

Supplement the reading with an opportunity for children to examine a liquid medicine-dispensing syringe from the drugstore. Let them practice filling it with water and emptying it. Set up a hospital play situation, including the syringe, for preschoolers. Invite a public health nurse to visit to provide information about immunization in a nonthreatening way.

Add a child-oriented message on immunization to the *About Me* booklets. Local offices of national health groups, or the public health office in your community, may have immunization promotional leaflets suitable for inclusion in the booklets. Immunization record booklets from the public health office could be sent home to parents to reinforce the classroom focus.

4. How can we take care of our teeth?

LEARNING OBJECTIVE: To inspire pride in caring for our teeth.

Introduction: Read aloud Paul Showers's humorous book *How Many Teeth?* Give children the opportunity to share their ideas about loosening and erupting teeth.

Invite a dental hygienist to present introductory dental health care information to the children. Some professionals are prepared to demonstrate good toothbrushing techniques with sets of plastic teeth and giant toothbrushes. If this is not possible, ask children to share what they already know and do to take good care of their teeth. Supplement their comments, as needed, to include regular dental checkups and eating the foods that make strong teeth and healthy gums, especially milk-group foods. Talk about smart snacks for healthy teeth.

5. *What do our teeth do?*
LEARNING OBJECTIVE: To appreciate the functions of our teeth.

MATERIALS:

Small mirrors

Tissues

Graham crackers

Slices of apple

Magazine pictures of tooth-paste, toothbrushes, and chil-dren brushing their teeth

About Me booklet pages

Paste

Scissors

GETTING READY:

Mark booklet pages "I Brush My Teeth."

Fold a tissue into a small pad for each child.

SMALL-GROUP ACTIVITY:

1. Encourage children to smile at themselves in the mirror. What does the smile look like? Are teeth useful for more than smiles? Are teeth all alike?
2. Let children carefully bite down on the tissue pads with all their teeth. "Look at the marks on the pads. Are they all alike? Which teeth would be best for biting? Which teeth would be best for chewing and grinding food fine enough to swallow?"
3. Encourage children to use mirrors to examine the grinding teeth. Give children bits of cracker to chew. Use the mirrors to view the grinding surfaces again. Can the tongue clean away some cracker crumbs?
4. Offer apple slices to the children to chew thoroughly. Check with mirrors again. Has the apple, "nature's toothbrush," changed the way the grinding teeth look?
5. Children may draw or paste magazine illustrations of toothbrushing on booklet pages.
6. Join the children at the sink to practice swishing water around in the mouth to rinse away food bits.

CONCEPT: **Strong, growing bodies need nourishing food.**

1. *What is a healthy, balanced diet?*
LEARNING OBJECTIVE: To take pleasure in eating healthy foods.

Large-Group Experience: Read, illustrate, and discuss the flannel board story, *"The Boy Who Wanted to Eat Upside Down."*

Getting Ready: To illustrate the story, form a yarn outline of the food group pyramid on the flannel board: Make an equilateral triangle, divided into four levels. Use smaller pieces of yarn to divide the two middle levels into appropriate sections. Cut out and mount pictures of a variety of foods on adhesive backing. Place pictures in appropriate food group sections as you read the story. Or, use an attractive Food Guide Pyramid poster, pointing to the foods as the story progresses. (See Figure 6–1.)

THE BOY WHO WANTED TO EAT UPSIDE DOWN

A boy was curled up in a comfy chair with his book when his grandma came back from the grocery store. She put down the bags full of groceries and pulled out a box of graham crackers. She said, "I have something important to show you. See this picture on the box? It's called the Food Guide Pyramid. It shows us how to eat for good health. From now on, we're going to follow this guide to healthy eating every day."

The boy looked at the triangle picture on the box. He saw that it had four levels. Two levels had two parts. Each part had food pictures in it. The biggest level

FIGURE 6–1 Food Guide Pyramid

was at the bottom. Grandma pointed to it. "The biggest part is called the Bread Group. A child your size needs to eat 6 servings of this kind of food every day, so I bought bread, cereal, rice, and macaroni for you." The boy said nothing.

"Above the bread level is the vegetable and fruit level." Grandma went on. "I bought carrots and broccoli and sweet potatoes from the Vegetable Group, and apples and oranges from the Fruit Group. I'm going to give you 3 servings of vegetables and 2 servings of fruit every day." Still the boy said nothing.

Next Grandma pointed to two groups in the protein and minerals level. "That's the Milk Group. A child your size needs 3 servings every day, so I bought milk and cheese and yummy yogurt for you. And this is the Meat Group. A child your size needs 2 servings every day, so I bought some chicken and some beans to make chili for you." The boy said nothing.

Grandma said, "Now you can see how the picture helps us figure out what you need to eat the most of, and what you need a bit less of, to be healthy, strong, and growing. You need to eat the most servings from the largest level at the bottom of the pyramid, and smaller amounts from the levels closer to the top. See what's at the very top in the smallest level? Foods like cookies and cake and chips and candy and sugary sodas are in that level. We don't need much of those foods at all. We'll just have them once in a while, and not too much then."

Then the boy spoke. "If we get to eat the most of what's at the bottom level, then this is the way I'm going to be." He scooted around so that his head hung down from the comfy chair. "I wish I could be a bat, or a three-toed sloth, or a nuthatch bird so I could eat upside down, like they do. You can just serve me all the sweets and desserts and chips and fizzy drinks that I want. When I eat upside down, they're on the bottom of the pyramid! That's what I want to eat every day for the rest of my life."

"Of all things!" Grandma said. "We can't have that wish coming true! It's a good thing you're not a bat or a nuthatch or a three-toed sloth hanging about upside down all day, just eating sweets and chips and buttery snacks and sugary drinks. If you didn't eat enough foods from the protein level, your muscles and bones wouldn't be strong enough to hang on to your perch upside down. Your fur or feathers would look terrible. Your teeth wouldn't be good enough to chew your fatty, sugary foods, and you wouldn't grow strong bones."

"Umm," said the boy. "I wouldn't like that!"

"If you didn't eat enough from the fruits and vegetables level, you wouldn't have the vitamins to help your body stay well," Grandma said. "You'd be hanging there half sick, coughing and sneezing and feeling miserable all the time."

"Oh," said the boy. "I wouldn't like that!"

"If you didn't eat bread and cereals like oats and wheat and rice, and pasta like spaghetti and macaroni, you wouldn't have the energy you need to move around up there. You would just be tired and droopy. Does that sound like much fun?" Grandma asked.

"No," said the boy. "I wouldn't like that at all!"

"And you need to know something else," Grandma added. "If you only ate desserts and crispy chips and fizzy drinks, you would grow so pudgy and heavy that you would finally collapse and fall from your perch."

The boy began to laugh and giggle so hard that he nearly slid right down off the chair in a heap. Just in time he caught hold of the chair and pulled himself rightside up. He said, "OK, Grandma. I guess I don't want to be a bat, or a nuthatch, or a three-toed sloth. I'm going to have what you bought for me, rightside up. When do we eat?"

2. How does each food group help us?

LEARNING OBJECTIVE: To appreciate how different foods keep us healthy.

Group Experience: Play this food group classification game.

MATERIALS:

Six grocery bags: 1 large-sized, 4 medium-sized, 1 small-size

Food replicas; mounted food pictures; empty food cartons and containers to represent all food groups

Food pyramid poster or model

LARGE-GROUP ACTIVITY:

1. Ask: "If we brought groceries home from the store in separate food group bags, how would we do it?"

2. Invite each child to choose a food carton or picture to place in a grocery bag. As the item is deposited in the appropriate bag, mention the daily nutritional need the group provides.

GETTING READY:

Label largest bag:
  BREADS AND GRAINS (6)

Label 4 medium-sized bags:
  VEGETABLE GROUP (3)
  FRUIT GROUP (2)
  MILK GROUP (3)
  MEAT GROUP (2)

Label smallest bag:
  FATS AND SWEETS

Breads and Grains Group:	"These provide energy and fiber. Cereals and pasta belong here, too. We need to eat the most from this group. Children need 6 servings each day."
Vegetable Group:	"Vegetables have lots of vitamins. Vitamins help good foods work to keep our bodies healthy and strong. Children need 3 servings each day."
Fruit Group:	"Each kind of fruit gives us special vitamins to stay healthy. Children need at least 2 servings each day."
Milk Group:	"Milk, cheese, and yogurt help build strong teeth and bones. Growing children need 3 servings each day."

| **Meat Group:** | "Fish, eggs, nuts, and all kinds of dried beans belong here. They help bodies grow and develop strong muscles. Children need 2 servings every day." |
| **Pyramid Tip:** | "Foods that have lots of fat or oil or sugar belong here. They are not a needed food group. 'Tip' foods don't help us grow well and strong, nor stay healthy. We should only eat a little bit of these foods." |

Note: Give this activity plenty of time. Empty the bags and repeat, so that each child has several chances to classify foods.

3. How are grains used as food?

LEARNING OBJECTIVE: To enjoy discovering the goodness of whole grains.

The Food Pyramid guidelines emphasize the importance of grain foods as the basis of healthy, balanced diets. Wheatberries (hulled wheat) are low in cost and highly nutritious. This is an interesting whole grain to explore in the classroom. Now returning into vogue, cooked wheatberries (such as a dish called *frumenty*) were introduced to this country by colonists and were a staple in pioneer diets. These food experiences link well with studies of early settlers. Whole grains can be purchased in natural food stores or ordered by mail. (See p. 141.) If a child in your class is allergic to wheat, whole hulled barley can be substituted. It can be ground into flour as with wheat. One pound (454 grams) of whole wheatberries will suffice for all of the following three whole grain activities. If possible, display a small bunch of dried wheat sheaves in the room.

Part 1: Cooking Wheat

MATERIALS:
Whole wheatberries
Measuring cup
Clean tray
Sieve
Water
2-quart saucepan
Salt
Electric crockpot
Alternative equipment, if class-
  room cooking is not possible:
Widemouthed quart thermos jug
Teakettle
Facility to boil water

Large-Group Experience: Show hulled whole wheat grains and wheat sheaves to class. Let them feel the hardness of the wheatberries. Invite children to share their knowledge of wheat as a familiar food. Near the end of the school day, have children measure 1 cup (200 ml) of wheatberries, then spread them out on the tray to sort out and remove broken grains and chaff. Save some grains in a small container for later comparisons with cooked, ground, and sprouted products.

Carefully transfer sorted wheatberries to the sieve, rinse under running water, put them in the pan, and cover with 2 cups (400 ml) of water to soak overnight. The next morning, let children watch as you drain off the soaking water. Put the soaked wheatberries in the crockpot, and add enough warm water to cover the berries. Stir in 1/2 teaspoon salt. Cover and cook at highest setting for 2-1/2 to 3 hours. Grains will have doubled in bulk and be tender. They will be somewhat chewier than corn niblets. Most of the water will be absorbed. Serve samples to each child.

Safety Precautions: Locate the crockpot and the cord in a safe place, blocked from the reach of children. Remove the hot cover carefully, away from children. Unplug the cord when the cooking period ends. Move the pot away from the electric outlet.

Alternative Preparation Method: Take the soaked berries home or to the school kitchen, away from children. Then:

1. Boil kettleful of water. Rinse the thermos bottle with some of the boiling water. Heat thermos by filling it completely with boiling water. Cover to keep warm. Empty the hot rinse water just before adding the heated wheat in the next step.
2. Heat wheat and soaking water in saucepan. Bring to a vigorous boil. Add salt.
3. Fill empty, warmed thermos with hot wheat and water. Add a little boiling water if needed to just cover the wheat. Leave some air space in the neck of the bottle. Screw on stopper and cap securely. Place bottle on its side. Leave for at least 8 hours. Soaked wheat placed in the thermos bottle in the evening will be ready to eat in the morning when you take it back to school.

Part 2: Grinding Wheat into Flour

This can be a satisfying activity when children can take turns using an old-fashioned coffee grinder, if one can be found.[*] They will still be impressed by the grinding process, even if they can only watch their teacher do the grinding with an electric food blender. (Do not use a food processor. It would be damaged by the tough kernels.) Place 1 cup of wheatberries in a glass (not plastic) blender container, and process at high speed for about 4 minutes, until all the wheat is ground. Sift the flour through the fine sieve into a bowl. The bits of grain that don't go through the sieve are called grits. They can be cooked as breakfast cereal.

[*]Alternatively, a small electric coffee grinder can be used by the teacher to grind 1/4 cup of wheatberries for 4 minutes. Safety Precaution: Unplug this appliance immediately after use. Always keep out of the reach of children.

Safety Precaution: Keep one hand on the blender throughout this period. Do not allow children to touch the blender. Unplug from the electric outlet when grinding is finished.

Mention that for thousands of years before newer grinders were invented, millers ground grains between heavy, grooved millstones to make flour. If possible, bake something at home with the whole wheat flour. Share it with the class.

Part 3: Sprouting Wheat

Sprout wheatberries, following the directions in the activity that follows (sprouting a vitamin crop). Wheat sprouts will be ready to eat in 2 days. (Sprouted wheat tastes quite sweet.) Mention that seeds develop vitamins as they begin to sprout.

In a summarizing group discussion, pass the small container of reserved wheatberries. Talk about the three ways wheat seeds were changed so they could be eaten. Encourage children to look for pictures of wheat or other grains in magazine ads, or on cereal, pasta, and cracker boxes when they grocery shop with their families.

4. Can we sprout a vitamin crop?

LEARNING OBJECTIVE: To delight in growing a nutritious snack.

Seed sprouting is probably the least expensive nutrition activity for the classroom. A few cents worth of seeds will produce enough sprouts to make an appealing snack for the whole class. The sprouts are rich in vitamins and minerals. The sprouting process can involve each child during the plant germination period.

MATERIALS:

Alfalfa seeds from a natural
  foods store
Small-mouthed quart jar
6-ounce foam cup
Thick needle
5-inch (12.5 cm) square of
  porous fabric
Rubber band
Cellophane tape, paper
Saucer

GETTING READY:

Method 1

Use a needle to pierce the bottom and lower half of the cup

SMALL-GROUP ACTIVITY:

1. Discuss the sprouting project with the children on a Friday. Tape a few dry alfalfa seeds to a piece of paper to use for a day-by-day comparison with the changing sprouts.
2. Let children measure 2 tablespoons of alfalfa seeds into the jar. Explain that you will add 1 cup of warm water to cover the seeds in the jar at your home on Sunday night.
3. On Monday morning, demonstrate how to cover the jar top with the fabric, then fasten it with a rubber band so the water can be carefully drained off. Refill the jar with cool water and let children gently swirl the seeds in the fresh water. Then carefully drain the water.

generously to form drain holes. (Figure 6–2.)

If class is large, prepare two sprouting jars to allow more child participation and to provide more sprouts.

Method 2

Follow the same procedures as for Method 1, except use a 2-liter plastic beverage bottle for a sprouting container.

Cut off the top quarter of the bottle and slide a nylon knee sock over the open end. Knot the top of the sock as shown in Figure 6–3.

Rinse and drain sprouts through the nylon mesh. Hold by knotted end to drain.

4. For Method 1, remove fabric and insert drain cup into the mouth of the jar as far as it will fit. Invert the jar so the cup rim serves as a stand, as shown in Figure 6–2. Place on a saucer. Keep it away from direct sunlight.

5. Set up a rinsing/draining schedule two or three times each day so that each child has a chance to care for the sprouting seeds. As the sprouts begin to develop, the foam cup can be used instead of fabric for draining and rinsing the sprouts in Method 1.

6. As tiny green leaves appear, the jar may be kept in sunlight to allow the sprouts to develop chlorophyll.

7. On Friday, empty sprouts into a deep bowl. Cover with fresh water. Any hard seeds that failed to sprout will sink to the bottom of the bowl. Scoop out only the sprouted seeds near the top. Drain on toweling. Serve to children.

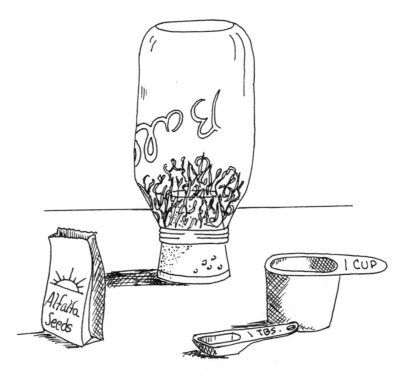

FIGURE 6–2

FIGURE 6–3

INTEGRATING ACTIVITIES

Math Experiences

1. Translate into concrete experience the evidence of growth from a child's birth weight to present weight. Do this for each child by stacking enough hardwood blocks on a bathroom scale to equal the two weights. Children may want to enter the following information in their *About Me* books: When I was a baby, I weighed as much as _____ blocks; now I weigh as much as _____ blocks. Children can feel good about their present state of growth when it is compared with past growth.

2. Establish a relative measure of muscle strength by weighing the number of blocks a child can lift. (Avoid competitive emphasis by using questions like, "How much weight are your muscles ready to lift now?")

3. To develop a sense of how long a minute is, let children use an egg timer or watch the second hand of a clock to time various enjoyable aerobic exercises. Have children count their heartbeats for 10 seconds before and after vigorous exercise.

4. Have children use their hands and feet to measure distances or dimensions: "This table is as wide as 11 of my hands."

5. Use fruit and vegetable shapes for flannel board math activities in set formation, one-to-one correspondence, and patterning.

6. Allow time for children to compare measuring spoons and cup sizes when they are used in cooking experiences. Try to have enough measuring equipment on hand so that all the children can participate in measuring ingredients. "We need one cup of flour for the dough. Will we have enough if two children each put in one-half cup of flour? Let's find out." Use sets of plastic measuring cups at the sand and water tables, so that children can practice using these utensils and develop a practical sense of their relative volumes.

Music (Resources in Appendix A)

1. *Raffi's Singable Songbook* offers "I Wonder If I'm Growing?" and "Brush Your Teeth" to extend human body study. "Popcorn" and "Peanut Butter Sandwich" extend nutrition concepts.

2. *Raffi's Everything Grows* offers "All I Really Need," "Oats, Beans, and Barley," and "Biscuits in the Oven" to extend nutrition concepts.

3. Listen to "You Are Special" from Mister Rogers' cassette, *Won't You Be My Neighbor?*, and "Everybody's Fancy" and "Everything Grows Together" from *Let's Be Together Today.*

4. Listen to how our bodies work in "What a Miracle" from Hap Palmer's cassette, *Walter the Waltzing Worm.*

5. "Here We Go 'Round the Mulberry Bush" provides a good pattern for improvising a song about health care. Children can sing, "This is the way I take care of myself . . . so I'll be strong and healthy." Add verses such as "This is the way I (brush my teeth, take my bath, wash my hands, go to sleep, eat good meals) . . . so I'll be strong and healthy."

Literature Links: Individuality

CARTER, ALDEN. (1997). *Big brother Dustin.* Morton Grove, IL: Whitman. Warm color photographs add meaning to this story of a child with Down syndrome welcoming his new sibling.

HAMANAKA, SHEILA. (1994). *All the colors of the earth.* New York: Morrow. A poetic text and warm illustrations show the physical diversity of children.

HARSHMAN, MARC. (1995). *The storm.* New York: Dutton. Jonathan wanted to be seen as himself, not as a boy disabled by an accident. His courage during a storm gains him this respect.

MAGUIRE, ARLENE (2000). *Special people, special ways.* Arlington, TX: Future Horizons. Acceptance of persons with disabilities is the focus of this book. It reminds us that every one of us is unique and special.

MCMAHON, PATRICIA. (1995). *Listen for the bus: David's story.* Honesdale, PA: Boyds Mills. We follow a sightless boy with limited hearing as his parents, teachers, and classmates help him through his day at school and home. Forthright color photograph illustrations.

MCMAHON, PATRICIA. (1996). *Summer tunes: A Martha's Vineyard vacation.* Honesdale, PA: Boyds Mills. Cerebral palsy limits Connor's mobility, but his family and his electric wheelchair help him get around. An unflinching look at social problems of children who use wheelchairs; also a spirited look at coping well.

MILLMAN, ISAAC. (2001). *Moses goes to school.* New York: Farrar, Strauss. Visit Moses' cheerful classroom in a school for the deaf. The children learn to sign a new song, following the rhythms of boom box vibrations. The text is paralleled with ASL signing illustrations for hearing children to learn.

MILLMAN, ISAAC. (2002). *Moses goes to a concert.* New York: Farrar, Strauss. School for The Deaf children watch and feel a concert featuring a deaf percussionist. Holding balloons in their laps helps them pick up vibrations. ASL signing illustrations accompany this fine text.

ROGERS, FRED. (2000). *Extraordinary Friends.* New York: Putnam. Mr. Rogers guides children toward feeling comfortable and finding friendships with disabled children.

RUSSO, MARISABINA. (1992). *Alex is my friend.* New York: Greenwillow. Alex has serious growth problems. His humor helps him cope with grim orthopedic surgery and a wheelchair-bound future.

Playing with assistive equipment helps children be more
accepting of others and value their own bodies.

Literature Links: The Body

ALIKI. (2001). *I'm growing!* New York: HarperCollins. It's all here: simple information about growth relevant to young children, presented in Aliki's clear, enjoyable style.

ANDERSON, KAREN, & CUMBAA, STEPHEN. (1993). *The bones & skeleton game book.* New York: Workman Publishing. Interesting, simple experiments will extend children's understanding and appreciation of human body intricacies.

BEELER, SELBY. (1998). *Throw your tooth on the roof.* Boston: Houghton Mifflin. Children in different cultures observe interesting traditions when baby teeth fall out. Tooth facts that are the same for all children are included.

BERGER, MELVIN. (2000). *Why I sneeze, shiver, hiccup, & yawn.* New York: HarperCollins. Clear, beginning ideas about the nervous system inform children about reflexes that take us by surprise. Reflex tests are included.

BONSIGNORE, JOAN. (2001). *Stick out your tongue.* Atlanta, GA: Peachtree. The amazing functions of various animals' tongues are compared to children's tongue experiences in this captivating book.

COLE, JOANNA. (1998). *Your insides.* New York: Putnam & Grosset. This wonderful book places information about body systems into meaningful child context. Cheerful illustrations with acrylic overlay pages offer an inside view of the location of organs and systems.

COLE, JOANNA. (2001). *The magic school bus explores the senses.* New York: Scholastic. Ms. Fizzle's class gets a whirlwind tour through the complex workings of six senses. To avoid factual overload, tackle this book one sense at a time.

FROST, HELEN. (2000). *Tasting.* Mankato, MN: Capstone Press. Cheery photographs and a simple text make it appealing to beginning readers. Other books in this sensory series are: *Hearing, Seeing, Smelling,* and *Touching.*

FROST, HELEN. (2001). *The skeletal system.* Mankato, MN: Capstone Press. Basic bone facts in this easy reader are amplified by clear graphics traced over pleasing photographs. Web sites are listed for further information.

HICKMAN, PAMELA. (1998). *Animal senses*. Buffalo, NY: Kids Can Press. Simple experiences help children understand how animals can hunt in the dark, underwater, or underground, perceiving sounds without ears.

O'BRIEN-PALMER, MICHELLE. (1998). *Sense-abilities: fun ways to explore the senses*. Chicago: Chicago Review Press. This is a great collection of classroom tested, clearly written activites. They will increase children's respect for their remarkable bodies.

PARKER, STEVE. (1994). *Human body*. New York: Dorling Kindersley. This Eyewitness Explorers book offers brief, well-chosen information about how our bodies work. Some simple experiments include a demonstration of why we need to wash our hands.

PRINGLE, LAURENCE. (1997). *Everybody has a belly button*. Honesville, PA: Boyds Mill. Soft illustrations and a personal text positively describe the first nine months of life. Reassuring to children who wonder what they were like before they were born.

RICE, CHRISTOPHER. (1995). *My first body book*. New York: Dorling Kindersley. Clear text, upbeat photographs, interesting activities, and see-through illustrations make this a fine reference.

ROJANY, LISA. (1992). *Exploring the human body*. Hauppage, NY: Barron's Educational Series. This book strengthens its clear text with pull tabs to move joints, flaps to lift, and transparent pages to view inner structures and systems. It also includes activities and experiments for this age group.

SHOWERS, PAUL. (1999). *How many teeth?* New York: HarperCollins. The amusing text and illustrations enliven the subjects of deciduous teeth and good dental care. The lisping story demonstrates how teeth help us speak. Paperback.

SHOWERS, PAUL. (1999). *Your skin and mine*. New York: HarperCollins. This book presents a simple treatment of the structure of the skin, the healing of scrapes, and the function of melanin. Paperback.

SHOWERS, PAUL. (2001). *Hear your heart*. New York: HarperCollins. To engage children in this topic, they are directed to use paper towel tubes as stethoscopes to hear this strongest muscle at work.

SHOWERS, PAUL. (2001). *What happens to a hamburger?* New York: HarperCollins. A diner chef carefully describes the amazing digestive process, suggesting some direct experiences as aids to understanding as he goes along. Paperback.

SIMON, SEYMOUR. (1997). *The brain: Our nervous system*. New York: Morrow. This factual book written for competent readers includes terrific photographs for the child who wants to know, "What's inside?"

WALPOLE, BRENDA. (1997). *See for yourself series: Touch, smell and taste, seeing,* and *hearing*. Austin, TX: Raintree. These four clearly written books present basic sense concepts, then extend them into the animal world and beyond. Beautiful color photographs underscore the text.

WIESE, JIM. (2000). *Head-to-toe science*. New York: Wiley. Though written for older students, the simple, interesting, and often funny activities in this book offer many ways to expand children's understanding of body systems. NSTA* recommended.

Literature Links: Health Care

BERGER, MELVIN. (1991). *Ouch! A book about cuts, scratches, and scrapes*. New York: Dutton. Written for older children, it can be read aloud selectively to younger listeners. Well-illustrated to add understanding of the body's healing capacities.

BERGER, MELVIN. (1995). *Germs make me sick*. New York: Harper. Children will be fascinated and relieved to learn about how our bodies fight bacteria and viruses. Paperback. A Reading Rainbow book.

BIRDSEYE, TOM. (1993). *Soap! Soap! Don't forget the soap!* New York: Holiday House. Sprightly illustrations add to the humor in this retold folktale. The title echoes through the story, so listeners can chorus the words. They can become a jaunty reminder for careful hand-washing.

Making nutritious food can be a prelude to eating and enjoying it.

DAVISON, MARTINE. (1992). *Robby visits the doctor.* New York: Random House. This book is part of the series written for the American Medical Association to prepare children for different health-care situations. Written by Davison, the series includes *Rita Goes to the Hospital, Maggie and the Emergency Room,* and *Kevin and the School Nurse.*

DEMUTH, PATRICIA. (1997). *Achoo! All about colds.* New York: Grossett. This book presents lively illustrations, clear facts, and debunked myths about catching colds. Unfortunately, careful handwashing to prevent spreading cold viruses was omitted. Paperback.

MANNING, MICK. (2001). *Wash, scrub, brush.* Morton Grove, IL: Whitman. Children's and animals' need for hygiene and grooming is tackled cheerfully and thoroughly in this book.

POWELL, JILLIAN. (1998). *Exercise and your health.* Austin, TX: Raintree Steck-Vaughn. This encouraging account of the daily exercise required for healthy body systems includes a breath-capacity experiment.

SHOWERS, PAUL. (2001). *Sleep is for everyone.* New York: HarperCollins. Color-drenched illustrations will keep listeners and readers awake and focused on sleep facts as we currently know them.

UNWIN, MIKE, & WOODWARD, K. (1993). *What makes you ill?* Tulsa, OK: EDC Publishing. Capsules of basic information, warmed with relevant illustrations, touch on a wide range of illness topics that interest children deeply. Paperback.

Literature Links: Nutrition

BROWN, MARC. (1995). *D. W., the picky eater.* Boston: Little Brown. Children will identify with D.W.'s amusing strategies for dodging unfamiliar foods. A good springboard for discussing healthy eating.

CHILD, LAUREN. (2000). *I will never, not ever eat a tomato.* Cambridge, MA: Candlewick Press. A girl uses her imagination to coax her sister into enjoying veggies.

DOOLEY, NORAH. (1991). *Everybody cooks rice.* Minneapolis: Carolrhoda Books. A comfortable narrative about neighboring families from eight different ethnic groups preparing their special rice dishes for dinner. Delicious recipes are given for this grain-group staple. Detailed illustrations of family life add to this book's usefulness in the integrated curriculum.

ERLBACH, ARLENE. (1994). *Peanut butter.* Minneapolis: Lerner Publications. Written for older children, the photographs and facts about growing and processing this interesting seed into a favorite food will intrigue prereaders when selectively read to them. It includes a recipe for making peanut butter from scratch and other smart snacks.

HOBERMAN, MARY ANN. (1997). *The seven silly eaters.* San Diego: Harcourt Brace. A happy accident settles the plight of a devoted mother catering to the fussy food demands of her growing brood. The cheerful illustrations double the delight this story poem offers.

HOLUB, JOAN. (2001). *The pizza that we made.* New York: Viking. A simple, rhyming text follows the progress of three children as they make, and eat, a pizza.

HOOPER, MEREDITH. (1997). *A cow, a bee, a cookie, and me.* New York: Kingfisher. Grandma explains where each ingredient comes from as she bakes cookies with Ben. Recipe included.

JENNINGS, TERRY. (1994). *Beans.* Ada, OK: Garrett. Good photographs accompany an informative text about beans as a worldwide nutritional staple. Activities and recipes are included.

KATZEN, MOLLIE. (1994). *Pretend soup and other real recipes.* Berkeley, CA: Tricycle Press. Nutritious recipes and clear, step-by-step drawings guide young classroom cooks.

LEEDY, LOREEN. (1994). *The edible pyramid: Good eating every day.* New York: Holiday. A maitre d' explains his restaurant menu in terms of the food guide pyramid.

MCGRATH, BARBARA. (1998). *The Cheerios counting book.* New York: Scholastic. Bright graphics illustrate using Cheerios to count by ones and tens.

MORRIS, ANN. (1993). *Bread, bread, bread.* New York: Lothrop, Lee, & Shepard. Marvelous color photographs by Ken Heyman show breads being made, sold, or eaten in 28 countries.

MURPHY, STUART. (1998). *Lemonade for sale.* New York: HarperCollins. A class could have some fun using the ideas from this book, doing some applied math along the way.

PAULSEN, GARY. (1995). *The tortilla factory.* San Diego, CA: Harcourt Brace. Rhythmic language leads this circular story of tortillas from the hands that work the earth to the mouth that eats the tortilla, to strengthen the hand that works the soil.

PETERSON, CRIS. (1994). *Extra cheese, please!* Honesdale, PA: Boyds Mills Press. Excellent photographs and a friendly text record mozzarella cheese-making from cow to store. A pizza recipe is included.

RATTIGAN, JAMA. (1993). *Dumpling soup.* Boston: Little Brown. Good foods from many cultures are involved as a Hawaiian family prepares a New Year's feast. Charming watercolors inform and delight. Winner: New Voices, New World Award.

RICCIO, NINA. (1997). *Five kids and a monkey solve the great cupcake caper.* Canterbury, NH: Creative Attic. Overindulging in junk food turns a boy into a cupcake. His friends learn about healthy eating and exercise to restore him.

ROBBINS, KEN. (1992). *Make me a peanut butter sandwich, and a glass of milk.* New York: Scholastic. To appreciate what really goes into a simple snack, the author photographed the whole production process starting with harvesting wheat and peanuts, and grazing cows.

ROCKWELL, LIZZY. (1999). *Good enough to eat: A kid's guide to food and nutrition.* New York: HarperCollins. Cheerful illustrations by the author help make basic nutrition information more accessible. The food pyramid and some good classroom cooking projects are included.

SOTO, GARY. (1993). *Too many tamales.* New York: G. P. Putnam. A well-plotted story centers on a child's first experience helping make tamales for a family festivity. Grains and meat groups combine in this tamale story.

THOMPSON, PEGGY. (1993). *Siggy's spaghetti works.* New York: William Morrow. From wheat field to the dinner table, the whole process for making spaghetti is revealed. Tucking in a bit of pasta history increases the cross-curricular usefulness of this grain-group story.

*National Science Teachers Association

Poems (Resources in Appendix A)

From *Now We Are Six* by A. A. Milne, read "Sneezles."

From *Egg Thoughts and Other Francis Songs* by Russell Hoban, read "Egg Thoughts."

From *I Thought I'd Take My Rat to School* by Dorothy Kennedy, read "Lunch."

From *Falling Up* by Shel Silverstein, read "We're Out of Paint."

From *Exploding Gravy*, read "Italian Noodles."

Children will enjoy all of the sprightly food poems on the menu in Lee Bennett Hopkins' collection, *Yummy Eating Through The Day*.

Fingerplays

Use this fingerplay to encourage handwashing:

This right hand is a very fine hand.

This left hand is its brother

Together they wash with soap and water.

One hand washes the other.

—AUTHOR UNKNOWN

Art Activities

Paper Doll Chain. To recall that people are alike in many ways, fold and cut out paper doll chains. Encourage children to use markers or crayons to make each paper doll different. "Make each one look special, just as each of you is special."

Individuality Collage. As a group project, make a collage poster by using pictures of persons of varying ages and races to emphasize the uniqueness of each person.

Fingerprint Art. Children's fingerprints can create all-over designs and patterns. Use a simple paint-stamping pad for prints. Suggest using crayons to add stems to print-petaled flowers, strings on fingerprint balloons, and so forth.

Clothespin Dolls. Plain wood clothespins form head, trunk, and legs of dolls; pipe cleaners twisted around the "neck" form arms and loop hands. Features can be drawn on the heads with ballpoint pen. Scraps of fabric can be fastened to the body with rubber bands. Compare the flexible and rigid parts of the doll bodies with the bone structure of the human body.

Play

Hospital Play. Provide props for hospital play such as bandages and a cot; add paper towel tubes so that children can listen to heartbeats. Add discarded plastic syringes (sterilized, needles removed) to allow children to play the role of shot-giver.

Grocery Store. Before and after the nutrition experiences, compare the ways that children arrange the food replicas provided for a play store.

Restaurant. Make picture menus from manila folders, using illustrations of wholesome foods marked with large-numeral prices. Provide restaurant workers with pads of paper, pencils, a toy cash register, trays, and food replicas (or pictures cut from cardboard food cartons).

Creative Thinking

Alike and Different Game. Ask one child to look around at the other children to find someone who is like her or him in one way. If Elena chooses Jenny because they are both girls, ask Jenny to stand next to Elena and find one way that she and Elena are different. Then Jenny has a turn to find someone who is like her in one way, and so on. End the game with a comment about no two people being just alike in every way. Mention the good thinking and choosing the children did.

Creative Movement

Try to find a marionette to demonstrate its stiff movements controlled by strings. Compare the differences between the carved figure and children's bodies. Encourage the children to dance to a record, using their bodies as though someone else controlled their movements with strings. End the dancing by saying that someone has "cut their strings."

Show the children a rag doll, whose body is so flexible that it can be bent and curled in many ways that the marionette and children could not move. Let the children dance like rag dolls without bones or muscle control. Change the movements to those of real people who have muscles to stretch.

Field Trips

Public Health Clinic. If a public facility can be toured, try to have the visit serve the children in a nonthreatening way, such as having children measured and weighed. Be certain that the children are prepared for what to anticipate at the clinic.

A Visit from the Field. Your community emergency medical service squad may be willing to bring a field trip to your school door. Children feel more at ease if a health professional visits them in a familiar setting. A careful look at the emergency vehicle can be fascinating and reassuring. The squad members evoke the awe of heroism, rather than the shadow of anxiety that may be aroused in some children when they meet health-care professionals.

PROMOTING CONCEPT CONNECTIONS

Maintaining Concepts

Teachers who are committed to the principle of accepting responsibility for one's own health and nourishment find it easy to use teachable moments to promote this goal. When a respected teacher joins the children in routine handwashing and toothbrushing, children emulate the patterns readily. When giving first aid to a scraped-knee victim, reassure the child that parts of the flowing blood are already beginning to make repairs so that new skin can grow over the scrape. Encourage children to discuss feelings about medical treatment when they have it, and express respect for the way they faced what had to be done to keep themselves healthy.

Teachers have an excellent opportunity to help children appreciate nonsweet foods when they have snacks or lunch with the class. This is a natural time to discuss food and to talk about the food groups represented in the menu. Use the simple rule that everyone (including adults) tries to taste each food being served, allowing (rather than requiring) children to eat as much as they can. Avoid using food as a punishment or as a bribe to force children to eat disliked food. This practice weakens trust between child and teacher and may fail to win compliance from the child as well.

Undue "preaching" of health care and nutrition messages to dictate home practices can become counterproductive. Young children are limited in their ability to change the habits or cultural patterns followed by their families. Therefore, pressing children to conform to healthful standards away from school may result in feelings of guilt or resentment. The common practice of requiring children to report what they have eaten at home each day can threaten feelings of acceptance and reduce self-esteem. Neither practice is likely to result in the goal of translating health-care knowledge into actual health-care practices. Teachers contribute most to this goal when they offer accurate information to children and parents, model sensible eating and health-care habits, encourage children to follow their lead, and support those who try.

Improving Schoolgrounds

Because North American children are suffering from lack of physical exercise, spruce up the asphalt playground with inviting exercise opportunities. Paint fresh graphics such as a curving snake, the segments of which invite hopping and number-counting, or a hundred square for jumping among numbers, or colored concentric circles that allow games where children follow directions such as "run into the yellow circle" or "throw the beanbag to the blue circle." See Sanders's *Active for Life* for ideas on movement programs.

Connecting Concepts

1. When children are learning about their sense of vision, think about how light passing through curved glass makes things look larger (see Chapter 15, Light). "This is how glasses help some people see better."

2. When discussing hearing, mention the delicate part inside of each ear that vibrates to let us hear sounds (see Chapter 14, Sound).

3. Identify the calcium that our bones and teeth get from milk and dark green vegetables as the same mineral that makes hard shells for some animals (see Chapter 5, Animals) and compresses or combines with other minerals to form certain rocks (see Chapter 10, Rocks and Minerals).

4. When children are learning about the muscles that keep the lungs expanding and contracting, mention that living things need air to stay alive.

5. Relate muscle development and exercise to simple machines by providing an inexpensive rope and pulley exerciser in the classroom.

6. Recall seed-sprouting experiences (see p. 129). Each seed contains enough nourishment to start a new plant. That same nourishment also helps all parts of our body grow. There would be enough food to feed everybody in the world if we all would eat more protein from plants and less from meat.

7. Relate the need for clean hands to the need for sanitary food preparation by using this comparison: Seal unrinsed wheatberries in one plastic sandwich bag, together with a damp paper towel. Seal thoroughly rinsed wheatberries in a similar bag. Leave flat and undisturbed for 2 or 3 days. Examine the seeds with a magnifier several days later for clear evidence of mold or bacterial growth.

8. Experiment with two pots of a fast-growing plant such as coleus. Provide only one plant with liquid fertilizer each month. The difference in growth in a few months' time will illustrate how proper nourishment helps living things grow. (Make it clear, however, that nourishing substances for plants can make humans very sick.)

9. For some classes it might be desirable to explore the concepts in this chapter more deeply over a longer period of time. (See Johnson, 1997.)

Family and Community Support

Two goals of this chapter—valuing oneself and assuming responsibility early in life for one's own health—cannot be achieved without parental involvement. Although few parents intend to neglect their children's health, there has been a marked decrease in communicable disease immunization for young children. The number of malnourished children in our affluent country is also discouraging. These problems are being addressed by the American Pediatrics Association campaign to urge prevention of illness through responsible self-care, rather than through reliance upon costly treatment to cure illness. Teachers and families together can encourage responsible attitudes in children. The *About Me* booklet can spur families' interest in promoting healthy development for their children.

Invite family members with bread-baking skills to make bread with the class.

Alert families to interactive anatomy exhibits in the nearest children's science museum and to local hospital preventive health-care programs designed for children.

RESOURCES

The Human Body

ALLISON, L. (1976). *Blood and guts: A working guide to your own insides.* Boston: Little Brown. Accurate information about anatomy and physiology is presented in a lively style. Experiments suggested for older children may be adapted for younger children.

COBB, VICKI. (2000). *Follow your nose.* Brookfield, CT: Millbrook Press. There's excellent information in this book for advanced students, but the easy experiments will fascinate all ages. Other books in this series include *Perk Up Your Ears* (2001); *Your Tongue Can Tell* (2000); *Feeling Your Way* (2001); and *Open Your Eyes* (2002).

GREENE, M. (1994). *A sigh of relief: The first aid handbook for childhood emergencies* (4th ed.). New York: Bantam Books. The easy, clear information and illustrations of first aid steps and child safety precautions make this a logical choice for every school's professional bookshelf.

JOHNSON, H. (1997). *The growing edge with the bodyworks.* Amherst, MA: Gemini Press. This book vividly documents young children's passion for figuring out how their bodies operate, and how to sensitively respond to it. Use it to develop a longer term, hands-on study of systems and structures. Write to Odyssey Book Shop, South Hadley, MA 01075, or call 1-800-540-7307.

KENDA, M., & WILLIAMS, P. (1990). *Cooking wizardry for kids.* Hauppauge, NY: Barron's. This fine cookbook contains mostly healthy, classroom manageable recipes, plus science experiments, folklore of food, and good nutrition projects for older primary children.

ROCKWELL, R., WILLIAMS, R., & SHERWOOD, E. (1992). *Everybody has a body.* Mt. Rainier, MD: Gryphon House. Further explorations and extensions for the classroom can be found in this book.

SANDERS, S. (2002). *Active for life: Developmentally appropriate movement programs for young children.* Washington, DC: NAEYC.

STEIN, S. (1992). *The body book.* New York: Workman Publishing. Intended for middle school children, this book provides excellent background reading about human anatomy and physiology. It informs without overwhelming the reader.

VAN CLEAVE, J. (1990). *Biology for every kid.* New York: Wiley. Experiments with lung capacity measurement are included.

Nutrition

BAIRD, P. (1994). *The pyramid cookbook.* New York: Henry Holt. This beautiful book takes us through each layer of the food pyramid. It provides sound nutrition background and lists pyramid equivalents for each recipe.

FURH, J., & BARCLAY, K. (1998). "The importance of appropriate nutrition and nutrition education." *Young Children, 53*(1), 74–79.

Additional Resources

Mail Order Grains Sources:

Arrowhead Mills
110 S. Lawton
Hereford, TX 79045

Meadowlark Grain Company
P.O. Box 93
Hingham, MT 59528 (Wheat only)

Air

How is the air around you right now? Chances are you hadn't noticed, unless it was too hot or cold. We move through air like fish swim through water, mostly unaware of it. Yet air is the medium of our existence. How can we help children understand air? This chapter will start you off.

Children become acquainted with hundreds of substances through sensory encounters. Air intrigues children because it is an invisible, ever-present substance that is not directly encountered by the senses until it affects something tangible. The activities in this chapter are designed to explore the following concepts:

- Air is almost everywhere.
- Air is real; it takes up space.
- Air presses on everything on all sides.
- Moving air pushes things.
- Fast-moving air keeps planes aloft.
- Air slows moving objects.
- Warm air rises.

In the experiences that follow, children will find air in empty containers and become aware of the air that they breathe. They will feel air enclosed in something, see how it occupies space, and note how it pushes on everything. Also, they will enjoy making things for moving air to push.

Introduce the topic of air to children by holding up your hands, cupped together, suggesting, "There is something important inside my hands. You may peek in, but you won't be able to see what it is. The important stuff is invisible! We'll be finding out more about it."

CONCEPT: Air is almost everywhere.

---

1. ♣What comes out of an empty can?

LEARNING OBJECTIVE: To enjoy finding that invisible air is almost everywhere.

MATERIALS:

Empty metal can
Nail
Hammer
Dishpan
Water
If indoors:
Plastic aprons
Inflatable wading pool (keep
   pan of water in pool; children
   outside pool)

SMALL-GROUP ACTIVITY:

1. Ask children to examine the can. Do they notice anything in it?
2. Use a hammer and nail to punch a hole in the bottom. Let a child do it, if possible.
3. Ask: "If there is something in the can, could we push it out through this hole? Let's see."
4. Invert can; slowly push it into the water. Ask a child to hold a hand just above the nail hole. What does the child feel being pushed out of the hole? A stream of air? "Could something real be in that empty can . . . something real that we can't see?"
5. Let the children experiment.

2. What can we find out about "empty" containers?

LEARNING OBJECTIVE: To confirm that invisible air is reliably almost everywhere.

MATERIALS:

Empty clear plastic shampoo
   bottles or tubes, uncapped
Downy feathers, milkweed fluff,
   or bits of tissue paper

SMALL-GROUP ACTIVITY:

1. Ask children to examine the bottles or tubes. Do they notice anything inside?
2. "Point the bottle top toward your chin and squeeze the bottle. Do you feel something? What? See if you can squeeze it out. Keep trying."
3. Offer a feather to each child. "If your bottle is really empty, nothing will come out to push the feather from your hand. See what happens if you point the bottle toward the feather." (This activity can be disorderly unless you set limits for a feather-blowing space.)

3. How does air get inside us?

LEARNING OBJECTIVE: To be impressed by our constant need to breathe in air.

Group Activity: Suggest that all the children take a deep breath, shut their lips tightly, and pinch their nostrils shut for as long as they can. "What happened? Why did you let go of your nose? What did your body seem to need so much that you had to let go? Let's try again.

"Our bodies need the part of air called oxygen. We need to breathe air into our bodies about every 6 seconds because it is used up so quickly inside of us." Guide the discussion to bring out the idea that all living things must have air to stay alive. Discuss the danger of climbing into boxes with heavy lids or other enclosed spaces that cannot be opened from the inside. Give examples.

Give each child an unfolded tissue to hold near the nose and mouth. "Let's see what happens to the tissue when you bring air into your body and then when you push this air out. Try it with your lips closed; now with your lips opened a bit. Are there two ways for the air to come in and out? Let's see if we can tell where the air is going inside our bodies." Ask children to take turns lying on the floor or putting their heads on the table so others can watch their chests go up and down as they breathe.

CONCEPT: **Air is real; it takes up space.**

1. How can we feel the substance of air?

LEARNING OBJECTIVE: To delight in containing air as tangible stuff.

MATERIALS:

Plain plastic sandwich bags, twist closures (or small zip-top bag)

Drinking straw

Transparent tape

GETTING READY:

Prepare a blowing bag for each child participating by gathering the top of a bag to form a neck, inserting a straw in the neck, and securing the neck of the bag to the straw with tape.

SMALL-GROUP ACTIVITY:

1. Ask: "Is the table real? How can you tell? If your eyes were closed, could you still tell that the table is real? Is feeling something a good way to know that it is real?"
2. Let children blow into the prepared bags. "What are you blowing into the bag? Look in the bag. Feel it. Do you think something real is in there?"
3. Remove straw and tie with wire closure, or zip seal so the children can keep their bags full of air to feel.

Children should leave the plastic bags at school so that younger children at home will not pick up the idea of playing with plastic bags.

2. What can a glassful of air do?

LEARNING OBJECTIVE: To be surprised by the force of air.

MATERIALS:

Clear plastic bowl (corn popper dome is fine) or 5-inch (12 cm) deep glass mixer bowl, if it can be safely used

Pitcher of water

Cork

Clear plastic tumbler

Splash catcher, aprons

GETTING READY:

If indoors, inflate wading pool. Put bowl in the center.

SMALL-GROUP ACTIVITY:

1. Put cork in the bowl. "The cork is touching the bowl now. What will happen if we pour water into the bowl? Let's see."
2. Fill half the bowl with water. "Notice if the cork is touching the bottom of the bowl now."
3. Ask: "Can someone put the cork back on the bottom?" Let children try to do this. "Will it stay if you let go?"
4. "See if something in the tumbler will push water away so that the cork can stay on the bottom of the bowl." Invert tumbler and push straight down to the bottom. "What could be inside the glass pushing the water away? Do you see anything?"
5. Let the children experiment.

Group Discussion: Ask the children to catch some air in their cupped hands. "Poke your nose into your hands. Can you smell the air? Peek in. Can you see it? Can you hear it? Try to taste it." (Children love to hang their tongues out for research purposes.) Ask those who have experimented how they know that air is real. Children are proud of their new information and are willing to repeat a discussion like this one. Next time, let a hand puppet be the skeptic who doesn't believe that invisible things can be real. The children will be happy to convince the puppet otherwise.

FIGURE 7–1

3. *What can a bag of air do?*

LEARNING OBJECTIVE: To take pride in using air as a force.

MATERIALS:

Large, sturdy paper bag

Wire twist closure, or tape

Bicycle tire pump, bellows-type
 pump, or hand pump

Heavy book or block

GETTING READY:

Gather bag top into a neck, fasten with wire twist, or tape.

Put bag on floor and stand book
 upright on it. Put the pump
 near the bag.

SMALL-GROUP ACTIVITY:

1. Demonstrate the pump if children don't
 know what it is or how it works. Look at
 the air intake hole where air comes in to be
 pushed out by the pump. (Remove intake
 valve cap from bellows pump.) Feel air being pushed out.
2. Ask: "Do you think a bag full of air could
 push that book over? How could we find
 out?"
3. Insert the end of the pump hose into the
 bag. (See Figure 7–1.) Tighten the closure,
 or simply hold bag firmly to hose while
 children take turns pumping air into it,
 pushing the book over. "Could air be doing that? Do you think air is real stuff,
 even though we can't see it?" Discuss car
 airbag rules.

 Read: Ups and Downs, by Joanna Cole.

CONCEPT: **Air presses on everything on all sides.**

1. *What can push up water in a narrow tube?*

LEARNING OBJECTIVE: To be amazed that air can press liquids in or out of nar-
            row tubes.

MATERIALS:

Baster (kitchen tool)

Medicine droppers (plastic or
 thick glass tubes are safest)

Small containers of water for
 each child

Pint jar half full of water

Sponge, pan, and newspapers
 for cleanup

Drinking straws, cut in half

Suction cups (desirable)

SMALL-GROUP ACTIVITY:

1. Let children examine baster. Is the tube
 empty? Squeeze bulb to feel what comes
 out.
2. Put baster in jar of water. Ask, "What do
 you see when I push air out of the baster?
 Watch the tube when I slowly let go of the
 rubber bulb on top. What is happening?"
3. Hold up the filled baster. Ask, "What's
 happening to the water now? What could
 be keeping the water in? Perhaps something invisible is in the baster with the
 water."

Learning to manipulate a tool of science

4. Squeeze bulb to push out water. Release bulb to pull in air. "What's happening now? Try it."
5. "Now let's try the same thing with straws." Insert a straw in water. Put your index fingers over the top and bottom of the straw and lift it from the water. Keep finger on top and remove finger from bottom. Most of the water will stay in the straw. Why? (Air pressure keeps it in.) See Figure 7–2.
6. "Nothing can get into the straw from the top with my finger on it. Watch as I let some air push into the straw." Remove finger from top. Water is pushed out of the straw. Let children experiment.

Note: Some children may believe that a dropper is filled with water if drops just cling to the outside. Help them hold the dropper tube in the water while releasing the bulb.

Listen for the squish of air forced out of the cup when you press a suction cup against a flat surface. Let children know that air pressing on the outside of the cup keeps it attached to the surface.

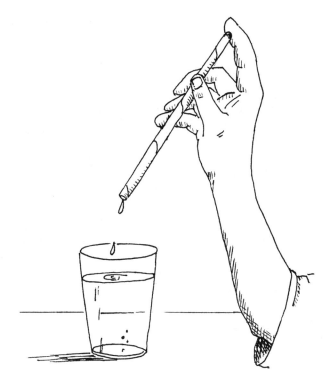

FIGURE 7–2

CONCEPT: **Moving air pushes things.**

Introduction: Ask the children to wave their hands back and forth in front of their faces. "Can you feel something on your skin? When air is moving you can feel it. You don't notice it when it isn't moving." Explain that we feel air moving against us in the same way whether we are moving when the air is still, or whether air is moving by itself (as wind) when we are still.

1. ♣ *What can we feel pushing on us?*
LEARNING OBJECTIVE: To revel in the effect of air moving and pushing against us.

MATERIALS:

Sheets of newspaper
Crepe paper streamers
Pinwheels or kites

OUTDOOR ACTIVITY:

Give children sheets of paper outside. "As you stand still, will paper stick to the front of you if you don't hold it there? Now see what happens to it when you run as fast as you can. Do you have to hold the paper to press it to yourself? What could be holding it?" Let children enjoy running with pinwheels or paper streamers. Launch the kite running toward the wind. Try flying the kite on a calm day and on a windy day.

Read about a struggle to fly a kite in *Days With Frog and Toad*, by Arnold Lobel.

2. How can we make a glider drift on moving air?

LEARNING OBJECTIVE: To be reassured that moving air can carry certain things.

MATERIALS:

A sheet of copier paper and a paper clip for each child

GETTING READY:

Draw a lengthwise line down the center of the paper.

Draw parallel lines 1 1/2 inches (4 cm) from the center line.

Draw a line 3/4 inch (2 cm) from the bottom across the paper.

SMALL-GROUP ACTIVITY:

1. Show the children how to fold up 3/4 inch (2 cm) from the bottom of the paper. Continue to fold this amount four times, forming a cuff.

2. With the cuff side down, fold the paper and cuff lengthwise on the center line, A. Form wings by folding back each side on B lines. Fasten the fold with a paper clip. (See Figure 7–3.)

3. Launch glider with cuff in front, holding the center. If the glider always nosedives,

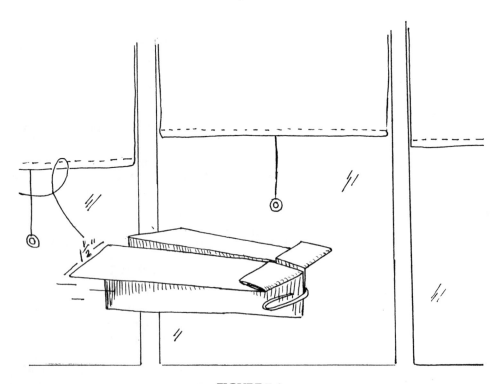

FIGURE 7–3

reduce the weight of the front end by re-moving the clip, or unfolding one fold of the cuff. Push the glider ahead by keeping the hand and arm straight, not sweeping downward, when launching the glider.

Note: Primary grade children may want to make more elaborate gliders. See *Fabulous Paper Airplanes* by Richard Churchill.

3. Can we make a helicopter spin in moving air?

LEARNING OBJECTIVE: To enjoy watching moving air twirl a helicopter.

MATERIALS:

Two duplicated templates of heli-copter for each child, plus extras

Scissors for each child

SMALL-GROUP ACTIVITY:

1. Show children the template for the heli-copter (Figure 7–4) and demonstrate cut-ting on the solid lines and folding on the

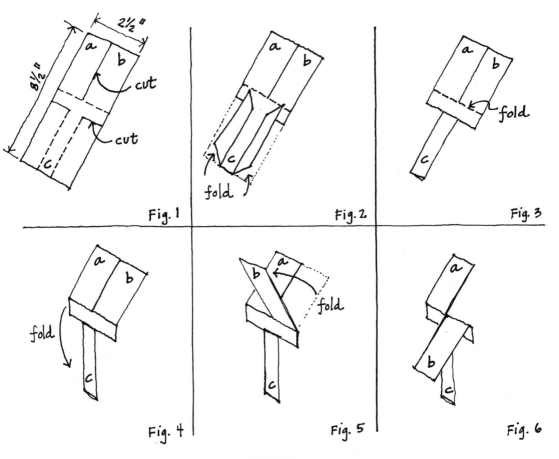

FIGURE 7–4

GETTING READY:

Enlarge and reproduce template from Figure 7–4.

Four templates will fit on a sheet of copier paper, using dimensions of 2 1/2 in. (6 cm) × 8 1/2 in. (21 cm)

dotted lines. Fold the longer vertical edges to form a single base piece. Fold one smaller blade section forward and one backward. (See Figure 7–4).

2. Stand on a chair or table, reaching up to add height, to drop the helicopter. It should twirl as it descends. Add that the air pushes on the helicopter as it falls. Each blade steers the air to the other one, causing the twirling.

3. ♣ Let children experiment outdoors on playground equipment, or an indoor stairwell.

? *Inquiry Activity:* Ask for predictions about what might happen when the helicopter is dropped upside down. Will it right itself? What might change when the blades are bent in the opposite direction? Will a different kind of paper change the twirling? Will different sizes of helicopters twirl differently? Can a really big one be made of a sheet of construction paper? How about a tiny one, tiny as a maple seed?

CONCEPT: Fast moving air keeps planes aloft.

1. What can fast and slow moving air do?

LEARNING OBJECTIVE: To diminish the mystery of how heavy planes can stay up in the air.

MATERIALS:

Hair dryer (preferably with cool setting)

Desk chair

Copier paper

Tissue paper

Transparent tape

GETTING READY:

Cut one 2-inch (5 cm) × 12-inch (30 cm) paper strip.

Cut a 1-inch (2.5 cm) × 6-inch (15 cm) tissue paper strip for each child.

LARGE-GROUP ACTIVITY:

1. Tape one end of a 2 × 12-inch (5 cm × 30 cm) strip of paper on back of chair allowing the other end to droop forward.

2. Position hair dryer so that it blows air across the strip starting at the chair back. Have children observe that the paper rises. What happens to the drooping end? *

3. Demonstrate holding one end of a strip of tissue paper between both hands, letting the other end droop forward. Bring the held end to your lips and blow over it, causing it to rise. What happens when you stop blowing? Let children experiment.

*This demonstrates Bernoulli's Principle that fast-moving air creates low-pressure zones into which paper—and airplane wings—can rise, pushed by the higher-pressure air below them.

Discussion: Explain that heavy airplanes are pushed ahead by their powerful engines but are lifted into the sky by their wings. The wings lift like the paper strips lifted when faster air was moving over the top. Air moves faster over the top of the curved wings than it does beneath the wings. This makes the air pressure above the wing lighter. The flow of air beneath the wing is slower, making the air pressure greater under the wings. This stronger pressure pushes the wings upward, lifting the plane and keeping it up in the air. Encourage children to simulate the effect with one hand lightly held out flat, representing lighter (low) air pressure and the other hand curled into a fist strongly pushing up beneath, representing greater (high) air pressure.

♣ To demonstrate how a curved wing creates fast air on the top and slow air on the bottom, chalk a large semicircle on the playground. One child can walk around the curved half-circle, one can walk across the straight diameter. Who gets to the other side first? Now the circle child should try to get to the other side at the same time. What does the child have to do to get there? Run—just like the fast-moving air. All children can try this.

? *Inquiry Activity:* Explore another airborne phenomenon. Ask children to sit with their eyes and ears closed while you do something mysterious for them to identify. Then puff a bit of hypoallergenic air freshener into the air. How long does it take for them to notice the drifting fragrance molecules? Suggest that children make a smell survey of the room, just sniffing the air, not touching anything. Discuss findings, and record on a class chart. If a stopwatch is available, find out and record how long it takes for moving air to carry the aroma molecules from a dish of vinegar all the way across the room. Compare with other scent-releasing things: peeling an orange, or slicing an onion, for example.

Read: In the Air, by Seymour Simon.

CONCEPT: Air slows moving objects.

Group Discussion: Show the children two pieces of copier paper: one piece lying flat and the other piece tightly crunched into a ball. Ask: "If I hold these two things up as high as I can reach and then let go of them, what will happen to them?" (Wait for responses.) "Do you think that both things will fall in just the same way? Let's find out." Repeat the action as needed to allow the children to carefully observe and report. "Which one fell more slowly? Can you think of anything beneath the wide paper that might have pushed against it and slowed its fall?" Mention that everything that moves above ground or above water must push air aside as it moves. Big things push more air aside than do small things.

1. ♣ *What does a parachute do?*

LEARNING OBJECTIVE: To enjoy discovering that air pressure can keep people safe.

MATERIALS:

For each child:

1 wooden thread spool or small
  toy figure*

12-inch (30 cm) square of light
  plastic (like grocery or
  drycleaner bags)

4 feet (1.2 m) light string

Extra wooden spool or toy figure

Masking tape

GETTING READY:

Cut squares of plastic for each
  child.

Cut two 24-inch strings for
  each child.

SMALL-GROUP ACTIVITY:

1. Demonstrate taping a string end to each
   corner of the plastic square, then gathering
   and tying the strings at midpoint. (See
   Figure 7–5.) Tape other ends of string
   around toy figure/spool. (Help with knots
   if needed.)

2. ♣ Let one child go to the highest point of
   the outdoor climber (or staircase) to drop
   the extra spool/toy and the parachuted
   toy/spool. Compare results.

3. Demonstrate folding the parachute and
   winding it with the strings on toy/spool.
   Let children throw them as high as they
   can into the air outdoors. Add weight to
   the spool or toy if parachutes fail to open.
   Safety precaution: Have children space
   themselves out to avoid their parachutes
   hitting others.

4. Discuss air bags that keep passengers
   safely back from serious injury if a car
   crashes.

*The spool/toy must be heavier than the plastic and string. Tie on metal washers or
nuts if more weight is needed.

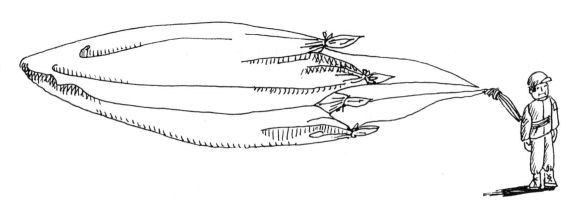

FIGURE 7–5

CONCEPT: **Warm air rises.**

LEARNING OBJECTIVE: To be astonished by the ways temperature affects air.

? *Inquiry Activity:* Ask, "How many different ways can we fill a bag with air?" Provide several thin plastic produce bags, twist ties, and as many kinds of air pumps as you can locate, such as a hand pump, bellows pump, or bicycle tire pump. Encourage other ideas. Compare what happens to those bags with what happens to a bag filled with air another way. Hold a bag upside down, fill it with a stream of hot air from a hair dryer for a few seconds, switch off the dryer, and release the bag. What happens? What made the difference? What do the children know about hot-air balloons? Have fun!

Safety Precaution: Keep children away from the dryer and the electric outlet.

INTEGRATING ACTIVITIES

Math Experiences

Measuring: Ask for children's ideas about what happens to the air inside a balloon over time. Blow up a balloon, tape it to a large piece of paper on the bulletin board, and trace around its shape. Record children's predictions about possible changes. Observe what happens to the balloon over several days. Record its shrinkage by continuing to trace around the balloon each day. Could air pressure from outside the balloon have helped squeeze the inside air together more tightly?

Music (Resources in Appendix A)

After children have finished clapping the rhythm of a song they enjoy singing, compare two styles of clapping. Listen to the sound made by clapping with palms open and flat, then to the sound made by clapping with slightly cupped hands. What is caught between the cupped hands to change the sound?

Sing this song to the refrain of "Goober Peas" (in *Folksong Festival*, Appendix A):

Air, air, air, air

air is everywhere.

We can't taste or see it,

but we know it's there.

Use appropriate tasting and peering gestures to add fun.

Listen to Joyce Rouse sing "The Same Air" from *Around the World With Earth Mama.* (See Appendix A.)

Literature Links

BALIAN, LORNA. (1990). *Wilbur's space machine.* New York: Holiday House. Wilbur builds a machine to create more space, filling every possible container with air. Then the containers take up too much space indoors. Will readers recognize that air-filled bags don't float up?

BENNETT, ANDREA, & KESSLER, JAMES. (1996). *Apples, bubbles, and crystals.* New York: Scholastic. Clear directions are given for making a simple paper helicopter. Paperback.

BORDEN, LOUISE. (2001). *Fly high! The story of Bessie Coleman.* New York: Simon & Schuster. This inspiring book chronicles a poor young girl's determination to become the first African-American to earn a pilot's license.

BRANLEY, FRANKLYN. (1986). *Air is all around you.* New York: Harper & Row. Simple air concepts and experiments are charmingly illustrated. Paperback.

BURTON, JANE, & TAYLOR, KIM. (1998). *The nature & science of bubbles.* Milwaukee, WI: Gareth Stevens. Photographs show air bubbles used as air supplies and floats for water animals, as hideouts for insects, and as part of plant life.

CALHOUN, MARY. (1981). *Hot air Henry.* New York: Morrow. Henry the cat has unexpected adventures in a hot-air balloon. Illustrations clearly show how the balloon's movement is controlled. A Reading Rainbow book. Paperback.

CHURCHILL, E. RICHARD. (1992). *Fabulous paper airplanes.* New York: Sterling. This book offers directions for making 29 paper airplanes, many easy enough for primary grade children to manage.

EVANS, D., & WILLIAMS, C. (1993). *Air and flying.* New York: Dorling Kindersley. Color photographs show young children enjoying the easy experiments that reveal nine air concepts.

GLOVER, DAVID. (1993). *Flying and floating.* New York: Kingfisher Books. Simple directions are given for making a paper hot-air balloon and pinwheel, an easy kite, and a helicopter rotor. Paperback.

GRIFFIN, MARGARET, & GRIFFIN, RUTH. (1993). *It's a gas!* Toronto, Canada: Kids Can Press. Experiments and information add to older children's knowledge about air, including the mixture of gases that make up air and how our bodies use only the oxygen from the air we breathe. Paperback.

LOBEL, ARNOLD. (1990). *Days with Frog and Toad.* New York: Harper. Toad and Frog persist, in spite of discouragement, and finally are able to fly their kite in the wind. Paperback.

MICHAEL, DAVID. (1994). *Making kites.* New York: Kingfisher Books. Careful instructions are given for making and flight-testing a variety of interesting kites, including one made from a plastic raincoat! A good book to recommend to families seeking a project to share with children. Paperback.

MILNE, A. A. (1961). *Winnie-the-Pooh.* New York: Dutton. Read this after children have made parachutes. Ask whether a small balloon could really slow Pooh's fall.

REY, H. A. (1995). *Curious George gets a medal.* New York: Scholastic. After a space flight, George drifts to earth under a parachute.

SHEA, GEORGE. (1997). *First flight: The story of Tom Tate and the Wright brothers.* New York: HarperCollins. Independent readers will enjoy this account of a Kitty Hawk boy who rode in the "flying machine."

SUHR, MANDY. (1991). *How I breathe.* Minneapolis, MN: Carolrhoda Books. Simple information for young readers describes the composition of air, and how our bodies need and use oxygen.

TAYLOR, BARBARA. (1992). *Up, up and away! The science of flight.* New York: Random House. Clear information and directions for simple activities cover several properties of air, as well as flight principles. Paperback.

WADE, ALAN. (1990). *I'm flying!* New York: Alfred A. Knopf. A boy fantasizes that a box of weather balloons and a tank of helium gas let him float away from earth's gravity pull to explore the world. A Reading Rainbow book. Paperback.

YOLEN, JANE. (1993). *The emperor and the kite*. New York: Philomel. In this satisfying retelling of a Chinese folktale, an imprisoned emperor is rescued by his daughter who puts the wind, her ingenuity, and her paper kite to use.

Poems (Resources in Appendix A)

The wind is a favorite topic in poems for children. The following are recommended:

> In *Poems Children Will Sit Still For* by de Regniers:
> "Who Has Seen the Wind" by Christina Rossetti
> "Wind Song" by Lillian Moore
> In *Now We Are Six* by A. A. Milne:
> "Wind On the Hill"
> In *Poems to Grow On* by Jean Thompson:
> "The Kite" by Harry Behn

Fingerplays

Seeds with silky wings are scattered by moving air (see Chapter 4, Plants). Recall the milkweed blowing that children may have enjoyed in plant life experiences, or try to find a milkweed pod to open outdoors now if it is a new idea.

Baby Seeds	
In a milkweed cradle	(cup hands)
Snug and warm	
Baby seeds are hiding	(make yourself small)
Safe from harm.	
Open wide the cradle	(open hands)
Hold it high.	
Come Mr. Wind	(blow in the hands)
Help them to fly.	

—AUTHOR UNKNOWN

Art Activities

Easel Painting. Cut newsprint into the shapes of things that move on the air, such as birds, balloons (tape a dangling string to the back), butterflies, and kites. Let the children choose shapes to paint with designs of their own creation.

Collage. Use airborne nature materials such as chicken feathers, milkweed fluff and seeds, and maple tree seeds. Cut some actual air bubbles from sheets of plastic packing material to glue on the collage.

Paper Fans. Make paper fans to move air. They may be accordion-pleated sheets of paper that the children decorate, or they may be small paper plates stapled to Popsicle sticks.

Jamal experiments with air-powered painting.

Gliders. Make simple gliders and decorate with crayon designs.

Air Pressure Art. With medicine droppers, make use of air pressure as an art medium. Let children use the droppers to make designs by dropping diluted food coloring onto absorbent paper. A fleeting, fascinating art form—snow painting—also makes use of droppers and food coloring. Gather a big bucket of snow. Store it on the windowsill. Quickly pack individual foam meat trays with snow, ready to receive the drops of color. Have another bucket ready for the sloshy end results.

Air Power Art. Let children use straws and air pressure to pick up tempera paint from jars and drop it on smooth-surfaced paper. The puddles of paint can then be changed in shape by blowing on them through the straws.

Play

Boat. Help the children create a block and plank boat, with two planks angled together to form a prow. Let them blow up a plastic ring for a life preserver.

Plane. Angled planks form the nose of the plane, hollow blocks form the tail and sides, and two more planks stretch out to form the wings. Children who have flown can contribute ideas about oxygen and air to the play.

Parachute Play. Children moving a group-size parachute up and down can see the lifting power of moving air. Children particularly enjoy one-at-a-time running across the circle under the billowing parachute before it falls. Taking turns holding and running cultivates cooperation. *Parachute Games* by T. Strong has many more ideas (see Resources, p. 161).

Air and Soapy Water Play. Let children make soap bubbles, using straws in cups of water and detergent. For younger children use baby shampoo, which won't irritate eyes, instead of detergent. Snip out a small notch above the middle of the straws to prevent sucking solution into mouths.

Air Cushion Play. Let children take turns pumping up a sturdy air mattress to use as a tumbling mat for somersaults.

Paper Dance Play. Cut a spiral from a sheet of paper to make one long, curving strip. Dangle it from the ceiling by attaching it to a long thread. Let children fan the air with a card to make the spiral twirl. Create a fantasy effect by dangling several spirals. Circulating air will keep them gently moving.

Creative Movement

1. Let children pretend to be balloons that are blown into large shapes. Suggest that they make themselves into flat, limp shapes on the floor. "Now I'm blowing, and blowing, and blowing some more. And you are getting bigger and bigger." When the shapes have been stretched as large as they can be, suggest that you will pretend to prick each imaginary balloon shape. Each shape is pushed about, then collapses into a limp piece of rubber on the floor as the air goes out of it.

2. Children can move like birds or butterflies soaring on moving air. They might enjoy holding a turkey wing feather in each hand to become a bird with out-stretched-arm "wings."

3. Some good ideas for leading creative movement about things that float on air can be found in *Creative Movement for the Developing Child* by Clare Cherry (see Appendix A).

Creative Thinking

Slowly guide a quiet imagery experience: "Close your eyes and take a very deep breath of air. Feel it fill your lungs. Let the air seep out slowly and imagine yourself getting lighter than air, so light you can just float out the window and drift above our school. How does it look from above? Catch an air current to let yourself drift over to your favorite place to play. Enjoy watching people below flying kites. . . Change into that air current and give the kites a strong, gentle push. Don't the kites look fine, tugging at their strings? . . . Now feel yourself getting smaller, until you're just a tiny handful of air . . . good. Now find some small spaces to fill. . . . Slip under a mosquito's wing . . . creep into a key hole . . . swing on a spider's web . . . slide into a French horn, up and around in the tubing and out the horn on a blast of sound. . . . Now ease yourself back into our classroom to open your eyes and share your air travels with us."

Food Experiences

If an electric mixer is available, whip up a treat. Explain that the beater is stirring many tiny air bubbles into the mixture. Watch it change and expand.

Combine: 1/2 cup instant dry skim milk

1/2 cup ice cold water

1 level teaspoon sugar-free gelatin

(berry flavors seem to work best)

Beat at highest speed 4 to 5 minutes until mixture forms stiff peaks. Makes about 3 cups, enough to provide each child a dollop to enjoy. Save some to examine quickly with a hand lens to see air bubbles. Edible science is impressive. Children really remember that air was part of the tidbit they enjoyed eating.

Field Trips

Small Airport Visit. If this is possible, keep the science focus simple. There will be too many exciting things to see to make lengthy explanations of flight principles bearable for the children. Be sure that any adult who offers a guided tour of the facility understands this.

PROMOTING CONCEPT CONNECTIONS

Maintaining Concepts

1. Make casual comments or inquiries about the function or presence of air when suitable opportunities arise. When outdoors with a class, observe planes or birds flying overhead, or leaves, seeds, or litter blowing past.

2. Suggest that children fill their mouths with a giant air bubble when the class needs to walk quietly through school corridors. Puff up your own cheeks to model this funny way to stay quiet. It's more positive than saying, "Be quiet!" Air takes up talking space.

3. Use medicine droppers to water tiny seedlings, to give moisture to insects in jars, and for art projects. If necessary, remind children to push the air out of the dropper while it is still in the liquid. Can they see the air bubbling into the liquid?

4. If you need to open a vacuum-sealed container, such as using a punch-type opener with a can of juice, let the children listen closely for the hiss of air rushing into the can. When using the bellows-type step pump, show the rubber cap on the air intake valve. Push the air out so the bellows are flat. Remove the cap so that air rushes in with a hiss, and watch the bellows expand dramatically.

Improving Schoolgrounds

If you are fortunate enough to have swings at your school, they are very useful for allowing children to experience the presence of air, especially on their faces as they rush through the air. (Swings are also excellent teachers of pendulums too—try to maintain them if at all possible.)

Connecting Concepts

1. Relate water concepts to air when investigating evaporation. Water droplets, or vapor, become part of the air. Speak of fog and clouds as very wet air.

2. Relate plant propagation (seed scattering) to moving air.

3. Relate sound to air concepts. Sound travels through air; moving air causes some things to vibrate and make sounds; air vibrates when enclosed in a column like a flute or a whistle (see Chapter 14).

4. Point out the crucial role of air in ecological relationships. Air is one of the non-living substances that all living things depend on to stay alive. Air that is spoiled by pollution makes problems for all living things. There is no way to make new air. It is used over and over again, so people must find ways to keep air clean.

Family and Community Support

A newsletter to parents can suggest ways to support and add to the air experiences at school. When families are out together, they can watch for soaring birds, planes, and clouds being pushed along by moving air. They can point out how air is heated in their homes to keep people comfortable in winter, and passed through coolers in summer.

Notify families about places in the area where gliders or small planes, windmills, fancy kite flying, hot-air balloons, or parasailing can be seen.

RESOURCES

HANN, J. (1991). *How science works* (pp. 115–123). Pleasantville, NY: Reader's Digest. This book provides basic information about the properties of air and air pressure and experiments.

HIRSCHFELD, R., & WHITE, N. (1995). *The kids' science book.* Charlotte, VT: Williamson. You will find a pattern and directions for making a hot-air-powered mobile in this book of easy science activities.

LEONARD, JACQUELINE. (2002). Let's go fly a kite! *Science and Children, 40* 4, 20–24. Urban children discover the science and mathematics behind the joys of kite flying.

LEVENSON, E. (1994). *Teaching children about physical science* (pp. 71–73). New York: Tab Books. Interesting air pressure experiments will intrigue children wishing to continue exploring air properties.

MANDER, JERRY. (1998). *The great international paper airplane book.* New York: Galahad Books.

MARKLE, S. (1990). *Exploring spring.* New York: Avon. To understand how kites fly and for the kite-flying safety tips, first-time kite flyers should read "Flights of Fancy" before heading outdoors with the class.

SAN FRANCISCO EXPLORATORIUM STAFF. (1996). *The science explorer.* New York: Henry Holt. Interesting ways to create air spinners and gliders are offered in this book of easy experiments, with detailed explanations of the principles involved.

STRONG, T., & LEFEURE, D. (1999). *Parachute games.* Urbana, IL: Human Kinetics Press. Enjoyable activites for playing with air in a group.

Water

Cascading waterfalls, cool relief scooped onto your face on a hot day, thirst-slaking spurts from a plastic bottle, blissful showers—you know the pleasures of water! Share them with children who will enjoy learning about water's surprising properties.

All living things require water to survive. Our planet could not exist without water. Young children delight in pouring, spraying, and splashing in water. Help them learn more about this fascinating substance to build lasting respect for a precious resource. The experiences in this chapter will explore the following concepts:

- Water has weight.
- Water's weight and upthrust help things float.
- Water goes into the air.
- Water can change forms reversibly.
- Water is a solvent for many materials.
- Water clings to itself.
- Water clings to other materials.
- Water moves into other materials.

It is hard for a child to imagine that sparkling, transparent water weighs something. When attention is focused on experiencing water's weight, children can then begin to understand how water can support objects. In the following activities, children experience the weight of water and explore buoyancy. Other activities deal with evaporation, condensation, freezing, and melting; water as a solvent; and water's cohesion, adhesion, and surface tension properties.

CONCEPT: **Water has weight.**

1. How can we feel water's weight?
LEARNING OBJECTIVE: To spark interest in the characteristics of water.

MATERIALS:

*As a warm weather
outdoor activity:*

Water source

Small wading pool

Large bucket

Large pitcher or milk cartons

For indoor use add:

Rubber boots

Plastic smock

GETTING READY:

♣ If outdoors, have children
remove shoes and socks and
roll up pant legs.

If indoors, have children wear
boots and smock.

SMALL-GROUP ACTIVITY:

1. Encourage children to dip fingers into water. "Think about this: Could water be
   heavy? Let's find out."
2. Let children take turns standing in the
   pool, holding the empty bucket.
3. Let others pour pitchers or cartons of water into the bucket until it becomes too
   heavy to hold. Conclusions about the
   weight of water are easily formed and
   communicated by this direct investigation.

CONCEPT: **Water's weight and upthrust help things float.**

1. ♣ Which things float; which things sink?

LEARNING OBJECTIVE: To enjoy exploring water's upthrust effect.

MATERIALS:

Dishpans of water

Plastic aprons

Assorted objects such as rocks,
twigs, corks, and washers

Pairs of objects of contrasting
weight: ping-pong/golf ball,
plastic/steel spoon,
plastic/steel paper clip

Old kitchen scale, postage scale,
or balance

Two trays

SMALL-GROUP ACTIVITY:

1. Let children gently place palms of hands
   against the water's surface to feel water
   pushing up against their hands (upthrust[*]). "Let's see if that push and water's
   weight will hold all these things up."
2. "Try to make a floating thing stay on the
   bottom of the tub. What happens when
   you stop holding it down?" (Water's
   upthrust pushes it up.)
3. Suggest classifying objects on float/sink
   trays. "Why do you think some things sank?"
4. Let children weigh matching objects to
   confirm that the objects' weight influenced
   the outcome.[**]

[*]Upthrust = the natural tendency of a body of water to push upward.

[**]Weight is an acceptable first explanation. Density is the accurate, but more difficult, explanation.

GETTING READY:

Tape card marked FLOAT on
   one tray; SINK on the other.

2. How does shape help some things float?

LEARNING OBJECTIVE: To be reassured by discovering that shape affects buoyancy.

MATERIALS:

Part 1

Dishpans of water

Plastic aprons

Postage or kitchen scale

2 sheets aluminum foil, almost
   dishpan size

Hammer

Cutting board

Part 2

Modeling clay

Rolling pin

Pennies

GETTING READY:

Prepare a 4-column chart headed:
   Weight, Shape, Float, Sink

SMALL-GROUP ACTIVITY:

1. Recall observations from Activity 1. "Did some things that seemed heavy float? Let's see if something else helped them float."
2. "Do you think these sheets of foil will float? Find out."
3. Next, crunch one sheet as small as possible. Pound the wad with hammer on the cutting board to make a tight, condensed lump. Ask for buoyancy predictions for the changed aluminum shape. "Find out." (The sheet's weight spreads out over more water. More water pushes up under the sheet than the wad.) Record observations for each condition: same weight, different shape; one floated, one sank.
4. Form two clay balls of equal weight and shape. Let children confirm the equivalence. "Do they float or sink?" Roll one ball flat. Form into a boat shape. "See if both shapes sink." Record observations. Let children enjoy forming and testing boat shapes.
5. "Can this boat hold pennies and stay afloat? Drop in one penny at a time and find out." Eventually, the spread-out shape became heavier than water's weight and sinks.) Discuss children's experiences with floating and sinking at the swimming pool.

Read: Who Sank the Boat? by Pamela Allen.

CONCEPT: **Water goes into the air.**

1. How can we tell that air and moving air take up water?

LEARNING OBJECTIVE: To take pride in noticing and hastening evaporation.

MATERIALS:

Two trays

Pans of water

Paper towels

Blackboard or other dark
  smooth surface

Cardboard or paper fans

Handheld hair dryer

Paper

GETTING READY:

Safety Precaution: prevent
  tripping over cord, or
  inappropriate dryer use.

Let children make folded paper
  fans.

SMALL-GROUP ACTIVITY:

1. "What do you think will happen if we
   wet some towels, and spread them out
   on these trays? Let's see." Put one tray in
   a sunny or warm place, the other in a
   cool, darker place. Check them in half an
   hour.
2. Meanwhile, show children the hair dryer;
   let them feel warm air coming from it.
   "What do you feel? This warm air can help
   us understand what is happening to the
   towels."
3. Let children dip a finger in water, then
   trace their names on the blackboard.
   "Blow warm air on your wet name. Watch
   closely to see what happens to the water.
   Where did it go? Only air touched it." The
   water has gone into the air in such tiny
   drops that they are invisible (vapor).
   When air takes up water, we say the water *evaporates.*
4. "Write your name with water on the black
   board again. Fold a paper fan and wave it
   near your name to make a breeze. Where
   does the water go? Let's see what happened to the paper towels. What happened
   to the wetness?"

? *Inquiry Activity:* Elicit children's predictions about where water will
evaporate fastest in the room. "Let's find out." Record all predictions. Provide children with numbered pieces of damp paper towel. Record on a group chart where
the towels are placed in the room. Check progress frequently. Chart drying times
for different locations. Record and compare observation data. How did the variables of temperature, moving air, sunshine, and proximity to a heat source affect
evaporation times?

CONCEPT: **Water can change forms reversibly.**

1. How does temperature change make water change?

LEARNING OBJECTIVE: To feel assured by the regularity of water changing/re-
                     versing forms.

MATERIALS:

Water

Two identical shallow plastic bowls (Do not use ice cube trays. In some parts of the country, children may believe that ice is formed only in cube shapes.)

Access to a freezing compartment or, better yet, to freezing weather

Or fill two or more small balloons with water. Children enjoy handling the "ice eggs" without getting wet

SMALL-GROUP ACTIVITY:

1. Early in the morning, let children fill bowls almost to the top with water. Help them deliver one bowl to the freezer or to the near-zero outdoor location. Leave the other bowl in the room (out of spilling range) for an hour or more.
2. Ask: "Do you think both bowls of water will stay the same or will one change? Let's check."
3. Bring ice back to the room when it is solid. Dump it out onto a pie pan for all to see.
4. "What do you think will happen if we leave the bowl of water in the cold place? Let's find out." Repeat the activity if the children request it.*
5. Bring snowballs or icicles indoors to melt in a pan, when possible. Collect snow in a coffee can and measure its depth. Measure the depth of the water after the snow has melted completely. Is it as deep as the snow was?

2. How does water change to vapor; vapor change to water?

LEARNING OBJECTIVE: To delight in demystifying the source of rain and fog.

MATERIALS:

Foil potpie pan

Clear plastic tumbler

Dark paper or folder

Water, ice cubes

Thermos of boiling water

Magnifying glass

SMALL-GROUP ACTIVITY:

1. Recall the earlier experience in which air temperature helped water change forms. "Let's watch what happens in this cup."
2. Let children examine the cup and pan to be sure they are dry and free of holes. Caution the children about staying back while hot water is poured into the tumbler. "The cup looks empty; do you think it is? Is it easy to see through the cup of air now?"
3. Let children add ice to the pan and feel the air temperature just below it. Pour hot water into the cup to the depth of 2 inches (5 cm).

---

*Some children have enough experience with water and ice to predict reversibility of this change. The transformation from water to vapor and back to water is less familiar. Both forms of reversibility may need repeating several times for less experienced children to grasp cause-and-effect ideas.

GETTING READY:

Experiment at home.

Form a backdrop with dark paper to make the water vapor more visible.

Try to provide more than one setup to avoid crowding observers.

Repeat as needed.

4. Let children feel the warm air temperature in the cup and the cold air temperature under the pan. "We'll watch for changes in the cup for a few minutes."

5. Immediately cover the cup with the pan of ice (Figure 8–1). "What's happening?" (Evaporation is occurring. Tiny bits of water are mixing with air to form water vapor.) "Is the water vapor moving up to the cool air? Let's lift the pan to see what's happening underneath. What does it look like?"

6. Look through the magnifier at the collected droplets. "How could those drops get on a dry pan?" There should be large drops falling before long. Help children recall water bits going into warm air; warm air rising up to the cold air; moist cooling air changing to larger and larger drops; and drops falling back down as water again.

Note: Children are likely to describe the collected condensation drops as rain. Using the same analogy, mention that the visible water vapor in the jar is

FIGURE 8–1

like a fog or a small cloud. To be accurate, condensation occurs in clouds when droplets collect on dust particles to form raindrops. We should say that the drops in the cup formed almost the same way as rain is formed. Be certain that children know that air far from the earth is cold because it is far from earth's warmth. Air close to the earth is warmed by reflected heat from the earth. (Be sure that children understand that there are no pans of ice in the sky.)

Read: Silver Morning by Susan Pearson.

Group Experience: Ask the children to breathe slowly into their cupped hands. Does their breath feel warm or cold when it comes from their bodies? Pass out small mirrors or foil pans for children to exhale on. Are these surfaces cool? Ask for predictions about the outcome of breathing on the cool mirror or metal. Find out what happens. Can the children see results? "How does the cloudy place feel? Is it wet or dry? Try it again. Feel the cloudy place, and then feel a place that wasn't breathed on. Why do we feel wetness?" Discuss common occurrences of condensation in homes: on bathroom mirrors after steamy showers, on kitchen windows when pots are boiling, and on eyeglasses when a dishwasher door is opened to let dishes air-dry.

CONCEPT: **Water is a solvent for many materials.**

1. Which things dissolve in water?

LEARNING OBJECTIVE: To enjoy discovering how water changes certain materials.

MATERIALS:

Muffin pans, or plastic ice cube molds

Pitcher of water

Assorted dry materials: salt, sand, cornstarch, flour, fine gravel, seeds, cornmeal

Spoons for dry materials

Salad oil

Small screw-top bottle

Plastic aprons

Newspaper

Sponge

Sticks for stirring

Cleanup bucket

GETTING READY:

Spread newspapers on work table.

Half-fill pans with water.

SMALL-GROUP ACTIVITY:

1. "See what happens when you put a little salt in one of your pans of water. Stir it. Can you see it? Feel it? Where is it?"
2. "Dip a finger in the pan. How does the water taste? The salt is still there, but it is in such tiny bits now, that it can't be seen. It dissolved in the water."
3. "Try the other materials; put each in its own pan of water. Find out which ones dissolve."
4. Half fill the bottle with water. Add some oil. Cap securely. Let the children shake it. "Does it seem to dissolve? Let it stand a while. Where is the oil now?"

Group Experience: Mix some sand, dirt, and gravel with water in a pint jar. Let it stand undisturbed for a day or more. Check the jar. Is the water still muddy looking? Did the sand and dirt really dissolve? Which is on the bottom?

CONCEPT: Water clings to itself.

1. How do water drops behave?

LEARNING OBJECTIVE: To be delighted by clinging or stretching water drops.

MATERIALS:

Water

For each child: small container, such as film canisters or Rx vials

Plastic droppers

Baster

Waxed paper

Popsicle sticks, grass blades, or bits of straw

Sponge to absorb spills

Pennies

GETTING READY:

Cut 5-inch squares of waxed paper for each child.

Fill individual containers with water. (Children like to help, using the baster.)

SMALL-GROUP INDOOR ACTIVITY:

1. Squeeze a single drop of water on each child's index fingertip. "What can you find out about your drop by looking at it?" Enjoy the perfection of water drops."Carefully touch that drop with your thumb. Pull it gently. What happens?" (Drop stretches, re-forms as its tiniest bits—molecules—cling together.)

2. Give each child a square of waxed paper. "What will happen if you squeeze a drop of water on this paper? Find out. Is your drop flat or curved?"

3. Add that the edges of a drop pull together tightly to act like an invisible "skin." The tiniest possible bits of water (molecules) cling tightly to each other. "Make more drops on your paper. What happens when you pull drops together with a grass blade?" Let children see how many drops they can fit on a penny.

Group Experience: Review small-group findings. Read aloud the charming poems "At the Window" from *Now We Are Six* by A. A. Milne, and "Ice Cycle" by Mary Anne Hoberman. Share at an appropriate level the outstanding book, *A Drop of Water,* by Walter Wick. Talk about how icicles form, one clinging drop at a time.

♣ *Outdoor Experience:* After the next rain, take magnifying glasses, a notebook, and a pen with you to the playground to record the places where children find raindrops clinging. Discuss the sightings with the group later.

2. How does the surface of water behave?

LEARNING OBJECTIVE: To be amazed by the strength of surface tension.*

*Tension describes the tightly clinging molecules on the surface of the water.

MATERIALS:

Clear plastic tumblers

Water

Syringe-type baster

Uncooked spaghetti bits, steel paper clips, twigs

Sponge and newspapers to absorb spills

SMALL-GROUP ACTIVITY:

1. Fill a tumbler to the top with water.
2. While children watch with heads close to the table, use the dropper or baster to slowly add drops of water to fill the tumbler. "What might happen if more drops are added?" Find out, drop by drop. (Curved dome stretches above rim as more drops are added, until surface tension weakens and breaks.)
3. "I wonder if those bits of water at the top are clinging tightly enough to let something rest on it?" Hold a dry piece of spaghetti horizontally: gently rest it on the surface. "Let's see if an upright piece rests on the surface." (No, it breaks through the surface.) Let children try steel paper clips and twigs.

See: Animals in Motion, by Pamela Hickman, p. 22–23, about water-walking creatures.

3. How does soap change water's surface tension?

LEARNING OBJECTIVE: To be surprised by changing surface tension effects.

MATERIALS:

Pitcher of water

Small foil pans

Shaker can of pepper or talcum powder

Cotton-tipped swabs

Liquid soap or slivers of bar soap

Liquid detergent

Small twigs, grass, and paper clips

GETTING READY:

Pour 1 inch (2.5 cm) of water in foil pans.

SMALL-GROUP ACTIVITY:

1. "We can't see the tiniest bits of water pulling tightly across this water, but perhaps we can see what the tightness does to other things.
2. Sprinkle pepper or powder onto the water. "What do you see happening? Try it."
3. Dab tip of swab into detergent or soap. "Let's see what happens when we touch the surface with a bit of soap." Be prepared to empty the pans often for re-experimenting.
4. Let pairs of children join hands and tug against one another like tightly clinging bits of water. "If I pushed through your grip, what would happen to you? That's almost like soap breaking up the pull between water bits."

CONCEPT: **Water clings to other materials.**

1. Where can we see water bits clinging?

LEARNING OBJECTIVE: To appreciate the beauty and strength of clinging water drops.

MATERIALS:

2-inch diameter coffee mug

2 clear plastic yogurt cup lids (unsmudged)

Try to have a clean lid for each child as well.

Tape

Magnifier

Water

4 more yogurt lids

Grass blades, twigs

GETTING READY:

Out of children's reach, put a clear lid on mug of hot water. Let steam condense on lid until it is covered with visible, tiny droplets. Join this lid to a dry lid with tape to make a sealed case. (See Figure 4–1 on p. 57.)

Collect condensation on single lids for children to observe and touch with blades of grass or twigs.*

Trim rims off of 4 yogurt lids.

SMALL-GROUP INDOOR ACTIVITY:

1. Recall condensation experience. Pass droplets case and magnifier. What is observed? "Let's see how long these beautiful droplets will cling to the plastic." Check at regular intervals.
2. "Do you think water can cling to something tightly enough for us to feel?" Sprinkle water on one rimless lid. Cover it with another. "Try getting these apart. What do you feel? Try getting two dry lids apart. How does that feel different?"
3. Let children dip their fingers in water and see how long it takes for water to drip off their fingertips.
4. ♣ Take a bucket of water and basters outdoors for children to see what water will stick to on the playground.

*This is such a simple, powerful way to help children appreciate the extraordinary laws of nature underlying ordinary, unnoticed events. Do it often.

CONCEPT: **Water moves into other materials.**

1. Which things can water move into?

LEARNING OBJECTIVE: To be intrigued by water spreading/climbing into things.

MATERIALS:

Water

Small Rx vial and plastic dropper for each child

Pressed foam meat trays

Small test materials such as:
bark, cotton, tissues, paper
towels, smooth paper, stones,
bits of fabric, dry sponge cut
into small cubes

Food coloring

Magnifiers

Plastic jar

Celery stalk

Clear straw or narrow pipette
(desirable)

GETTING READY:

Fill vials with water.

Tint water in jar and one small
container with food coloring.

Arrange a tray of test materials
for each child.

SMALL-GROUP ACTIVITY:

1. "What happens when you put drops of
water on different things in your tray?"
Discuss results.
2. "Let's see if paper towels and smooth paper look the same under the magnifier.
Which has tiny holes for water bits to
move into?" (Water sticks to both, but
there are more places for water to fill and
cling to in the toweling.)
3. Offer fresh toweling, tinted water, and
magnifiers so water can be better observed
as it crawls through the soft paper. Use the
term *absorbs* when discussing how the materials let water travel through.

Group Experience: Recall with children how water clung and crawled through some test materials. "Would you imagine that water might also cling in-side and crawl UP narrow tubes?" Listen to children's ideas. " Let's find out whether or not water can crawl up these tiny tubes in the celery stalk." (A small capillary effect can be seen immediately by inserting a clear drinking straw or pipette in a tumbler of tinted water.) Check celery for several days until the col-ored water has traveled into the leaves. Cut slices from the stalk for children to examine with magnifiers. Talk about moisture in the soil traveling up roots and tubes in stalks to help trees and plants grow.

INTEGRATING ACTIVITIES

Math Experiences

1. Provide a set of measuring cups or three sizes of paper milk cartons for casual use by children playing with water. Ask how many small containers of water it takes to fill a cup or carton this size, and so on.
2. Let the children record the weight of different materials in dry and wet states. Weigh a dry sponge on a kitchen scale. Drop it in a bowl of water. Ask children for predictions about the weight of the wet sponge. Reweigh the sponge. Let the

children decide what made the weight difference. Squeeze the water out over a dry bowl. Weigh the sponge again. A discussion of the results could bring in more-than/less-than comparisons.

3. Measure water absorption with dried beans. Early in the day, begin to soak 1/4 cup of dried beans in 1 cup of water in one container; 1/4 cup dried beans and 2 cups of water in another. Drain off, measure, and return the water after 2 hours, 6 hours, and next morning. How much water did the beans absorb? Several small groups can do this with different kinds of beans and different amounts of water. Results can be compared and charted.

Music (Resources in Appendix A)

1. Sing "Row, Row, Row Your Boat," with children joining hands with a partner and touching feet to pull back and forth. Ask, "Does water hold boats up? Is water heavy to push?"

2. Sing "The Eency Weency Spider" after the evaporation experiences, making an adaptation in lyrics. Change "and dried up all the rain" to "and evaporated the rain." Look for rain spouts near the school for children to watch after a rain.

3. Sing this song, after experimenting with forms of water, to the tune of "Twinkle, Twinkle, Little Star":

> *Water, water from the stream*
> *When it boils it turns to steam.*
> *Water, water is so nice;*
> *Freeze it cold, it turns to ice.*
> *Cool the steam; warm the ice*
> *It's water again, clear and nice.*

Literature Links

ALLEN, PAMELA. (1996). *Who sank the boat?* New York: Putnam & Grosset. Amusing illustrations clearly demonstrate that every substance has weight in this funny, beginning reader book. Paperback.

BELL, J. L. (1993). *Soap science.* Reading, MA: Addison-Wesley. Surface tension is explored and stretched even more with detergent, providing fun with bubble-making. Additional experiments for the fascinated older child.

BERGER, MELVIN. (1993). *All about water.* New York: Scholastic. The author's crystal clear, focused narrative style makes this an excellent resource for youngsters. Paperback.

BERGER, MELVIN, & BERGER, GILDA. (1995). *Water, water everywhere.* Nashville, TN: Ideals. This is an easy-to-read book about the water cycle, forms of water, treatment systems, and conservation. Paperback.

BRANLEY, FRANKLYN. (1997). *Down Comes the Rain.* New York: HarperCollins. Cheerful children join the discussion of evaporation and condensation as it occurs naturally. The size of a droplet of water vapor is approximated. Paperback.

BUNTING, EVE. (1997). *Ducky.* New York: Clarion Books. This story is based on an actual load of bathtub toys that washed overboard during shipment from China. Floating characteristics are an asset to the toys and to oceanographers who studied their journey to shore.

DURANT, PENNY. (1993). *Bubblemania!* New York: Avon. The most complete, least expensive bubble book includes good experiments to enhance understanding of surface tension, and offers a myriad of explorations and purely pleasurable bubble activities. Paperback.

FLACK, MARJORIE. (1970). *The story about Ping* (Seafarer Edition). New York: Viking Press. In this classic story, a barrel full of air tied to his back keeps a houseboat boy afloat after he tumbles into the Yangtze River.

GLOVER, DAVID. (1993). *Floating and flying.* New York: Kingfisher Books. Easy directions are given for making a water wheel and a soap-powered boat, as well as a new recipe for bubble-blowing.

HOOPER, MEREDITH. (1998). *The drop in my drink.* New York: Viking. A boy reflects on the history of the tiny parts of water that have come together for the first time into a single drop. NSTA* Outstanding Trade Book.

LEVINE, SHAR, & JOHNSTONE, L. *Bathtub science.* New York: Sterling. Extend the explorations of water properties, i.e., surface tension and siphon-making. The scientific principles are explained.

LOCKER, THOMAS. (1997). *Water dance.* San-Diego: Harcourt. Locker's luminous paintings and lyrical prose portray dramatic aspects of the water cycle. End notes explain the science behind each scene.

LOBEL, ARNOLD. (1975). *Owl at home.* New York: Harper & Row. In this classic, Owl lets freezing air into his house. His soup freezes in the bowl. It thaws when Owl starts a new fire in the fireplace.

MARKLE, SANDRA. (1993). *A rainy day.* New York: Orchard Books. Charming illustrations capture the curiosity of a child enjoying the effects of rain. Objects absorb, repel, or dissolve in the rain, and the water cycle is traced in this pleasant story.

MARZOLLO, JEAN. (1996). *I am water.* New York: Scholastic. This attractive book for beginning readers shows the uses of water in the young child's world. Paperback.

MILNE, A. A. (1961). *Winnie-the-Pooh.* (Chap. 9, "In Which Piglet Is Entirely Surrounded by Water"). New York: E. P. Dutton. Pooh and Christopher Robin use unorthodox means of floating through flood waters.

MURPHY, BRIAN. (2001). *Experiment with water.* Princeton, NJ: Two Can Press. Lively illustrations and a good level of information will attract independent readers to this activities book. The explorations include surface tension and bubbles. Directions include an easy bubble blower.

MURPHY, P., KLAGES, E., SHORE, L., & SAN FRANCISCO EXPLORATORIUM STAFF. (1996). *The science explorer.* New York: Holt. Intriguing new additions to the bubble-making repertoire are offered and explained.

PEARSON, SUSAN. (1998). *Silver morning.* San Diego, CA: Harcourt Brace. A mother and child are engulfed by a shimmering fog during their walk through the woods.

RELF, PAT. (1996). *The magic school bus wet all over: A book about the water cycle.* New York: Scholastic. Its tie-in with the Magic School Bus TV series will motivate reading.

REY, H. A. (1997). *Curious George rides a bike.* New York: Scholastic Book Services. George forgets to deliver newspapers because he is so absorbed in making newspaper boats and floating his fleet downstream.

ROBBINS, KEN. (1994). *The elements: Water.* New York: Holt. All of the forms of water are reverently shown in lovely, soft photographs, accompanied by a lyrical text.

SHUURMANS, HILDE. (2001). *Sidney won't swim.* Watertown, MA: Charlesbridge. Beginning readers will recognize Sidney's fear of sinking in this enjoyable story, but they will have to figure out the "whys" of buoyancy in a group discussion afterward.

SPEED, TOBY. (1998). *Water voices.* New York: Putnam. Soft watercolors and read-aloud rhythms describe seven forms of water young children love, including mud puddles and ocean waves.

WICK, WALTER. (1997). *A drop of water: A book of science and wonder.* New York: Scholastic Press. Striking, delicate photographs by the author let us marvel at the properties of water from dewdrops, to frost, to clouds of steam. Clearly written explanations and experiments are offered. NSTA* Outstanding Tradebook Award.

*National Science Teachers Association.

Poems (Resources in Appendix A)

From *Poems Children Will Sit Still For,* read "Dragon Smoke" by Lillian Moore.
From *Now We Are Six* by A. A. Milne, read "Waiting at the Window."
From *Once Upon Ice and Other Frozen Poems,* read "Ice Cycle" by Mary Ann Hoberman.

The 34 poems in Constance Levy's book, *SPLASH! Poems of Our Watery World,* consider all aspects of water in nature and in ourselves—from teardrops to ocean waves—in fine, read-aloud rhythms.

Fingerplays

Here is a fingerplay about evaporation:

In soapy water	(scrubbing motion)
I wash my clothes,	
I hang them out to dry.	(pantomime)
The sun it shines,	(hands form circle)
The wind it blows,	(wave arms, sway)
The wetness goes into the sky.	

—J. H.

Art Activities

Ice Cube Painting. Use finger paint and glossy paper, but do not wet the paper as you would to prepare for finger painting. Instead, offer the children ice cubes, frozen with a popsicle stick "handle" with which to spread and dilute the paint while making designs.

Tempera Painting. Let children watch or help you mix dry tempera paint with water. When the finished paintings are hung to dry, use the term evaporate to explain how this drying occurs.

Cohesion/Adhesion Effects. Tint water in cups, so drops of different colors can be mixed together on their papers. The cohesive action of different colors jumping together is exciting to watch. Add adhesion to the experience another time, comparing what happens with different papers, such as finger paint paper, paper towels, and coffee filters.

For more water-in-art ideas, see *Water: Science Through Art* by Hilary Devonshire.

Play

Housekeeping Play. Wash doll clothes. If possible, hang some to dry in the sunshine, some in a shady location, and some indoors. Compare drying times. Add a bowl of soapy water and one of plain water with an eggbeater for each. Encourage children to notice that much more air can be beaten into the soapy water. Encourage explanations.

Outdoor Water Play. ♣ Place two or three tubs of water in the water table. Provide plastic pitchers, funnels, small containers, and lengths of tubing. Let barefooted children transfer water from buckets to the wading pool using plastic tubing and a small plastic squeeze pump from the automotive supply section of a variety store. Raise the bucket of water on a pile of hollow blocks next to the wading pool for further experimentation. Add a water play pump, available from school equipment sources, if possible.

Read *Curious George Rides a Bicycle* by H. A. Rey. Then help children make newspaper boats to float in the wading pool, following the techniques George uses in the story.

Bubble-Making. Choose some of these ways to have fun with surface tension:

- ♣ Use commercial bubble solutions and ring-tipped wands to wave or blow bubbles. Replenish the solution with a concentrated mixture of 1/4 cup of liquid dishwashing detergent (Joy and Dawn are good) and 1 cup of water. Glycerin, from the drugstore, about one teaspoon for the above

Jessie blows carefully, observing the surface tension in her bubbles.

recipe, extends bubble strength. If available, try the commercial set of giant rings and multiple bubble template, or try plastic berry baskets. Use these outdoors. (Bubbles last longer on cloudy days.)

- Provide straws and cans of detergent/water solution to blow bubbles into. This is easier for children who aren't able to manage blowing bubbles into the air. **Safety Precaution:** Prepare individual plastic straws. Print children's names on straws with a permanent felt pen. Flatten the straw, then cut a tiny notch 1 inch from mouth end to prevent accidentally sucking up soapy water.
- Try using fat drinking straws as pipes for blowing detergent/water solution bubbles into the air. Show the children how to dip the end of the straw into the solution to let a film collect across the bottom of the straw. Suggest holding the straw slightly downward to avoid dripping solution into the mouth.
- Try using soft plastic funnels to blow giant bubbles. (Have several ready and be prepared to wash mouthpieces before sharing.) Put the funnel upside down into a bowl of detergent solution. Gently blow a few bubbles into the bowl to allow a film of solution to coat the inside of the funnel. Lift out the funnel and softly blow a bubble.
- Talk with the children about how the outside surface of the soap film pulled together, almost like a balloon around the air. The soap or detergent mixture makes a more flexible, stretchier "skin" than the water makes alone.

More intriguing bubble experiences are offered in the 1993 paperback *Bubblemania,* by Penny Durant. (Do not confuse it with a more recent book of the same title, about bubblegum.)

Creative Movement

Bubbles. Add a soap bubble movement stimulus to your collection of emergency ideas (i.e., ideas to use when you have a group of children ready to do something that isn't quite ready for the children). Tell the children that you will blow imaginary bubbles to them to catch. "Here's a high one . . . catch this one on your elbow . . . your shoulder . . . your chin. Don't let this one touch the ground. Catch this one on a fingertip and blow it back to me. Pretend that your hands are made of soap film. Blow into them until they can't stretch any more and they pop."

Snowmen. Guide the children as they roll imaginary snowmen, rolling more and more slowly as the ball gets larger. "Let's make a smaller ball for a chest . . . now a smaller ball for a head . . . . Lift them into place. Oh! There it goes! Snowballs this size are very heavy. Now, be the snowman yourself, all curvy and cold and tall. But wait, the sun is beginning to shine and warm the air. Oh! What's happening to your arms and your body?" Continue with your suggestions and the children's responses until the snowman is a puddle that will soon evaporate and vanish without a trace.

Cohesion. Use this activity to help children grasp the concept of water molecules being attracted to, and bonding to, one another. "Let's pretend to shrink into the tiniest bits of water possible, so tiny we can't be seen without a microscope. Move around now and find ways to connect with other water bits to form droplets (linking elbows, arms, and feet inventively). Now let's find ways for everyone to connect into a single drop of water. Make as many connections as possible. Now let's see what happens when the water bits on the outside edges pull together tightly, linking elbows. Look, the outside edges are pulling us into a circle. Now, outside droplets disconnect those elbows. Reach out your arms and hold hands to stretch that drop of water. Good. We're still clinging together, but we've stretched into a bigger drop now."

Creative Thinking

Invent a story mixup that includes references to water concepts. Illustrate the story with mounted pictures cut from magazines or catalogs. When the concept is referred to, let it be in the form of an obvious misstatement for the children to catch and correct. Perhaps it could be a camping story where "the children could hardly wait to cool off by skating on the lake in the summer sunshine . . . " or "John and Anne filled the boat with heavy rocks to help it float on the water . . . " or "Dad put the teakettle in the icebox to boil the water for soup."

Food Experiences

Water is—or has been—part of everything we eat. Children put many water concepts to use when they cook, such as boiling water to dissolve gelatin, melting ice cubes to thicken it, and freezing fruit juice into popsicles. Cooking rice for lunch offers both water absorption and volume measurement experiences. Popping corn is an exciting edible way to illustrate a property of water: high temperature changes water to steam. Children are surprised and pleased to learn that moisture inside the kernels of corn changes to steam so fast that it pops the kernel open. The steam is very evident in a plastic domed corn popper.

PROMOTING CONCEPT CONNECTIONS

Maintaining Concepts

1. Discuss evaporation whenever clothes have to be dried at school—after play in the snow or a fall into a puddle. It's especially reassuring to a child who is worried about staying neat to know that an accidental stain can be washed out, the moisture will evaporate, and the garment will look fine again. When children come to school in raincoats and boots, look for drops of water still on the outside of the garments—evidence that these materials don't absorb water.

2. Examine puddles in the playground after a rain. Using stones, mark the outline of the puddle size when it is at its fullest level. (Make a chalk outline if the puddle is on concrete or asphalt.) This will make it easier for the children to make comparisons from day to day as they watch for changes in the puddle. They will remind you if you should happen to forget the puddle-checking ritual. Those in the northern latitudes might be able to see the puddle freeze and thaw as well as evaporate. Relate that cold air causes the water to freeze.

With a hill, a pump, and a riverbed, children can play in the "Snake River" in Idaho.

Improving Schoolgrounds

Standing water is banned from many childcare centers, but running water is permitted. At Idaho State University, a miniature Snake River flows through the campus child care. A shallow, curving concrete trough lined with river rocks carries water that children have pumped down the hill, under a bridge, and into an underground aquifer where children can send a little bucket or cup down and draw up water. At two places children can insert boards to make dams, just like on the real river. Children can float objects down the river, and can observe that water flows faster in narrow spaces. Similar intriguing water features can be seen elsewhere; also we notice that playground equipment manufacturers are beginning to add interesting water play features.

Connecting Concepts

Some of the relationships between air and water can be observed in caring for classroom fish and plant life; some can be effectively demonstrated with simple experiments.

1. Children can see evidence of air in water when they watch a covered jar of water that has been allowed to stand in the room. Rows of tiny air bubbles will appear on the sides of the jar. Point out that fish must have air to live and that water takes in air. Fish have their own way of getting the air they need from the water. Point out the safety fact that children cannot get air from the water when

they swim. They must learn how to breathe, how to let the water hold them up, and how to use their arms and legs to move along when they swim.

2. Plant dependence upon water can be seen quite well in thin-leaved plants that have gone without water for a weekend. An avocado plant droops dramatically, but recuperates within an hour or so after a good watering.

3. Air pressure (see Chapter 7, Air) can be used to empty the aquarium, to drain water from a large water play tub, or to provide outdoor water play. Make a siphon by completely filling approximately a yard (1 meter) of tubing with water, pinching the ends together to keep air from entering the tube. Place one end of the tube in the water and the other in the bucket below. The water will drain into the bucket, unless air entered the tube. Explain that air presses on the surface of the aquarium water, pushing water up the tube. Read about how liquids are moved from one place to another in *Messing Around With Water Pumps and Siphons* by Bernie Zubrowski. (See Resources.)

Family and Community Support

There are many opportunities for families to point out examples of water and water/air concepts at home: moisture condensing on mirrors and windows at bath time, steamy kitchen windows when dinner is cooking, and the "smoke" of moisture condensation that emits from clothes dryer vents in cold weather. All of these amplify the classroom experiences.

During family visits to the swimming pool or beach, children can stride through shallow water to test its weight and substance. With encouraging parents standing by, children can learn that the buoyancy principles work to support their own floating bodies.

Notify families if popular giant bubble performances and other bubble activities are offered at an area children's science center, or as part of community summer programs.

RESOURCES

AGLER, L. (1990). *Involving dissolving.* Berkeley, CA: Lawrence Hall of Science. Dissolving, evaporating, and crystal activities are found in this book. Paperback.

AGLER, L. (1990). *Liquid explorations.* Berkeley, CA: Lawrence Hall of Science. See above. Explorations of liquid properties are carefully organized for classroom use. Paperback.

BARBER, J., & WILLARD, K. (1999). *Bubble festival: Presenting bubble activities in a learning station format,* Grades K-6. Berkeley, CA: Lawrence Hall of Science. Terrific teacher's guide, explaining very clearly how and why bubbles manage to exist, and providing lots of variation for exploring and playing with them.

DEVONSHIRE, H. (1991). *Water science through art.* New York: Franklin Watts. This excellent book first defines, then demonstrates, certain properties of water as art media: Water flows, is wet, evaporates, can be absorbed, and forms crystals.

FITZSIMMONS, P., & GOLDHABER, J. (1997). Inquiry at the water table. *Science and Children, 34,* 17–19. Suggestions are offered for setting up more elaborate water table investigations.

HANN, J. (1991). *How science works* (pp. 130–143). Pleasantville, NY: Reader's Digest. This book provides good background information on the properties of water.

LEVENSON, E. (1994). *Teaching children about physical science* (pp. 146–167). TAB Books. Further experiments extend understanding of salt water buoyancy and capillarity.

WARD, A. (1992). *Water and floating.* New York: Franklin Watts. Intended for older children, this book provides fresh, practical ways of exploring the properties of water. It can provide interesting challenges for children who are ready for enrichment activities. The clear, concise scientific explanations can be helpful for beginning teachers as well.

ZUBROWSKI, B. (1981). *Messing around with water pumps and siphons.* Boston: Little Brown. This book will still be on children's library shelves; it hasn't been supplanted.

Weather

What's the science topic that everyone talks about? Weather! You have a lifetime of knowledge about it. This unit will be a natural for you as you unpack some of the familiar phenomena with children.

"Who turns on the sun? Where does the wind come from?" Early in life, children wonder and worry about the weather. Exploring simple concepts about the sun, water cycle, and moving air makes weather something interesting to observe rather than something to endure. Understanding something about the nature of lightning can soften fearfulness about storms. The following concepts are presented in this chapter:

- The sun warms the Earth.
- Changing air temperatures make the wind.
- Evaporation and condensation cause precipitation.
- Raindrops can break up sunlight.
- Weather can be measured.
- Lightning is static electricity.
- Charged electrons make sparks when they jump.

In the activities that follow, children feel the sun's effects, observe the effect of warm-air movement, observe a small cloud in a cup, simulate a rainbow, record the weather, and imitate the movement of Earth around the sun.

CONCEPT: **The sun warms the Earth.**

1. What feels warm on a sunny day?

LEARNING OBJECTIVE: To experience and appreciate the sun as a source of warmth.

? *Inquiry Activity:* Do this activity on a mild, sunny day. You will need sand, water, and two containers of equal size. For older children, provide two thermometers.

1. Encourage children to share ideas about the day's temperature. How did they decide what to wear? "What's happening to make the temperature pleasant today? Let's see if we can find out."
2. Let children spread a layer of sand in each container. Let younger children touch the sand to decide if both pans of sand feel about the same temperature. Have older children check sand temperatures with thermometers. ♣ Move outdoors with the containers. Place one container in heavy shade; place the other container in the sun. Plan to return to these places in an hour. "Do you think both pans of sand will feel the same when we come back?" Return to check predictions. Which feels warmer? What might have caused the difference? Where do the children feel warmer, in the sunlight or in the shady place where a building or tree blocks the sunlight? (The sun warms our Earth—the land, air, and everything the sunlight reaches.)
3. "What else can you find out about how the sun warms our world?" Move around the school area and have children touch the building, blacktop, and sidewalks on the sunniest side; then repeat on the shadiest side. Which side feels warmer? Feel a car parked in the sunlight, then one parked in the shade. Feel the top of a rock on the ground; turn the rock over to feel the underside. "Where are things warmest? What could cause the difference?" If it's possible to dig a hole on the school grounds, let children compare temperatures on the surface of the ground and at the bottom of the hole. Continue with other surface temperatures children may suggest. Record findings.

Group Discussion: Summarize children's findings and conclusions about how the sun affects the temperature. Expand the topic to think about which feels warmer on bare feet: the sand or the water at the beach? The deck of a pool or the water? Help children decide whether some things take up (absorb) more warmth from the sun than others.

CONCEPT: Changing air temperatures make the wind.

1. What makes air move as wind?

LEARNING OBJECTIVE: To experience the surprising effect of heat on air.

Introduction: The A. A. Milne poem "Wind on the Hill" makes a nice introduction to this activity. Encourage children to tell how they know the wind is blowing, as wind is invisible. Summarize their ideas with a comment about knowing that wind is blowing because of what it does to things we can see.

MATERIALS:

Part 1

Unshaded table lamp (regular 60 or 75 watt bulb)

Strips of crisp tissue paper about 3/4" × 4" (2cm × 10cm)

SMALL-GROUP ACTIVITY:

Part 1

1. Children can find out something about how air moves as wind by experimenting with air that is heated.
2. Let children feel the air just above the unlighted light bulb. Give each child a strip of paper to hold steadily by one end just above the bulb. What happens to the other end of the paper? (A strip of crisp tissue paper will droop down.)
3. Repeat after the bulb has been turned on long enough to become hot. (Urge caution near the hot bulb.) How does the air above the bulb feel now? What happens to the paper in the warm air?
4. Recall that when air is moving, it pushes against things. We can tell which way the air is moving because of the direction it pushes things. Encourage children to observe which direction the hot air pushes the tip of the paper strip. **Safety Precaution:** Be sure to tell children, *"We must never allow anything that could burn to touch a hot light bulb."*
5. Does the free end droop down or is it being pushed up so that it is straight or moving up somewhat? (Hot air rises.) Ask children if they have seen other evidence of hot air rising. Smoke (carbon particles mixed with heated air and gases) goes up chimneys; steam rises from a teakettle on the stove; balloonists heat the air in their balloons to make the balloon rise off the ground. (See p. 155.) Add, "When the sun heats the earth, the air above the warm parts of the earth heats up, too. All the air above warm land rises, just like the air above the bulb moves up. The rising air is part of the reason for wind."

Part 2

Clear plastic tumbler
Chilled water
Steaming water

Part 2

1. "Another thing happens to air that causes it to move as wind. We can see something like it using water instead of air."

Small, clear prescription vials
Food coloring

GETTING READY:

If water is heated in the classroom, use a safely located electric pot.

Safety Precaution: *Do not use
immersion water-heating coils directly in a cup.* They are too
hazardous to use.

2. "Let's pretend that the cold water in this
glass is cold air and the hot water I pour in
is like hot air." Add two or three drops of
food coloring to the vial of hot water to
make it distinguishable. (Children can observe the effect better when they are at eye
level with the tumbler.)

3. "How is the dyed hot water moving?"
Watch for a few minutes without disturb-
ing the tumbler. Repeat with the glass of
cold water and a few drops of dyed cold
water. What happens? Does the cold, dyed
water move slowly upward and stay
around the top in a layer, or does it mix
with all the water right away?

Comment, "Water and air get lighter when they are heated. Cold water and
cold air move under the heated water or heated air and push the hot air or hot water upward. We saw it happen with the colored water model but we can't see the
same thing happening in the invisible air outdoors. Hot air is lighter than cold air,
so cold air rushes under hot air and pushes it up. When that happens, we feel the
cold air rushing under the warm air. The air moves fast. This is wind. *Air is always
moving like this somewhere around the earth.* Warm air moves up and cooler air rushes
in under it, pushing against leaves, flags, people, *everything.*"

Encourage children to find out at home what happens when freezer doors are
opened in warm, steamy kitchens. Which way does that foggy air move?

Note: In a follow-up discussion, mention that the movement of suddenly
heated air and fast rushing cold air is the cause of thunder. When lightning streaks
through a cloud, it moves so fast that it heats air around it very quickly. The cold air
pushes under the hot air so fast that it makes the loud sound we call thunder. Let
children listen to the very small popping noise they can make by drawing their lips
over their front teeth, compressing their lips together, then pushing air out as they
would to make the sound of a *b.* A small popping noise is made by fast-moving air
from a small space. Thunder is made by huge amounts of fast-moving air.

CONCEPT: Evaporation and condensation cause precipitation.

1. How is rain formed?

LEARNING OBJECTIVE: To reassuringly affirm the continual evaporation/con-
densation water cycle.

MATERIALS:

Zip-top plastic bag
Small, clear plastic vial
  such as a film canister or

Children enjoy gathering data firsthand.

protective cap from a spray-top
  product
Tape
Cranberry juice, or water and
  food coloring

Group Experience: Ask children, "How do you think rain gets up in the air?" Responses will vary with age and experience with prior evaporation/condensation/precipitation activities (see Chapter 8). Accept all responses tentatively. "Let's make a model to see what we can find out for ourselves."

Make a demonstration kit. Place a container half-filled with juice or tinted water inside the plastic bag and seal it shut. Tape the bag to a sunny window. (See Figure 9–1.) Ask for predictions about what might happen to the liquid and air in the bag after a few days. "Let's find out." Children can observe water vapor clinging to the inside of the bag, then forming into a few drops that eventually slide down to the bottom. Ask children to draw and report what they observe. Does the bag look different on a cloudy day, or early in the day compared to noon sunshine? Are the raindrops the same color as the juice?

Leave a small amount of juice out in the room in a shallow container for a day or so, until all the moisture evaporates. Did air pick up the solid bits from the juice or just the water in the juice? Does air pick up salt water over the oceans to make salty rain? Evaporate a small amount of salted water for a few days to

FIGURE 9–1

find the answer. Recall with the group that air picks up water as vapor. Sun-warmed air in the bag picked up just the water part of the juice.

Warm air can hold more vapor than can cool air. Did the water vapor in the bag look different on a cloudy day? Outdoors this happens all the time, all over Earth. The sun warms the air and hurries the evaporation process. Air picks up bits of moisture everywhere. Vapor collects into clouds as it rises high into the sky. Droplets in the clouds collect into larger drops. Cool air temperatures high above the Earth hurry this condensation process. Eventually, the drops fall to Earth as rain. Then the evaporation and condensation cycle happens again, and again, and again.

2. How do water drops change in freezing air?

LEARNING OBJECTIVE: To enjoy facilitating reversible water changes.

MATERIALS:

Medicine dropper (narrow tips make more spherical drops)

Cookie-baking pan

Aluminum foil

Water

Freezer or below-freezing weather

SMALL-GROUP ACTIVITY:

1. "We've seen water vapor in the bag get cold and change to drops of water. What do you think might happen to the drops if they got freezing cold before they fell? Let's find out."

2. Place foil on the baking pan. Carefully squeeze out a drop of water onto the foil for each child, spacing drops so they can't touch. Carry the pan to the freezer or, on a freezing day, to a sheltered spot outdoors.

3. Return to the freezer in 10 minutes. Show the frozen drops to the children. "Is this how they looked before? What happened?" Quickly spoon a frozen drop into the palm of each child's hand. "What's happening now?" Later comment that large frozen raindrops become ice (sleet). Frozen water vapor becomes snowflakes.

CONCEPT: Raindrops can break up sunlight.

1. What makes a rainbow?

LEARNING OBJECTIVE: To delight in creating exciting rainbow effects.

Introduction: Open a discussion about rainbows and the joy of being lucky enough to see one, or even a part of one. Comment that rainbows form when sunlight happens to shine just the right way into air that holds just the right amount of water vapor after a rain. "We don't often see rainbows, but we can use a mirror and water to send back some sunlight through the water to make a bit of a rainbow."

MATERIALS:

Shallow baking pan
White cardboard
Small pocket mirror
Small pitcher of water
A sunny location

SMALL-GROUP ACTIVITY:

1. Place the mirror at a 45-degree angle at one end of the baking pan. Let children take turns holding a piece of white cardboard near a sunny tabletop or windowsill while other children take turns trying to reflect a spot of sunlight from the mirror to the cardboard.

2. When the spot of light hits the cardboard, slowly pour water into the pan to cover about 2 inches (5 cm) of the mirror. Small adjustments to the angle may be needed until the white light is broken up into the spectrum ("like a bit of rainbow") on the cardboard.

3. Verify that it is light refracted through the water that caused the light to separate into the spectrum colors. To do this, hold a hand above the submerged portion of the mirror, blocking the reflection. What happens to the spectrum reflection?

CONCEPT: Weather can be measured.

1. How does a thermometer work?

LEARNING OBJECTIVE: To take pride in recalling how temperature changes affect liquids, making thermometers understandable.

MATERIALS:

Cooking thermometer
Hot water
Ice cubes
Small container
Outdoor thermometer

LARGE-GROUP ACTIVITY:

1. Recall the experience of feeling warm in the sunshine and cool in the shade. "How else can we find out how warm the air is?" Show the thermometer. Record the level of the liquid column (the current indoor temperature). Ask for predictions about where the liquid column might move if the thermometer is taken outdoors for a while. Place the thermometer outside and compare the difference after a while.

2. Examine the cooking thermometer. Note that the numbers start with higher readings than the outdoor thermometer because food is cooked at hotter temperatures than the weather reaches.

Put the thermometer into a container of hot water. "Is the liquid going up or down?" Record the final temperature. Ask for predictions of what will occur if ice cubes are added to the water. Let children add them. Check the results. Read thermometers and record new temperatures. Make a plan to check the outdoor thermometer daily. (Thermometer must be in the shade.) Keep a record of your readings and the daily water forecast. Guide children through the thermometer creative movement found on p. 173.

2. How fast is the wind blowing?

LEARNING OBJECTIVE: To become engaged in discerning wind speed.

Group Activity: Move the group to the windows. Can children tell if the wind is blowing? How? What do they see? In a group discussion, introduce the idea that the wind, the heat of the sun, and water work together to make the weather. Winds move rain clouds and dry air.

Weather is more interesting to observe when we know many ways to describe and compare it. For generations, people have judged the wind's speed by observing its effect on things around them. The following chart is part of the Beaufort scale of wind velocity and provides visual guidelines for determining the wind's speed.

End the group discussion with the measures we take to stay safe in storms. Assure children that weather forecasters collect information very carefully so we can be warned about serious storms and find safety when necessary.

Plan to make a daily check at the windows to decide how fast the wind is moving. Record the children's description of the wind on a wind chart. Children can check the direction of the wind each day by observing the school flag or by holding

What to Look For	Description	Miles per Hour
Leaves don't move. Smoke rises straight up from chimneys.	Calm	Less than 1 mph
Light flags blow; leaves and twigs move constantly.	Gentle Breeze	8–12 mph
Large branches sway. It's hard to hold an open umbrella.	Strong Breeze	25–31 mph
Whole, large trees move. It is hard to walk against the wind.	High Wind	32–38 mph
Whole trees uprooted.	Full Gale	55–63 mph

up a wet finger to see which side is cooled by the wind. Wind is named for the direction it blows from. (A north wind pushes the flag south.)

3. How much rain falls?
LEARNING OBJECTIVE: To arouse curiosity about weather measurements.

Group Activity: Elicit children's ideas about why rain is needed. Emphasize that every living thing needs water to survive, and also that lakes, rivers, reservoirs, and underground water stores are filled by rain. Explore the reasons *why* it is important to many people to know how much rain falls. (Farm children, those living in flood areas, or those living in cities dependent upon reservoirs for water supply may have information to share about rainfall amounts.)

Tell children, "Weather forecasters use special measuring equipment to find out how much rain has fallen. We can make something like it. We can put our rain gauge outside in a safe, open place. After each rain we can check to see how much rain fell." (This will be a relative measurement. It will allow comparisons of the amount of rain collected in the jar from day to day.)

Use rubber bands to attach the ruler to the jar. Place the jar in a safe, open place where it will be undisturbed. Check the level of water in the jar as soon as possible after a rain. Empty the jar. Keep a record of the number of inches (centimeters) of rain that falls for several weeks during your rainy season.

MATERIALS:

Widemouthed glass or
 clear plastic jar
Heavy rubber bands
Small plastic ruler

CONCEPT: **Lightning is static electricity.**

Introduction: Encourage children to share what they understand about lightning. Add, "Lightning is a powerful spark of static electricity. It develops when huge quantities of water droplets and tiny particles of ice in rain clouds rub together. Every one of those droplets and ice bits has something invisible that gets active this way: *electrons.* Electrons are part of everything. The activity caused by rubbing together is called *charging* the electrons. We can't see electrons, but we can see how they make things behave."

Show the children a 2-inch square of plastic wrap, held between your thumb and forefinger. "What do you think might happen when I let go of this plastic?" Find out.

"Let's see if rubbing (friction) might make a difference in what happens to the plastic." Rub the plastic on a piece of wool or nylon fabric. Pick it up again and let go. "Look at this. I have let go, but the plastic hasn't let go this time. Friction did change some things in the plastic, things so very tiny they are invisible. They are *electrons.* Electrons are *even part of us.* Friction gets the energy of the electrons ready to move.

That builds up an electric charge called *static electricity.*" Encourage children to share their ideas about static electricity. They may mention hair flying up when a sweater is pulled off or the crackle of static when the TV screens or computer monitors go off. Allow children to apply static-cling window decals decorations, if you use them.

Give children their own pieces of plastic to try. A sample of nylon carpeting or garments that children are wearing can be good synthetic fibers to rub the plastic against. "Electrons are part of everything, but we don't notice them until they are charged enough to move. You can have fun building an electric charge to make some little things jump."

1. How can we build up an electric charge to make things move?
LEARNING OBJECTIVE: To have fun creating static electricity.

MATERIALS:

Clear, flat plastic boxes

Tissue paper

Combs (plastic or nylon)

Small pieces of cotton thread

Scraps of wool, fur, silk, or nylon

SMALL-GROUP ACTIVITY:

1. Ask children to tear up tissue paper into rice-sized shreds. Put some shreds in the boxes.
2. "Let's rub a box top with a bit of fabric very fast to see what happens to the shreds of paper." (The shreds are attracted to the top. See Figure 9–2.)
3. Gradually add these ideas: "Rubbing two things together (friction) makes invisible bits, called *electrons,* in one thing (the fabric) leave it and jump to the other thing

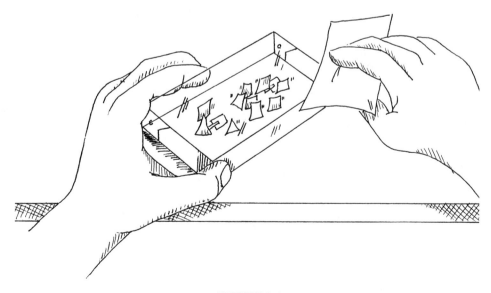

FIGURE 9–2

(the box top). The jumping is called a *static electricity charge.* The charge can pull or push other things. The charged box top pulled the paper shreds to it."

4. Suggest turning the boxes over to build a charge on the bottom of the box. What happens?

5. "Now try to build a charge on the comb with the fabric. Hold a thread near it. What happens? Did the static charge pull the thread to the comb?"

6. "Hold the charged comb near your hair. Does the static charge pull the hair toward the comb?"

CONCEPT: Charged electrons make sparks when they jump.

1. How can we make a tiny lightning flash? (This is a dry-weather activity.)

LEARNING OBJECTIVE: To ease fear of lightning by making and managing a spark of static electricity.

Introduction: "We saw how something charged with static electricity pulled other things to it. Now let's find out if we can see a spark when jumping electrons make a static electricity charge. Perhaps we can see a spark in a dark place. The spark will be like a tiny flash of lightning. We'll pretend that balloons are storm clouds full of water and tiny ice crystals. The water droplets and crystals are blown about and rubbed together in a storm cloud. The energy builds up to make a huge spark: a big charge of electricity."

MATERIALS:

Small, long balloons

Small wool or nylon rug or carpet sample

Heavy blanket

Table

GETTING READY:

Drape table with the blanket to make a very dark place.

Place rug on the floor under the table.

Blow up balloons.

SMALL-GROUP ACTIVITY:

1. Show children how to stroke the balloons on the rug to build the electric charge. Count 20 strokes with them.

2. "Now pretend my finger is another cloud or the Earth. I'll bring the charged balloon close to it. Watch! Listen! Did you see the spark jump to my finger? Now you try it."

A bar graph records weather facts for the group to recall and compare.

Group Discussion: "You can make a tiny lightning flash at home in a room that is almost dark. Scuffle your feet on a wool or nylon rug, then touch something metal. You can feel, hear, and see a small charge of electricity jump from yourself to the metal.

"A small spark like this is not dangerous, but lightning from storm clouds is very powerful when it strikes the Earth. That is why we take shelter in a building or car during an electrical storm."

Note: The experiences with electric charges will not be successful in a humid atmosphere. Save these experiences for dry weather.

Read: Lightning, by Seymour Simon.

INTEGRATING ACTIVITIES

Math Experiences

Weather Charting. For the remaining months of the school year, weather data gathering lends itself to chart-making.

For younger children: Mark off a calendar on a large sheet of newsprint. Make a yellow sun symbol in each square to remind children that the sun is shining whether we can see it or not. (Speak accurately when asking children about the day's weather: "Can we see the sun today?" not, "Has the sun come out today?") Cut squares of white tissue paper to tape over the sun on foggy days and opaque white cloud shapes to cover the sun on rainy and snowy days, according to the children's decision about the day's weather.

For older children: Record the weather on the calendar by charting the temperature, the class estimate of the wind speed, and sky conditions (clear, cloudy, rainy, sunny). At the end of the month, summarize the total number of days of each condition. A bar graph makes comparisons of the month's weather easy, providing ready answers to questions such as, "Which kind of weather did we have the most often?" and "How many more days were cloudy than sunny?" Go back to compare monthly or seasonal summaries. Children can learn to identify cloud types and graph the number of days each type was seen. They can watch the weather forecast at home or bring in the newspaper forecast and compare it with the data gathered by the class the next day, recording when the two agree.

Music (Resources in Appendix A)

1. Sing the songs that children have been singing about the weather for generations: "One Misty Moisty Morning," "Rain, Rain, Go Away," and "The North Wind Doth Blow."
2. Sing "The Eency Weency Spider," remembering to change "dried up all the rain" to "evaporated the rain." Check the rain spouts around your building after a rain.
3. Play "Air Cycle Swing" from the Banana Slug String Band cassette, *Adventures on the Air Cycle.*
4. Hang a melodic wind chime near or in your classroom on a breezy day. Let the weather provide the music.
5. Expand the lyrics for "It's Raining, It's Pouring" with Kin Eagle's book by that name.

Literature Links

BRANLEY, FRANKLYN. (1999). *Flash, crash, rumble and roll.* New York: Thomas Y. Crowell. Clear information about thunderstorms helps reassure fearful children. Paperback.
BRANLEY, FRANKLYN. (1990). *Tornado alert.* New York: Harper & Row. The nature and incredible power of tornadoes will intrigue children. The safety tips will reassure them. Paperback.

BRANLEY, FRANKLYN. (1997). *Down comes the rain.* New York: HarperCollins. How big is a droplet? Find out in this freshly illustrated classic, with its approachable presentation of the water cycle.

BREEN, M., & FRIESTAD, K. (2000). *The kid's book of weather forecasting: Build a weather station, 'read the sky', and make predictions.* Charlotte, VT: Williamson. The accurate information, lively writing, clear activity directions, and attractive format are sure to appeal to capable readers.

CALHOUN, MARY. (1997). *Flood.* New York: Morrow. A family deals with powerful flood-waters that engulf their home.

CASEY, DENISE. (1995). *Weather everywhere.* New York: Macmillan. Appealing photographs of children experiencing weather conditions and making simple discoveries will communicate well to preschoolers.

EAGLE, KIN. (1994). *It's raining, it's pouring.* Boston: Whispering Coyote. This version of the traditional song goes on to show what happens to the old man in all kinds of weather.

FARNDON, JOHN. (1998). *Weather.* New York: Dorling Kindersley. The brief, well-chosen information in this beautiful book includes simple cloud form identification and easy activities. Paperback.

HAAS, JESSE. (2000). *Hurry!* New York: Greenwillow. Subtle weather changes foretell a damaging rain. The rhythm of both the prose and illustrations capture an urgent race to save the hay crop on Gramp's farm.

HARSHMAN, MARC. (1995). *The storm.* New York: Dutton. A storm-loving boy, who uses a wheelchair, fearlessly rescues the farm horses from the path of a tornado.

HENDERSON, KATHY. (1999). *The storm.* Cambridge, MA: Candlewick. A boy feels exhilarated by the strong ocean wind, until it becomes a raging storm that threatens his home.

HESSE, KAREN. (1999). *Come on, rain!* New York: Scholastic. Young listeners will delight in a lyrical text and exuberant watercolors of city children reveling in a long awaited rain.

HISCOCK, BRUCE. (1993). *The big storm.* New York: Atheneum. Meteorology concepts are skillfully embedded in context with this fascinating story of one storm as it slowly sweeps from the West Coast to the East Coast. This mind-stretcher is beautifully illustrated by the author.

HOWELL, WILL. (1999). *I call it sky.* New York: Walker. Young listeners will identify with the engagingly portrayed children who are putting together their emerging ideas about weather. End notes provide clarification for those seeking answers.

KURTZ, JANE. (2000). *River friendly, river wild.* New York: Simon & Schuster. A series of engrossing poems capture the anxiety, losses, and rebuilding experienced by an actual family during the 1997 Grand Forks, ND flood.

LAUBER, PATRICIA. (1996). *Hurricanes: Earth's mightiest storms.* New York: Scholastic. With excellent photographs and an informative text for older children, this is an important book for children living in hurricane-prone areas.

LESSER, CAROLYN. (1997). *Storm on the desert.* San Diego, CA: Harcourt Brace. This satisfying, lyrical book describes a storm and its effect upon desert plant and animal life.

LOCKER, THOMAS. (1997). *Water dance.* San Diego, CA: Harcourt Brace. Placid illustrations and the "voice" of the water convey the water cycle.

LOCKER, THOMAS. (2000). *Cloud dance.* San Diego, CA: Harcourt. Paintings shimmer and glow to match the poetic images portraying various cloud formations. Scientific information on cloud types is provided on endpages. NSTA* Outstanding Science Trade Book.

LLEWELLYN, CLAIRE. (1997). *Wild, wet, and windy.* Cambridge, MA: Candlewick. This well-written book contains factual bits about weather extremes and how they affect people. Good illustrations add to making this a book that independent readers will enjoy browsing.

MARTIN, JACQUELINE. (1998). *Snowflake Bentley.* Boston: Houghton Mifflin. Read about this self-taught man who dedicated his life to studying snow crystals. He invented a way to photograph single flakes, to share their beauty with all of us. NSTA* Outstanding Trade Book; Caldecott award-winning woodcut illustrations.

*National Science Teachers Association

MILLER, WILLIAM. (1997). *A house by the river*. New York: Lee & Low Books. Belinda's house is threatened by flooding during a terrible storm. Her mother lends courage to help her cope with the torrents of rain.

PEARSON, SUSAN. (1998). *Silver morning*. San Diego, CA: Harcourt Brace. A mother and child watch for deer on a quiet walk through the woods completely transformed by a silvery fog.

PFEFFER, WENDY. (2001). *The big flood*. Brookfield, CT: Millbrook Press. The damaging power of a serious midwestern flood is captured in this true story for independent readers. End notes explain how man-made changes cause flooding after heavy rains.

POLLACO, PATRICIA. (1990). *Thunder cake*. New York: Philomel Books. A wise grandmother dispels a child's fear of thunder as they bake together before a storm breaks. Appealingly illustrated.

SAUNDERS-SMITH, GAIL. (1998). *Rain*. Manketo, MN: Capstone. The clear information in this small book is focused only on the rain cycle. Easy reading for beginners.

SIMON, NORMA. (1997). *Wet world*. Cambridge, MA: Candlewick. Wet-looking watercolors update this classic for preschoolers. Alliterations and simple text help beginners read it. Paperback.

SIMON, SEYMOUR. (1997). *Lightning*. New York: Morrow. Clear text and spectacular photographs will help children acquire knowledge about this fearsome and beautiful phenomenon.

SINGER, MARILYN. (2000). *On the same day in March: A tour of the world's weather*. New York: HarperCollins. Perspective altering, child-level information on climates and geography is presented in charming prose and warm illustrations. End notes explain the how and why of changing seasonal weather patterns.

Poems (Resources in Appendix A)

From A. A. Milne's *Now We Are Six*, "Wind on the Hill" reveals a child's problem-solving logic about where the wind blows, and the unsolved question of where the wind comes from.

From Robert Louis Stevenson's *A Child's Garden of Verses:*

"The Wind," in which another child tries to understand the wind
"Rain," four classic lines of verse.

Lee Bennett Hopkins has compiled readable, likeable poems in his book, *Weather.*

Dorothy Kennedy has collected breezily illustrated poems about the wind in *Make Things Fly.*

Jane Yolen has compiled poems appealing to a wide range of tastes in *Weather Report.*

From *Sing a Song of Popcorn,* compiled by DeRegniers et al., read "Dragon Smoke" and "Wind Song" by Lillian Moore.

"Snowflakes" by David McCord, is in Lee Bennett Hopkins's latest poetry collection, *Spectacular Science.* (Read it before heading outdoors with magnifiers in hand during a gentle snowfall.)

Art Activities

Weather Mobile. Let children help you create weather symbols to hang in your classroom. Cut out pairs of cloud shapes from newsprint. Staple them together over a wire coat hanger. Let children stuff them with shredded paper or polyester fiber to create a soft sculpture appearance. Place ends of plastic silver tinsel on strips of tape. Fold the tape lengthwise over the bottom of a white wire coat hanger to simulate rain. Let children crayon spectrum colors on a cardboard rainbow arch. Add a yellow construction paper sun to the mobile.

Fog Pictures. Let children draw outdoor scenes on light blue paper. Attach a sheet of white tissue paper of matching size to the top edge to give the effect of fog. The "fog" can be lifted by folding back the tissue paper.

Rain Painting. See what changes will be created by holding children's finger paintings outdoors in a light rain for a few seconds.

Sidewalk Painting. Give children wide brushes and cans of water to paint huge designs on the sidewalk on a cloudy day. Ask for predictions about what will happen to the designs when the sun comes out or a warm wind blows over them.

Good directions are given for making sun prints in *Good Earth Art* by Mary Ann Kohl and Carolyn Gainer.

Creative Movement

Thermometers. "Find a space where you can stand without touching anyone. Pretend that you are a special liquid that gets bigger when it is warm and smaller when it is cool. Now you are going into a long, skinny tube with a round space at the bottom. Are you standing straight up with stomachs pulled in tight so that you fit into the thermometer tube? I'll tell you when the sun is warming the air around you. When you get warm and grow bigger, you can only go up in your skinny tube. When you shrink and get smaller in cold air, you can only sink straight down.

"Now the sun is shining in a clear blue sky. It is lunchtime. The air is getting hotter and hotter. You have to get bigger and bigger because the air is so warm. Oh! Your fingertips have reached all the way up to 40 degrees C on the number marks. I'll pretend to carry you indoors where it is cooler. The sun isn't shining inside. Ah, it feels cooler here. What will happen inside the tube when you are cooler? There you go shrinking down a bit. It must be about 25 degrees C in here. Now I'll take you outdoors again. It's getting warmer. But wait, a big cloud comes between me and the sun. I can't see the sun now. What happens to you? Do you get bigger or smaller? I see some liquid columns starting to shrink down when the sunlight is blocked and the air feels a bit cooler. Now it is night; the sun isn't shining on our part of the Earth. You are shrinking down more and more because it's cooler than it was in the daytime sunlight. Let's see what happens when there is a snowstorm. Look, there are icicles and snowmen. Now I see liquids shrinking down. Let the liquid slide all the way down to the floor. Now become yourselves again."

Creative Thinking

Print as a story, or tape-record children's responses to stimulus phrases such as "If I could drift on the wind like a bird . . . ," "If I were a raindrop . . . ," "If I could sail away on a cloud . . . " Read the completed story or play the finished tape for the whole class to enjoy. Make a booklet of the ideas evoked by the children, including illustrations by each idea's author.

Food Experiences

For centuries, warm air has been used to preserve fruits, vegetables, fish, meat, and herbs. Children enjoy preparing dried apple rings. Let them wash several apples. Then you core the apples and slice them crosswise into 1/4-inch (0.6 cm) rings. Children then drop the apple rings into a bowl of water to which 2 tablespoons of lemon juice have been added. Pat rings dry. String them on a long, clean dowel or on a heavy cord. Tie the cord or place the dowel across a warm corner of the classroom, away from direct sunlight, to dry for several days. Cover loosely with cheesecloth to discourage insects. Apples will be dry to the touch, darker in color, and slightly rubbery. Rinse slices, dry, and eat. Read about apple and berry drying during pioneer days in *The Little House Cookbook,* by Barbara Walker.

Experiment with drying small clusters of grapes on a towel-covered tray placed in the sun. Turn grapes each day. Cut fresh corn from the cob. Dry in the same way. Feed the dried corn to the birds, or soak it overnight, simmer for 15 minutes, and serve. Bring samples of dried legumes, dried fruits, dried vegetables, and dried beef, if possible.

On a really hot, sunny day, consider making herbal sun tea or constructing a simple solar cooker to toast marshmallows. (See Kenda & Williams, Resources.)

Field Trips

♣ After a rain stops, tour the school neighborhood to examine the effects of wind and rain on the environment. Where has water collected in a puddle? Why there? Is a wooden sandbox seat as wet as a blacktop area? Is the ground under the playground swings as dry as a graveled area? Have leaves been blown down (small branches, large branches)? What might these signs indicate about the speed of the wind? Was there enough rain to flood the gutters or to wash earthworms out of their tunnels?

PROMOTING CONCEPT CONNECTIONS

Maintaining Concepts

1. Expand the weather chart with questions about adaptations children may have made to cope with the day's weather. It can become part of the day's routine to inquire about how the weather affected their lives positively or negatively.

2. If a small dehumidifier is available, examine it on a humid day with the children. See how this adaptation to change a room's climate uses the process of condensing water vapor to water. Unless your dehumidifier poses a special safety hazard, let the children feel the condenser coil before turning on the unit.

Switch on the unit and let children hold a piece of paper next to the condenser, then in front of the blower screen, to discover which way air is being moved. Watch the changes gradually taking place on the condenser coils. Does the coil feel the same after the unit has run for a while as it did before? Let children help empty the water from the collection pan. Help them relate this process to the cloud in a jar and to clouds in the cold atmosphere.

Improving Schoolgrounds

To teach water conservation and to reduce rain run-off, install a rain barrel under a downspout of your building. The captured water can be used to irrigate school gardens and lawn. Modern barrels have spigots near the bottom for attaching a hose, and run-off valves at the top to prevent overflow in unwanted areas; they are covered to prevent insects, larger animals, and debris from getting in. Garden centers sell them; cooperative extension agents can provide advice, as can the Internet.

To show which way the wind is blowing, install a windsock. Windsocks are used by air traffic controllers, meteorologists, and NASA engineers helping the space shuttle land. The Internet (e.g., NASA's site) provides directions for making windsocks as well as the names of various vendors.

Connecting Concepts

1. A miniature water cycle can be observed in a classroom terrarium. At times condensation will be visible inside the glass enclosure. At other times it will appear to be dry. The plants survive without additional watering for many weeks. Why?

2. Recall the experiences with water changing forms; with air taking up water; with the effects of moving air; with water pushing up objects that are less heavy than water; and with air supporting gliders.

3. Note that the water cycle (the evaporation/condensation process) is one of nature's ways of keeping our limited supply of water clean.

Family and Community Support

Encourage families to show children the cold, wet air that rolls down from an open freezer door on a humid day, or the direction hot steam takes when it escapes from pots of simmering food or from a teakettle. Suggest that families owning Swedish holiday candle chimes examine the before-and-after effects of heating the air below the figures with the small candle flames. Note how the blades of the candelabra are bent to catch the rush of hot air and begin to move. Tell families what nearby homes or businesses have visible solar energy panels on their rooftops. You could mention that the sun's energy can be used to heat water in those homes. Mention the location of local windmills used to generate electricity.

An urban TV meteorologist may be available to present a forecasting program for your classroom. Alert families to small weather stations in your area that might encourage visits.

RESOURCES

FRANKLIN INSTITUTE SCIENCE MUSEUM. (1995) *Ben Franklin book of easy & incredible experiments.* New York: John Wiley. Building on Ben Franklin's fascination with weather, the chapter on exploring the weather offers ideas to extend weather activities. It includes directions for making a hygrometer using one's own hair. (Bad hair days put to good use!)

FRANKLIN, S. (1995). *Power up!* Glenview, IL: Goodyear. This book describes one of the easiest ways to make solar cookers.

KAHL, J. (1998). *National Audubon Society first field guide to the weather.* New York: Scholastic. This is a highly recommended resource.

KENDA, M., & WILLIAMS, P. (1990). *Cooking wizardry for kids.* Hauppauge, NY: Barron's. Simple solar cooking is detailed.

LEVENSON, E. (1994). *Teaching children about science.* Blue Ridge Summit, PA: Tab Books. Good ideas are offered for explaining the water cycle, as well as an excellent analogy experience for understanding the expansion of warm air.

MANDELL, M. (1990). *Simple weather experiments with everyday materials.* New York: Sterling Publishing. Readable background information on weather phenomena is presented with additional experiments to illustrate more advanced concepts.

McVEY, V. (1991). *Weatherwisdom.* San Francisco: Sierra Club Books. General background information on weather is given, plus activity suggestions that could be adapted for Early Childhood classrooms.

PERRY, P. (1993). *Rainy, windy, snowy, sunny days: Linking fiction to nonfiction.* Englewood, CO: Teacher Ideas. This is a sensible approach to multidisciplinary integration, though many of the selected books may be out of print.

VANROSE, S. (1994). *Earth.* London: Dorling Kindersley. This excellent Eyewitness Series book includes basic background information on weather.

Rocks and Minerals

Are you wearing a rock or mineral on your hand? Are you writing with rocks? The Earth is an enormous rock. Rocks are literally the foundation for our lives. You already know a lot about rocks. Now learn how to introduce basic rock knowledge to children.

". . . Oooooh! This one has shiny speckles! Look! This one is all little rocks joined into one. These three are a family. This one has a stripe all around and around." Children relish sifting through piles of rocks to find favorites. They are awed to hear that our Earth is a giant ball of rock and that rocks can be millions of years old. Learning about the importance of rocks seems to promote feelings of security in youngsters, just as the Rock of Gibraltar symbolizes trust and stability to some adults. Activities in this chapter explore the following concepts:

- There are many kinds of rocks.
- Rocks slowly change by wearing away.
- Crumbled rocks and dead plants make soil.
- Old plants and animals left prints in rocks.
- Minerals form crystals.

An unstructured experience in washing and examining ordinary highway gravel is suggested as a beginning activity. This is followed by classifying and hardness testing. Basic information is given about rock formation. Other suggested experiences include grinding soft rocks, breaking rocks open to compare the fresh surfaces with the worn exteriors, pulverizing rock to compare it with complete soil, and forming crystals.

Introduction. Tuck a small rock into your hand, then comment quietly, "I have something quite small but very old in my hand. It is so old that it might have been here long before any people lived on Earth or even before the dinosaurs were alive. Can you guess what it could be?" Slowly open your hand to reveal the humble, but now significant, rock.

CONCEPT: There are many kinds of rocks.

1. *How do rocks look when dry and wet?*

LEARNING OBJECTIVE: To enjoy examining rocks.

MATERIALS:

Bucketful of #67 washed gravel
  (builder's supply warehouse)*

Dishpans, water

Few drops of detergent

Old, small brushes

Magnifiers

Trays for clean rocks

Cleanup sponge

Smocks for children

GETTING READY:

Fill dishpans one-quarter full
  with water.

SMALL-GROUP ACTIVITY:

1. Let children wash and scrub some of the rocks to discover whether or not they look the same wet or dry.
2. Have children choose and get acquainted with the shape, texture, and color of a favorite rock.
3. After they have examined it carefully with the magnifier, have children write, draw, or dictate a description of their favorite rock. Leave the gravel out for children's independent examination during center times.

Note: Children seem to be drawn to a material that is available in quantity for them to explore freely. A heaping dishpan of common rocks will have more appeal than a box of neatly labeled special rocks.

2. *Can we find rocks that are alike in some ways?*

LEARNING OBJECTIVE: To appreciate and organize rocks by characteristics.

? *Inquiry Activity:* Suggest sorting rocks that are alike in some way into the same container. Classifying decisions are easy for many children to make (by color, size, shape, texture). If children can't get started on their own, offer a suggestion like, "The flat rocks could go here; rocks that aren't flat could go there. How would you like to group the ones that seem to be alike?" Record and discuss the categories that children devise.

MATERIALS:

Bucketful of #67 washed gravel*

Sorting containers (egg cartons,
  margarine tubs, divided plastic
  snack trays, old muffin tins)

---

*#67 washed gravel consists of varied rocks (from old riverbeds) that range from almond to egg size. For school use, some building suppliers might give you a bucketful without charge. It is usually sold by the ton.

3. Which rocks are hard? Which are soft?

LEARNING OBJECTIVE: To introduce a satisfying way to group rocks.

MATERIALS:

#67 washed gravel

Blackboard chalk (pressed gypsum)

Pumice (from the drugstore)

Pennies

Three trays or boxes

GETTING READY:

Make two labels: *Soft* and *Hard*.

Place trays next to each other.

Put *Soft* and *Hard* labels in first and third boxes; leave middle box unlabeled.

SMALL-GROUP ACTIVITY:

1. "Some rocks are soft enough for a fingernail to scratch them. Rocks just a bit harder can't be scratched that way, but a penny edge will scratch them."
2. Let children experiment with scratch tests. Suggest sorting rocks by degree of hardness: "Put rocks scratched by your fingernail into the tray marked *Soft*; put rocks scratched only by the penny into the unmarked tray; put rocks that can't be scratched by a penny into the tray marked *Hard*."

If children find it hard to form three classes of rocks, simplify the experience to form two classifications of hardness: hard rocks, not scratched by a penny; and softer rocks, scratched by a penny. Make a separate activity to find soft rocks, scratched by a fingernail; and harder rocks, not scratched by a fingernail. Perhaps a teacher is wearing the hardest rock of all on her finger—a diamond (crystallized pure carbon). Read *Rocks in His Head*, by Carol Hurst.

ROCK FORMATION

As children engage in the suggested experiences, they can be given bits of simple information about the mineral content of rocks and about the way rocks were (and are) formed.

Mineral Content

When children question the specks and streaks of color they see as they sort rocks, tell them that most rocks are mixtures of many kinds of material. The materials are called *minerals*. There are about 2,000 different minerals, but only about 20 minerals are abundant. Different mixtures of minerals make different kinds of rocks. (You might want to recall baking experiences with children. Talk about how sometimes the same materials are put together in different ways to make different things to eat. Cornbread and cookies are almost alike in ingredients.) Sometimes the mineral mixtures are easy to see as specks, sparkles, and stripes. Rocks may contain many different combinations of minerals. Small amounts of minerals are also important for healthy growth of plants, animals, and humans.

Three Types of Rock Formation

Igneous. Millions of years ago, some rocks were mixtures that melted deep inside the Earth. When they cooled, they formed very hard rocks. As worn-down pebbles, they are usually somewhat ball-shaped.

Sedimentary. Some rocks were formed in layers or parts, like a sandwich. Layers of sand, clay, and gravel were pressed together very hard at the bottom of old lakes, rivers, and oceans. Sometimes animal shells were mixed into the rock. It takes many thousands of years of very hard pressure to form rocks this way. Some sedimentary rocks have stripes of color or line marks in them. Some feel sandy. Some have tiny rocks stuck together. They were all made under pressure. Bits may break off in thin layers. As worn-down pebbles, they are shaped like flat discs.

Metamorphic. Sometimes rocks that were already formed by pressure or by the cooling of melted mixtures were changed again by more heat and pressure, changing the rocks into still different types. Bits break away as slabs. As worn-down pebbles, they also are flat, disk-like shapes.

Try to find out something about the rocks in your area, both the visible outcroppings and the rocks beneath the soil. Were rocks heaved up into mountains and hills in your area millions of years ago? Did ancient rivers wear away rocks and carve out valleys? Mention this to the children when a suitable time arises.

CONCEPT: **Rocks slowly change by wearing away.**

1. ♣ How can we wear away bits of rock?

LEARNING OBJECTIVE: To enjoy the power to change rocks.

MATERIALS:

Pieces of soft, crumbly rock
  (shale, soft sandstone)

Coffee cans with lids

Wrapped hard candy (one for
  each child)

Hammer

Bowl of replenishable water

GETTING READY:

1. Crack each wrapped candy
   with a *light* hammer tap.

SMALL-GROUP ACTIVITY:

1. Put several soft rocks in each can. Ask children to feel the rocks. Cover the cans tightly. Let children hold them tightly and shake them as long and as hard as they can. Open cans. Ask, "Has anything changed? Is there dusty stuff at the bottom?"

2. If this must be an indoor activity, try briskly rubbing two crumbly rocks together over a piece of white paper.

3. Have children wash their hands. Let each child un-wrap a cracked candy. "Pretend this is a broken rock. Keep one broken bit in the wrapper. Swish another bit in the bowl of water for several minutes. "What

do you think will happen in the water?"
Compare the edges of the water-tumbled
bit with the edges of the dry bit. "It takes
much, much longer for moving water to
smooth edges of real rocks." Eat results.

Group Discussion: Talk about the results of the rock-shaking activity in terms of wearing away pieces of rock. Talk of how pieces of rock break from large rocks. Over hundreds of years, the surfaces of the rocks are worn by wind or water. Encourage children who have visited natural beaches to recall whether they found smooth pebbles or jagged rocks on the sand. Discuss how waves or running streams tumble the rocks against each other and smooth them, and how bits are slowly, slowly rubbed off. If there are nearby rock formations with which children are familiar, speak of how they were slowly changed and worn by winds or running streams of water.

2. How can we draw with rocks?

LEARNING OBJECTIVE: To enjoy the results of rocks wearing away.

Group Activity: If there is a safe sidewalk area where this activity can be performed, give children assorted soft rocks to use for outdoor sidewalk art. Mention that cave dwellers made pictures on rock walls with soft rocks of different colors.

Later, show the children two other rocks we use for writing: pencil "lead" (graphite) and blackboard chalk (pressed gypsum). They make marks because they are so soft that worn-away bits are left as the drawing or writing we see.

Does your schoolroom have an old-fashioned slate blackboard to draw on? (Slate is a metamorphic rock.) Perhaps you can buy an inexpensive one at the variety store. Slabs of slate can sometimes be found in salvage stores after wrecking crews have taken off old slate roofs. (They are fine to use under flowerpots on the windowsill after the writing experience is over.)

3. How can we tell that rocks have changed?

LEARNING OBJECTIVE: To be fascinated by and wonder at the differences between the inside and weathered outside of rocks.

MATERIALS:

Rocks (ball-shapes are hard to crack; avoid them)

Hammer

Old jeans fabric (precaution against flying rock chips)

Safety goggles

Magnifiers

Sidewalk or hard surface

SMALL-GROUP ACTIVITY:

1. **Safety Precaution:** All children must wear safety goggles. Place a rock on the sidewalk. Cover with two thicknesses of the fabric. Strike it hard with the hammer. (Children experienced with hammers can do this successfully. A two-handed grip may help.) Very hard, round (*igneous*) rocks may not split well. Other rocks will split with one hammer blow.

2. Examine the inside; compare it with the outside appearance.

Note: This is a very exciting activity that may lead to "rock fever." Children will be curious to discover what is inside a rock: the glint of mica flakes, a streak of mineral, a sleek surface, a glittering bit of quartz crystal. Engage children's imagination by stating that the worn outside surface of the rock was once the same color and texture as the inside. Ask: "What might have happened to change the outside of these rocks?"

If there is access to a rock-tumbling machine and appropriate school permission, the class can embark on an intriguing 6-week rock-polishing project. This will help them understand how slowly rocks change. Each stone will be transformed into a smooth, gleaming gem, perhaps one for each child to have. The machine can be placed in a covered, inexpensive foam picnic cooler to muffle the noise. Children can appreciate the changes in appearance every 2 weeks when the grit size is changed. (See Resources for information on purchasing a machine by mail.)

CONCEPT: Crumbled rocks and dead plants make soil.

1. What happens when we pound soft rocks?

LEARNING OBJECTIVE: To take satisfaction in converting rocks to part of soil.

MATERIALS:

Pieces of crumbly rock (shale, soft sandstone, etc.)

Discardable jeans

Hammers

Newspapers

Sieve

Empty can

SMALL-GROUP ACTIVITY:

1. Put one jeans leg inside the other. Put a few rocks in the double jeans leg and place on sidewalk. Let children take turns pounding rocks, checking results often.
2. Spread newspaper on the ground. Fit sieve over the can. Shake contents of bags into sieve, catching spills on newspaper.
3. Keep pulverizing until children are tired.
4. Examine the powdered rock in the can and save for the next experience.

2. What does soil look like?

LEARNING OBJECTIVE: To enjoy exploring what makes up fertile soil.

MATERIALS:

Trowel

Container

Newspapers

Topsoil

Sieve, sticks

Magnifying glasses

SMALL-GROUP ACTIVITY:

1. Let children scoop up a trowelful of soil from a permitted digging area to bring indoors.
2. Spread the soil on newspapers; examine with a magnifying glass. Compare with rock pulverized by children.
3. Put soil through sieve. Good topsoil contains bits of leaves, twigs, roots, and

Container of pulverized rock
    from previous experience
2 paper cups
Water

worms. Some of this matter will be left in the sieve.

4. Put some sifted soil and powdered rock in separate cups. Stir a bit of water into each. Compare.

Note: Clay is like moist powdered rock. It must have lots of old vegetable and animal matter (and perhaps sand) added to it to make good soil for growing things.

CONCEPT: Old plants and animals left prints in rocks.

Recall splitting rocks open to find unexpected color, sparkle, and texture inside. Add that prints of animals, shells, and plants that lived on Earth millions of years before people did can be found pressed between layers of rocks. These rocks are called *fossils*. (Perhaps there are some fossils in the bucket of highway gravel that the children have been using.)

Children can have fun making prints of their hands, shells, or leaves using the kind of powdered stone that became clay. They can make prints similar to fossils, though they won't be as old or as hard as fossils, of course.

1. How can we make a "fossil" print?
LEARNING OBJECTIVE: To take pride in leaving one's mark like a mold fossil.

Let children use small rolling pins to roll out moist clay slabs about 1/4 inch (1 cm) thick. Show them how to press a leaf, shell, or their hand firmly into the clay. It may take several tries to get a clear print. "Erase" unsatisfactory leaf prints by rubbing the clay with water and lightly rerolling. Cut the slab into a plaque shape by using an empty coffee can as a cutter. Poke a hole through the top of the slab for a hanging loop of string. Scratch the child's initials in the clay. Allow several drying days. Mention that fossils took even longer to form. Teacher may shellac the dried clay to preserve it, if desired.

Read: Stone Girl, Bone Girl, by Lawrence Anholt.

CONCEPT: Minerals form crystals.

1. How do mineral crystals form?
LEARNING OBJECTIVE: To be intrigued by crystal formation.

Introduction: (Do this after children understand evaporation.) Try to bring in a geode or other intriguing crystal formations, perhaps borrowed from a rock collector, to share with the children. Include rocks the class broke open to reveal glittering bits of mica, or tiny, sparkling quartz crystals, or gemstone jewelry. Tell the children that when minerals dissolve in water, which then evaporates, or when minerals melt and cool slowly, they form such *crystals*. Each type of mineral forms into its own special crystal pattern. "Let's see what will happen if we dissolve some ordinary minerals in hot water and leave the solutions out to evaporate for a few days."

(Be sure to try the following activities at home, to see whether adjustments will be needed for your climate, and to determine the approximate length of time required for crystals to form.)

Point out that solutions need to be undisturbed for crystals to slowly form, so this needs to be a "hands-off" observation for several days.

MATERIALS:

Measuring cup and spoon

1/4 cup (60 ml) *steaming* hot water (bring to class in a thermos jug)

1 tablespoon (15 ml) plain salt (not light salt)

8″ (20 cm) aluminum foil piepan

LARGE-GROUP OBSERVATION:

Let children help measure salt and carefully stir into *steaming* water until salt dissolves. Pour solution into piepan. Place pan in a location where the pan can be undisturbed. Have children make *Hands Off! Science in Progress* signs to indicate a designated science zone. Check the next day for changes. Let children use the magnifier to examine the residue that formed as water *slowly* evaporated. Already, a few beautiful salt crystal cubes may have formed. More should continue to form for another day or so.

2. Do all crystals look alike?

LEARNING OBJECTIVE: To be amazed by unique differences in crystal formations.

Introduction. Ask students, "Do you think other minerals will form crystals just like the salt crystal cubes?" (This will be another *"hands-off"* experiment at first.) Explain that when scientists experiment and compare different samples in the laboratory, they must be careful to use separate equipment for each mixture so the results will be accurate.

MATERIALS:

Small containers of:

Epsom Salts*

Table salt

Borax**

Measuring spoons

3 plastic spoons

Three small cups

6 clear plastic yogurt cup lids

Indelible marker

? WHOLE GROUP INQUIRY

1. Put 2 T *steaming* water in each of 3 cups.
2. To each cup, stir in one of these: 1/2 t salt; 1/2 t Epsom salts; 1/2 t Borax.
3. Carefully spoon each solution into corresponding marked plastic lid.
4. Leave tray of solutions undisturbed for 2 days. When crystals have formed, cover with clean lids. Tape edges together (see Figure 10–1).

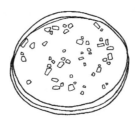

FIGURE 10–1

Clear tape
Tray or cookie sheet
Waxed paper
Strong magnifier; 40X micro-
   scope

GETTING READY:

1. Label 1 lid for each mineral.
2. Line tray with waxed paper.
3. Put marked lids on tray.

5. Examine with magnifier, and, if possible
   a 40X microscope. Compare results! If
   possible, repeat this experience to
   confirm the unique shape of each
   mineral's crystals.

3. *How do stalagmites and stalactites form in caves?*

LEARNING OBJECTIVE: To delight in watching a miniature crystal pillar form.

MATERIALS:

18-inch (45 cm) cotton or wool
   yarn or heavy string
2 small keys
Sheet of dark colored paper
Paper towels
Tray or cookie sheet
2 pint jars
2 cups (500 ml) steaming hot
   water
¼ cup (60 ml) Epsom salts
Magnifier

WHOLE-GROUP OBSERVATION:

Learn what children may know about how
icicles form from dripping, freezing water. If
available, read aloud *Caves*, by Diane Siebert,
or show reference illustrations of stalag-
mites/stalactite formations. Discuss how
mineral solutions can drip into underground
limestone caves for millions of years to form
these crystal columns. "Perhaps we can watch
something like this happening in a much
faster way." Set up observation as shown in
Figure 10–2. Leave it undisturbed where it
can be watched for several days by the children. Marvel at the results!

---

*Available at drug stores
**Available at supermarkets, shelved with laundry aids; also sold as "washing
soda" **Warning:** *Neither should be ingested.*

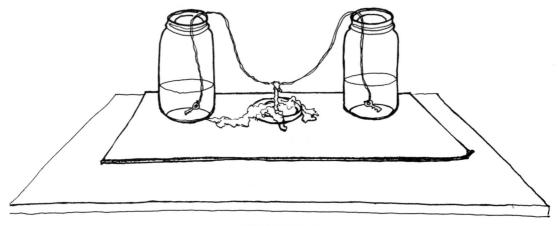

FIGURE 10–2

GETTING READY:

1. Tie keys to each end of string.
2. Put colored paper over 2 layers of paper towels on tray.
3. Pour 1 cup of steaming water into each jar.
4. Stir 2 T Epsom salts into jar, adding as much more as can be dissolved into the water. Place on ends of colored paper.
5. Soak string in one jar briefly. Then put one key in each jar, letting string curve over the paper. (See Figure 10–2). **Leave undisturbed.** Measure dripping column daily to watch crystal buildup. It takes several days to form a solid column.

Read: "Plink by Plink" from Constance Levy's book, *SPLASH! Poems of our Watery World.*

Note: To explain how ancient trees, shells, and bones turned to stone (petrified), fill a jar with a cup of hot water and as much Borax as can be dissolved in it. Twist one end of a colored pipe cleaner into a tight spiral. Twist the other end around a pencil, adjusting the length so the spiral doesn't touch the bottom of the jar when the pencil is suspended across the jar. (See Figure 10–3.) Allow crystals to build for several weeks. Remove and let the rock-hard

FIGURE 10–3

spiral air dry. Tiny holes in dead trees and animal shells and bones filled with mineral solutions are turned into stone this same way.

INTEGRATING ACTIVITIES

Math Experiences

Counting. The Grab Bag Game may be played with stones. Place a container of stones in the center of a circle of children. Let them take turns reaching in to scoop out as many stones as they can hold in two hands. Then count the results. Keep score with an abacus or a handheld calculator.

Buried Treasure. If a sandbox is available, bury a specific number of stones (or stones and shells, if you wish to include classifying) for children to hunt. A large sandbox may be "staked out" with string to form separate territories for several children to use amicably.

Counting Cans. Mark numerals from 1 to 10 (or more) on the sides of low metal cans. Line up the cans in order on a table or shelf. Place a coffee can full of gravel beside them for independent counting of appropriate quantities of stones to put in numbered cans.

Ordering. Search through the bucket of gravel to find stones of conspicuously different sizes. Place them in a paper bag. One child at a time can reach into the bag to choose a stone to order by size. Allow time for much fingering and feeling in choosing. Ask for the smallest stone found. Next ask children to compare their stones with the smallest one to find a stone just a bit larger to put next to it. Build up to the largest stone. Older children who have had experience measuring with rulers could use them for this activity. Suggest ordering rocks according to texture, from smoothest to roughest; and color, from lightest to darkest.

Weighing. Keep two coffee cans full of stones near the classroom balance for independent use by the children.

Music (References in Appendix A)

1. A familiar folk song can be easily adapted to help children remember that mountains are rock formations. Sing "The Bear Went Over the Mountain," substituting ". . . But all that he could see was the rocky part of the mountain" for ". . . But all that he could see was the other part of the mountain." You could mention that some mountains are covered with soil and growing things while other mountains are bare rock on top.

2. Hear Michael Mish sing "Center of the Earth" on his cassette, *I'm Blue.*

Literature Links

ADDY, SHARON. (1999). *Right here on this spot.* Boston: Houghton Mifflin. Thoughtful children will enjoy this gentle speculation about the geological and social history of the farm where a child's grandfather finds an Ice Age fossil, an arrowhead, and an old button. An archaeologist helps to identify the treasures.

ALIKI. (1990). *Fossils tell of long ago.* New York: HarperCollins. This book offers a cheerful presentation of fossil formation and how they inform about the ancient past. Paperback.

ANHOLT, LAWRENCE. (1999). *Stone girl, bone girl: The story of Mary Anning.* New York: Orchard. The interesting story of a determined young English girl who unearthed the rare fossil of a giant fish-lizard in the 1800s.

BANKS, KATE. (2001). *A Gift from the sea.* New York: Farrar, Straus. A lovely text follows the history of a boy's favorite rock from its ancient volcanic source to the beach where he found it.

BARTON, J., & TAYLOR, K. (1998). *The nature and science of rocks.* Milwaukee, WI: Gareth Stevens. Basic concepts of rock formation types, plus information on small plants and creatures that live on rocks are found in this reference.

BIAL, RAYMOND. (2000). *A handful of dirt.* New York: Walker. This respectful tribute to soil as an essential building block of life is comfortably presented. Meant for older children, it can be read aloud selectively to others. NSTA[*] Outstanding Science Tradebook.

BLOBAUM, CINDY. (1999). *Geology rocks!* Charlotte, VT: Williamson. Enthusiastic writing, manageable and informative activities, plus a lively layout brighten this topic and make it easily accessible to youngsters.

BOCKNEK, JONATHAN. (1999). *The science of soil.* Milwaukee: Gareth Stevens. Emphasizing our dependence on soil, this well illustrated book includes the makeup of soil, the role of earthworms, and soil-identification activities.

BRANLEY, FRANKLYN. (1994). *Earthquakes.* New York: Harper & Row. Children will be impressed by the nature and power of earthquakes. They will be reassured by learning what they can do to take care of themselves, should they experience an earthquake. Paperback.

CHRISTIAN, PEGGY. (2000). *If you find a rock.* New York: Harcourt. Children are sure to connect with the personal meaning of special rocks charmingly photographed in this Zolotow award-winning book.

COLE, JOANNA. (1988). *The magic school bus inside the Earth.* New York: Scholastic. The author and her illustrator, Bruce Degen, entertain as they present information about Earth's interior.

DEWEY, JENNIFER. (1998). *Mud matters: Stories from a mud lover.* New York: Marshall Cavendish. Intriguing tales describe the author's fascination with mud in the arid ranch home of her childhood.

DUKE, KATE. (1997). *Archaeologists dig for clues.* New York: HarperCollins. Amusing illustrations and factual text describe the field work of archaeologists as a bright ten-year-old would experience it (which means seven-year-olds will admire it). Paperback.

GALLANT, ROY. (2001). *Minerals.* New York: Cavendish. Striking color photographs and comfortably clear descriptions of minerals and their properties will have special appeal for independent reader rock hounds. Web site listings are provided.

GALLANT, ROY. (2001). *Rocks.* New York: Cavendish. An unpedantic, conversational style leads readers by the hand into the basic facts of rock formation and identification. Handsome photographs offer an almost close-enough-to-touch view. Relevant Web sites are listed.

GANS, ROMA. (1997). *Let's go rock collecting.* New York: HarperCollins. Two children explore rocks around the world to learn about their formation and simple identification. A Reading Rainbow selection.

HOOPER, MEREDITH. (1996). *The pebble in my pocket.* New York: Viking. A girl wonders where her pebble came from. The answer traces the pebble's formation over 480 million years. Vivid illustrations add power to this book for competent readers.

HURST, CAROL. (2001). *Rocks in his head.* New York: Harper. A boy's fascination with rock collecting eventually leads him from adversity to becoming a museum curator. His daughter wrote his inspiring story. NSTA[*] Outstanding Trade Book.

LIONNI, LEO. (1995). *On my beach there are many pebbles.* New York: Mulberry. Whimsical drawings of rocks are found in this reissued paperback.

LOCKER, THOMAS. (2001). *Mountain dance.* San Diego: Harcourt. Children living near mountains will be surprised to learn of different mountain formations in other parts of the world. The art is acclaimed; the geological facts are clearly explained. NSTA[*]-recommended.

McLARREN, ALICE. (1992). Illustrated by Barbara Cooney. *Roxaboxen.* New York: Puffin Paperback. Classic story about children's rock village.

MURPHY, STUART. (2000). *Dave's down-to-earth rock shop.* New York: Harper. Here's a cheerful way to pull readers into classifying concepts as Josh and Amy get excited about rock collecting.

NAYER, JUDY. (2000). *Rocks and Minerals.* Cleveland: McClanahan. Spectacular photographs one can almost touch, and diecut board pages enliven brief, basic concepts about rock formation and minerals. An excellent companion to crystal forming experiences.

PELLANT, CHRIS. (2000). *Fossils, rocks, and minerals.* New York: Kingfisher. This reference, with inviting illustrations, is written at a good level for independent readers.

PRAGER, ELLEN. (2000). *Sand.* Washington, DC: National Geographic. A lighthearted sandpiper sleuth guides this clearly focused investigation about the origins of different kinds of sand. Simple directions for making sand are included.

SIEBERT, DIANE. (2000). *Cave.* New York: Harper. A poetic text accurately describes limestone cave formation, the special creatures that live within, and the "crystal world from weeping stones" (stalactites and stalagmites).

STEELE, PHILIP. (1997). *Rocking and rolling.* Cambridge, MA: Candlewick. A clear text, well-illustrated in a nice format, informs about volcanoes, earthquakes, mountains, and rock formations.

TEJADA, SUSAN. (2001). *Dig It: How to collect rocks and minerals.* Pleasantville, NY: Readers' Digest. The activities in this book include a helpful one for understanding how freezing breaks rocks. It also lists museums and national parks in the U.S. with outstanding rock and mineral collections.

[*] National Science Teacher's Association

Poems (References in Appendix A)

Read "Plink by Plink," a poem about stalactite formation by Constance Levy, in *SPLASH! Poems of our Watery World.*

Read the profound poem "Rocks" by Florence Parry Heide, in *Spectacular Science: A Book of Poems.*

Read "Rock Tumbler" by Constance Levy, in *A Tree Place.*

Read the following poem with a box of your favorite rocks at hand.

My Rocks

Here in this box

I keep my rocks.

They came from under the ground.

Some are striped, some are plain,

Some are tiny as a grain.

My favorite is round.

—J. H.

Art Activities

Rock Sculpture. Let children create additive sculpture by joining rocks of assorted sizes using white glue. The resulting sculpture forms may be painted with tempera. Sculptures that have been coated with shellac (adult work) can be used as paperweights.

Sand Mosaics. For temporary pleasure, provide small, flat stones and small shells for children to create designs on dampened sand.

Zen Garden. Keep the connection with rocks alive during the rest of the school year by setting up a shallow tray of sand, one or two interesting rocks, and a toy rake or comb. Each day let a different child arrange satisfying sand patterns around the rock to create a peacefulness reminder.

Rock or Sand Collage. Small stones, painted if desired, can be glued in patterns onto heavy cardboard. Color sand by shaking it in a tightly covered jar with dry tempera paint. Punch nail holes in the lids to make sand shakers. Let the children paint swirls of diluted white glue on construction paper using cotton swabs, then sprinkle colored sand over the glue patterns. Surplus sand can be tipped onto a small tray and reused.

Chalk Drawings. When children use chalk as an art medium, recall that the chalk material was once a rock.

Sand Painting. Prepare four colors of sand as you did for the collages above. Give children each a clear, screw-topped container. Let them spoon successive layers of sand into the container, being careful not to disturb the container. Probe gently along the inside of the container with a toothpick to produce interesting designs. My student, Peggy Robinson, uses these layers to help children understand how the time when dinosaurs lived is determined. Add one layer each day, recording the date and color of sand. Place a small chicken bone on one layer. After 5 days ask, "Which is the oldest layer of sand? Which is the newest? How do you know?" Explain that Earth's crust is made up of layers of rock that have built up on top of each other. Scientists can tell how old dinosaur remains are by the layer of rock in which they are found.

"Found-Clay" Making. Try to locate a natural source of clay: a stream bank, a ditch, or an eroded place are often good sources. (Ask a local potter for suggestions.) Dig out some clay together with the children, if possible. Notice the texture. Are there rocks in it? Do the children have ideas about how to make it as smooth as commercially available clay? One way is to soak the clay in a bucket of water for several days, until it becomes liquid. Strain it, and allow it to settle into layers. This process takes several days, so be patient. When the clay dries somewhat, it can be worked and shaped.

Play

Introduce rocks as a play material in the indoor or outdoor sandbox. Rocks can be formed in lines to make the floor plan of a house. They can also be piled up to make furniture, and sticks or clothespins can become the people who live in the house. Lines of rocks can also outline highways for toy cars to travel through sand-table dunes and deserts. In addition, children find relaxed enjoyment using sifters to separate the rocks from the sand at cleanup time. *Roxaboxen*, by Alice McLarren, is the charming story of children who built a play town of rocks.

Creative Movement

Take a "rock walk." Children enjoy moving in a circle, interpreting movement suggestions, and following the rhythm of the teacher's drumbeats or clapping. Adult participation in the activity encourages the involvement of children. Suggest ways to move in a story form such as this: "Let's go for a rock walk. Let's pretend to be barefooted. We'll start on this gravel path. Oh! It's hard to put our feet down on the broken rocks. We'll have to move quickly and lightly to the end of the path. Step, step, step, step. There, that's better. We've come to a sandy place. Let's scuffle our feet in the sand. Scuffle, scuffle, push up little piles of sand with each step. Oh look! We've come to a wet place where we have to walk on moss-covered rocks. They are so slippery to walk on; let's move very carefully with each step. Look at that huge rock. Let's try to climb it, bending way over to hold on with our hands. Climb slowly, slowly. Now we're at the top. Let's run down the other side to the beach ahead. Run, run, run to the sandy beach. But this sand is hot from the sunshine. We can't move slowly here. Let's move quickly down to the edge of the water to cool our feet. Now let's sit down to rest."

Creative Thinking

Encourage children to bring a favorite small rock to school, or choose a special rock from the classroom supply. "Pick up your rock, feel its shape and texture. Now close your eyes and imagine that your rock has become 20 times larger than it is. . . . It's huge! It's large enough to climb and explore. Is it a steep climb? How does it feel under your feet? Your hands? Are there crevices to explore? Can you find a flat place to sit on your rock?" Continue offering sensory ways to get acquainted with the rock, then let the rock resume its usual size so the children can return from their rock climb to the classroom.

Food Experiences

Children are surprised to find that we eat small amounts of one kind of rock every day—salt. Show them some rock salt (available in grocery and hardware stores as "halite"). Mention that all the salt that is mined under the ground was once part of ancient oceans.

Another link between food and rocks is the use of grainy-surface rocks to grind seeds into meal and grain. Perhaps you can find a bag of stone-ground flour or cornmeal in a natural foods shop. (One teacher let fascinated children grind dried corn between two rocks as part of a study of Native Americans.)

Bring in a cereal box, then read aloud the minerals listed in the nutrition facts label. Calcium, potassium, sodium, zinc, iron, and copper all play a part in keeping our bodies strong and healthy. They are found in small amounts in the nutritious foods we eat.

Field Trips

✤ Walk around the school neighborhood to look for the following: rocks in their natural setting, rocks that have been cut for use in buildings, and products made from rocks and minerals. Look closely at the natural rock for signs of weathering, such as cracks or surfaces worn smooth by years of exposure to heat, cold, wind, and rain. Young children personalize familiar rocks according to the events they associate with them: our picnic rock, our sitting-on rock, our story time rock, and our where-we-found-the-turtle rock. Use the special rock names when you can.

Look for old stone steps or stone curbings that have been worn down into sloping shapes by thousands of feet treading upon them. Look for monuments, stone walls, and stone windowsills in old brick buildings, and flagstone or crushed limestone paths.

Man-made materials containing rocks and minerals are everywhere. Concrete or blacktop playground surfaces contain coarse or fine gravel bonded together with concrete or asphalt, both derived from rocks. Cement blocks, bricks, tiles, terrazzo flooring, porcelain sinks, glass, iron railings, steel slides, and fences around school playgrounds are made with rock or mineral raw materials. No school is without structures of this sort to visit. Talking about these strong, solid parts of their environment seems to contribute to children's feelings of security.

Make an ecological scavenger hunt the focus of a field activity, as Margaret Drysdale does. She takes her classes to an empty lot where they check the area for debris. They classify their collected materials into two piles: man-made materials and natural materials. She explains that only the things from nature can be left on the ground, because they will decompose and eventually become part of the soil. The class carries the man-made materials back to the school recycling/trash bin because those things won't decompose. She emphasizes that a discarded aluminum can or plastic item could still be littering the land when the children are old enough to be grandparents.

PROMOTING CONCEPT CONNECTIONS

Maintaining Concepts

Because rocks and minerals are so commonplace, the topic would become tedious if reference were made to them at every opportunity. Do mention rocks when something a bit different prompts a comment, such as, "Is Lynn wearing a very special rock in her bracelet today? Tell us about it." Bring interesting rocks to share with the children whenever you come across one. Talk about its texture, color, or whatever appeals to you. The children will respond similarly with their favorites when they know of your appreciation of rocks.

Improving Schoolgrounds

Think about developing the geologic features of the schoolgrounds. A Boston school has a huge piece of native "puddingstone." At Coombes School, head Sue Humphries has trucked in rocks and boulders from every part of Great Britain. The local boulder sits by the school's front door for the children to pat and look at every day. A large throne-shaped rock from the area associated with King Arthur is at the edge of the school field where children can climb and sit on it. A more modest project is at Washington School in Little Rock, Arkansas, where labeled basketball-sized rocks from across the state are placed on the path leading to a wildlife habitat. Such projects provide children with ongoing opportunities to learn about rocks.

Jensen and Bullard (2002) urge us to "recapture childhood" by establishing "mud centers" in our schoolyards.

Connecting Concepts

The inclusion of rocks as materials for experimentation is suggested for the topics of water and the effects of gravity. It could be pointed out in discussing the effects of magnetism that the original source of magnetic material is a rock called *lodestone* (magnetite). Magnetite is found in this country near Magnet Cove, Arkansas.

The tie between soil formation and growing things is an easy relationship to mention. Wet sand is sometimes used as a growing medium for rooting stems such as begonias or pineapple tops. The powdered rock made when children pounded soft rocks could be used in a seed-germinating experience. Compare the results with seeds growing in good topsoil containing humus and other rotted organic matter.

Discuss how thoroughly rotted natural materials improve the soil so that healthy, strong plants will grow. Ask: "Do people use some plants for food?" Talk about renewing the soil this way as one of the wonderful cycles of nature: from living plants to decomposition, from enriched soil to living plants and food again . . . and again. . . and again. Talk about saving and improving the soil with compost as one way that people help to renew our planet.

If possible, in early fall bury several nonbiodegradable materials such as a plastic spoon, a foam cup, or an aluminum can in a marked location on the schoolgrounds. Also include a paper bag and a regular plastic bag. Dig them up in late spring to see if the biodegradable and nonbiodegradable materials were affected differently in the soil. Encourage the children to make the connection between what they observed and our need to reuse and recycle man-made objects that do not decompose. Celebrate Earth Day, April 22.

Family and Community Support

Invite families to share special rocks or fossils with the class. Masking tape name labels are helpful for ensuring the safe return of borrowed rocks. Suggest that they point out to their children areas of rock exposed by highway construction or special rocks that are landmarks in the area. Win the hearts of parents by forewarning them to check the pockets of their children's jackets and jeans for rocks before laundering them, now that the children's interest in rocks has been whetted.

Many local museums have rock displays, some more engaging than others. A natural history museum in your area may have a dazzling display of crystals, or mysterious phosphorescent rocks glowing in a darkened room. A nature center may have hands-on rock exploration tables. Local rock hobbyists may have an annual show.

RESOURCES

CHALLONER, JACK. (1999). *Rocks and minerals.* Milwaukee: Gareth Stevens. Many projects in this attractive book for upper grades can be adapted for early childhood classrooms.

GIBBONS, G. (1987). *The pottery place.* San Diego: Harcourt. A young friend watches a potter as she mixes clay, throws pots on her wheel, fires, and glazes her wares. Three methods are described for children to make simple pottery, a fine extension of rock study.

HAUSER, J. (1997). *Super science concoctions.* Charlotte, VA: Williamson. Directions are given for some intriguing crystal-making activities.

HORENSTEIN, S. (1993). *Rocks tell stories.* Brookfield, CT: Millbrook Press. The level of concise information in this book for older children makes good background preparation for teachers.

JENSEN, BECKY J., & BULLARD, JULIE A. (2002). The mud center: recapturing childhood. *Young Children, 57* (3), 16–19.

LEVENSON, E. (1994). *Teaching children about life and earth sciences.* New York: Tab Books. This is a helpful resource for more sophisticated rock-testing and soil-erosion activities.

MEYER, C. (1975). *Rock tumbling: From stones to gems to jewelry.* New York: Morrow. This book may still be on your library's shelves. You will need its complete directions for the rock-tumbling process if your polisher lacks manufacturer's instructions.

PELLANT, C. (1992). *Rocks and minerals.* New York: Dorling Kindersley. The excellent color photographs in this Eyewitness Handbook make it possible to identify any rock brought in by children, but the descriptions are highly technical.

POTTER, JEAN. (1998). *Science in seconds at the beach.* New York: John Wiley.

RICCIUTI, E. (1998). *Rocks and minerals: A National Audubon Society first field guide.* New York: Scholastic. This compendium includes characteristics of 50 common rocks, plus identification of 125 more specimens. Softcover.

SEXTON, U. (1997). Science learning in the sand. *Science and Children, 34,* 28–31.

STACE, ALEXA. (2002). *The atlas of the Earth.* New York: Friedman. General information about the forces that continue to shape our planet.

STANGL, JEAN. (1990). *Crystals and crystal gardens you can grow.* New York: Franklin Watts. A general discussion of crystals and specific recipes for a variety of crystal "gardens" are offered.

VAN CLEAVE, J. (1996). *Rocks and minerals.* New York: John Wiley. Some of the 20 experiments could be adapted to help younger children understand rock formation. Good background for teachers. Paperback.

VANROSE, S. (1994). *Earth.* London: Dorling Kindersley. This Eyewitness Science book combines fine illustrations with concise nuggets of basic geological information about rock formation, earthquakes, volcanoes, erosion, and more. An intriguing reference for background reading.

Additional Resources

CHILDREN'S TELEVISION WORKSHOP. *The Big Bird gets ready for earthquakes kit.* Earthquake safety information is provided with a board game and an audiocassette of a song, "Beatin' the Quake." The cost is $2.25 for a single copy. Make your check payable to: Children's Television Workshop, Dept. NH, One Lincoln Plaza, New York, NY 10023.

FEDERAL EMERGENCY MANAGEMENT AGENCY. *Coping with children's reactions to earthquakes and other disasters.* FEMA #48. Single copies are free. Write to: FEMA, P.O. Box 70274, Washington, DC 20024.

NATIONAL SCIENCE TEACHERS ASSOCIATION. (1988). *Earthquake curriculum.* Federal Emergency Management Agency. This extensive K–6 multidisciplinary curriculum actively involves children in learning about the nature of earthquakes, recognizing an earthquake, and earthquake safety and survival. It is free of charge by writing to: Susan McCabe, FEMA SL-NT-EN, 500 C Street SW, Washington, DC 20472.

ONLINE RESOURCES

MRS. STEWART'S BLUING. The recipe for developing a salt crystal "garden," its scientific explanation, and information for ordering a Salt Crystal Garden Kit is available at this Web site: *http://www.mrsstewart.com/pages/msbscg.htm?86,23*

ROCK TUMBLERS. Order from the Hearthsong catalog at: *www.hearthsong.com.*

Magnetism

Attractive people can draw us to them; others can repel us. Magnets behave that way toward other magnets, but to children the terms North Pole *and* South Pole *may seem to apply more to cold places and Santa Claus. Activities in this chapter offer experiences and vocabulary to clear up the confusion.*

Magnets attract iron, steel, and the attention of young children. Although magnetic attraction cannot be seen or felt, its effects can be seen and felt. Children can accept the reality of this invisible force when they have experience putting that force to work. The following concepts underlie the experiences in this chapter:

- Magnets attract some things, but not others.
- Magnets vary in strength.
- Magnets pull through some materials.
- One magnet can be used to make another magnet.
- Magnets are strongest at each end.
- Each end of a magnet acts differently.

In this chapter, children will experiment with familiar objects to see what magnets will pull and what they will pull through, make temporary magnets, and discover how opposite magnetic poles affect each other. For all magnet experiences, teachers are cautioned that computers, discs, peripherals, credit cards, and tapes rely on magnetic force to operate. Children experimenting with magnets near these objects can seriously disrupt them.

CONCEPT: Magnets attract some things, but not others.

1. What will magnets attract?

LEARNING OBJECTIVE: To enjoy investigating and drawing conclusions about magnetic effects.

MATERIALS:

Magnets of assorted shapes
  and sizes

Small foam meat tray filled
  with test items for each child
  (Iron/steel suggestions: keys,
  key chains, bolts, screws, nails,
  paper clips, lipstick cases;
  non-iron/steel items: pennies,
  brass fasteners, rubber bands,
  plastic, glass, wood, aluminum
  objects)

Two large trays or box covers

GETTING READY:

Have only magnets on the table
  when children gather. Count
  them together. (Tiny magnets
  are easily misplaced.)

Prepare a mixed collection of
  objects for each pair of
  children.

Tape a *yes* label on one tray and
  a *no* label on the other.

SMALL-GROUP ACTIVITY:

1. Give each child a paper clip and a small magnet to try out. To see the effect well, slide the magnet toward the clip on the tabletop. To feel the effect, hold clip in the palm of the hand.
2. "Do you think the magnet will pull everything to it? Find out with the things on the small trays."
3. After some exploration, suggest sorting objects pulled by the magnets from those that are not. Use the *yes/no* trays.
4. "Things on the *yes* tray do not look alike, but they are made of the same stuff." Children may note that all items are metal. You can use the specific terms iron or steel: "Magnets pull only on the iron or steel objects." (Magnets also attract cobalt and nickel, two minerals not commonly used alone in manufactured articles.)

♣ Take magnets outdoors for pairs of children to investigate which objects in the natural and built environments are attracted by magnets. One child in each pair can work with the magnet, and the other can take notes on a notepad. You may want to block off part of the school parking lot to allow children to investigate car bumpers, license plates, hubcaps, and tires. (Caution against the rest of the car because magnets can scratch paint and make you unpopular in the school!) Include the school building in the investigation.

Note: Toy magnets are rarely strong enough for school use. School suppliers and scientific equipment suppliers sell sturdy magnets. A reusable magnet source is old sound system speakers. Scientific equipment outlet stores carry as many as 40 shapes (rings, cylinders, bars, horseshoes) and kinds (steel, ceramic, rubber) of magnets. (See Appendix A for catalogs.)

Felicia and Eric test their magnets' strength.

CONCEPT: Magnets vary in strength.

1. Which magnet is strongest? Which is weakest?

LEARNING OBJECTIVE: To take satisfaction in controlling variables and making accurate assessments.

? *Inquiry Activity:* Set up a center for pairs of children to compare the strength of several magnets of different sizes and shapes. Number the magnets with nail polish. On a strip of paper, trace around a paper clip to indicate where investigators should put a paper clip. Mark a line a few inches away where the end of a magnet should be. Do this for each magnet. Investigators slowly slide the magnet toward the clip. When the clip is attracted to the magnet, investigators mark where the end of the magnet is; then they measure the distance between the two magnet marks with a ruler and record the results for each magnet on a class record sheet. The strongest magnet will pull the clip that is farthest away. The weaker magnets need to be closer to attract the clip. Encourage children to bring in well-marked magnets of all sorts from home to test.

CONCEPT: Magnets pull through some materials.

1. How well can magnets pull through things that are not attracted?

LEARNING OBJECTIVE: To enjoy investigating materials through which magnetic force can pass.

MATERIALS:

Magnets*

Steel wool pad

Iron and steel objects (nails, washers, bolts, clips)

Paper, cardboard, aluminum

Shoe box

Drinking glasses

Sand or dirt

Water

GETTING READY:

Put steel object in tumbler.

Put steel objects in box; cover with sand.

Put water in another tumbler; drop a washer in it.

Put water in a third tumbler; drop a washer in it.

SMALL-GROUP ACTIVITY:

1. "Do you know what this (steel wool) is made of? Could a magnet help you find the answer?"
2. Tear off bits of steel wool. Give some to each child. Find out if a magnet can pick up steel that is covered with a piece of paper. Try cardboard and aluminum. "Will magnetism pull through these things to pick up steel?"
3. Touch the magnet to the outside of a dry tumbler. Does it attract the steel object inside the tumbler? Try different magnets and different objects.
4. Suggest dipping the magnet into the sand-filled box and the tumbler of water. Can magnetism pass through materials that it does not attract? Later, if the classroom has an aquarium, use a magnetic scraper to clean off algae inside the tank.

Note: Children can help keep magnets strong by remembering to put a steel "keeper bar" across both ends of a horseshoe magnet. They can also keep magnets strong by not jarring them. A child may believe that a keeper bar is also a magnet—one that just doesn't happen to work right when it is separated from the magnet. From the child's experience, a plain bar of metal has no assigned function. Find a familiar iron or steel object to use as a temporary keeper bar. "Children's scissors are not magnets. Will a magnet attract them? If so, then we can leave this pair of scissors across the ends of the horseshoe magnet to keep it strong, while you experiment with the other keeper bar." Experience may clarify a child's ideas about the keeper bar, while verbal persuasion from an adult may not.

*The thickness of the non-iron material and the strength of the magnet are factors in the success of this experiment. A strong, new magnet will attract a paper clip through one's fingertip, or a magnetic earring through one's earlobe. A weak magnet will not attract a paper clip through cardboard. To keep magnets strong, always store two bar magnets together with opposite poles touching (north to south and south to north) when not in use.

CONCEPT: **One magnet can be used to make another magnet.**

1. How can we make a magnet?
LEARNING OBJECTIVE: To take pride in creating a temporary magnet.

MATERIALS:

2-inch (5 cm) needles or
  straightened paper clips
Strong bar magnet
Paper clips, steel wool, steel
  straight pins (not brass pins)

SMALL-GROUP ACTIVITY:

1. Let children use the magnet to determine if
   needles or clips are made of steel.
2. "Try to pick up steel wool bits with the
   needles or clips. Are they magnetic?"
   (They won't be, yet.)
3. Show children how to pull the needle
   across one end of the magnet in one direction. Count aloud about 25 strokes.
4. "Now try to attract steel wool with the
   needle. It should be magnetized. It has become a temporary magnet."

Note: This is a good time to demonstrate how jarring a magnet weakens it.
Hit the magnetized needle against something hard a few times. Now try to pick
up some light steel object. The pull will be very weak.

CONCEPT: **Magnets are strongest at each end.**

1. Which parts of a magnet are strongest?
LEARNING OBJECTIVE: To be fascinated by the location of power in magnets.

MATERIALS:

Bits of steel wool
Paper clips, steel key chain or
  light switch pull chain about 3
  inches (7.5 cm) long
Horseshoe and bar magnets

GETTING READY:

Cut the steel wool into fine bits.
  (Did some of the steel cling to
  the scissor edges? The scissors
  became a temporary magnet.)
Open the key chain full length.

SMALL-GROUP ACTIVITY:

1. Hold the curved end of the horseshoe
   magnet over steel wool. Notice if any steel
   is attracted to the middle of this magnet.
   "Now hold the ends of the magnet over
   the steel wool. Do the ends act differently
   from the middle?" Try with a bar magnet.
2. Touch the chain with both ends of a bar
   magnet. Notice whether the whole chain
   clings to the magnet or if the middle part
   dangles free. (Chain should be longer than
   the bar magnet.)
3. Dangle the key chain 1/4 inch (1 cm) above
   the center of a bar magnet. (The pull of a
   strong magnet will visibly curve the end of
   the chain toward one end of the magnet.)

CONCEPT: **Each end of a magnet acts differently.**

1. How do the ends of magnets act?

LEARNING OBJECTIVE: To see and feel the intriguing pulling power of unlike magnet ends and the push of like ends.

MATERIALS:

2 strong bar magnets
String
Nail polish or tape
Compass (desirable)

GETTING READY:

If using lightweight magnets, tape the string to a tabletop or chair seat.

Tie the string to any horizontal bar or chair back that will allow a heavy magnet to swing freely.

SMALL-GROUP ACTIVITY:

1. Tie the string to the center of a magnet, balancing it.
2. Let the magnet hang and swing freely. When it stops moving, one end of the bar (or one side of the horseshoe magnet) will be pointing north. Mark this end with tape or a dot of nail polish. Do the same for the second magnet. If a compass is available, place it on a level surface so children can see the pointer swinging to the north.[*]
3. Let the children hold a magnet in each hand, then try to touch like ends (north to north, south to south). "What do you feel? Try to touch unlike ends. What happens?" Give children lots of time to explore the attraction and repulsion effects. With strong magnets, results are fascinating.

2. How strong are magnets of different shapes?

MATERIALS:

Play dough
Table knife
3 ring magnets
Disc magnets

LARGE-GROUP ACTIVITY:

1. Show ring, disc, and horseshoe magnets. Learn what children think about the positive and negative ends of these magnets. (It can be confusing to perceive the sides of a flat disc as the ends of a magnet.)
2. Point to each end of a horseshoe magnet. "This magnet was bent, bringing the two ends close together to make the pulling power stronger. Let's find out how a disc magnet is made, using a play-dough model." Roll a handful of dough into a long cylinder. "A long magnet is made

[*]The magnetic compass pointer lines up the same way. When the compass is flat, the pointer swings freely and comes to rest with the tip pointing north. This happens because Earth is a gigantic magnet with a magnetic north pole and a magnetic south pole. Its force is pulling the north-seeking tip of the pointer that way. (The legendary Santa is at the geographic North Pole, not quite the same location.)

FIGURE 11–1

first. The power is in each end. Where are the north and south ends?"

3. Cut the cylinder in half. "Now there are two magnets, each with north/south ends. The power collects at each end, no matter if the magnet is long or short." (See Figure 11–1.)

4. Cut a narrow slice from a cylinder. Find the north/south ends of the still vertical slice. "The power still collects in each end. Ring and disc magnets are slices of a longer magnet."

5. Stand several disc or ring magnets side by side, north/south poles together to form a cylinder. Then "float" three ring magnets by slipping them onto a vertically held pencil, with like ends facing to repel. "The power is always in the ends, no matter how they are turned." Let children explore the power of an assortment of disc and ring magnets to attract paper clips and other magnets.

INTEGRATING ACTIVITIES

Math Experiences

Magnet in the Grab Bag. Half-fill a large grocery bag with used steel bottle caps, common nails, paper clips, or other small steel objects. Use a string to tie a strong magnet to a stick, fishpole style. Let children take turns dipping the magnet into the bag, then counting aloud the number of objects they have pulled up. A numeral recognition version of this game can be played by cutting out colored paper fish, writing a numeral on each, and fastening a paper clip or safety pin to each fish.

Magnetic Numerals. Plastic numerals and counting shapes are made with magnets to use on coated steel bulletin boards. Use them to form sets of objects, labeled with corresponding numerals. Make a game of this by letting children draw the numerals from a paper bag, choose the corresponding quantity of objects, and place them on the bulletin board. You may have an old, tin-coated steel baking sheet in your kitchen that would substitute well for the commercial steel bulletin board.

Music

Mention to children that we couldn't hear sounds from a stereo, VCR, radio, television set, or tape recorder without magnets. Recording tape is coated with magnetized powdered iron, and the other four devices have magnets in their mechanisms.

Sing the "Magnet Song."

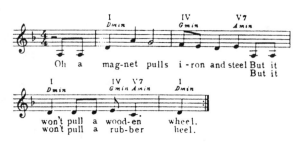

Literature Links

ARDLEY, NEIL. (1991). *The science book of magnets.* San Diego, CA: Harcourt Brace. The clear, well-organized text and clearly illustrated experiments make this book intriguing and useful for the independent reader.

ARDLEY, NEIL. (1995). *How things work.* Pleasantville, NY: Reader's Digest. Older children interested in technological applications of magnetic force will find many well-illustrated examples in this reference.

BOCKNEK, JONATHAN. (2000). *The science of magnets.* Milwaukee, WI: Gareth Stevens. Excellent photographs of familiar things, including migrating birds and butterflies, that magnetic force helps function will reinforce the importance of magnetic force. Related Web sites are given.

BRANLEY, FRANKLYN. (1996). *What makes a magnet?* New York: HarperCollins. Magnetizing a needle leads to easy compass-making and other magnetic properties discoveries. Sprightly illustrations and Branley's usual clear prose will pull in primary children like a magnet. Paperback.

CHALLONER, JACK. (1992). *My first batteries and magnets book.* New York: Dorling Kindersley. Clear instructions and excellent color photographs of magnet explorations and interesting toymaking have their own pulling power for children.

COLE, JOANNA, & DEGEN, BRUCE. (1997). *The magic school bus and the electric field trip.* New York: Scholastic. Wacky Ms. Frizzle shows how magnets generate electricity and their importance in motors.

EDOM, HELEN. (1992). *Science with magnets.* Tulsa, OK: EDC Publications. The general information and experiments with simple magnets also includes electromagnet experiments.

GIBSON, GARY. (1995). *Playing with magnets.* Brookfield, CT: Millbrook Press. Basic information about magnets is threaded through this book of homemade magnet games and toys for children.

JENNINGS, TERRY. (1992). *Electricity and magnetism.* New York: Smithmark. Familiar objects that depend on magnetic force to operate and magnet projects are featured in this book.

NANKIVELL-ASTON, SALLY. (2000). *Science experiments with magnets.* New York: Franklin Watts. This activity book will attract independent readers.

PARKER, STEVE. (1997). *Magnets.* Milwaukee, WI: Gareth Stevens. This is a comprehensive, kid-size look at the nature of magnets, their importance in operating computers and loudspeakers, their role in generating electricity, and the fun they offer.

PFEFFER, WENDY. (1995). *Marta's magnets.* Parsippany, NJ: Silver Press. Marta shares her magnet collection with children in her new neighborhood and helps solve the problem of a down-the-drain key.

ROYSTON, ANGELA. (2001). *Magnets.* Plymouth, NH: Heinemann. Written at a comfortable level for independent readers, this book describes and illustrates uses of magnets in familiar contexts. NSTA[*] recommended.

TAYLOR, BARBARA. (1993). *More power to you! The science book of batteries and magnets.* New York: Random. This book offers some advanced magnet experiments for children ready for more.

WHALLEY, MARGARET. (1994). *Experiment with electricity and magnetism.* Minneapolis, MN: Lerner Publications. Standard beginning experiments are offered, plus a timely awareness of the potential harm magnets can cause to electronic equipment.

[*]National Science Teachers Association

Poems (Resources in Appendix A)

Read "Magnet," by Valerie Worth, in *Spectacular Science: A Book of Poems,* compiled by Lee Bennett Hopkins.

Storytelling With Magnets

Tell a story featuring practical uses of magnetic gadgets that could also be props for the telling. A small magnet could save the day when father drops his keys down the register, when sister's box of hair clips spills in her bubble bath, when someone upsets a box of pins, or when a glass jar of nails breaks on the garage floor. These and other calamities could be resolved with an upholsterer's tack hammer, a magnetic-holder flashlight, a paper clip or pin box with a magnetized top, or other magnetic equipment that may be available.

The effects of magnetism can be used throughout the school year as a storytelling device in the following three ways.

Magnetically Directed Puppets. Tape a paper clip to the bottoms of small wooden dollhouse dolls. Put an open shoe box on its side to make a platform for

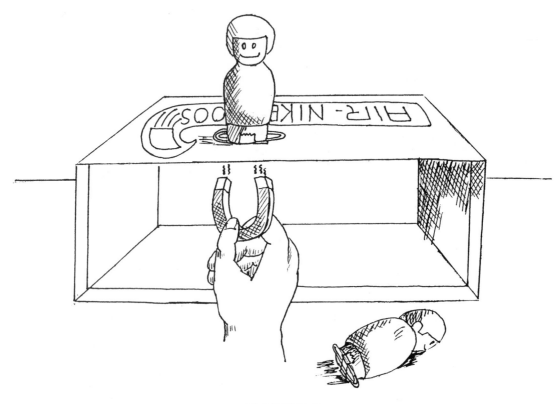

FIGURE 11–2

the puppets (Figure 11–2). Make the puppets move by holding magnets in each hand beneath the platform. (Puppets can be thread spools with button heads glued on, clothespin dolls with paper clip feet, or pipe cleaner dolls.) Children love using magnet puppets to retell familiar stories or to create their own plays.

Paper Doll Stories. Cut out paper figures to illustrate a story. Tape paper clips or small safety pins to the backs. Invert a large grocery bag (plain or decorated) as a backdrop, and manipulate the paper figures with magnets held inside the bag.

Magnetic Bulletin Board Stories. Use fabric or paper figures as you would for a flannel board story. Hold them in place with a shirt-button-sized magnet. Try to fit one of the whimsical magnet insects into the story. Sheet steel bulletin boards with colorful magnet disks are sold in office supply stores. Use one for creating messages from magnetic poetry sets.

Art Activities

Make junk sculpture with iron or steel.

1. Prepare steel bottle caps by punching two nail holes into each one.
2. Prepare sculpture bases using mounds of damp clay, chunks of foam, or cardboard fruit trays.
3. Put out a tray full of iron and steel discards (paper clips, nails, steel bottle caps, hairpins, pipe cleaners, twist bag closures, washers, soft wire. Put out several magnets so that the children can test materials for magnetic attraction. Explain that the sculpture for today will be made only of iron or steel.
4. Show how wire can be threaded through the punched bottle caps, how paper clips can be opened, and how wire pipe cleaners can be coiled around a finger to make interesting shapes.

Play

Automobile Service. Tie a small magnet to a toy tow truck for children to use in hauling steel cars to the garage.

Block Play. Fasten disc magnets with rubber bands to the front of small plastic cars, some with north-seeking poles facing outward, others with south-seeking poles facing outward.

Fascinating Attractions. If magnetic marbles are available, prepare a dozen of them after school, making the poles evident. Choose six marbles of two different colors. Carefully separate the outside of the marbles at the seam, using a butter knife. Find the north pole of the small magnets inside. Then reconnect the marbles as two-tones, consistently using one color for the north pole, and the other color for the south pole. Let children enjoy rolling marbles toward each other, sending them spinning, making chains and patterns, and holding one marble above the others to see what happens. Help them make the connection between the colors and the poles, if they don't figure this out for themselves. (Confine this activity to a tray with sides. Also, announce the number of marbles that should always be on the tray, as pockets have a way of attracting these charming toys.)

Magnet Construction Box. Collect three or four small, strong magnets with keeper bars (or nails to serve that purpose). Find iron and steel discard items similar to those suggested for the junk sculpture. Try to include steel key chains, notebook rings, old keys, and cocoa box lids. Children enjoy combining odd shapes that are held together by magnetic attraction. Try to find a tin cookie box for storing the game. The lid and the box can serve as bases for the constructions, since the tin is a coating for steel.

Commercial magnetic building sets are available through school equipment catalogs. Magnetic games and magnet sculpture sets are available in toy and specialty stores. The Magna Doodle toy uses a magnetic wand to make iron filing designs on a screen. A fine magnetic play set is available through HearthSong and Childcraft: Magnuts. These sturdy, flexible action figures wearing magnetic boots are ready to do acrobatics, climb steel cabinets, grasp cords, ride a cable car, and more.

Creative Thinking

I Am a Magnet. Collect a tray of assorted objects: key, steel bottle cap, spool, stick, rock, nail, bolt, paper clip. Sit with the children in a circle on the floor. Place the tray in the center. Start off as the leader when introducing the game. Ask the child next to you to choose one of the objects to pretend to be. Say, "I am a great, strong magnet. What are you, Maria?" If Maria replies that she is a bottle cap, say, "Then we'll cling together," and hold her hand. Encourage Maria to say to the child next to her, "Josh, I'm a magnetized bottle cap. What are you?" If Josh decides to be a rock, Maria goes on to the next child until she finds someone to cling to. End the game with, "Now I am a teacher again and my pulling strength is gone."

PROMOTING CONCEPT CONNECTIONS

Maintaining Concepts

Point out magnets in use around the school whenever they come to your attention: refrigerator door sealing strips, car seat belt clasps, fancy buckles on children's belts, cupboard door latches. For the latter example, it is a good idea to suggest that children using those cupboards try to close them gently, without banging them, so that the magnets won't lose their strength. Show how the force of magnetism is used for banking, shopping, and other purposes by pointing out the magnetic strip on an ATM or credit card.

Make magnets a standard part of classroom cleanup equipment. Hang a magnet and keeper bar on a low peg near the workbench if you have one. Let the children use it on the floor, in workbench drawers, or on the workbench to gather up stray nails. Use it to sort out tiny nails from wooden shapes after children have worked with hammer-on design kits. Use the magnet to locate small steel cars that have become buried in the sandbox.

Improving Schoolgrounds

A compass showing the directions, N-S-E-W, can be painted on the asphalt. Upper elementary children can design and paint this graphic. Children can check pocket compasses against it.

Connecting Concepts

1. When discussing the effect of magnetism passing through materials, ask the children whether air is one of the substances that magnetism passes through.

How can they tell? Recall with the children that even though we cannot see air or magnetism, we have discovered that both are real things.

2. Set up a water play game that depends upon magnetic force passing through water. Let the children make barge-shaped boats from pressed foam, and fasten a paper clip to each boat with a rubber band. Stack three blocks under each end of a shallow cake pan. Fill the pan with water and launch the foam boats on it. Children can guide their boats through the water with magnets held beneath the pan.

3. Combine buoyancy and the principle of attraction and repulsion of like magnetic poles in a water play activity. Help the children magnetize 2-inch (5 cm) blunt needles, then place them on top of barge-shaped foam boats. Float the boats in a pan of water. Push the boats ahead by approaching the end of the needle with the like pole of a magnet; pull boats back with the unlike pole of the magnet. If a needle rolls off a boat, the children can go fishing for it in the water with a magnet.

4. Make a simple marine compass model for a Columbus Day observation. Float a magnetized needle, which has been taped to a bit of styrofoam tray, in a cereal bowl filled with water. Gently tilt the bowl back and forth, noting that the water level, and therefore the needle compass, is constant. (Gravity pulls on all things, so both shallow and deep water in a container are pulled down to the same level.) Explorers had a reliable compass to guide them when the stars or sun weren't visible, and storms rocked their ships. See *Science Through the Ages,* by Janice VanCleave or *Reinvent the Wheel,* by Ruth Kassinger.

Family and Community Support

Ask families to lend interesting souvenir or advertising magnets to a classroom steel cabinet or desk display. Label the collection with magnetic letters, or put together a display slogan with words from a magnetic poetry set.

Notify families about the nearest children's museum or science museum that has interactive magnet exhibits. When families visit a public library with a magnetic scanning system at the exit, ask the librarian to explain how it works.

RESOURCES

BERGER, M. (1988). *The science of music.* New York: Thomas Y. Crowell. Learn how microscopic magnets turn into audiotapes.

HANN, J. (1991). *How science works.* Pleasantville, NY: Reader's Digest. Historical background and the relationship between magnetism and electricity are interestingly presented.

KASSINGER, RUTH. (2001). *Reinvent the wheel.* New York: John Wiley. Magnets have been used to guide fishermen for about 2000 years. Read the history of the marine compass and make a simple model (see p. 83–85). Columbus couldn't have discovered the New World without one.

LEVENSON, E. (1994). *Teaching children about physical science.* New York: Tab Books. Ideas are offered for making a compass and for "floating" ring magnets.

WOODRUFF, JOHN. (1998). *Magnetism.* Austin, TX: Raintree. Good photographs and advance information and experiments with magnetism, including electromagnets.

VANCLEAVE, J. (1993). *Magnets.* New York: John Wiley. Intended as a science fair project book for older children, a good range of background information on magnetism is also offered. The demagnetizing experiment can help children understand why they shouldn't bang magnets.

VANCLEAVE, J. (2002). *Science through the ages.* New York: John Wiley. The history of compass development is offered in this book, together with directions for making simple wet and dry compasses.

The Effects of Gravity

Do you remember wondering, as a child, if people living on the bottom of the globe might fall off? Knowing about the force of gravity is a comforting revelation to children, so you will enjoy offering these activities.

Children who have felt the tug of invisible magnetic attraction with their own hands can move from this awareness to simple understanding about the effects of gravity. These children are ready to put credence in the far stronger invisible pull that holds people, houses, and schools on the ground—the force of gravity. The learning experiences in this chapter amplify one central concept:

Gravity pulls on everything.

Drawing children's attention to an ever-present effect that is rarely noticed or labeled calls for more preliminary description than we usually offer to action-loving children. The first suggested gravity experience is a story that provides basic information. The active experiences involve measuring and comparing gravity's pull on objects, trying a pendulum, and bringing things into balance.

Introduction

Lead into the gravity story by crushing a piece of paper into a ball and holding it between your fingers. Ask children, "What will happen to this ball of paper if I turn my hand over and open my fingers?" Find out if the children's predictions are correct. "Do you think the ball might do the same thing another time, or might it fall up instead? Did you ever stumble and fall up? Here is a story about the reason for this."

Use a flannel board and felt figures to illustrate your story. It could be stated something like the following.

> Once a girl had a dream. Everything seemed very strange. The girl was floating in the air, looking for her house. She saw her friend floating close by with a ball in his arms. They wanted to play catch, but when the boy threw the ball, it drifted up out

of reach. Then the girl saw her house bobbing up and down gently in the breeze. Her mom was very upset because somebody had spilled milk all over the ceiling. When the girl woke up, she was glad that her house was standing still.

"Something important was missing in that dream. Houses and balls and children don't float around. Milk doesn't spill up! There is a reason why those things don't happen. There is a very powerful force pulling down on everything in the world: the force called gravity. We can't touch gravity or see it. We can just see what gravity does.

"Can you think of something else invisible that pulls some kinds of things? Gravity reminds us of the way magnets pull on iron and steel. But gravity is much, much stronger than magnetism. Gravity pulls from inside Earth. It pulls on everything all of the time. We are so used to it that we don't even notice it happening."

Show a picture of an astronaut in his space suit. "The astronauts who walked on the moon had a strange experience. They had to wear very heavy boots to stand on the moon, because the moon's gravity pull is weaker than Earth's gravity pull.

"At the science center you can find out how much Earth's gravity is pulling on you."

CONCEPT: Gravity pulls on everything.

1. How can we become aware of gravity pulling on us?

LEARNING OBJECTIVE: To invite dawning awareness of the invisible force of gravity.

Invite a volunteer child to be the demonstration subject to introduce this activity. Have the child sit on a straight chair. Make sure both his feet are flat on the floor, his back is touching the chair back, and his hands are in his lap. Now ask the child to try to stand up without swaying his body forward nor moving any other muscles—not even a tiny bit. Encourage the child to try very hard to stand up, then report to the class what he is experiencing. Ask, "What will you have to do in order to stand up? Think about it."

Let the rest of the class take turns trying the experience in their small groups, while others observe for motionlessness. Afterward, discuss what the children noticed. "What do you think held you to the chair when you didn't move a muscle? What did you need to do to stand up?"

Guide the discussion to the conclusion that it is gravity's force that holds us down in the chair. The force of gravity always pulls on everything. We have to use our energy to push ourselves out of the chair and stand up. It takes energy to move the muscles we use to stand up. It always takes energy to work against gravity's pull.

2. How does gravity's pull affect our body positioning?

LEARNING OBJECTIVE: To enjoy noticing how our bodies accommodate gravity's pull.

This child is feeling gravity's inexorable pull.

MATERIALS:

Bathroom scale

Kitchen scale

4 small, sturdy bags

Sand, pebbles

Market bag with handles

Containers, scoops

Long mirror, if possible

Low balance beam

GETTING READY:

Fill each small bag with 2
  pounds of sand or stones.

SMALL-GROUP ACTIVITY:

1. "When we weigh ourselves on a scale, we are finding out how much gravity pulls on us."
2. Find out how much gravity pulls on each child. Record the weights.
3. Weigh the children again while they hold a sandbag in each hand. Compare with first weight record. Which way does gravity pull more?
4. Put both sand bags in the market bag. Have children hold it in one hand so the weight is on one side. Weigh each child again.
5. "Look in the mirror. Are you standing up straight now or leaning over? You lean away from the heavy side to keep your balance."

Let children discover how they use their arms as they walk, turn, and stand on one foot on a low balance beam.

Let children weigh objects on both scales. Containers of sand make good materials to weigh. Provide objects of varying weights and sizes. Let children discover that size does not always determine weight.

Group Discussion: Recall the earlier discussion about gravity holding everything down. Encourage children to share ideas about things that they see being
pulled down from the sky by gravity (leaves, seeds, snowflakes, raindrops). Recall
that, as long as it is moving, air can lift and keep gliders, kites, birds, and planes
aloft for a while against gravity's pull. Can the children lift themselves all the way
off the ground momentarily by using their energy to push against gravity?

3. How can we compare gravity's pull on objects?

LEARNING OBJECTIVE: To enjoy exploring how much gravity pulls on different
materials by achieving equilibrium.

MATERIALS:

Scrap lumber: 2-foot (60 cm)
  piece of dowel or broomstick;
  8-inch (20 cm) × 8-inch
  (20 cm) piece of shelving

Nails: 6d and 4d sizes

Yardstick (meterstick)

Pipe cleaners

2 small, reused yogurt cups

Small objects to weigh: shells,
  washers, acorns, etc.

GETTING READY:

Drill holes or saw small notches
  3 inches apart on yardstick
  (8 cm on meterstick).

Make a hole at 18 inches (50 cm)
  and mark with the 6d nail.

Make 2 holes on opposite sides
  of each container.

SMALL-GROUP ACTIVITY:

1. To make base: Mark center of shelving
   square. Nail dowel perpendicular to center
   of base. (Let children do the hammering.)
2. Nail yardstick (meterstick) loosely near the
   top of the upright stick, driving a 4d nail
   through hole at the 18-inch (50 cm) mark.
   Yardstick (meterstick) should swing easily.
3. Insert pipe cleaners into yardstick (meterstick) holes. Hook them into paper cups. (Put
   one cup on each side. Let children add more
   cups as they wish.) If notches were made instead of drilled holes, make pipe cleaner handles for cups and hang in notches.
4. Let children fill cups with small items to
   balance.
5. Provide materials as different in weight as
   cotton balls and shells. Do five cotton balls
   balance five shells? Is the balance arm lower
   on the shell side? What does this mean?
   (Gravity pulls more on shells; thus, we say
   they weigh more than the cotton balls.)

Set up a center with balances and containers of materials to weigh for independent investigations.

? *Inquiry Activity:* Show children a pebble and a palm-sized stone. Ask for,
and record, their predictions and reasoning about whether or not the two objects
would land on the floor at the same or different times if you dropped them simultaneously from the same height. With arms extended outward, drop the two objects. Without comment, ask children what they observed. ♣ Take the class
outdoors, equipped with notebooks and pencils, to conduct and record their own
experiments in small groups, with each child having at least one turn to experiment. Provide two containers of indestructible objects to test: small objects such as
pebbles, marbles, acorns, sweetgum tree balls, pinecones, cotton balls, washers,

Kathleen considers how to balance blocks.

foam packing chips, old keys; and larger objects such as a baseball, rocks, a solid metal paperweight, or a #2 hand weight. Discuss safety precautions, then let children experiment with items from each container, or with found objects from whatever heights are safely available on the playground. Back in the classroom, compile observations and draw conclusions.

Tell children they have carried out a gravity experiment that astonished the scientific world about 400 years ago. It was devised by the famous scientist, Galileo. Legend tells us that he dropped two sizes of brass balls from the Leaning Tower of Pisa to show that the force of gravity pulls all falling objects down at the same rate of speed, no matter how much they weigh. Read *Science Through the Ages,* by Janice VanCleave, and *Galileo's Treasure Box,* by Catherine Brighton, to place this experiment in historical perspective.

4. Can we keep objects in balance?

LEARNING OBJECTIVE: To discover satisfying strategies for balancing unequal weights.

MATERIALS:

12-inch ruler

Half-circle blocks

Small rocks

Tinkertoys

Acrobat balance toy sold by import gift shops (optional)

SMALL-GROUP ACTIVITY:

1. Gently place a ruler on a block, with the 6-inch mark resting on top of the curve. "Let's see if the ruler will tip or balance. Can you try this?"

2. "Can we balance two rocks on the ruler?" Show how to slide a heavier rock toward

the center (resting point) to balance a lighter rock at the other end of the ruler.

3. Make a platform of two Tinkertoy wheels and one long stick. Insert two sticks in a connector wheel and add small connectors to the stick ends. Rest connector wheel on the platform edge as shown in Figure 12–1.

4. Remove one stick, then the other, from the connector wheel. What happens? Is the connector wheel stable without them? (The location and weight of the sticks change the way gravity pulls on the connector wheel.)

5. How do pendulums work?

LEARNING OBJECTIVE: To wonder at and delight in pendulum action.

Group Experience: Tie a small doll at the end of a foot of string. Hold the other end of the string, letting the doll dangle. "How could I make the doll go higher without lifting up the string? Good! I could swing the doll higher. Look, it is going high now, but it doesn't stay high. Why? Let's watch what happens when I stop swinging the string. Is it moving up as high now? It's going slower and lower, and it has almost stopped swinging. What could be helping to stop it?

"Is this what happens to you when you're on the swing? What happens to you when you start to pull and push with your muscles? What happens when you stop using your energy to keep the swing moving back and forth? Are you close to the top of the swing set or close to the ground when the swing stops? Why?" (The force of gravity is part of the reason.) Tape the string and doll pendulum to the edge of a table for children to try later.

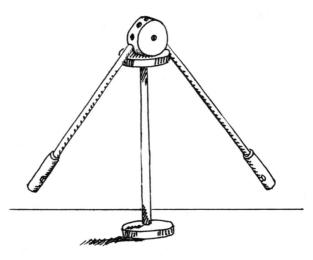

FIGURE 12–1

Continue the pendulum investigation another day, making a sand pendulum so the children can observe the beautiful pattern of the pendulum arcs. Make a funnel by cutting off the bottom of an empty dish detergent bottle. Make three evenly spaced holes near the cut edge. Tie three strong strings to the holes; bundle the strings and tie them to a sturdy cord (Figure 12–2). Suspend the up-ended funnel by the cord from a doorframe or ceiling beam. The capped end of

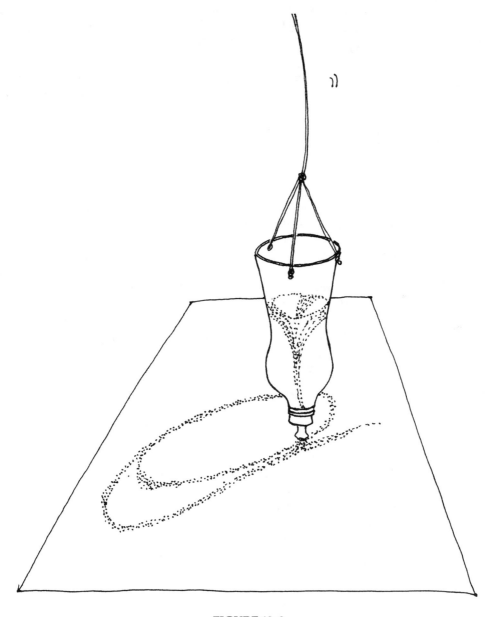

FIGURE 12–2

the funnel needs to be close to the floor, about one-half inch above, so that the sand doesn't bounce.

Spread a large plastic sheet under the pendulum. Fill the funnel halfway with sand. Pull the cap open, give the funnel a push, and watch the sand flow into interesting arc patterns below. (To make the sand flow more smoothly, you may need to remove the bit of plastic that has been put there to slow down the flow of detergent.)

"Do the swings start to go out wider and wider, or do they get smaller? Find out." Vary the way you push the pendulum to create different patterns. Leave the pendulum set up as a center for children to explore.

♣ To reduce cleanup and still have fun, rig up the sand pendulum from a tree limb or hanging bars. Allow a thicker stream of sand to flow. Experiment with different colors of sand, mixing dry tempera paint with sand. Try layering two or three colors in the bottle.

? *Inquiry Activity:* ♣ Take a stopwatch or a watch with a second sweep, a clipboard, and paper and pencil to the swing set. Choose a child from the class and a bigger child borrowed from an older class as subjects. Choose a third child to time one minute with the stopwatch, and a fourth to record data. All other children count aloud the number of swings accomplished in one minute.

Then have the bigger child start swinging very slowly. Children count and record each full swing as it reaches the top of the forward motion. Next, ask the child to swing hard and fast as the others count swings per minute.

Ask the group for predictions about whether a smaller person will have different swinging results. Count this child's slow and fast swings. (Each swing of pendulums of the same length will be the same, if the count is accurate.) Keep the inquiry going with all the children who want to participate. If the swing chain can be shortened, experiment again under this new condition. (There will be more swings per minute, but again, all children will have the same number.)

INTEGRATING ACTIVITIES

Math Experiences

When they experiment with a pan balance and weights, children can strengthen their understanding of numerical equivalence. Make a pan balance available as a center for experimenting with equal and unequal quantities of cube blocks. Provide sets of commercial standard weights for which size and weight are related. To devise substitute weights, fill screw-top plastic or metal containers with sand and gravel to equal 1-, 2-, and 4-ounce (25-, 50-, and 100-gram) weights as desired. Mark the corresponding numeral on each container.

Numeral balance equipment is made in several forms. One type uses weighted plastic numerals to make the mathematical equation balance as the weight balances. Keep a set of weights, along with boxes of materials to weigh, next to a pan balance for children to use when time permits.

Music

Listen to Michael Mish's "Gravity" song on his *I'm Blue* cassette.

When children are investigating the effects of gravity, they enjoy singing three nursery rhymes as though gravity were not operating. "Jack and Jill Went Up the Hill" might be sung ". . . Jack fell up, and broke his cup, and Jill bent over with laughter." "London Bridge" might be sung ". . . London Bridge is floating up," and "Ring Around the Rosy" might be sung ". . . One, two, three and we fall up in the tree."

Here is a gravity song to sing:

Literature Links

ARDLEY, NEIL. (1992). *The science book of gravity.* San Diego, CA: Harcourt Brace. Colorful photographs of needlessly fussy activities and bits of information will hold browsers' attention.

BRANLEY, FRANKLYN. (1998). *Floating in Space.* New York: HarperCollins. Astronauts traveling in a space shuttle can lift tons of gear easily beyond Earth's gravitational pull. Ordinary activities are harder to manage. Paperback.

BRANLEY, FRANKLYN. (2000). *Gravity is a mystery.* New York: HarperCollins. Although this book doesn't explain what gravity is (because no one has been able to explain it yet), it hasn't been surpassed for sharing what is known in good, child-level style. Paperback.

BRIGHTON, CATHERINE. (2000). *Galileo's treasure box.* New York: Walker. In this charming fictional portrayal, Galileo's small daughter investigates souvenirs of his famous experiments. Richly detailed illustrations of a Renaissance household place the story in historical perspective.

COBB, VICKI. (1989). *Why doesn't the earth fall up?* New York: Lodestar. Gravity and the laws of motion are explained simply.

EVANS, DAVID, & WILLIAMS, C. (1992). *Make it balance.* New York: Dorling Kindersley. Vivid photographs invite the youngest explorers to try open-ended balancing challenges. Explanations of gravity's role are listed separately for adult guidance.

FALCONER, IAN. (2001). *Olivia saves the circus.* New York: Atheneum. Olivia steps in for sick circus performers. Balance is critical in tightrope acts, stilt walking, and unicycle riding. School Library Journal Best Book of 2001.

GETZ, DAVID. (1997). *Floating home.* New York: Henry Holt. This lively story is about a girl determined to sketch her home from a distant perspective: outer space. Her weightless adventure in a space shuttle is accurately described, based on NASA information.

KNAPP, BRIAN. (1991). *Falling.* Danbury, CT: Grolier. Good photographs illustrate intriguing explorations of the force of gravity and the ways we work with it and against it.

LEONTOVICH, M. (1995). *Force, of course.* Glenview, IL: Goodyear. Further experiments with pendulums, balance, and gravity are carefully described.

McCULLY, EMILY. (1992). *Mirette on the high wire.* New York: G. P. Putnam's Sons. A venturesome girl persists and learns to concentrate and balance as a highwire walker. She saves a performer. A Caldecott Award winner.

McCULLY, EMILY. (2000). *Mirette and Bellini cross Niagara Falls.* New York: G. P. Putnam's Sons. This story about famous 19th century highwire balancers and immigration problems has good social studies links.

MINARIK, ELSE. (1961). *Little bear.* New York: Harper & Row. Children will enjoy Chapter 3, "Little Bear Goes to the Moon." Paperback.

PINKNEY, BRIAN. (1997). *The adventures of sparrowboy.* New York: Simon & Schuster. A sparrow gives Henry the super flying power to save others from the neighborhood bully. Read it aloud to inspire creative thinking responses to the question, "What if gravity didn't keep you down?"

RIDE, SALLY, & OKIE, SUSAN. (1986). *To space and back.* New York: Lothrop. Young children will enjoy hearing the portions of this book portraying the peculiarities of doing ordinary life routines weightlessly in an orbiting space capsule. Excellent color photographs of the astronaut/author in space.

ZUBROWSKI, BERNIE. (1993). *Mobiles: Building and experimenting with balancing toys.* A Boston Children's Museum Book. New York: Beech Tree. Interesting experiences with body balance, and finding balance points with various objects, are included with directions for simple and complex balance toy making. Paperback.

Swinging, sliding, blockbuilding, and falling down are part of many other children's stories as well. Casually refer to the effects of gravity's pull whenever possible.

Poems (See Appendix A)

From *A Child's Garden of Verses* by Robert Louis Stevenson, read "The Swing."
From *The Llama Who Had No Pajama* by Mary Ann Hoberman, read "The Folks Who Live in Backward Town," where gravity doesn't seem to operate.
For beginning readers, see *Blast Off! Poems About Space,* selected by Lee Bennett Hopkins.

Art Activities

Create nature mobiles. Collect fallen sticks outdoors. Let children help, if the schoolgrounds have trees. Using tape and string, suspend each stick at a level that allows children to work on it. Provide two small objects from nature, such as cones and pods, to hang by a string from each stick. Children can experiment to achieve a balance by moving the objects' strings closer or farther away from the center of the stick, or by winding one string around the stick to make it shorter than the other (Figure 12–3). Shapes cut from pressed foam plastic can also be used.

Play

Store. Put a pan balance or old kitchen scales, containers of materials like horse chestnuts, and artificial fruit and vegetables in the play store area.

Block Play. Help block builders think about why their structures collapse. Suggest making broad, sturdy bases for tall towers, so that gravity will pull more on the bottom of the tower than on the top. When appropriate, ask if gravity is pulling equally on both sides of the weight-supporting blocks or whether an unbalanced load will tip over.

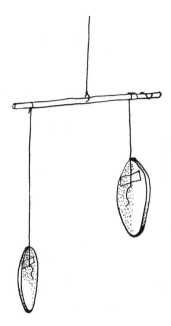

FIGURE 12–3

Spaceship. Try to find a refrigerator shipping carton for the children to convert into a spaceship. Help them improvise space helmets by using small cartons and coils of telephone cable wire, like the one worn by Little Bear on his imaginary trip to the moon. Before setting up the spaceship play, supply play ideas by reading *Little Bear* by Else Minarik, or another one of the astronaut books.

Creative Movement

Help the children recognize, when they dance or exercise, the way their bodies involuntarily adjust to changes in body position to maintain their balance. When they lean in one direction, their bodies automatically compensate for gravity's pull by extending an arm or leg in the opposite direction.

Let the children pretend that they are on a ship in a storm, rocking from side to side. They will stretch their legs into a wide-based stance or tip over. Suggest moving like ice skaters, swinging arms and bending bodies as they glide and stride on the ice. Now they are tightrope walkers sliding one foot in front of the other on a swaying rope, arms extended. Next, imagine that they are going to lift a heavy rock, working very hard with their muscles to force it up against gravity's pull, bit by bit. Now put the rock down carefully and push it ahead slowly. Then move like the astronauts on the moon where the gravity pull is weak.

In *Creative Movement for the Developing Child,* Clare Cherry suggests two poems as stimuli for balancing movements: "The Cat on the Fence" and "The High Wire Walker."

Whenever tension seems to be mounting in the classroom, or when excited children need help shifting from physical activity to a learning situation that requires concentration, use this "anti-gravity relaxation fantasy." Guide it slowly and quietly, saying: "Let your eyelids slide down now to close . . . and let your hands be loose and comfortable in your lap . . . Let your arms be loose . . . and limp . . . and light . . . so light they seem to float . . . so light that it seems that gravity isn't pulling on them much at all . . . And now . . . notice . . . just notice how loose and light your neck and shoulders feel . . . There is just enough gravity pull to help them keep your head above them . . . But your head might want to move all around slowly, until it finds a comfortable place to rest. There, it feels soooo comfortable now . . . There is almost no heaviness in your body now . . . Everything feels easy now . . . Let your mind take you on a floating journey now . . . You might want to have a cloud to rest on, feeling all that softness around you . . . or you might want to be an astronaut floating inside a space capsule, far, far, away from Earth's gravity pull . . . It's your floating journey, so you can have it be just the way you want it to be, because gravity doesn't pull on your thoughts—ever . . . so you can float as easily as you like in your imagination . . . And then gradually, slowly, you begin to notice gravity's pull again . . . You notice how well you are breathing now as you drift down closer, closer to Earth . . . feeling rested and fresh and relaxed now. . . . And you take three long, slow, deep breaths . . . and then your eyes open again, so that you can see what we will be doing next in school."

Creative Thinking

Use gravity pull as a topic to stimulate creative thinking. Ask, "What if there were no gravity pull from Earth? What would be different? What would it be like to play on the playground? What if we had to eat our meals as the astronauts do on space flights? Would we be sitting in our room?"

Food Experiences

Take the class to the nearest food store where purchases are weighed on a balance beam scale. Buying and sharing a half pound of sweets with the children is a good investment in gravity learning.

In *Cooking Wizardry for Kids* by Kenda and Williams, read the chapter, "Food for Astronauts," which is about requirements of successful foods for spaceships. Then follow the recipe to bake "Space Cookies," just the right size to pop into the mouth in one bite, without danger of letting a single crumb float away to cause problems for the astronauts.

If a science museum field trip is a possibility, be sure to purchase the astronaut ice cream, "Dip 'n Dots," to share a taste with the class. Packets of astronaut meals may also be available for purchase.

Field Trips

Knowing how much gravity pulls on objects is an important part of many businesses and services. Try to include a look at weighing devices during the field trips you plan to the post office, grocery store, feed store, airport, drugstore, medical offices, or the loading docks of factories. It can be great fun for a whole class of children to be weighed together on loading dock scales.

PROMOTING CONCEPT CONNECTIONS

Maintaining Concepts

One child applied gravity concepts in a judgmental way when he picked himself up from a fall complaining, "That ol' grabbity pulled me down!" Many of the large-muscle play activities provide opportunities to point out how gravity's pull makes some of our fun or work easier, such as balancing block towers; enjoying a slide, teeter-totter, or swing; or playing catch. Some activities are difficult to do because of gravity's pull. This is why children become tired when they put away blocks, climb the jungle gym, walk up the stairs, or trudge up a hill. Comment on how the force of gravity is affecting children's activities. When a tumbled block structure needs rebuilding, ask the builder where gravity's pull requires the heaviest blocks.

Improving Schoolgrounds

Good playground equipment, especially slides and swings, provides lasting learning about the inexorable force of gravity: the child's body absorbs the knowledge that "What goes up must come down." A hill is a tremendous asset in a playspace, persuading a child of the energy required to climb up against gravity, and the "almost-flying" feeling of a running descent. Even a small, specially built hill is useful; cover it with sod.

Connecting Concepts

Gravity/Air Relationship. Balancing two air-filled balloons is a vivid way to demonstrate that gravity pulls on air. To make a long balance arm, insert one drinking straw partway into another straw. Insert a hanging loop in the center as you did in making the mobile. Blow up two balloons to equal size; tie one to each end of the arm. Be sure that the balloons are the same color. Some children may believe that balloons of different colors are also different in the amount of air they contain.

Hang up the arrangement and let the arm come to rest. To achieve balance, add bits of tape to the light side. It is hard to blow exactly the same amount of air into two balloons. Explain to the children that you are going to prick one balloon. "What will happen to that balloon?" Some children become scared when the balloon pops and forget to watch what happens to the balance. "Put your hands over your ears if the noise might bother you." Pop the balloon. Ask, "Which side of the balance went down? Why did that happen? Gravity pulls on air, too!" (If the pricked balloon flies apart, gather the pieces and tape them onto the end of the balance stick so a comparison of empty and air-filled balloons can still be made.)

Gravity/Water Relationship. Introduce the idea that gravity's pull plays a part in determining which objects sink and which float. Gravity pulls on water more than it pulls on corks, for instance. Recall that raindrops are pulled down to Earth when they become too heavy to float as droplets of vapor in clouds (see Chapter 9, Weather). Watch gravity's effect on raindrops clinging to classroom windows. Read A. A. Milne's poem "Waiting at the Window," from *Now We Are Six*. (See Appendix A.)

Family and Community Support

Families often have opportunities to show their children things that go up and away from gravity's pull. Big motors help elevators and escalators lift people. Heavy motors are needed to lift loads of materials at building construction sites that families could visit together. Families can watch TV presentations of gymnastics, ballet, and figure skating, pointing out how the athletes and dancers use their arms and legs to maintain their balance.

Check with the closest children's science museum about their interactive gravity displays, such as spinning coins down a gravity well.

RESOURCES

GERTZ, S., PORTMAN, D., & SARQUIS, M. (1996). *Teaching physical science through children's literature.* New York: McGraw-Hill. The best of the books integrating science with literature offers hands-on gravity activities using *Mirette on the High Wire* as a starting point.

SUMNERS, C. (1994). *Toys in space: Exploring science with the astronauts.* Blue Ridge Summit, PA: Tab Books.

TAYLOR, B., POTH, J., & PORTMAN, D. (1995). Teaching physics with toys. Middletown, OH: Terrific Science Press. The National Science Foundation supports this book. Clear directions for classroom activities with balance pans and making balance stick toys are included.

VANCLEAVE, J. (1993). *Janice VanCleave's gravity.* New York: John Wiley. Additional gravity experiments in this book extend this topic.

Simple Machines

Does the term simple machines *make your eyes glaze? Does it revive memories of formulas like, "distance × weight = work"?*

Relax! Activities in this chapter will let children in on a great discovery: simple machines can help them do things more easily.

Throbbing motors and turning wheels make little-noted daily background noises in the Western world. Children are proud to learn how to move and lift things with the help of simple machines. The knowledge invites interest in the complex machines they have previously taken for granted. The learning experiences in this chapter explore the following concepts:

- Friction can heat, slow, and wear away objects.
- A lever helps lift objects.
- A ramp shares the work of lifting.
- A screw is a curved ramp.
- Simple machines help move things along.
- Some wheels turn alone; some turn together.
- Single wheels can turn other wheels.
- Single wheels can help us pull down to lift up.

Experiencing the advantages and disadvantages of friction is a useful preliminary to the experiments that follow. The simple machines experiments illustrate the lever, ramp, screw, wheel and axle, and pulley.

Introducing Friction: "Rub the palms of your hands together as fast as you can. Keep going. Do you feel something happening to your hands? What we are doing makes heat. The reason for the heat is a force called *friction.*"

CONCEPT: Friction can heat, slow, and wear away objects.

1. How does friction slow sliding objects?

LEARNING OBJECTIVE: To enjoy direct research on the slowing effect of friction.

MATERIALS:

Gum erasers

Small pieces of waxed paper

Magnifying glass

Outdoor slide or smooth plank, propped against a table

Sheets of waxed paper

Rubber sink or tub mat

LARGE-GROUP ACTIVITY:

1. Pass around pieces of waxed paper. Tell children, "Try rubbing this on your arm. Does it slide fast? Try sliding the rubber eraser on your arm. Does it slide fast? Can you think of a reason for this?" (The rubber makes more friction.)
2. "Look at the paper and the eraser through the magnifying glass. Which is smooth? Which is fuzzy?"
3. ♣ Let children take turns on the slide out-doors, sitting first on waxed paper, then on the rubber mat. "Smooth paper doesn't make much friction, so you move fast."

2. What can we feel and see friction do?

LEARNING OBJECTIVE: To spark immediate interest in the heat-producing, wearing-away effects of friction.

MATERIALS:

6-inch (15 cm) pieces of scrap lumber

Coarse sandpaper, cut into 3-inch (7 cm) squares

Hammer

Nails

Magnifying glass

GETTING READY:

Hammer a few nails half their length into a chunk of wood. (To use the hammer as a lever, catch nail in claw and roll hammer back on curve of claw. Pull *down* on handle to lift nail *up* and out.)

SMALL-GROUP ACTIVITY:

1. Give each child sandpaper and scrap lumber. "Feel these. Are they smooth or rough? Do they look smooth or bumpy with the magnifier? Rub them together hard and long. See what happens."
2. "Are your fingers feeling warm? (Rough things rubbing together make lots of friction.) Are bits of wood wearing away? Look at your wood. Feel it. Is it getting smoother? Is the sandpaper changing? What does friction seem to do to things?"
3. "I'm going to pull a nail from this wood. Do you think that will make friction? Let's feel the nail quickly after it comes out. Is it warm or cool? Do you think the nail and wood rubbed together? How do you know?"

3. *How can we cut down on friction?*

LEARNING OBJECTIVE: To savor finding ways to reduce friction.

MATERIALS:

Coarse sandpaper

Petroleum jelly

Meat trays

Cream cheese or jelly

Soda crackers

Waxed paper

Table knives

GETTING READY:

Cut sandpaper into 2-inch (5 cm) squares.

Put a spoonful of spread or jelly on pieces of waxed paper for each child.

SMALL-GROUP ACTIVITY:

1. Give children two pieces of sandpaper. "Rub these together fast. What happens to the bits of sand?"

2. "Look at the sandpaper. Is it bumpy and rough? Do you think it would be smoother if something filled up the bumpy places? Try this petroleum jelly on it. See if the pieces of sandpaper slide past each other smoothly now."

3. Give each child two crackers on a tray. Repeat steps 1 and 2, offering cream cheese or jelly as a lubricant. Let the children eat this experiment.

Group Discussion: Show the children a small can of household oil. Ask what they know about it and why it is used at home. Develop the idea that oil makes a smooth sliding surface on objects that rub together. It cuts down friction that makes heat, wears bits away, makes things difficult to use, and makes things squeak.

Year-round programs can reduce friction and add cooling pleasure on the playground by hosing down the slide with water. As a safety tip, remind children that splashed water reduces friction, thus increasing slippery falls on tile surfaces near swimming pools.

4. *How can friction be useful?*

LEARNING OBJECTIVE: To find satisfaction in using friction to do work and stay safe.

MATERIALS:

Chalk

Dark-colored paper

Small pieces of waxed paper

Pencils

Petroleum jelly

Screw-top plastic containers, such as small paste jars

Two pans of water

Soap

Towels

SMALL-GROUP ACTIVITY:

A

1. Give children paper and chalk. "What sound does the chalk make on the paper? Why do you think this happens?"

2. "Try dipping your chalk into the petroleum jelly. Now does it rub and scrape? What happened to the chalk mark? Do you need friction to draw?"

3. Let children try to draw on waxed paper with pencils. Explain that the wax coating is like a lubricant.

B

1. "Are your hands strong enough to un-screw this jar cover? You can do it well."
2. "Try it again, but this time get your hands wet and soapy first. Why is it hard to do now? What is missing?"
3. "Try the doorknob with wet hands. Can you turn it?"

Group Discussion: Ask the children to check each other's shoe soles. Are some smooth and slippery? Do some have rubber heels? Do others have one-piece rubber bottoms? Are sneakers good for running and stopping, or do they skid? Are car tires smooth and slippery, or more like the soles of sneakers? Why? Talk about slippery road conditions, slippery bathtubs, and wet bathroom floors. How does friction make these places safer?

CONCEPT: A lever helps lift objects.

1. What can a lever do?

LEARNING OBJECTIVE: To gratify the wish to be powerful, using a lever and a resting point.

Open a discussion about machines and the work they do. Elicit children's information. Add that all of these mechanical inventions use one or more simple machines to make work easier. Children are surprised to know that they, too, use simple machines. "One day I watched Sophia on the playground pushing *down* to lift David *up* in the air. Then David pushed *down* to lift Sophia *up*. What were they doing? Did you notice how the seesaw worked? Did the board rest on something? Let's see what we can find out about making the work of lifting easier."

? *Inquiry Activity:* Develop background information by identifying the lever* as one of the simple machines that makes work easier. Ask for predictions about whether or not it will be easier to lift a book bundle with one finger through the string loop than to press that finger on a ruler resting on a pencil to raise the books. Ask for ideas about how to make the ruler a lever, with a pencil resting point (*fulcrum*). If necessary, demonstrate sliding the ruler under the books, placing the pencil beneath it (Figure 13-1), pressing the end of the ruler. Let children experiment independently at the science center, comparing lifting the bundle by one finger slipped through the string loops, with pressing that finger on a lever to lift the books at the other end. Encourage experimenting by placing the pencil under different measurement marks on the ruler, recording their findings on the "Highest Lifting" chart. Discuss results. Were the books raised higher if the pencil resting point was closer to the books or farther away?

*There are three types (classes) of levers for different uses. The locations of the load, the fulcrum, and where the force is applied differ for various uses. This activity uses a first-class lever.

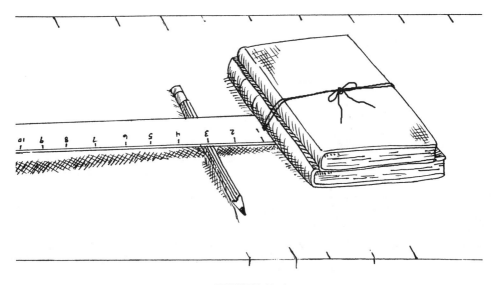

FIGURE 13–1

♣ Later, place the plank and block on the floor or outdoors. Ask one volunteer to stand on one end of the board, another to use the board to lift the child. Ask for predictions about success, and for suggestions about finding a way to do this. (Use the block as a resting point (fulcrum) to make the plank a lever. Stand by to steady the child.) After a success, ask for predictions. "Can two volunteers be lifted exactly the same way?" Find out. "Why not? What is different?" (Their weight.) "What could be changed to make it work? Find out." After discovering that a change in the block location makes lifting possible, point out the length of the lever on the pushing end from the resting point. Did that also change? Let small groups of children experiment and record their results on the "Lever Length" chart. Tally the results for the load weight and the length of the lever needed to lift it. At the end of the experimenting, restate the principle: *The longer the lever, the easier the lifting. A load must be close to the resting point to make it easy to lift up.*

MATERIALS:

Books

Sturdy 12-inch or 35-cm rulers

Pencils

String

6-foot seesaw plank or balance
  beam board

Large block

Empty paint can

Short screwdriver

GETTING READY:

Make bundles of two or more books tied with string in a single bow. Place in science center with rulers and pencils and chart.

Make "Easiest Lifting" chart with 3 columns: *Finger, Lever,* and *Same* for the class to record ease of book lifting results.

Make "Lever Length" chart with columns: *Short* and *Long*; and rows for *Light* and *Heavy* to record experiment results.

Read: Reinvent the Wheel, by Ruth Kassinger, (pp. 27, 28) about Archimedes's interest in levers more than 2000 years ago.

♣ On the playground seesaw, continue the inquiry about the weight of the load and the length of the lever by observing what happens when partners change their locations on the seesaw.

Group Discussion: At another group time, ask a volunteer to lift the lid off a small paint or similar can. Have a small screwdriver nearby. Did the child push

Changing where we stand changes how the lever works.

down to lift the lid up? Show that the resting point was the edge of the can. Many other things can be used as levers. Have the children seen other levers being used? Read relevant parts of *How Do You Lift a Lion?* by Robert Wells.

CONCEPT: **A ramp shares the work of lifting.**

The inclined plane (ramp) is another simple machine that helps us lift things against gravity's pull.

1. How can a ramp help us lift?
LEARNING OBJECTIVE: To take pride in raising a heavy load using a ramp.

MATERIALS:

Old, sturdy suitcase

Heavy objects to fill suitcase

Plank, at least 4 feet (1.2 m) long

Table

GETTING READY:

Fill the suitcase with enough
  weight to make it hard for a
  child to lift by the handle.

SMALL-GROUP ACTIVITY:

1. "See if you can pick up this heavy case by the handle and lift it onto the table."
2. "See if this plank can make it easier to get the case up on the table." Lean the plank from the floor on the tabletop. Place the suitcase near the bottom on the plank. "We call this a ramp."
3. "A ramp holds some of the weight of the suitcase as you slide it along. Now you can get the suitcase up there."

♣ Take a fun variation of this activity to the playground, if a slide is available. Tie a rope the length of the slide to the suitcase handle. Let children take turns trying to lift the suitcase as high as possible, then compare with climbing to the top step of the slide and pulling the suitcase up the slide by the rope. Which way gets the suitcase the highest with the least work? (See Wieseman, et al., 2002.)

Keep a running record of ramps that the children observe in the community. Ramps also help us take loads down safely and easily, as shown in the dump truck photo.

CONCEPT: **A screw is a curved ramp.**

Introduction: Draw a thick crayon line diagonally from one corner of a sheet of 8 1/2" × 11" paper to the other. Cut along the line, leaving a crayon-edged triangle. Bring the triangle, a pencil, a large screw, and a collection of nuts and bolts to a class discussion. "Does the line on this paper triangle look like a ramp? Let's see what we can do with it." Wind the triangle around the pencil so the line looks like a screw thread. Trace the spiral path from the bottom of the ramp to the top. Compare it with a screw. Give children the bolts and nuts. "Can you make the nut go up the ramp that curves around the bolt? Try it."

We watch dump truck's ramp do work outdoors.

1. *How can screws help us?*

LEARNING OBJECTIVE: To be surprised by the uses of screws to move things.

MATERIALS:

(Use as many as possible)

Screw-type cookie press

Tissue

C-clamps

Modeling clay

Old lipstick tube

Screw-type nutcracker

Screw-top plastic jars

Plastic pipes and joints

Old food grinder

Old piano stool or office swivel
  chair

GETTING READY:

The bottom half of a lipstick
  tube is usually two pieces.
  Separate them to reveal the

SMALL-GROUP ACTIVITY:

1. Remove design plate from the cookie press.
   Stuff a tissue in the press. Let children see
   what happens when the screw knob is
   turned. "What lifted up the tissue?"
2. Put a small ball of clay on the end of the
   C-clamp, turning the screw. Hold clamp
   upright; turn the screw until the clay rides
   up to be squashed by the top.
3. Show how two screws can be threaded together so they can't be pulled apart. (Use
   jars with matching lids, or a hose and noz-
   zle, or large bolt and nut.)
4. Let children experience being lifted by a
   screw with a piano stool or office chair.
   Examine the emerging screw as it turns.

spiral ramp that the lipstick moves along as it is twisted up.

Set up an exploration center for taking apart and assembling the activity objects.

Read *Reinvent the Wheel,* by Ruth Kassinger, (pp. 23–26) about Archimedes's screw. Consider following the directions to make an inexpensive, simple model for the classroom.

CONCEPT: **Simple machines help move things along.**

1. How do rollers move things?

LEARNING OBJECTIVE: To enjoy comparing ways to be moved: dragging, using rollers, and using wheels.

MATERIALS:

Grocery cartons

Jump ropes

4 cutoff broomsticks or cardboard cores from newsprint rolls to use as rollers

Platform dolly or board and 4 caster wheels

GETTING READY:

If the school custodian doesn't have a platform dolly for scrub buckets, make your own by screwing four swivel casters into a 1-inch (2.5 cm) thick plank.

SMALL-GROUP ACTIVITY:

1. Loop jump ropes around cartons. Let children take turns pulling each other in boxes, using jump rope handles in each hand. (Cardboard boxes fall apart soon, so have many.) "Is pulling easy or hard?"
2. Place rollers side by side on the floor. Put box on top. Repeat step 1. "See if rollers help move the box." (They don't stay under the box. Put them back for the next child's turn.)
3. "Which way made less friction?" Feel box bottoms after the dragging and after rolling.
4. "Now let's try rolling wheels that will stay under the box." Put box on the platform dolly. "Which is the easiest way to pull the box: dragging with rollers or with wheels?"

Group Discussion: Recall the rollers experiment. "Was the carton moved very far by four rollers? Would rollers be a good way to move cars and trucks? What if someone had to keep putting rollers in front of the car to keep it moving? Rollers are used that way when whole houses are moved a short distance. They give good support to the house. Rollers are also used to unload big trucks at the grocery store. Rollers are part of conveyor belts and escalators."

Read: Reinvent the Wheel, by Ruth Kassinger, (pp. 10–12).

CONCEPT: **Some wheels turn alone; some turn together.**

1. How do single wheels and pairs of wheels work?

LEARNING OBJECTIVE: To enjoy comparing the ways single and paired wheels work.

MATERIALS:

A light piece of furniture on 4 swivel wheels (office chair, typewriter stand, utility table, crate on casters, platform dolly)

Toy car with axles exposed

Small paper plates

Masking tape

Plastic drinking straws

Compass

GETTING READY:

Find the exact centers of paper plates with a compass. Mark each center; with pencil tip, push out a 1/4-inch (1 cm) hole. Have one for each child.

Cut 1-inch (2.5 cm) pieces of tape; stick lightly on a nearby table edge for children's use.

SMALL-GROUP ACTIVITY:

1. Divide children into two facing rows at least 5 feet apart.
2. "Let's take turns pushing the chair to children across the room. Watch what happens. How does it move?"
3. "Now let's push these cars across. Do they move like the chair wheels?" Compare with the swivel again, watching the wheels very closely. Turn the swivel and the cars upside down to see if they look the same. Supply the word *axle* if a child doesn't offer it. Point out pairs of wheels that turn together on an axle.
4. Let children try to roll their plates across to another child. Offer straws and tape, suggesting that two children could join wheel plates to see if they will roll better as a pair with an axle.

Group Discussion: Talk about the advantages of single wheels and pairs of wheels. If your classroom has an old upright piano or a classroom storage chest on casters, have children push it. Tiny, single wheels can make it easier to push something very heavy for a short way in all directions. "Do you think wagons, cars, buses, and trucks have a single wheel on each corner?" Show some pictures of wheeled objects cut from catalogs. "Do these things use single wheels or pairs of wheels on axles?" Children are surprised to learn that doorknobs are pairs of wheels on an axle. Bring in an old doorknob or unscrew one at school. Look together at a manual typewriter for rollers, wheels, and axles. Try to bring in a conventional roller skate to compare with the single wheels of in-line skates.

Set up a center for inventing wheeled vehicles with Lego® bricks or K'nex® construction sets.

Oops! Pairs of wheels can't make tight turns. We have to back away from the fence.

CONCEPT: Single wheels can turn other wheels.

1. How do gears work?

LEARNING OBJECTIVE: To delight in the details of meshing gears at work.

MATERIALS:

Eggbeater (hand operated)

2 deep mixing bowls

Soup spoons

Water

Detergent

Gear toys, visible clockwork, visible music box works, old clock to open

Crayon

Newspapers

Sponge

GETTING READY:

Put 1/2 cup water and 1 teaspoon detergent in each bowl.

Spread papers on the floor.

SMALL-GROUP ACTIVITY:

1. Ask children "Let's look very closely at a beater. How many wheels do you see? (Some wheels may look different.) Watch what happens to the little wheel when the big wheel is turned." Introduce the term *gear,* explaining that this is a wheel with teeth that mesh with teeth on the wheels next to it.

2. "Let's take turns using the beater to find out how the gears work. Let's compare beating bowls of soap suds with the beater and with a spoon to find out which works more easily."

3. Help children see that the big gear turns the little gears on the beater blades much faster.

Set up a center for exploring gear toys. If possible, include an old wind-up clock, a tiny screwdriver, and safety goggles to wear when children take apart the clock. **Safety Precaution:** The clock's coiled steel main spring has sharp edges. It should be unscrewed and removed only by an adult.

Group Discussion: Try to borrow a *one-speed* bicycle to examine with the group. Turn the bicycle upside down and look at the gears. Tell children, "Sometimes gears turn each other without touching each other. Instead they fit into a chain that moves them. Is one gear large and one small, like the eggbeater? Let's turn the pedals and watch the chain make the small gear turn. Count how many times the back wheel turns while I turn the pedal one time." Count one turn when the air valve reaches the top.

Look at the tire tread. "Could friction help stop a bicycle? Why do you think the chain looks greasy? Would it need grease? What do you think is inside the tires?"

CONCEPT: Single wheels can help us pull down to lift up.

1. How does a pulley help us lift things?

LEARNING OBJECTIVE: To take pride in finding that a pulley helps with heavy lifting.

MATERIALS:

Small pulley

Firm cord, double the length of floor-to-pulley distance

Bucket and blocks

Stopwatch

Screw hook

GETTING READY:

Install screw hook in a ceiling beam or door frame (ask custodian).

Pass the cord over the pulley wheel; hang pulley on screw hook.

SMALL-GROUP ACTIVITY:

1. Show children the pulley. "Do you suppose this single wheel could make it easier to lift a bucketful of blocks?"
2. "First let's see how long you can lift up and hold this bucket with one hand. Lift it as high as you can. I'll time you." Record length of time each child can hold bucket.
3. Tie cord firmly to bucket handle. "Now try pulling down on this cord to lift the load. I'll time you to see how long you can hold it up." (Demonstrate careful lowering of bucket, but stand by in case someone lets it down too fast.) "Are you pulling down on the rope, or lifting the rope to lift the bucket up? Does the pulley make the lifting job easier?"

Group Discussion: (Try to find pictures of the following things to show.) "Pulleys help people load big ships, trains, and barns. Pulleys are used on steam shovels, on sailboats, on flagpoles, on scaffoldings, in draw-drapery rods, and inside the casings of windows. A pulley arrangement moves people up in large buildings on elevators and escalators. Single wheels help people and machines pull *down* to *lift up* or *pull across.*" David Burnie's *Machines and How They Work* is an excellent source for pictures. Read relevant parts of *How Do You Lift a Lion?* by Robert Wells.

INTEGRATING ACTIVITIES

Math Experiences

Screws, Bolts, and Nuts Grouping. Set up a sorting center with many sizes of nuts, bolts, and screws for children to match, seriate, and group. Many variations are possible. Children can explain their reasons for groupings.

Wheel Quantity Classification Game. Cut out and mount catalog pictures of wheeled objects. Ask children to sort them into groups according to the number of wheels each object has. (A record player turntable could be used as an example of a one-wheeled object.)

Music (Resources in Appendix A)

1. Sing this song about friction to the tune of "Here We Go Round the Mulberry Bush" while rubbing hands together.

Friction Song

This is the way we warm our hands, warm our hands, warm our hands.

This is the way we warm our hands, out in chilly weather.

Friction is what warms our hands, warms our hands, warms our hands.

Friction is what warms our hands, rubbing them together.

—J. H.

2. "Little Red Wagon" is a lively reminder of the usefulness of wheels and axles. One child created these three verses for his favorite song:

Both wheels are off and back end's dragging . . .

Four wheels are off and we're not even moving . . .

Now we're going to the repair shop . . .

3. Listen to Tom Paxton sing "Ride My Bike" on his cassette, *Suzy Is a Rocker.*

Literature Links

ANHOLT, LAURENCE. (2000). *Leonardo and the flying boy.* London: Barrons. A true story of the unsuccessful flight in 1502 of Leonardo da Vinci's first flying machine. Pulleys and gears are visible in the illustrations.

ARDIZZONE, EDWARD. (2001). *Little Tim and the brave sea captain.* New York: Scholastic. Watch for heavy pulleys in the illustrations of lifeboat launching and the rope rescue of Tim and the Captain. Paperback.

BINGHAM, CAROLINE. (1998). *Monster machines.* New York: Dorling Kindersley. This is a big book about big machines: dump trucks, cranes, and tractors. The text is informative and the photographs are terrific. A good browsing book.

BURNIE, DAVID. (1991). *Machines and how they work.* New York: Dorling Kindersley. Excellent color photographs and intricately detailed drawings allow children a clear view of wheels and gears in use in a clock, windmill, and 10-speed bike.

DAHL, MICHAEL. (1996). *Levers. Pulleys. Wheels and axles.* Mankato, MN: Capstone. Each book deals with a different simple machine. The photos have a contemporary flair, as in showing a skateboard axle, though the text is basically definitions.

FALCONER, IAN. (2001). *Olivia saves the circus.* New York: Atheneum. When the circus performers have become sick, Olivia, the intrepid piglet, steps in to perform as the unicycle performer.

FOWLER, ALLAN. (2001). *Simple machines.* New York: Children's Press. This small book of simple machine concepts for beginning readers has an easy text and attractive photographs.

FROST, HELEN. (2001). *What are wheels and axles?* Mankato, MN: Pebble Books. Very basic information about the topic is provided in this small book for beginning readers.

GIBSON, GARY. (1995). *Pushing and pulling.* Brookfield, CT: Copper Beech. Ideas are offered for projects for primary children to do with some help from adults.

HARSHMAN, MARC. (1995). *The storm.* New York: Dutton. Jonathan wheels his chair at top speed to save horses from a tornado's path. Friction from the turning wheels burns his hands.

HOBAN, TANA. (1997). *Construction zone.* New York: Greenwillow. This is a great source for photographs of rollers at work.

HODGE, DEBORAH. (1998). *Simple machines.* Buffalo, NY: Kids Can Press. This book has clear drawings and text, along with bright photographs showing children exploring simple machines.

KORMAN, JUSTINE. (1998). *Tonka: Building the new road* and *Tonka: Working hard with the mighty crane.* New York: Scholastic. The vocabulary and concepts about what those big machines do will be used in sandbox play. Some children will memorize these books.

KUHNE, HEINZ. (1999). *Leonardo da Vinci: Dreams, schemes, and flying machines.* New York: Prestel Verlag. Older children will be intrigued by the range of inventions created by the genius best known for his paintings. His drawings of levers, gears, and the "airscrew" illustrate the book.

LEONTOVICH, M. (1995). *Force, of course!* Glenview, IL: Goodyear. Straightforward text describes the functions of simple machines. Experiments take intrigued children a bit further.

MASON, JANE. (1995). *Hello, two-wheeler!* New York: Grosset & Dunlap. A boy who still needs training wheels withdraws from bicycling with his two-wheeling friends until the training wheels fall off when he isn't looking. Lots of wheels and a wrench lever in this familiar situation. Paperback.

MORRIS, ANN. (1998). *Tools.* New York: Mulberry. Color photographs show tools being used around the world to make life easier. Paperback.

OLLERENSHAW, CHRIS, & TRIGGS, PAT. (1994). *Gears.* Milwaukee, WI: Gareth Stevens. The photographs of gears in use will increase awareness of their importance. Most of the activities seem too labor-intensive for classroom use, but may work as independent projects.

PARKER, STEVE. (1997). *Making tracks.* Cambridge, MA: Candlewick. The brief text and good illustrations show ancient uses of the wheel, early trains and bicycles, and today's wheels.

REY, H. A. (1997). *Curious George rides a bike.* New York: Scholastic Services. A hammer is used as a lever to open a crate. Gears, chain, and pedals on George's bike, and pulleys on a circus wagon cage are shown in this adventure.

RICHARDS, JON. (2000). *Work and simple machines.* Brookfield, CT: Millbrook. Simple machine principles are clearly explained with each suggested experiment, although the rather labor-intensive projects are more suitable for home than classroom use.

SOMMERVILLE, LOUISA. (1999). *The science of cogs and pulleys.* Laguna Hills, CA: Walter Foster Publishers. The clear text and excellent photographs will be interesting long after the accompanying stickers and paper model cutouts are used up. This book illustrates the working parts of escalator pulleys and cogs.

Sullivan, George. (1993). *In-line skating.* New York: Dutton. Written for advanced readers, it illustrates the maneuverability of single wheels as the basis for this popular sport.

Walker, Sally, & Feldman, Roseann. (2002). *Inclined planes and wedges.* Minneapolis: Lerner. Great photographs of age-mates having fun with experiments will invite young readers to try them. Careful descriptions and background information, as well as useful Web sites, complete the value of this book, as well as the others in the series by these fine authors: *Levers; Wheels and Axles; Screws;* and *Pulleys.* NSTA* recommended.

Wells, Robert. (1996). *How do you lift a lion?* Morton Grove, IL: Albert Whitman. In this fresh approach, the author/illustrator shows lively kids solving unusual lifting and moving problems with simple machines. A pleased lion, giggling baboons, and a jubilant panda will lock in wheel, pulley, and lever concepts. Paperback.

Welsbacher, Anne. (2001). *Levers.* Mankato, MN: Bridgestone Books. Clear writing and bright photographs in this book provide basic information about how levers work.

Williams, Bryan. (1992). *On the move.* New York: Random House. This small, clearly illustrated book on transportation includes drawings of bicycle gears, rollers moving airport baggage, rollers on paving equipment, rollers in the car wash, and various wheels—from unicycles to double-wide race cars.

*National Science Teachers Association

Poems (Resources in Appendix A)

To stimulate children to invent machines they may wish existed, read "Homework Machine," from *A Light in the Attic,* by Shel Silverstein.

Fingerplays

The familiar fingerplay, "The Wheels on the Bus," calls for arm rolling and active bouncing.

Art Activities

Collage. These collage materials are strongly suggestive of simple machines: macaroni wheels; pieces of thick string; bottle caps; popsicle sticks; and round, triangular, and rectangular construction paper shapes. (The macaroni wheels may become essential parts of pulleys and gears, or they may be quietly eaten by a child whose inspiration is not as strong as his curiosity about new tastes.)

Cutting and Pasting. Young children enjoy making their own books or contributing pages to a group book for classroom use. For individual books, staple a few sheets of folded paper together. For group books, use cardboard punched with holes at the top. Fasten with leather thongs or notebook rings. Provide scissors, paste, and pages cut from catalogs illustrating things with simple machine parts: clocks, eggbeaters, wheelbarrows, wheeled toys, mechanical toys, tools, carts, pepper mills, and so forth. If the supply of pictures is sufficient, they could be part of a math experience, making separate pages to show one-wheeled objects, two-wheeled objects, and so on.

Friction as an Art Medium. Sometimes when children are drawing with pencils and crayons, or making chalk rubbings, remind them that friction is involved in making colors stay on the paper.

A Friction Project. This project requires at least 2 days. Let the children sand 3-inch × 5-inch (8 cm × 12 cm) pieces of scrap lumber to satin smoothness. Next, use markers to draw a design on paper to cut out and glue to the sanded wood. The teacher can coat the plaque and picture with clear varnish. Allow at least a day of drying time. Insert a small screw eye in the top edge of the plaque for hanging. This makes an appreciated gift for parents.

Play

Packing Carton Vehicles. Young children usually need little more than grocery cartons, paper plate wheels, and paper fasteners to create play cars and trains. A real steering wheel from an auto salvage yard, an inner tube and tire pump, and some sets of discarded keys add fun to the play.

Elevator. A tall refrigerator packing carton can become an elevator with a door cut in one side and numerals marked above it to indicate floors. It can be part of block or housekeeping play as desired.

Pulley Fun. Make an elevator for a skyscraper. Ask children to build a three-sided block tower directly below a pulley. Fasten a milk carton elevator to one end of the pulley cord. Cut a door in one side of the carton and fill it with toy passengers.

Attach two small pulleys to opposite sides of the block play area, a few feet above the floor. Tie the handle of a small basket to the pulley cord and knot the cord into a continuous, taut loop running between the two pulleys. It can be an aerial tramway for toy passengers or a conveyor belt for block construction workers. A pulley-operated cable car kit is available by mail from HearthSong (see Appendix A). A pulley and cable car are available with Childcraft *Magnuts* toy sets.

Other Indoor Fun. A toy conveyor belt ramp is sold commercially. It can be an airplane baggage loader or a piece of play farm equipment. The two rollers that move the belt are operated with a small crank.

Many commercial toys with visible working parts extend the simple machine concepts in play. Examples include construction sets, gear sets, clocks, music boxes, and locks with visible working parts. Add a toy sand or water wheel to sandbox or water table.

PVC pipes and elbows screw together to create "inventions." Provide pieces of perforated hardboard and hardware odds and ends to attach to it: cupboard doorknobs and hinges, nuts, bolts, and washers. Short screwdrivers are easiest for children to control. Supply the workbench with bottle caps, metal ends from food container tubes, and discarded spools to inspire the construction of wheel-, gear-, and dial-encrusted inventions.

Creative Movement

Mechanical Toys. Children enjoy acting out the stiff, jerking movements of windup toys. Offer to wind up one child toy at a time so that other children can guess what kind of toy they are watching, or wind up all the toys at once so they can all move to music. In addition, children can try to move like the Tin Man in the

Many toys have simple machines in them.

story *The Wizard of Oz*, both when he was too rusty to move and after friction was cut down by oil so that he could move. Encourage children to improvise other simple machine actions. (See Thompson, 1998.)

Creative Thinking

Read Shel Silverstein's poem "Homework Machine." Then ask children to imagine a new machine that would help them solve a problem. "What would it do? What would it look like?" Read the E. L. Konigsburg book, *Samuel Todd's Book of Great Inventions*. Encourage drawing pictures and/or writing a description of children's inventions. Collect them into a class book of great inventions. Or let children write about a simple machine they like, or have used, and make a "What We Have Found Out About Simple Machines" class report.

What If? Collect pictures to illustrate a family picnic outing: getting food ready, climbing into the car, and gathering fishing poles and playthings. Ask, "What if there weren't any friction anywhere one day? What would be different for this family on a picnic? Yes, the mother would have trouble opening the peanut butter jar to make the sandwiches, the children would skid and fall down trying to walk to the car, the baseball bat would slip out of the boy's hand when he hit the ball, and the fishing poles might slide out of their hands."

Food Experiences

Children feel very important when they turn a crank that contributes to good eating. Several simple machines can be used to prepare food in the classroom. Make molded cookies with a cookie press. Use a hand-cranked grinder to make graham cracker crumbs for unbaked cookies or to make toast crumbs for the birds. Use a rolling pin to make cutout cookies and a gear-driven eggbeater to mix instant pudding. Grind wheatberries in a hand-cranked coffee mill. Borrow an apple paring/slicing machine to prepare apples for a snack.

Field Trips

1. Field trips to see simple machines in action can be as simple as a walk to the school kitchen. A well-timed visit might allow the children to see a food order being unloaded on a hand truck from a delivery truck. Hand trucks have one pair of wheels on an axle and use the lever principle to lift loads. The kitchen may have a swivel-wheeled utility cart and a large can opener that has a sharp wheel to cut metal, gears to turn the can, a crank that turns an axle, and a screw to clamp the opener to a table.

2. The school office may have an electric typewriter that has wheels, gears, axles, and a roller inside. Ask permission to lift the top for children's visual inspection (no touching!). Examine the gears of the plastic correction tape reels and the ribbon cartridge. Find the corresponding gears inside the typewriter that mesh with and turn them.

3. A repair worker in the building could show children an array of tools and equipment that apply simple machine principles.

4. The nearest driveway could be the scene of an impressive sight if the teacher can demonstrate the screw or lever principle by jacking up her car. (Be sure to observe the safety precaution of blocking the wheels on the ground with a brick, and keeping children a safe distance away.)

   Safety Precaution: Be sure to check for safety hazards when planning the following field trips. The locations are not intended for general public use. Children should be well supervised.

5. Many pulleys are visible on weight training machines at a health club, and treadmills use rollers, not always visibly.

6. Many wheels, rollers, conveyor belts, and pulleys are used in the work areas of the post office. Each one also has a flagpole with a pulley to raise the flag.

7. Backstage supermarket operations include hanging meat from overhead rolling tracks, using sets of rollers enclosed in metal frames to slide cases of food from trucks to storerooms, and moving groceries on checkout counter conveyor belts.

8. An older retail store in your community might still use a hand-operated dumbwaiter to bring stock upstairs from a basement storage room. In some types of dumbwaiters, the pulleys and ropes are visible. See if there is an enclosed freight elevator near your school where the whole class could take a ride together. It's fun to do!

There are so many opportunities to see simple machine principles in action that it would be easy to overdo the effort. Don't risk wearing down children's interest by taking too many field trips.

PROMOTING CONCEPT CONNECTIONS

Maintaining Concepts

There are countless opportunities to bring simple machine principles to light during everyday school activities. When we want things to move or spin or slide easily, we can mention the need to cut down friction with a few drops of oil. There are times when too little friction poses safety hazards for young children: shoeless children moving fast on slippery floors or unwary children crossing streets on rainy or icy days.

For a vivid application of the lever and a pair of wheels, let children use a hand truck to help trundle heavy sandbags to the sandbox. Encourage them to try moving the sandbags without the hand truck so that they will realize how much the hand truck helps them.

Simple machine concepts are part of workbench use. Examples include the friction of sanding and sawing, the lever action of pulling out nails with the hammer, and the interlocking screw threads that hold wood tightly in a vice or clamp.

Whenever possible, let children watch the repair and maintenance of classroom and playground equipment. Better still, enlist the help of a shy child or one who needs a chance to get positive attention and approval. One child who broke toys and mistreated other children to attract attention was able to give up these undesirable behaviors when he became our chief mechanic. He took such pride in manning the oilcan and tightening tricycle bolts that he became a good steward of school property and a friend to other children.

Improving Schoolgrounds

Provide some 6-foot planks for children to devise their own ramps and levers. Screw 2 × 2 pieces of wood under each end so that when plank is on a climber cross-bar it will not slip. Establish safety rules about the height planks can rise to.

A slide and a balance beam are good additions. If you are making a walled garden area, make the wall have a wide top for balancing walks.

Connecting Concepts

Simple machines help overcome the effect of gravity's pull. This can be brought out by speaking about the weight of the objects being lifted or moved in terms of gravity's pull. The effect of magnetism could be used to discover what a strong axle or wheel frame is composed of or to learn what kind of hinge rusts and needs oiling when it works hard and squeaks from too much friction.

Simple machine principles are used to move boats on water. Easy examples are the levers called *oars* and the paddle wheels that power the swanboats seen in Robert McCloskey's book, *Make Way for Ducklings.*

Family and Community Support

Ask families if they would be willing to lend equipment or demonstrate skills that involve simple machines. Todd's mother loaned us a butter churn that her grandmother had used. Jenny's mother made bread with us, using her hand-cranked kneading bucket. Both children gained new status as a result of their parents' contributions.

Identify the interactive simple machine exhibits available at the nearest children's or science museum. Using a giant lever to heave up a boulder, hoisting themselves up in a rope-and-pulleys display, and turning wheels to make big things happen are impressive hands-on learning activities.

RESOURCES

FRIEDHOFFER, BOB. (1996). *Physics lab in a hardware store.* New York: Franklin Watts. This is very useful background reading if you need a brush-up on simple machines.

KASSINGER, RUTH. (2001). *Reinvent the wheel.* New York: John Wiley. Develop awareness for the historical importance of simple machines with the fascinating anecdotes and models in this book.

MACAULAY, DAVID. (1998). *The new way things work: A visual guide to the world of machines.* Boston: Houghton Mifflin. This book gives the teacher the same revelations of "so-that's-how-it-works" that children gain from their study of simple machines.

THOMPSON, W. (1998). A moving science lesson. *Science and Children, 36*(3), 24–28. The fundamentals of creative movement for concept learning are given here, as well as simple machine improvisation suggestions.

VAN CLEAVE, JANICE. (1993). *Machines.* New York: John Wiley. The projects and explanations provide additional experiences with pulleys, an inclined plane, the wheel and axle of a pencil sharpener, and more.

WIESE, JIM. (1994). *Rollercoaster science.* New York: John Wiley. This book for advanced-level students can be used selectively as a fascinating illustrated reference for simple machines, light, and gravity principles at work in the amusement park.

WISEMAN, K., CADWELL, D., & PIKE, L. (2002). It's time for adventure buddies. *Science and Children, 39*(6), 40–46.

Teaching Resource

Moving machines. Videotape. Bo Peep Productions, P.O. Box 982, Eureka, MT 59917. Parallels are shown between heavy construction machines at work and young children playing with toys like them.

Sound

Have you ever tried making a scary movie less scary by plugging your ears? It works! Sound impacts our emotions, maybe even more than sight, so it's good to explore this phenomenon with children.

The discovery that sound occurs when something vibrates can help children overcome fears about scary noises. Vibrations cause sound whether they originate in the distant clouds or in our own throats. The following concepts are explored in this chapter:

- Sounds are made when something vibrates.
- Sound travels through many things.
- Different sizes of vibrating objects make different sounds.

The experiences begin with a group activity to clarify the term *vibration* and to establish the idea that vibrations cause sounds. This is followed by experiencing vibrations, experimenting with mediums through which sound travels, and relating the pitch of sound to the size of vibrating objects.

Introduction: Help children understand what a vibration is by producing one. Say something like this: "Can you lift your arm and let your hand dangle from your wrist? Now, shake your hand as fast as you can. What do you call what is happening to your hand? Shaking? Wiggling? Jiggling? Wobbling? Those are good words. *Vibration* is another word that means moving back and forth very fast. Does your hand look different when it is vibrating? Some vibrating things move back and forth so fast that they look blurry. Another thing happens when something vibrates. You can find out if you listen very quietly. Hold your hand near your ear, then vibrate your fingers and hand very fast. What happens? Does someone hear a soft, whirring sound?

"Now put your fingers very lightly on the front of your throat, near the bottom. Very softly sing a sound like *eeeeee.* Do you feel something with your fingertips? Try it again. Did something inside your throat vibrate? Yes, you made a sound in there. Whenever we hear a sound, it is being made by something vibrating. Try touching your lips while you say *hummmmmm*. What's happening?"

CONCEPT: Sounds are made when something vibrates.

1. What's happening when we see things vibrate?

LEARNING OBJECTIVE: To make the surprising connection between sound and vibrating materials.

MATERIALS:

Binding strip from vinyl folder cover, or flexible ruler

Coffee can with plastic lid, or sturdy drum

Sand, rice, or foam packing chips

Quart milk carton

Rubber bands

GETTING READY:

Cut window opening in one side of milk carton.

Stretch rubber band around length of milk carton.

SMALL-GROUP ACTIVITY:

1. "Watch and listen to this." Extend folder strip from edge of table or chair, like a diving board. Bend free end down, then release. "What did you see and hear?"
2. Show the milk carton. "What will happen if you pluck the rubber band? Watch and listen. You try it."
3. "It was easy to see the plastic strip and the rubber band vibrate. Some vibrations are hard to see. Let's put light things on this can lid to find out if the lid vibrates." Put sand, rice, or chips on lid. Tap the lid. "What happens? Now you try it."

2. What's happening when we feel things vibrate?

LEARNING OBJECTIVE: To enjoy memorable ways of associating sound with vibrations.

MATERIALS:

One or more of these: windup alarm clock, kitchen timer, toy music box

Combs

Waxed paper (tissue paper disintegrates when damp)

GETTING READY:

Cut pieces of waxed paper to fold over teeth of combs.

SMALL-GROUP ACTIVITY:

1. Pass unwound clock, timer, and music box among the children. "Do you feel these things vibrating now? Are they making sounds?"
2. Wind the equipment and pass again. "Now what do you feel and hear?"
3. "Try making some music with vibrating air and paper. Hold the paper at the bottom of the comb lightly between your lips. Now try to hum and blow a tune at the same time. The vibrations feel funny, but the sound is nice."
4. Tour the room and halls to feel vibrating electric motors (aquarium water pump, sound system speaker, water cooler, etc.).

CONCEPT: **Sound travels through many things.**

1. How can we tell that air carries sound?

LEARNING OBJECTIVE: To have fun confirming that air carries sound vibrations.

MATERIALS:

12-inch (30 cm) pieces of plastic
  garden hose
Clear PVC tubes

SMALL-GROUP ACTIVITY:

1. "What could be inside the pieces of hose? Put one end next to your mouth; put the other next to your ear. Whisper your name into the hose. Could you hear yourself? What could be vibrating inside the tube?"
2. "You can *feel* what is vibrating if you put your hand at the end of the hose. Try saying words like *toot* and *tut*. Can you feel something pushing on your hand each time you say a word?" (Air carried vibrations from their throats through the tubes.)
3. Let seated children enjoy speaking to each other through the PVC tubes.

☘ Take a silent listening tour of the schoolyard. How many sounds can be heard?

Group Discussion: "Peek into the ear of the child sitting next to you. Do you see anything inside the ear that is vibrating? Could something invisible be in there?"

Recall how the sand or foam chips bounced around when someone tapped the coffee can lid. One vibrating thing made the things next to it vibrate. "Air vibrates when something next to it vibrates. That is the way sound is carried by air. It is the way sounds usually come to our ears. The air inside our ears also vibrates so we hear the sounds." Let children experiment with this idea by covering and uncovering their ears with their hands as they listen to some music. Could the air inside their ears vibrate very well when their hands were covering them?

Safety Precaution: "Our ears have an outside part that we can see and an inside part that we can't see. The inside part is so delicate that vibrating air can vibrate it. That is how we hear. We must be very careful with our ears to keep that delicate part working well. Can you think of some good safety rules for our ears?"

2. How can we tell that water carries sound?

LEARNING OBJECTIVE: To make the surprising discovery that water can carry sound vibrations.

MATERIALS:

Two similar containers, such as
  plastic buckets

SMALL-GROUP ACTIVITY:

1. "Take turns pressing one ear to the side of the bucket to listen to the sound I'll make."

Pair of blunt scissors

Sponge, plastic sheet, or newspaper for spills

PVC tubes

GETTING READY:

Half-fill one container with water

Open and shut scissors to make a steady clicking noise while holding them inside the empty bucket.

2. "I'll make the same sound in the water in this bucket. Listen the same way here. Listen for clicks. Are they louder or softer in the water? Put the PVC tube in the wa-ter, then put your ear at the other end to listen. Is the sound louder coming through the air or through water?" Let the children make the scissors clicks for each other.

Note: If children in your class have gone fishing, they will understand now why people try to be very quiet when they are fishing. Mention that whales can hear other whales miles away.

3. How can we tell that sound travels through solids?

LEARNING OBJECTIVE: To be amazed that solid objects can carry and intensify sounds.

MATERIALS:

Table

Bottle caps, sticks, small rock, to
  tap on the table

Clock, timer, or musical toy
  works

SMALL-GROUP ACTIVITY:

1. "We're going to make sounds for each other. Some may be very soft, so we'll have to listen closely." Tap one fingernail on the tabletop. "Does this sound seem loud? Now cover one ear with your hand and press the other ear on the tabletop while I do the same thing again."

2. "Which way was the sound louder, through the air or through the wooden table? Now put your ears to the table and close your eyes. Each one of you can take a turn tapping on the table with these things. We'll try to guess what made the sound."

3. Later compare sounds made by the clock, motor, or music works when held in the hand, placed on the table while heads are up, and on the table while ears are pressed to the table. Which sounds loudest? Finding out takes time. Keep the learning pace relaxed. Listen to the children's ideas.

? *Inquiry Activity:* Establish a center for ongoing investigations about how well various materials carry the sound of a small ticking object. Investigators cover one ear, and hold the material and the ticker next to the other ear. Test materials should include a metal pot lid, a square of wood, a mugful of air to be cupped over the ear, and a pillow. What other materials will children want to test? Record findings on a class chart.

4. How does string carry sound?

LEARNING OBJECTIVE: To enjoy discovering that tight strings carry sounds well.

MATERIALS:

Light string

Metal spoons

Bar of soap

Empty frozen juice cans, 2 for each telephone

1 1/2-inch (4 cm) nails

Hammer

GETTING READY:

Cut string into 2 1/2-foot (75 cm) lengths for spoon chimes.

Make a hole in center of each can bottom.

Cut string into 5-foot (1.5 m) lengths for metal can telephones. (String can be longer for use at home. Short lengths are best when many children will be using phones in the same room!)

SMALL-GROUP ACTIVITY:

1. Dangle short string over a finger. "Do you think loose string will vibrate to make a sound if you pluck it? What if it is held tightly by both hands? Try it both ways with your string." (Loose string vibrates too slowly for audible sound.)
2. "Let's add heavy vibrating metal to the string ends and listen to find out if tight string will carry sound." Tie a spoon to each end of string. Fold string in half; press folded end to ear. Lean over so that spoons dangle freely. Swing string to make spoons strike each other. Listen to the sounds traveling up the string.
3. Make frozen juice can telephones along with children. To stiffen string ends, pull them across a soap bar or wrap with clear tape. Put a string through the holes in two cans from the outside. Pull string into the can and tie around a nail. Wedge the nail inside the can. "Keep the string straight and tight. You talk into one can and your friend listens through the other can."

Group Discussion: Give each child a rubber band to pluck when it is limp and when it is stretched. What did the spoon chime and metal-can telephone makers find out about how string vibrates to carry sound? How many things vibrated to carry the sound of their voices? (Air in cans, the cans, and the string.)

CONCEPT: **Different sizes of vibrating objects make different sounds.**

---

1. How do different vibrating string lengths sound?

LEARNING OBJECTIVE: To take pleasure in discerning pitch differences and associating them with vibrating string lengths.

Vibration turns ordinary string and ordinary spoon into sound.

MATERIALS:

Three sizes of plastic boxes, such as 3-inch, 4-inch, 5-inch (8 cm, 10 cm, 13 cm)

Egg carton

Rubber bands large enough to stretch around the length of boxes and egg carton

Pencil

Autoharp or guitar (desirable)

SMALL-GROUP ACTIVITY:

1. Pluck rubber bands on the plastic boxes. "Do these all sound alike? Which one sounds highest? Lowest? Try it."

2. "Now try this." Stretch long rubber band lengthwise over the egg carton. Slip pencil under band near left end of the box. Pluck the length of rubber band to the right of the block. Listen. Continue plucking and slide the pencil slowly toward the other end of the box. "Is it changing? Is it higher or lower? Does the whole rubber band length vibrate, or just the side being

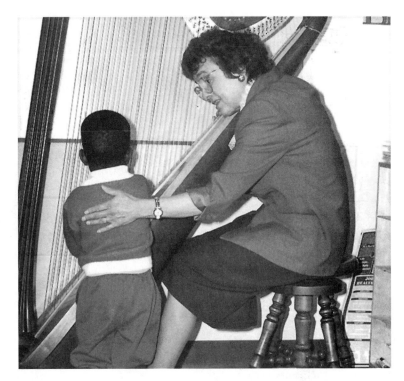

Vibrating strings, long and short, captivate Steven.

GETTING READY:

Stretch small rubber band over each opened plastic box, the smallest band on smallest box, etc. (The effect won't be the same if same size rubber band is used on all three boxes. Try to find out why.)

plucked? Is the part that vibrates getting shorter and higher?" Let children experiment, sliding the block and plucking. "Can you play the scale this way? Play a tune?"

Group Discussion: The autoharp very clearly shows the relationship between string length and pitch. (A real harp and an upright piano with the front panel removed, or a grand piano with the top raised, will show the same thing.) If a guitar is used for this purpose, be sure to make clear which part of the string is vibrating, so that the relationship between vibrating string length and pitch can be understood.

2. *How do different vibrating air column lengths sound?*

LEARNING OBJECTIVE: To enjoy associating differences in pitch with varying columns of vibrating air.

MATERIALS:

8 empty 16 oz. (480 ml) bottles

Extra bottle to demonstrate
  blowing technique

Pitcher of water

Funnel

Masking tape

Sponge

Rubbing alcohol

Paper towels

GETTING READY:

Experiment at home with levels
  of water needed to produce
  tones of the octave. Internal
  shapes of bottles vary, but
  these water levels may be
  about right:

1. empty

2. 1 ¾ inches (4.5 cm)

3. 2 ½ inches (6.5 cm)

4. 4 inches (10 cm)

5. 4 ½ inches (11.5 cm)

6. 5 ¼ inches (13 cm)

7. 5 ½ inches (14 cm)

8. 6 inches (15 cm)

Place band of tape around each
  bottle, with upper edge of tape
  at measurement level.

Let children pour water to
  marked levels of bottles, if
  possible.

SMALL-GROUP ACTIVITY:

1. "What is inside these bottles? What will
   happen if the air inside the bottles vibrates? When air moves across the top of
   the bottle, the air inside vibrates."
   Demonstrate producing a tone.[*]

2. "We put some water in these bottles.
   Which bottle has space for more air? Let's
   see what happens when we make different
   amounts of air space vibrate."

3. Arrange bottles in order, 1 through 8. Have
   eight children, one per bottle, blow across
   them in order, playing the scale. Can they
   play a tune? Wipe tops with rubbing alcohol before others have turns.

Note: Listen to a beautiful recording of Romanian pan flute music. Zamfir
plays this ancient pan-pipes instrument. Many of the covers for his recordings
illustrate the graduated-size pipes he blows across.

[*]Demonstrate pressing your lower lip taut against your teeth, holding the bottle top
to your lower lip, blowing *"toooooo"* across, *not* into, the bottle. Experiment at home.
Consult a flute player if you need help producing a tone.

Soundmaking is fun for everyone.

INTEGRATING ACTIVITIES

Math Experiences

Ordering by Pitch and Size. The mathematical relationship between the size and the pitch of vibrating objects is fun to explore. Sets of bells and sets of detached metal chimes, available commercially, can be placed on a molded framework to form a xylophone. The bells and chimes can be arranged by children in one-step tone order visually according to size, largest to smallest; or according to tone, lowest to highest.

Music

Many familiar children's songs are easy extensions of the vibrations and pitch concepts, as they describe bell sounds and animal sounds. The concepts can be applied when rhythm instruments are used. "Charles, try holding your triangle by the string loop instead of with your hand. See if it vibrates more now." Prolong the life of school drums by suggesting that they will vibrate better when lightly tapped than when thumped very hard.

Children can make simple instruments to play. Directions are offered in *Making Music: Shake, Rattle and Roll with Instruments You Make Yourself* by M. Jackson.

The following song is about the cause of sounds:

Sounds

—J. H.

Literature Links

ANDERSON, KAREN C., & CUMBAA, STEPHEN. (1993). *Bones and skeleton game book.* New York: Workman. This book includes an illustrated description of how sounds reach hearing centers in the brain, and offers an experiment to sense sound vibrations going through the bones in the head.

ARDLEY, NEIL. (1991). *The science book of sound.* San Diego, CA: Harcourt Brace Jovanovich. Lively color photographs illustrate directions for a variety of sound activities. A paper noisemaker toy suggests how a thunderclap is heard. A Reading Rainbow selection.

BERGER, MELVIN. (1994). *All about sound.* New York: Scholastic. Simple activities are offered, together with explanations of vocal cord functioning and how a stethoscope works. Paperback.

BRETT, JAN. (1991). *Berlioz the bear.* New York: G. P. Putnam's Sons. A buzzing bee causes one problem for the village band and solves another. Rich detail and whimsy of the author's illustrations add visual delight to this Reading Rainbow selection.

COLE, JOANNA. (1999). *The magic schoolbus explores the senses.* New York: Scholastic. Travel the ear canal with Ms. Frizzle's class to discover how sound reaches the brain.

CRAATS, RENNAY. (2000). *The science of sound.* Milwaukee: Gareth Stevens. Advanced readers can browse this collection of brief facts about how sounds occur and how we hear them.

DILLER, HARRIETT. (1996). *Big band sound.* Honesdale, PA: Boyds Mill. Arlis is fascinated by the dance band drum sets. She creates her own set from discarded cans and buckets.

EVANS, DAVID, & WILLIAMS, C. (1993). *Sound and music.* New York: Dorling Kindersley. Bright color photographs of children engaged in simple explorations of soundmaking will lead young story listeners into experimenting.

GERSTEIN, MORDICAI. (2002). *What Charlie heard.* New York: Farrar, Straus. Spilling over with sounds, this book chronicles the childhood and later life of the composer Charles Ives. It's sure to inspire careful listening to sounds around us.

JACKSON, MICHAEL. (1993). *Shake, rattle, and roll: Making music with instruments you make yourself.* New York: HarperCollins. This book offers directions for making and playing, no-cost instruments, as well as instructions for playing the harmonica. Paperback.

JEUNESSE, GALLIMARD, & DELAFUSSE, C. (1993). *Musical instruments.* New York: Scholastic. Lavish, intriguing illustrations of instruments, and clever peek-inside features clarify the relationship between the length of vibrating strings or air columns and the pitch they produce.

KEATS, EZRA JACK. (1999). *Apt. 3.* New York: Viking. Varied sounds guide Sam to a sightless new friend who knows his neighbors by the sounds he associates with them. Paperback. A Reading Rainbow book.

KETCHAM, SALLIE. (1999). *Bach's big adventure.* New York: Orchard. This legend of J. S. Bach's boyhood determination to be a great organist illustrates persistence, and pictures arrays of organ pipes.

KROLL, VIRGINIA. (1998). *Faraway drums.* Boston: Little Brown. Two girls imaginatively transform the scary sounds of their gritty urban neighborhood into sounds of Africa: wildebeest herds thundering by, and monkeys screeching in the treetops. Warm illustrations add comfort.

LEVINE, SHAR, & JOHNSTONE, LESLIE. (2000). *Bathtub science.* New York: Sperling. The engaging activities in this book explore the way sound travels through water.

LITHGOW, JOHN. (2002). *The remarkable Farkle McBride.* New York: Simon & Schuster. This delightfully silly story of a temperamental young musical genius brings a light touch to the study of sound, as well as fine illustrations of musical instruments.

LONG, MELINDA. (2000). *When papa snores.* New York: Simon & Schuster. The household responds hilariously to the vibrations caused by the snoring vibrations of Grandpa and Grandma.

MILLMAN, ISAAC. (2002). *Moses goes to a concert.* New York: Farrar, Strauss. Children from a school for the deaf watch and feel the concert by a deaf percussionist. Holding balloons in their laps helps them pick up vibrations. American Sign Language illustrations accompany this fine story.

ORGILL, ROXANNE. (1997). *If only I had a horn: Young Louis Armstrong.* Boston: Houghton Mifflin. Children who enjoy music will be inspired by this warmly illustrated account of the famous musician as a child.

PFEFFER, WENDY. (1999). *Sounds all around.* New York: HarperCollins. Young readers can feel vibrations as they speak, learn how sound guides bats in flight, how snakes feel sound, how whales and dolphins communicate, and how sound is measured. Simple sound activities are included. An NSTA[*] Outstanding Trade Book.

PINKNEY, ANDREA. (1998). *Duke Ellington.* New York: Hyperion. Brian Pinkney's distinctive, powerful illustrations enliven this story of The Duke's musicality, with its childhood beginnings.

PINKNEY, BRIAN. (1994). *Max found two sticks.* New York: Simon & Schuster. Max captures the joy and rhythm of the sounds of life around him with his two special sticks.

WALPOLE, BRENDA. (1997). *Hearing.* Austin, TX: Raintree. This book presents simple sound concepts, animal sounds, and bright color photographs of children exploring sound.

[*]National Science Teachers Association

Poems (Resources in Appendix A)

Many poems for children re-create sounds and extend the learning activities about sound.

> From *Poems to Grow On* by Jean McKee Thompson, read "Kitchen Tunes" by Ida Pardue and "The Storm" by Dorothy Aldis.
> Paul Fleischman's "Joyful Noise" captures the sounds of familiar insects.

Fingerplays

Recall the juice can telephone fun with this fingerplay.

Juice Can Telephone

I called my friend on a juice-can phone.	(Make cylinders with hands)
Two juice cans were joined by a string.	(extend little fingers to touch each other)
I put it to my mouth,	(put one cylinder up to mouth)
I put it to my ear *I could hear my friend* *say everything!*	(put other cylinder to ear)

—J. H.

Art Activities

Drums. Use salt or oatmeal boxes, or cans with airtight plastic lids. Glue construction paper to the side of the drum, slipping rubber bands around the paper to hold it firmly while the glue dries. Children can decorate with markers and fancy materials.

Horns. Let children wind and glue lengths of yarn around paper towel tubes, or decorate with markers. An adult can punch an air-vent hole near one end. Help children fasten a single piece of waxed paper over one end of the tube with a tight rubber band. A reedy sound is made by tooting tunes into the open end of the tube.

Rainsticks. Linda Schaffer offers directions for making a mailing tube rainstick. (See Resources, p. 286.)

Play

1. A pair of juice can telephones can add interest to many dramatic play situations.
2. Medical play can include the experience of actually hearing each other's heartbeats. Use a real or improvised stethoscope to "gather" the sound so it can be heard more clearly. Insert the tube ends of two soft plastic funnels into a short length of narrow-gauge plastic tubing. Place one funnel on a child's chest. Hold the other funnel close to the ear to hear the beats.

Listening Activities

Match My Sound. Gather pairs of matching items that will produce sounds, such as metal spring "crickets," two squares of sandpaper to rub together, small brass bells, jingle bells, two bottle caps to tap together, blunt scissors to click, small pieces of corrugated paper to scrape with a fingertip, pocket combs and waxed paper to blow on, and two finger cymbals. Put one complete set of soundmaking items in a teacher's bag. Distribute the matching items as evenly as possible into lunch-size paper bags. Fold down the tops and present a bag of secret sounds to each child at the table. While children keep their eyes tightly shut, the teacher reaches into her bag and makes a sound with one of the items. The children then search through their bags to see who can find things that produce a matching sound. Allow plenty of time for this activity.

Sound Matching Tray. Use a divided cutlery tray and 35mm film cans or small opaque plastic bottles to adapt a Montessori sensory exercise. Loosely fill two matching containers with materials that make distinctive sounds when shaken, such as gravel, sand, pennies, rice, or puffed cereal. Mark matching pairs with matching numerals or letters on the container bottom as a self-correcting aid. Put one set of containers on one side of the tray; have children find the matching sound containers and place them next to their mates on the other side of the tray.

Creative Movement

Children can show their perceptions of high or low sounds by moving to the tones of an instrument played by an adult. When the notes are low the children move in a low position close to the floor; when they are high the children move in a stretched-up position. They can also rise from a crouch to tiptoes in response to a slowly ascending scale, and return to the crouch as the descending scale is played. Use a drumbeat to indicate varied movement tempos and rhythms as children move in the same direction around the room.

Creative Thinking

Pacing your comments softly and slowly, begin with something like this: "Close your eyes and let your imagination tune in to remembered sounds. Hear a loud bell ringing. . . . Where are you when you hear that bell? . . . What is it telling you? . . . Now hear a softer bell ringing. . . . What does its sound mean? . . . Now listen for the blowing wind on a stormy day . . . will you hear rain coming down soon? . . . the crack of thunder? . . . Will the wind blow through your window and make the blinds rattle? . . . Now listen for sounds coming from the kitchen as someone fixes your breakfast. . . . Do you hear the toaster popping up? What else do you hear?" Create other auditory images. Then let children report the sounds and their personal meanings.

Food Experience

Sound is a critical part of microwaving popcorn without burning it. If a microwave oven is accessible, let children time the pops.

Field Trips

Look around your school area for a place that will produce an echo. An empty gymnasium or a high, windowless wall that borders an empty lot might be good places. Tell children that when they shout their names toward the walls, the vibrations touch the walls and bounce back to them. Try it.

As you walk together for any special purpose, suggest walking very quietly so that you can listen for sounds to identify. An old church or auditorium with visible organ pipes, within walking distance of the school, is a good destination for this study.

PROMOTING CONCEPT CONNECTIONS

Maintaining Concepts

Occasionally, two of the loudest and most frightening sounds occur while children are in school: thunder and sonic booms. When lightning moves through the air, that air suddenly gets warm and it swells so fast that it vibrates. Thunder is the way we hear the vibration from that fast-swelling air far up in the clouds.

The unexpectedness of sonic booms adds to the scariness of that particular sound. Adults can agree with frightened children that surprise noises startle us. That acknowledgment and the example of our calm response are helpful to children. You could explain that when a jet goes very, very fast, it sometimes bumps into the air ahead that is already vibrating with its own sound. Sound travels fast, but sometimes a jet can travel faster than sound. People on the ground below hear that bump like a big explosion of air.

Improving Schoolgrounds

Hang a set of windchimes in a quiet area of the yard. Children can construct chimes from shells or other recyclables. Install a talk tube, available from playground equipment suppliers, which is installed underground with vertical aboveground talking stations (see photos on p. 285).

Connecting Concepts

1. Some of the suggested experiences relate to the children's existing concepts about the presence of air in empty-looking places and moving air pushing things (see Chapter 7, Air).

2. Friction is also involved in the production of some sounds, such as rubbing sandpaper together and unlubricated metal parts rubbing together to produce squeaks from the vibrations (see Chapter 13, Simple Machines).

3. Nature-based musical instruments traditionally are made from plants, such as gourd horns, bamboo flutes and pan pipes, dried cactus rainsticks, and hollow log drums. Animal skins form drum heads, animal horns and conch shells are wind instruments and animal bones are used as percussion instruments.

Family and Community Support

Any parent who is able to bring in and play a musical instrument can enrich the children's awareness of soundmaking. Families could be encouraged to lend things like a bell collection or wind chimes for the children to enjoy. Suggest events

Maya and Justin converse through the talk tube.

of soundmaking interest in the locality that parents might attend with their children, such as a bell-ringing choir or children's concerts.

Families will enjoy hands-on soundmaking exhibits, such as whisper chambers and floor keyboards where children can hop out tunes, in the nearest children's museum.

RESOURCES

FRANKLIN INSTITUTE SCIENCE MUSEUM. (1995) *Ben Franklin book of easy and incredible experiments.* New York: Wiley. This book devotes a chapter to making musical instruments. It portrays Franklin's invention of the armonica, an instrument for which Mozart wrote music. It makes a good social studies connection possible.

HANN, JUDITH. (1991). *How science works.* Pleasantville, NY: Reader's Digest. Excellent background "how" and "why" information about sound is given, including the difference between sound and music.

LEVINE, S., & JOHNSTONE, L. (2000). New York: Sterling. *Science experiments with sound and music.* Written for middle school students, this attractive book is a reliable source of scientifically accurate information about sound, and of additional hands-on activities adaptable for younger children.

MOOMAW, SALLY. (1997). *More than singing: Discovering music in preschool and kindergarten.* St. Paul, MN: Redleaf Press. Lots of ideas for instrument making and sound exploration are found in this well-illustrated book. Cassette included.

MURPHY, P., KLAGES, E., & SHORE, L. (1996). *The science explorer.* New York: Henry Holt. Easy creative activities for exploring soundmaking are found in this San Francisco Exploratorium book.

SCHAFFER, L., PINSON, H., & KOKOSKI, T. (1998). Listening to rain sticks. *Science and Children,* 35, (5), 22–27. Directions are given for an inexpensive, teacher-made rainstick and related class activities.

SELLER, MICK. (1992). *Sound, noise, and music.* New York: Glouster Press. This book provides good background information about sound as a form of energy, how sound travels and is heard, and how music is made.

Light

Are you awed by a rainbow? Do you think flashlight tag is fun? Do you enjoy the sparkle of sunlight reflected on a stream? Then it will be a pleasure for you to help children acquire fundamental concepts about light.

On the day of birth, infants are able to perceive light. Later, the playpen explorer may try to catch a sunbeam. The toddler may try to pounce on a shadow. Growing young children are fascinated by the sparkle of reflected light and the beauty of the spectrum. The experiences that capture some children's closest attention, however, are those that help to allay their worries about darkness—the absence of light. The following concepts are suggested for investigation in this chapter:

- Nothing can be seen without light in everyday experience.
- Light appears to travel in a straight line.
- Shadows are made when light beams are blocked.
- Night is Earth's shadow.
- Everything we see reflects some light.
- Light contains many colors.
- Bending light beams make things look different.

Children can experiment by examining a box full of darkness, using a flashlight beam to note the straight path of light, creating shadows, and looking through filters. Other experiences explain night and day, reflection, and refraction.

Introduction: To lead into these experiences with light, read one of these stories about the mastery of nighttime anxiety: *Flashlight,* by Betsy James, or *Switch on the Night,* by Ray Bradbury.

CONCEPT: Nothing can be seen without light.

1. What can we see in a dark box?

LEARNING OBJECTIVE: To soften anxiety about the dark: it's dispelled by light to let us see.

MATERIALS:

Pen flashlight

Extra batteries

Shoe box with cover

Small picture

Old, heavy blanket

Low table

GETTING READY:

Cut a dime-size peephole in one end of the shoe box.

Cut a flap in top of box.

Paste picture to inside of box at end opposite the peephole.

Cover table with the blanket so it drapes to floor on all sides, making a dark place.

SMALL-GROUP ACTIVITY:

1. Tell children, "Let's stretch out on the floor and put just our heads into the dark place under the table."
2. "Here is a dark box. It has a hole in one end to look into. What do you see in there?" Pass the box to everyone.
3. "Now I am going to change something; then you can look into the box again." Turn on the flashlight and push it under the flap on the top of the box. "Can you see something in the box now? It was there before, but you couldn't see it. Let's try to find out why."
4. Remove the flashlight; pass the box again. "The picture is still in there. Can you see it? What happens when the light goes off? We always need light to see anything. *Nothing can be seen without light.*"

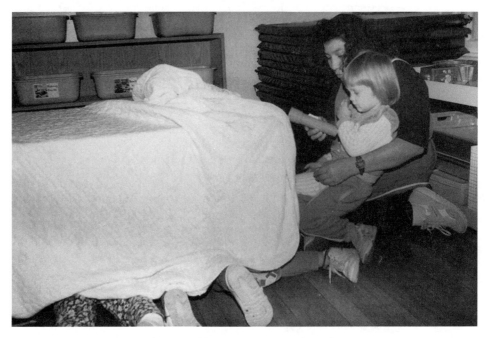

A blanket-covered table adds intrigue to light experiments.

Be prepared to repeat this experience. Children are impressed with, and re-assured by, their ability to make the dark go away and come back at will.

Read: The Bird, the Frog, and the Light by Avi.

CONCEPT: Light appears to travel in a straight line.

1. How does a flashlight beam travel?

LEARNING OBJECTIVE: To confirm the intriguing way light seems to travel in a straight line.

MATERIALS:

Pen flashlight

Extra batteries

3 sheets of white paper

Blanket and low table

Blocks

Masking tape

GETTING READY:

To prepare 3 screens:

- Stack the 2 blocks and tape the flashlight to the top block. Turn the flashlight on.
- Fold paper as shown in Figure 15–1. Stand it in front of the light.

SMALL-GROUP ACTIVITY:

1. Tell children, "Let's find out how a beam of light travels. Lie down along the sides of the table. Put your heads under the blanket. I'll be at this end; no one will be at the other end."

2. Turn on the flashlight. "Notice the light shining on the blanket at the end of the table? It passes through each hole in the screens."

3. "Liz, will you put your hand in front of one hole, please? What happened? Did Liz's hand block the light or did it curve around the paper to shine through the next holes?"

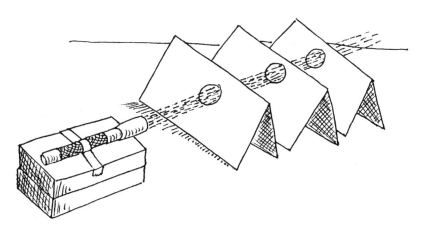

FIGURE 15–1

- Cut a small hole where the beam hits the center of the paper.
- Cut holes in the same location in the other screens.

Line up screens a few inches apart so that the light beam can pass through all the holes.

Cover table with blanket.

4. "Take turns blocking the light beam as Liz did. Does the light curve around things or does light travel in a straight path?" Let children use the flashlight to check and recheck the path of light.

CONCEPT: **Shadows are made when light beams are blocked.**

---

1. Which things let light pass through?

LEARNING OBJECTIVE: To enjoy seeing how light passes through different materials and forms shadows when blocked.

MATERIALS:

Small flashlight

Blanket and low table

Waxed paper

Cardboard

Large shoe box

Clear glass jar

Water

Colored tissue paper

Clear acetate folder

GETTING READY:

Cut a large opening in shoe box bottom.

Cut simple 3-inch (7.5 cm) cardboard doll figure.

Fill jar with water.

Cover table with blanket.

SMALL-GROUP ACTIVITY:

1. "Let's find out what light will shine through. You stretch out along that side of the table and I'll be across from you."
2. Put the box on its side with the opening facing the children. Shine the light through the opening. "Let's see if light shines through air."
3. Put the water jar in the opening. "Let's see if light shines through water."
4. "Let's see if light will shine through waxed paper in the same way." Cover the opening with waxed paper. "Does the light shine in one spot or spread out?" Try colored tissue paper and clear acetate at the opening.
5. "Let's see if light will shine through this cardboard doll." Remove box; place doll so that it makes a shadow on the blanket.
6. Tell children to notice that light shines on only one side of the doll. "There is a dark place where the doll blocked the light. It's a shadow."

Large-Group Activity: ♣ Move outdoors on a sunny day. Use chalk to trace the outline of children's shadows on a paved area. As you trace, ask other children, "Is sunlight shining right through Nina, or does she block the light? I'm tracing the darkness that Nina's body makes where the sunlight can't shine through her."

"Look, we're blocking the light!"

Note: A child may notice that a transparent glass window sometimes *reflects* light like a mirror. This occurs as a result of the way light strikes the surface of the glass. The surface of a still pond or shallow swimming pool can also show a mirror-like reflection. This happens when sunlight reflects back *up* from the bottom of the pond or pool.

CONCEPT: Night is Earth's shadow.

1. Why do we have day and night?

LEARNING OBJECTIVE: To be reassured that night's darkness is the turning Earth's shadow.

Large-Group Experience: (You will need a globe or ball, projector or flashlight, chalk, and a darkened room.) "We had fun blocking the sunlight to make shadows. Did you know that the whole Earth does the same thing? That is the way day and night happen. Let's pretend that this light is the shining sun. This globe is a model of our huge Earth. I'll put a chalk mark here on the globe to show where our part of the world is. Watch the mark as I turn the globe the way the Earth always slowly turns. Is the mark in the light now? Does the light curve around the globe to keep shining on our part of the world? No, the light shines in a straight line. Our part of the world is in a shadow now—the shadow of the other side of the Earth."

Continue to turn the globe, so that children can see the marked part of the globe alternately in the light and in the shadow. "What do we call the time when our part of the world is in Earth's shadow? When it is in the sunlight?" Let the children turn the globe.

When your class encounters mention of the sun's *rising* or *setting* in stories, poems, or songs, point out that such was the old, imaginary way of thinking about night and day. *We* know that it only *looks* like the sun is traveling around Earth. We have daylight when our part of the traveling Earth spins toward the sun. After a while, rely on the class to correct such misconceptions they may find.

CONCEPT: Everything we see reflects some light.

Introduction: Put a lighted purse-size flashlight into your cupped hands. Open your hands to let the children see where the light is coming from. "Is the flashlight making this light?" Hold a pocket mirror in your hands. "Is the mirror making a light?" Now shine the flashlight beam onto the mirror. Tilt the mirror so that the light is reflected onto the walls or ceiling. "Which thing made the light that is bouncing up there, the flashlight or the mirror?" Turn the flashlight off and on several times so children can verify that the spot of light is reflected by the mirror to the ceiling only when the flashlight makes the light.

1. Which things reflect light better than others?

LEARNING OBJECTIVE: To enjoy bouncing light beams and exploring differences in reflecting surfaces.

MATERIALS:
Strong sunlight or spotlight lamp
White paper
Easel
Aluminum foil pans
Cardboard
Aluminum foil
Colored paper: yellow, red, black
Dark carpet sample, velveteen,
 or bath towel

GETTING READY:
Cover cardboard with a smooth
 piece of foil.

? *Inquiry Activity:* Ask if anyone has suddenly had light shining into their eyes while riding in a car at night when no car was coming the other way. "How could that have happened?" Introduce a way to reflect light by fastening the paper on the easel and placing it at a right angle to a sunny window or the spotlight lamp. Facing the window or lamp, hold a pan so that it reflects light onto the sheet of paper on the easel. What do children observe? Offer the term *reflection*. Would other materials reflect light this way?

Arrange for small groups to reflect light on the white paper and the other materials. Have them decide and record their comparison of how well different materials and colors reflect light. Encourage experimenting with other materials. Post and discuss the final results.

♣ Take the aluminum foil pans outdoors on a sunny day to play reflection tag. **Safety Precaution:** Avoid directing reflected sunlight into anyone's eyes.

Whole-Group Experience: To use aluminum foil conservatively, do this for all to observe: Reflect light onto the smooth, new sheet of aluminum foil. Then crumple the sheet and reflect light onto it to compare the diffused reflection with the first reflection. (The crumpling created many small surfaces.)

CONCEPT: Light contains many colors.

1. Which things bend light to show its colors?

LEARNING OBJECTIVE: To be awed by light's hidden colors spreading out
through a prism.

MATERIALS:

Magazine

Strong sunlight, or a projector

Small piece of thick plate glass
  or plastic, edges taped[*]

Prisms or chandelier drops

Small, clear plastic boxes

Water

Soap bubble materials

Aquarium (desirable)

Diffraction grating cards, if
  available

2 freebie CDs

String

SMALL-GROUP ACTIVITY:

1. "There is a surprise in light beams. This magazine can help us find it." Hold the magazine with cut edges toward children and the bound edge toward you (Figure 15–2). "When pages are pressed together, does the edge look like one thick line? I'll bend it back toward me. Notice the line spread out to show many edges of paper. Try it."

2. Hold plate glass in front of light source. "When light comes through this glass, it looks clear. Let's see how light looks when it is spread by glass that bends it."

3. Hold prism edge in front of light beam and rotate until a spectrum can be seen in the room. "Now you see the secret! Light really has seven colors in it (spectrum), but we only see them when light shines through something clear that is bent or curved." Let the children try it.

[*]Do *not* use a magnifying glass.

FIGURE 15–2

4. If possible, place an aquarium near sunny windows. Fill with water. Help children stand where they can see the spectrum through the aquarium corners.
5. On a sunny day, let children experiment with water in small plastic boxes outdoors. Can they see the spectrum through the corners?
6. Try to make soap bubbles near a sunny window to see colors.
7. Let children examine diffraction grating cards and CDs to see the rainbow effects reflected by the patterns of lines.
8. Tie together pairs of free Internet CDs, label sides facing. Hang from strings near windows to reflect light around the room. Some reflect spectrum colors as well.

Read: "Crystal Vision", by Lawrence Schimel, a poem about prisms, in Lee Bennett Hopkins's collection, *Spectacular Science.*

CONCEPT: **Bending light beams make things look different.**

1. How do things look through a curved drop of water?

LEARNING OBJECTIVE: To wonder at how light bending into a curved path lets us see things differently.

MATERIALS:

Small bottles

Water

Medicine droppers

Waxed paper

Newspapers

plastic "Card Lens"

2 strong magnifiers

Toilet paper tube

Sponges

Small objects to examine

GETTING READY:

Fill bottles with water for each child.

Cut waxed paper and printed sections of newspaper into 3-inch (7.5 cm) squares.

Give each child a square of newspaper with waxed paper covering it.

SMALL-GROUP ACTIVITY:

1. "What happens when you put *just one* drop of water on your piece of waxed paper? Look at the newspaper through the drop of water. What do you see? Is the water drop curved or flat?"

2. "Now add more water to the drop. Is it still curved, or is it a flat spot of water? Do words beneath still look bigger? Why not? What has changed?"

3. "Absorb the water with a sponge and try again."

4. Show children the curved profile of a magnifying lens. "Hold up the curved water bottle. Look at your finger through the bottle and water. How does it look?" (The path of light bends when it goes through curved glass or a curved drop of water. Things seen through them look different.) "We looked through curves that made things look bigger." Look at the curved grooves in the plastic "Card Lens" magnifiers.

5. Explore the effect of holding the paper tube between two strong magnifiers (a simple microscope). Compare looking at newspaper type through a single magnifier, then through the tube-joined two magnifiers.

   Make the lenses and magnifying glasses freely available for children's own independent explorations from now on. Teach children to hold magnifiers close to the eyes and to bend close to the viewed object for best focus.

Note: Children are intrigued by the upside down reflections they see in the concave (inside) surface of a shiny spoon, or the odd magnification made by the convex (outer) surface of the spoon. Point out that the curved path of light changes reflections on these curved surfaces.

INTEGRATING ACTIVITIES

Math Experiences

Shadow Math. ♣ Early on a sunny morning, move outdoors and have children find a place to stand along a line with their backs to the sun. Let them trace one another's shadow outlines with chalk. Mark with the owner's initials. Measure the length of each shadow with a meter stick and record the data indoors on a chart. At noon, return to the marked places and repeat the tracing and data collecting. Abstract explanations of Earth's spinning will not make much of an impression on most children. But this experience with changing shadows will contribute to eventual understanding.

Return to the marked places at the end of the school day. Where are the children's shadows? Measure the length of the afternoon shadows. Add to the chart. (As our part of Earth spins away from the sun, shadows change in direction as the day goes on. They change in size as the angle of sunlight reaching Earth changes.)

Make a Sundial. In late spring, older children will be intrigued by creating a primitive sundial on the schoolgrounds that can be closed off for this purpose. Directions for making a sundial can be found in *Great Experiments With Light*, by Phyllis and Noel Fiarotta.

Mirror Math. Explore easy symmetry experiences with mirrors. Provide small, rectangular mirrors to children. Give them pictures cut from magazines to see if they can make the same pictures in the mirror. Provide objects like half circles to see if they can make whole circles in the mirror.

Further ideas for making these activities more challenging for older children are found in the Delta publication, *Mirror Explorations*. (See Appendix A.)

Energy Conservation. (Adding tens in a useful context.) Show children the wattage numbers on lightbulbs, explaining that the numbers mean different degrees of brightness. Using a small, shadeless lamp, demonstrate the brightness of different wattages. Calculate with the children the total wattage used in the classroom so they can understand the reason for turning off the lights when the classroom is empty.

Explore Angles. As a background experience for future geometry study, let children play with a flashlight and plastic mirror to explore how the angle of light hitting the mirror is the same as the angle of light bouncing off the mirror. Pose problems for them, "Can you use the mirror to make the light shine on the door . . . on the ceiling . . . on the big table?"

Music (Resources in Appendix A)

Mention that laser light beams are used instead of needles to play compact disc recordings. Sing this song after children have used prisms (to the tune of "Good Morning, Merry Sunshine"):

Prism Song

Good morning, merry sunshine,

Your light comes straight to me.

When glass or water bend your line,

Your colors I can see.

—J. H.

Literature Links

ANACONA, GEORGE. (1998). *Fiesta fireworks*. New York: Lothrop. Fireworks, the most exciting kind of light, are part of this account of a Mexican festival.

ARDLEY, NEIL. (1993). *Great science experiments*. New York: Dorling Kindersley. This collection of science activities includes directions for making a periscope and a kaleidoscope.

AVI. (1994). *The bird, the frog, and the light*. New York: Orchard Books. In this satisfying fable, an arrogant frog king can't see his dark underground kingdom. He asks a bird to bring a ray of sunshine into his tunnel with disillusioning results.

BERGER, MELVIN. (1995). *All about light*. New York: Scholastic. This clearly presented book offers activities revealing the nature of light, reflection, refraction, how lenses work, and more.

BRADBURY, RAY. (2000). *Switch on the night*. New York: HarperCollins. A child learns to control his fear of darkness. Read after exploring darkness as the absence of light. Paperback.

BRANLEY, FRANKLYN. (1998). *Day light, night light: Where light comes from*. New York: Harper Collins. Cozy illustrations and clear prose place difficult concepts into the context of ordinary events. Paperback.

BRIGHTON, CATHERINE. (2001). *Galileo's treasure box*. NY: Walker. In this gorgeously illustrated book, Galileo's small daughter plays with souvenirs of his famous studies of magnification and construction of the first astronomical telescope.

BULLA, CLYDE. (1993). *What makes a shadow*. New York: HarperCollins. A simple text informs preschoolers about shadows as blocked light paths, and night as Earth's shadow. Paperback.

BURTON, JANE, & TAYLOR, KIM. (2000). *Reflections*. Milwaukee: Gareth Stevens. Aspects of reflection, refraction , scattered light, phosphorescence found in nature, as well as mirror activities are laid out for advanced readers.

CARLE, ERIC. (1995). *The very lonely firefly*. New York: Philomel. A solitary firefly hatches alone and searches through the night to join others of his kind. Light's straight path shows up well.

CHORAO, KAY. (2001). *Shadow night: A picture book with shadow play*. New York: Dutton. Essentially a hand-shadows story, this book makes a fine extended activity for light study.

COLE, JOANNA. (1999). *The magic schoolbus explores the senses*. New York: Scholastic. Join Ms. Frizzle's class to discover how light reaches the brain's optic center as vision. Paperback.

DOROS, ARTHUR. (1990). *Me and my shadow*. New York: Scholastic. Simple, clear explanations are presented for night as Earth's shadow, and the phases of the moon as its own shadow. Shadow tag and other shadow fun are included.

FIAROTTA, PHYLLIS, & FIAROTTA, NOEL. (2000). *Great experiments with light*. New York: Sterling. This book pulls together a fascinating array of activity extensions, a brief history of the uses of light, as well as poetry. Older children will enjoy browsing. NSTA[*] recommended.

HELLER, RUTH. (1995). *Color*. New York: Putnam & Grosset. Heller's dramatic graphics delight, as always.

JAMES, BETSY. (1997). *Flashlight*. New York: Knopf. An understanding grandfather offers his flashlight to help his visiting grandchild take charge of the dark.

JEUNESSE, GALLIMARD, & DELAFOSSE, CLAUDE (1994). *Light.* New York: Scholastic. Clever graphics illustrate basic facts about light in this child-size book for small hands.

KRUPP, E. (2000). *The rainbow and you.* New York: HarperCollins. Useful ideas for youngsters about rainbows are in this book. NSTA[*] recommended.

LIONNI, LEO. (1994). *Little blue and little yellow.* New York: Morrow. This color story, which intrigues the youngest children, is convincingly told as a light story. Paperback.

MURPHY, BRIAN. (2001). *Experiments with light.* Princeton, NJ: Two Can Publications. Activities in this book include light refraction, periscope making, and mirages. Paperback.

MURPHY, PAT. (1993). *Bending light.* Boston: Little, Brown. Find out from this engaging book how to make a magnifying lens with lemon Jell-O! Try some of the other neat lens activities devised by the San Francisco Exploratorium Museum staff.

MURPHY, PAT, & SAN FRANCISCO EXPLORATORIUM STAFF. (1996). *The science explorer.* New York: Henry Holt. Let this book guide you in taking apart a disposable camera and in carrying out intriguing light refraction and reflection activities.

ONTARIO SCIENCE CENTRE. (1987). *Having fun with magnifying.* Toronto: Kids Can Press. This activities book includes making and using a simple, failure-proof magnifier. Paperback.

ROSENBERG, LIZ. (2001). *Eli's night light.* New York: Scholastic. When Eli's night light burns out, he notices other reassuring sources of reflected light in and around his darkened room. The youngest listeners and beginning readers will find comfort in this simple story.

SAYRE, APRIL. (2002). *Shadows.* New York: Holt. In this pleasant story, two youngsters' playful search for shadows is interrupted when clouds "sponge shadows away." Striking illustrations and a lively, rhyming text add charm.

SELSAM, MILLICENT. (1991). *Greg's microscope.* New York: HarperCollins. Greg's new microscope reveals exciting aspects of everyday materials in this easy reader. Paperback.

*National Science Teachers Association

Storytelling with Lights

1. Tell Leo Lionni's story, *Little Blue and Little Yellow,* using a small study lamp and blue and yellow plastic paddles to blend and separate the color families in the story. Let the children experiment with the light and paddles afterward. Have a sheet of white paper under the lamp. A set of colored plastic construction squares can also be used this way.

2. Use a small high-intensity lamp and three-dimensional objects to animate and tell a simple shadow story. Do this on the floor of a darkened room with the children sitting in a circle around the story setting. Small dolls can be children playing shadow tag outdoors. A cardboard tree or a wall of blocks can form a shady place for the dolls to rest after the game. A cardboard cloud could pass between the dolls and the lamp to perplex the story children. They can't find their shadows for the tag game and think they've lost them. Walk the dolls over to the children watching the story to ask them for help finding the shadows.

Poems (Resources in Appendix A)

There are many poems about light.

From *A Light in the Attic* by Shel Silverstein, read "Shadow Race" and "Reflection."

From *Poems to Grow On,* compiled by Jean McKee Thompson, read: "Shadow Dance" by Ivy O. Eastwick; "Kick a Little Stone," by Dorothy Aldis; "Mirrors," by Mary McB. Green; and "I Wonder," by Virginia Gibbons.

From *Sing a Song of Popcorn,* compiled by Beatrice deRegniers, read "8 A.M. Shadows," by Patricia Hubbell.

From *A Child's Garden of Verses,* by Robert Louis Stevenson, read "My Shadow."

From *I Thought I'd Take My Rat to School,* compiled by Dorothy Kennedy, read Lillian Moore's "Recess," about children scribbling their shadows on the schoolyard.

From *Out and About,* by Shirley Hughes, read "Squirting Rainbows."

From *Flicker Flash,* by Joan Graham, read all 23 poems honoring forms of light familiar to children.

From *Spectacular Science,* read "Crystal Vision," by Lawrence Schimel, and "Under the Microscope," by Lee Bennett Hopkins.

Art Activities

A Reflecting Collage. Let children use pieces of foil gift wrap, aluminum foil, sequins, glitter, and gummed stars to make collages.

Reflector Hanging. Let children cut pairs of simple shapes from foil paper or aluminum foil. Help them place three or four shapes face down in a line. Put a few drops of white glue in the center of each shape. Place a 15-inch (38 cm) length of string on the glue spots, then let the children cover each shape with its mate. Tie a gold plastic thread spool to the bottom of the string. Tape to the ceiling or to a doorframe.

"Stained Glass" Medallions. Cut apart separate rings of plastic "six-pack" holders from frozen juice or drink cans. Pierce a hole at the top of each ring with a heavy threaded needle. Tie a thread loop. Let children dot glue around the ring and press colored tissue paper and cellophane over it; then trim away excess paper. Hang the medallions in the windows. "Does light come through?"

Waxed Paper Translucents. Let children cut shapes from colored tissue paper and arrange them as they wish between two sheets of waxed paper. Children seal the papers together by placing them on a newspaper-covered food-warming tray and rubbing firmly across the waxed paper with a pizza roller.

Color Blending. After reading *Little Blue and Little Yellow* by Leo Lionni, children may be interested in blending paint colors. Younger children can try two primary colors at a time. Older children can try to create all the colors of the rainbow with three primary colors.

Play

Ship Play. The crew of a building-block ship will enjoy using a periscope. Let them see how mirrors reflect light to create this interesting effect. Instructions for making a periscope are found in *Great Science Experiments* by Neil Ardley.

Shadow Fun. Draw the shades during active playtime on a rainy day and set up a projector at one end of the room. Turn on dancing music and let the children enjoy creating shadows as they dance in a designated area. ♣ Play shadow tag outdoors with the children on a sunny day.

Reflection/Refraction Attraction. Follow up the reflection and refraction experiences by bringing in as many of these fascinating toys and practical items as you and your class can supply. Kaleidoscopes, octoscopes, and homemade milk-carton periscopes all depend upon mirrors within to create intriguing patterns and views. The Dragonfly Octoscope has 25 planes in its lens to imitate that insect's view of the world. Diffraction grating lenses and novelty items produce rainbow effects. One popular miniature figure has such a lens that creates an appearing/disappearing face. These items are usually sold in nature stores and museum shops. Add old binoculars, varied plastic card magnifying lenses and other magnifying lenses, and a container of small things to examine.

Creative Movement

Be My Mirror. Suggest to the children that they pretend to be your reflection in a mirror. They silently move as you move. You may be surprised at the number of movements you and the children can invent while you are seated, using your head, neck, shoulders, arms, hands, and fingers. This is a good activity to calm a restless group.

Creative Thinking

What If? Start a story for the class to complete. "What if you wake up one stormy night and find that the electricity isn't working? The moon isn't shining, and the stars are hidden by clouds. Your light won't click on. You don't have a flashlight. You don't feel sleepy. Feel around your room for your favorite book. Do you have the right book? Can you read it? Feel around for your box of crayons and some paper. Can you draw a picture? Which colors would you use? Can you see yourself in your mirror? How could someone in your house make some light for you? Does the light fill the room? Can you think of a way to make that light bigger? What else would seem different?"

PROMOTING CONCEPT CONNECTIONS

Maintaining Concepts

1. Point out reflections when you notice them in the classroom: in doorknobs, in a child's shiny brass button, in the spoons at lunchtime, or in the rain puddles on the playground.
2. Hang a prism in a classroom window that gets direct sunlight. Experiment with balance and location to produce a good spectrum.

3. Use the opportunities that arise to comment on the need for light to see well: when raising the shades after rest time, when looking closely at a scraped knee, and so on. Comment that we need light to see our wonderful world.

4. Store magnifying glasses in a place where children will have access to them when they want to examine something. If you have a classroom microscope, let the children know that you will get it out for them when they want to examine a specimen. Talk about reflecting more light onto the specimen with the adjustable mirror.

5. Keep track of the length of the shadow made by a special tree or building near the school playground. Use a chalk mark on a paved surface, or stones on a grassy area, to compare its length when you are outdoors in the morning, at noon, and in the afternoon. Assign this responsibility to specific children, who then demonstrate the change to the others.

6. When the subject of lasers is brought up by children in terms of the destructive weapons they see in television programs or in certain toy advertisements, balance these ideas with the constructive uses of laser light. Tell them that this form of synthetic light is used by doctors to heal people. It is a powerful tool with many good uses. It is also used to "read" the special marks on grocery packages at the supermarket checkout counter. A tiny laser beam shines on compact discs to produce sound.

Improving Schoolgrounds

Make the schoolgrounds more interesting and inviting by altering the light and shadow patterns. An arbor of vines creates both welcome shade on sunny days and shifting leafy patterns on the group. In the fall or spring, plant the largest shade trees possible and make them places to play under by encircling them with decks that protect the root system and provide level cool places for quiet activities. If you have a garden, cast-off CDs suspended from strings between stakes catch sunlight intriguingly.

Connecting Concepts

Relate the bending of light beams to the surface tension experiences (see Chapter 8, Water). Recall that the pull on the outside of the water drop makes it curved. Light coming through this curve of water bends and changes the way in which we see through it. Surface tension keeps soap bubbles curved and lets us see rainbow colors of spread-out light beams. In caring for classroom plants, remind children that all plants need light to stay alive and grow. Animals and humans need light to live, too, because they need plants for food.

Family and Community Support

Encourage families to notice light coming through stained glass windows, the path of nighttime searchlights, car headlights on both clear and foggy nights, a lighthouse beacon, and the paths of stadium lights. Point out solar panels on home roofs, storing the sun's energy for heating. Families may have pocket calculators that use photovoltaic material to change light into electricity. At the supermarket, families can show children the electric-eye door openers and point out how the laser scanner units signal the price of groceries to the computer cash register.

If there is an observatory or planetarium in the community, find out if family programs are offered. Scout the nearest children's museum for interactive light and optics exhibits and notify families.

RESOURCES

BENNETT, A., & KESSLER, J. (1996). *Apples, bubbles, and crystals.* New York: Scholastic. Cartooned directions are given for making a rainbow and using a plastic box and flashlight in a darkened room.

DOHERTY, P., RATHJEN, D., & EXPLORATORIUM TEACHER INSTITUTE. (1995). *The magic wand and other bright experiments on light and color.* New York: John Wiley. Interesting activities and helpful background information are offered.

FRANKLIN INSTITUTE. (1995). *The Ben Franklin book of easy and incredible experiments.* New York: Wiley. Chapter 6 has good directions for making simple optical toys.

HANN, J. (1991). *How science works.* Pleasantville, NY: Reader's Digest. The carefully written chapter on light and sound presents clear, understandable background information on light as a form of energy, shadows, reflection, and refraction.

KEPLER, L. (1996). *Windowsill science centers.* New York: Scholastic. Good suggestions for preparing and cataloging microscope slides are found in "Tiny Worlds."

LAUBER, P. (1994). *What do you see and how do you see it?* New York: Crown. This book presents clear information and illustrations for teachers.

LEVENSON, E. (1994). *Teaching children about physical science.* New York: Tab Books. Background information (p. 94–124) for teachers is set out clearly in brief definitions of terms.

VAN CLEAVE, J. (1993). *Microscopes and magnifying lenses.* New York: John Wiley. This book of science fair projects for advanced students provides good background information about lenses.

Teaching Resource

SUNPRINT KIT. Create images using sunlight and light-sensitive paper. Museum stores or nature stores carry these. Also may be ordered from Lawrence Hall of Science (see Appendix A).

The Environment

Are you concerned about the environment?

Who isn't! How do we help children learn to take care of this beautiful planet without making them worried and afraid of the future? Activities in this chapter will help you guide them to positive attitudes and solid knowledge.

Plants, animals, air, water, weather, rocks, and the human body are the primary elements of the environment that are accessible to children. Learnings from these topics can serve as the basis for constructing an understanding of the environment, the system in which each of us participates. The experiences suggested for this chapter will help children create connections between concepts studied earlier. To help develop an understanding of the overarching concept of the environment, these subconcepts will be explored:

- There is an interconnectedness among things: plants, animals, air, water, weather, rocks, and ourselves.
- The environment is where we are. We can study it, as well as live in it.
- We can work together to sustain the environment by restoring, reusing, repairing, and recycling.

These concepts can be presented after the primary elements have been studied, or they can be used as an introduction to the year's science study, as they provide a framework for considering the other elements. Because the broad topic of the environment is complex, it is better suited to second and third graders than to younger children. Some of the activities can be successfully used with younger children. Teachers can best decide for their own classes when and how to use them.

In the experiences that follow, children will explore connections among themselves and their surroundings, examine a microclimate carefully, construct terrariums, develop an affinity for a tree, and feel proud of taking care of the environment by participating in recycling in various ways. Our aim is to develop a lasting affection for and interest in the natural world (see Wilson, 1996).

This chapter also contains additional suggestions for teachers and schools to rehabilitate their schoolyards to offer more natural elements to children. This will provide a setting both for environmental education and for the informal play experiences with nature that children once had more commonly in their neighborhoods. We list concrete suggestions and helpful references.

CONCEPT: **There is an interconnectedness among things: plants, animals, air, water, weather, rocks, and ourselves.**

1. What is connected to what? (Indoor activity)

LEARNING OBJECTIVE: To feel security in being connected to others.

MATERIALS:

Index cards

Paper clips or tape

Markers

Scissors

Ball of string or yarn with some 6-foot (about 2 m) lengths precut

Bulletin board or wall space as background for web (or form web on the floor within a circle of children)

SMALL-GROUP ACTIVITY:

1. Ask children to tell what they know about the word *connections*. You may need to offer some examples, such as Lego bricks or train cars being connected to one another, or give one end of a string you are holding to a child: "Now you and I are connected." Ask children to think of connections they have to other persons in the class, or in their families. Use the connections they offer to begin shaping a web of index cards and string.

   For instance, if Sarah says she is connected to her mommy, write *mommy* on one card and *Sarah* on another card. Tape the cards to the background and attach a length of string between the cards. Perhaps Sarah's mom drives a car pool for Tyler, so a *Tyler* card is taped to the background. Mom's card is connected to Tyler's card with another length of string, and so on. If Tyler goes to play at Andrew's house after school, they are connected. Continue to join strings and cards as long as you can keep it up. Answers will vary, but a web of connections should develop from the conversation.

2. To ensure that each child has a connection of some kind firmly in mind, accept responses for all kinds of connections. Discuss things outdoors that children can think of as "connected."

3. Leave the web in place for children to study. Leave extra string and cards nearby for children to add new ideas. Older children can also add written explanations of the connections they make.

2. ♣ *What is connected to what?*

LEARNING OBJECTIVE: To enjoy an awareness of the interconnectedness of the outdoor environment.

MATERIALS:

Index cards or sticky labels, 3 or 4 per child

Pencils or markers

Sheets of cardboard or heavy fabric or plastic for background, one per group of 3–4 children

SMALL-GROUP ACTIVITY:

1. Indoors, recall the first "connections" experience with children. "Today we are going outside to study the connections between things around us in our schoolyard." Ask children for their ideas about the "environment." "Where we are and everything that surrounds us here are called an *environment*."

2. ♣ Outdoors, the children sit in a circle and brainstorm about things they can see, hear, smell, and touch, as well as other things they know exist in this particular environment (the air, a nearby creek, etc.).

3. Work with younger children to make cards for the things children have discussed. Join them into webs of relationships, attaching the webs to the background material. Older children break into their small groups to do this independently.

4. In a discussion, consider ways that webs of each group differ. Are there connections no one has thought of yet? Are some connections more direct than others? One purpose of the discussion is to raise questions that individual children may want to pursue. "What if. . . . " questions can provoke fresh thought. "What if there were no water? What if the sun shone all day?" Encourage independent questioning. Follow up on individual children's queries (e.g., "What do ants eat?") to help them find classroom books and other resources.

3. ♣ *Living in the web of life.*

LEARNING OBJECTIVE: To feel attached to elements of the environment and appreciate the sense of belonging.

MATERIALS:

Ball of string

LARGE-GROUP ACTIVITY:

Have children stand in a circle. You stand in the middle with the ball of string in hand. Ask a child to name a plant growing in the area. Give that child the end of the string to hold. Ask, "Who eats that plant?" Take the string to a child whose response is reasonable (e.g., rabbit), so the rabbit can be connected with the string to the plant. Continue with a food or shelter question (e.g., "What eats the rabbit?" "Where does the fox live?" etc.) until everyone is connected in the web. Ask a child (perhaps one who mentioned a tree) to sit down. Ask, "If the tree falls down, who feels the tug on his or her string?" etc. Through this activity, children can physically experience interconnectedness.

Read one of the following books: *The Gift of the Tree*, by Alvin Tressalt; *Once There Was a Tree*, by Natalia Romanova; *Hungry Animals: My First Look at a Food Chain*, by Pamela Heckman; *This Is the Sea That Feeds Us*, by Robert Baldwin; or *The Missing Sunflowers*, by Maggie Stern.

"Where do you think this little guy lives?"

CONCEPT: **The environment is where we are. We can study it, as well as live in it.**

1. ♣ *What is the environment of creatures like?*

LEARNING OBJECTIVE: To enjoy imagining being a very small being in the grass and to empathize with small creatures.

? *Inquiry Activity:* "Do you know the story about Thumbelina? She was as tiny as your thumb. Let's see what it would be like to take a Thumbelina walk." Provide each child with a magnifier and a 4-foot (or 1.3 m) piece of string or yarn. Take children to a nearby grassy or wooded area. Let each child choose a section to explore. "Lay out your string and crawl along next to it, pretending you are tiny Thumbelina. Look how tall the grass is. Is it bigger than your head? Use your magnifying glass and keep your head down low to see every detail. Do you see any other tiny creatures here? What are they doing? Do you see an ant scurrying home? Too busy to talk to you, is she? Is there a drop of water to drink or anything to eat? Where would you like to rest here? Is there any soft moss for a pillow?"

Children can report to the group what they saw. Encourage children to draw their miniworlds afterward.

Read about a child lying in the grass exploring the eye-level world nearby in Rose Wyler's book, *Grass and Grasshoppers.* Read about a place "where clover tops are trees" in Robert Lewis Stevenson's classic poem, "The Little Land," from *A Child's Garden of Verses.* (See Appendix A.) Read about a child who feels safe and private in a grassy spot in Shirley Hughes' poem, "The Grass House," from *Out and About.*

2. *How can we make a microclimate?*

LEARNING OBJECTIVE: To imagine a little world and to enjoy constructing and sustaining a terrarium.

MATERIALS:

Tiny plants dug from the grassy area, if permitted; or small seedlings started earlier as class activity (see p. 58)

Bits of moss

Small sticks or bark bits, shells, small rocks

2-liter soda bottle for each pair of children, or each child

Potting soil

Gravel

Crushed charcoal bits (*not* chemically treated briquettes)

Old spoons

SMALL-GROUP ACTIVITY:

1. "Can you imagine making a tiny world where it rains by itself? Plants can live there, and you could pretend to live under a tiny leaf." Show children how to just cover the bottle base with a layer of pebbles, cover them with bits of crushed charcoal, and then spoon in a deeper layer of soil. Carefully arrange a few small plants in the soil. First, make a hole for each rooted plant. Then press soil down over roots. Decorate with bark or other natural objects. A shell could be a tiny pond.

2. Dampen plants with a few sprays of water. Replace the top 2/3 of the bottle, tucking the top into the base. Tape top and bottom together. If the bottle cap is missing, tape

FIGURE 16–1

Newspapers, if working indoors
Spray bottle of water

GETTING READY:

Prepare bottles: Soak off labels
  with warm water.
Use scissors or blade knife to
  cut off top 2/3 of bottle.

over **the top** opening as well. (See Figure 16–1.) Place in a warm, light place, but not in direct sunlight.

3. The next day, watch for evidence of water evaporating and condensing inside as drops of "rain" that return to the soil. (See Chapter 9, p. 167.) If children sprayed their plantings too generously, the domes will be covered heavily with condensation. If you suspect the terrarium will start to mold from excess moisture, untape the top opening for a few hours. By contrast, if *no* moisture condenses inside the dome, spray plants again. Talk about the self-sufficiency of this microworld. Think about how these plants get their food and water.

3. ♣ *What can we learn about a tree without using our eyes?*

LEARNING OBJECTIVE: To develop an affinity for a tree; to be able to see trees as individual organisms.

MATERIALS:

Freestanding trees (without poison ivy growing around them); a park may be needed for this activity

Folded soft paper towels to use as blindfolds, one per child

Large clips or paper clips

Read Joanne Ryder's book, *Hello Tree.* Read Harry Behm's poem, "Trees," from *Land, Sea and Sky,* by Catherine Paladino.

SMALL-GROUP ACTIVITY:

1. Outside with the children, ask, "Would you like to get to know something old and big? It's something that can't talk or see, so we'll get to know it without looking at it or talking to it. Have any ideas what this thing might be?"

2. Have children work in pairs. One child leads the blindfolded partner to a tree. The blindfolded child feels the tree with her hands. (Blindfolds frighten some children—they can try to keep their eyes closed instead.) Encourage multisensory exploration. Ask, "What is the bark like? Do you find branches? Are there leaves? Are roots sticking out? Are there holes in the tree? Can you reach all the way around the tree trunk? How does your tree smell? Does it feel sticky?"

3. When the blindfolded child has finished exploring, the partner leads her or him away from the tree, rotates the child a bit, and removes the blindfold. The child can try to recognize his or her tree. Reverse the roles of the children.

4. Indoors, let children draw how they remember their tree. Encourage them to keep track of their special trees through the school year. Children become attached to individual trees in this way, and begin to think of trees as alive and unique, not merely backgrounds to life. Discuss the relationships of trees to other animals and to ourselves (see Maintaining Concepts, p. 320).

CONCEPT: **We can work together to sustain the environment by restoring, reusing, repairing, and recycling.**

1. What can we do to reduce waste and conserve water?

LEARNING OBJECTIVE: To feel strong and useful in protecting the world, and to take pride in working with others.

MATERIALS:

Discarded cardboard cartons
Markers
Bathroom scale

LARGE-GROUP ACTIVITY:

Part 1: Reducing Waste

1. Ask children to recall all of the things they throw into the wastebasket at school. List the items on the chalkboard. Ask children to group their responses. A variety of groups is possible. Provide and label a carton for each category, so children can collect separately each of those throwaways for several days. (Alert the custodial staff not to empty the boxes at day's end. Food wastes should be removed each day, but the amount should be recorded.)

2. At the end of the collecting period, weigh and graph the amounts of trash in each carton. Extend the graph on the chalkboard to show what the amounts would look like after 9 months of school. (You can help with the calculations.)

3. See if children think there is a problem. Have groups of children brainstorm how to reduce the amount, and reuse different types of trash. If they do not think that there is a problem with trash, ask: "What would happen if the garbage truck never came to our school to whisk our trash out of sight? What did people do with trash in the days before there were garbage trucks?" Consider ways to reduce waste in the classroom, such as cutting paper towels in half, keeping a box of paper used on one side for reuse by children, and cherishing pencils and crayons. Plan with children how to carry out their ideas on reducing waste. Almost every idea is worth trying for a day or two. Some ideas will really work. Keep a running record or estimate how much waste was avoided by the class

at the close of the school year. Consult *50 Simple Things Kids Can Do to Recycle* for other ideas. (See Resources.)

4. Undertake a school building and yard environmental improvement activity. Figure out together what might make this environment a cleaner, more life-enhancing place. Talk about everyone's part in taking care of our schoolyard environment by "putting waste in its place." Think of a slogan for the school to adopt to help remember that "every litter bit hurts." Such environmental activism can be schoolwide, providing interaction between younger and older students for their mutual benefit. Read *Miss Rumphius*, by Barbara Cooney, as an example of how one person can enhance the environment. Many state governments provide resources for habitat improvement, particularly Fish and Wildlife departments. (See Resources.)

5. Explore the concepts of *biodegradable* and *nonbiodegradable* in terms of materials that can or cannot easily rot to become part of the soil. In a place on the schoolgrounds that won't be disturbed, bury several items that won't degrade, such as a styrofoam cup, a plastic bag, and a soda can, along with a paper bag. Check several months later to see how different things were affected by the damp soil. Encourage children to make the connection between what they observed and our need to recycle and reuse man-made materials that won't degrade. Start a compost pile in the schoolyard. (See Soil Composition Relationships, p. 77.) To amplify the discussion, read the last half of Vicki Cobb's book, *Lots of Rot*; Elizabeth Ring's *What Rot: Nature's Mighty Recycler*; or Linda Glaser's *Compost! Growing Gardens from Your Garbage.*

6. Put broken classroom equipment in a fix-it box to be repaired instead of discarded. Children gain satisfaction and a sense of importance from making repairs to restore equipment. Prevail upon the custodian, or

an amenable parent, to restore things that are beyond the children's or your own skills. Older children can tape torn book pages. They can learn to do simple sewing repairs if you have an emergency kit with safety pins, thread, and large enough needles. Preschoolers and kindergartners take pride in maintaining school bicycles. Keep an oil can handy for squeaky axles, and a crescent wrench for tightening handlebar bolts.

Part 2: Conserving Water

Introduction: Talk about the crucial role of water in ecological relationships. It is one of the nonliving substances that all living things depend on to stay alive. It is used over and over again in nature. Recall the evaporation, condensation rain cycle in the terrarium domes. (See Concept: Evaporation and condensation cause precipitation, p. 186.) When too many waste materials are emptied into lakes, streams, and rivers, or when chemicals seep into underground water supplies, living things may have less water than they need. *No way has ever been discovered to make new water,* so we must use the world's supply carefully to keep it clean. Investigate the way water is cleaned in your area.

1. Try out a simple way your children can keep from wasting this resource. Using empty half-gallon milk containers, collect the amount of water that runs from a school sink for 1 minute. Translate this amount in terms of numbers of glasses of water that can be wasted each time children wash their hands under running water.

   Afterward, talk about using a stoppered basin of water for handwashing. Talk about the need every person, animal, plant, tree, and the land itself, has for water. Children who do not let water run needlessly are helping our planet Earth.

2. As aware stewards of Earth's nonrenewable resources, celebrate Earth Day, April 22!

INTEGRATING ACTIVITIES

Math Experiences

1. Use found natural objects for ordering by size: twigs, stones, leaves, feathers. Interesting questions can arise when working with natural objects that manufactured manipulatives do not present. For instance, is a short, thick stick "smaller" than a long, thin one?

2. Use found objects to count big numbers. How many autumn leaves can you fit into a berry basket? How many does it take, stacked one on top of the other, to make an inch-high stack? How many leaves are on a tree? How many acorns? How many seeds in a pod? Point out the abundance of nature. Read *How Much Is a Million?*, by David Schwartz.

3. Compare leaf areas. Give children sets of various sizes of cardboard and ask them to find leaves that approximately match each piece. Older children can work with graph paper to estimate how many square units each leaf covers.

4. Estimate measurements. Count out the steps it takes to walk around the perimeter of the schoolyard or blacktop area. Does everyone get the same measurement? Discuss differences. How could those measurements be standardized?

5. Look for symmetry in natural objects. For instance, are both sides of a leaf alike? Look at deciduous trees after the leaves have fallen. Are they symmetrical? Compare freestanding trees with those in a more crowded area.

6. Read George Ella Lyon's *Counting on the Woods*, a walk through an eastern woodland where natural objects are countable.

7. Read Ruth Brown's *Ten Seeds*, which shows the impact of natural forces on ten sunflower seeds so that only one survives, but it in turn makes ten seeds. Good for counting and comforting.

Music (Resources in Appendix A)

Listen to the Tickle Tune Typhoon group sing "A Place in the Choir" on their *Hug the Earth* cassette. It cheerfully affirms every being's right to live. "Oh Cedar Tree" is a Native American chant that even the youngest children could sing well.

Listen to several ecology songs on Mary Miche's *Nature Nuts* cassette, including "Bats Eat Bugs," "Recycle Blues," and "Garbage."

Raffi's cassette, *Raffi on Broadway*, has numerous songs about Earth, the most singable being, "Big, Beautiful Planet," "May There Always Be Sunshine," "One Light, One Sun," and "KSE Promise Song," the song for a children's environmental group.

Joyce Rouse presents some very singable, understandable songs on *Around the World With Earth Mama*, such as "Only Take What You Need" and "Trees."

The Banana Slug Band has several CD's with environmental songs, including "Dirt Made My Lunch." Their Web site is at *www.bananaslugband.com*.

Literature Links

AYRES, PAM. (1989). *When Dad fills in the garden pond.* New York: Alfred A. Knopf. In this realistic story, a family considers the value of a messy, fun pond against that of a pretty flower garden.

BALDWIN, ROBERT. (1998). *This is the sea that feeds us.* Nevada City, CA: Dawn. This cumulative rhyme is based on the food chain relationships in the sea.

BANG, MOLLY. (1996). *Chattanooga sludge.* San Diego, CA: Harcourt Brace. This account of a scientist's effort to use biological processes to detoxify the industrial sludge at the bottom of Chattanooga Creek is delightfully illustrated and inspirational.

BOSVELD, JANE. (1997). *While a tree was growing.* New York: American Museum of Natural History. This beautiful book places human events within the life span of an ancient redwood. For teachers and older children.

Brother eagle, sister sky. (1992). Attributed to Chief Seattle. (See p. 344, Project Learning Tree.) New York: Scholastic. Wonderful illustrations by Susan Jeffers accompany this beloved environmental credo.

BROWN, RUTH (2001). *Ten seeds.* New York: Alfred A. Knopf. A counting book that shows how ten seeds are reduced by natural forces, such as insects, slugs, and a mouse, until finally the one plant that has survived produces ten seeds. The cycle can start all over again.

CADUTO, MICHAEL J., & BRUCHAC, JOSEPH. (1991). *Keepers of the Earth: Native American stories and wildlife activities for children.* Golden, CO: Fulcrum Publishers. The environmental emphasis is well-illustrated.

CHERRY, LYNNE. (1990). *The great kapok tree.* San Diego, CA: Harcourt Brace Jovanovich. A woodsman is persuaded not to destroy the rich natural community of the great kapok tree in the rain forest.

CHERRY, LYNNE. (1992). *A river ran wild: An environmental history of the Nashua River.* San Diego, CA: Harcourt Brace Jovanovich. This is a beautifully illustrated story of a river that is pristine, becomes polluted, and is restored.

CHERRY, LYNNE. (1995). *The dragon and the unicorn.* San Diego, CA: Harcourt Brace. Older readers will linger over the author's gorgeous illustrations and illuminated page borders as they discern the lesson on preserving old-growth forests in this original fable.

CHERRY, LYNNE. (1997). *Flute's journey: The life of a wood thrush.* San Diego, CA: Harcourt Brace. A wood thrush seeks places to live from Maryland to Costa Rica, finding few as woods disappear to forestry and development.

CHERRY, LYNNE., & PLOTKIN, M. (1998). *The shaman's apprentice: A tale of the Amazon rainforest.* San Diego, CA: Harcourt Brace. This lushly illustrated story about the use of native plants for healing is respectful of indigenous knowledge.

COBB, VICKI. (1981). *Lots of rot.* New York: Lippincott. Read aloud selectively to develop appreciation for the role of decomposers in the soil-renewal cycle.

COLE, JOANNA. (1993). *The magic schoolbus at the waterworks.* New York: Scholastic. Ms. Frizzle takes the class on her usual zany-style, informative trip through the waterworks.

COLLARD, SNEED B., III. (2002). *Butterfly count.* New York: Holiday House. A prairie habitat for butterflies is portrayed in beautiful illustrations by Paul Kratter in this story of a girl who participates in the annual butterfly count, sponsored by the North American Butterfly Association. She wonders where her grandmother's favorite butterfly has gone. Pesticides and habitat reduction are discussed.

CONE, MOLLY. (1992). *Come back, salmon.* San Francisco: Sierra Club. This is the inspiring true story of an elementary school in Washington State that cleaned up a creek and restored the salmon migration.

COOMBS, KAREN. (1995). *Flush: Treating wastewater.* Minneapolis, MN: Carolrhoda. The facts about modern sewage treatment are important to know for improving the environment.

COONEY, BARBARA. (1982). *Miss Rumphius.* New York: Viking. This book tells how one person made her environment more beautiful by planting wildflowers in nearby meadows.

CURTIS, PATRICIA. (1997). *Animals you never even heard of.* San Francisco: Sierra Club. Photographs and descriptions of 12 little-known animals will interest the child who loves to know off-beat facts.

DEWEY, JENNIFER. (1994). *Wildlife rescue: The work of Dr. Kathleen Ramsay.* Honesdale, PA: Boyds Mill. Older children who worry about wildlife survival will appreciate this account of a doctor who does everything possible to save animals.

FOSTER, JOANNA. (1991). *Cartons, cans, and orange peels: Where does your garbage go?* New York: Houghton Mifflin. Various methods for handling garbage are described.

FRASIER, DEBRA. (1998). *Out of the ocean.* San Diego, CA: Harcourt Brace. The Florida coast is revealed in photographs, paper-cuttings, and a child's voice about what the ocean provides her.

GARLAND, SHERRY. (1995). *The summer sands.* San Diego, CA: Harcourt Brace. Two children spend the summer on a sand dune, learning about its ecology. They participate in a conservation effort to restore the sand dune after a bad storm. Encourages children to take constructive action.

GIBBONS, GAIL. (1992). *Recycle! A handbook for kids.* Boston: Little Brown. A sprightly introduction to the topic of recycling, with basic suggestions for action at the end.

GILMAN, PHOEBE. (1992). *Something from nothing.* New York: Scholastic. A resourceful grandfather and boy keep reusing his blanket until nothing remains. (Check the mice in the border illustrations.)

GLASER, LINDA. (1996). *Compost! Growing gardens from your garbage.* Brookfield, CT: Millbrook. A family composts their table scraps and yard wastes and uses it to create a garden.

GODKIN, CELIA. (1998). *What about ladybugs?* San Francisco: Sierra Club. A gardener learns to use ladybugs instead of chemicals to control aphids "nature's way," with good results. Paperback.

GRINDLEY, SALLY. (1996). *Peter's place.* San Diego, CA: Harcourt Brace. Young Peter's pristine ocean beach is fouled by an oil spill. He helps with the cleanup. Though the cleanup is never complete, the book's tone remains hopeful: the beach is still "full of life."

GRUPPER, JONATHAN. (1997). *Destination: Rainforest.* Washington, DC: National Geographic. Excellent photographs of the rainforest habitat explain how plants and animals relate to one another.

HECKMAN, PAMELA. (1997). *Hungry animals: My first look at a food chain.* Toronto, Canada: Kids Can Press. The rhythm of this cumulative story builds the food chain flow from seed, to bug, to toad, to snake, to owl. A well-designed small book with lovely, child-focused illustrations and fold-out sidebar pages.

HISCOCK, BRUCE. (1997). *The big rivers: The Missouri, the Mississippi, and the Ohio.* New York: Atheneum. This book presents the causes, consequences, and experience of the Great Flood of 1993. You may question the tranquil conclusion that the flood was a once-a-century event.

HUGHES, SHIRLEY. (1992). *The big Alfie out of doors story book.* New York: Lothrop, Lee, & Shepard. Alfie and his family enjoy being outside: camping, playing store, walking in the country, cherishing a special rock, and playing on the beach.

JOHNSON, D.B. (2002). *Henry builds a cabin.* Boston: Houghton Mifflin. Henry the bear is a stand-in for Henry David Thoreau. In this book, he builds the famous tiny cabin, explaining to his friends Emerson and Alcott that he can use the outdoors for lots of his living.

KANE, TRACY (2001). *Fairy Houses.* Lee, NH: Great White Dog Picture Co. Do you believe in fairies? This is a book about creating woodland homes for them using natural materials.

LASKY, KATHRYN. (1997). *She's wearing a dead bird on her head!* New York: Hyperion. This award-winning book is about real women who helped stop the use of feathers on clothing and hats in the United States around 1900. It encourages children to speak up for the environment. Paperback.

LASKY, KATHRYN (2001). *Interrupted Journey: Saving endangered sea turtles.* Cambridge, MA; Candlewick. Photo essay on the life-cycle of a sea turtle, emphasizing the constructive role of concerned adults and children in saving them.

LYON, GEORGE. (1998). *Counting on the woods*. New York: Dorling Kindersley. This book presents beautiful, restful eastern woodland photographs of natural objects (vines, stones, etc.) to count. A lap-held child will enjoy doing the counting.

MARZOLLO, JEAN. (1997). *Home sweet home*. New York: HarperCollins. This picture poem of blessings on the diverse beauties of the world is short, sweet, and very pretty.

PATENT, DOROTHY HINSHAW. (2000). *The bald eagle returns*. New York: Clarion. Good photographs and much information for an interested reader.

PIROTTA, SAVIOUR. (1997). *Turtle bay*. New York: Farrar, Straus, Giroux. Taro and his old friend collaborate to help sea turtles lay eggs and survive for another generation.

POSADA, MIA. (2002). *Dandelions: Stars in the grass*. St. Paul, MN: Carolrhoda. A poem about the life cycle of a dandelion.

RING, ELIZABETH. (1996). *What rot: Nature's mighty recycler*. New York: Greenwillow. This book reveals all the creatures who decompose natural materials and keep the world clean.

ROMANOVA, NATALIA. (1989). *Once there was a tree*. New York: Dial. This lovely ecosystem tale from Russia is enriched by soft, detailed illustrations. *New York Times* Notable Books of the Year Award. Paperback.

SCHWARTZ, DAVID. M. (1993). *How much is a million?* New York: Lothrop, Lee, & Shepard. The author uses the natural environment to help convey the meaning of big numbers.

STEINER, BARBARA. (1996). *Desert trip*. San Francisco: Sierra Club Books. A girl and her mother go camping and "leave only footprints" as they explore and enjoy the desert hills.

STERN, MAGGIE. (1997). *The missing sunflowers*. New York: Greenwillow. A boy plants sunflowers and discovers that other creatures want them, too.

TAFURI, NANCY. (1997). *What the sun sees/What the moon sees*. New York: Greenwillow. This cleverly designed book, with simple text, turns upside down halfway through.

TRESSALT, ALVIN. (1992). *The gift of the tree*. New York: Lothrop, Lee, & Shepard. This fine story describes the hundred-year life cycle of an oak tree as it shelters and promotes new life.

WYLER, ROSE. (1990). *Grass and grasshoppers*. New York: Julian Messner/Simon & Schuster. The text and illustrations move from good feelings about lying in grassy fields to wondering, observing, experimenting, and learning about grass and the small creatures it shelters.

YOLEN, JANE. (1992). *Letting Swift River go*. Boston: Little, Brown. This is an account of an actual event: the damming of a river to provide water for Boston and its effect on the people who lived by the river.

Poems (Resources in Appendix A)

From Robert Lewis Stevenson's *A Child's Garden of Verses,* read "The Little Land."

From Catherine Paladino's *Land, Sea, and Sky,* read "Trees," by Harry Behm.

George Shannon's *Spring: A Haiku Story* is brilliantly illustrated for the quick thoughts of haiku.

Art Activities

Modeling Beeswax. Children soften pieces of beeswax by warming it with their hands until it is pliable. They can model and shape it as desired, stretching it thin for translucency. Beeswax hardens when it cools. It can be reused by softening it again. Because it melts, avoid putting finished work in direct sunlight or leaving it in a hot car or other places. This natural material is obtainable in many colors from craft stores. For an ecology experience, buy a piece of natural comb honey and let the honey drip out of the comb. What remains is beeswax, in a very sticky state. Wash it carefully with warm water and use it for modeling.

Sun Prints. ♣ Arrange leaves or other nature finds on dark-colored construction paper. Weight it down with rocks on the leaves and on each corner of the paper. Leave for about an hour in bright sunlight. The paper shaded by the objects will stay the same color, while the rest of the paper will be faded by the sunlight. Solar print (light sensitive) paper is commercially available for the same purpose. Follow the package instructions.

Outdoor Chalk Making. ♣ Mix powdered tempera paint with 6 tablespoons of plaster of paris. Stir in 1 cup of water. Pour quickly into a plastic ice-cube tray and let it harden. This will take about 1/2 hour. Children can use the chalk on the sidewalk or asphalt.

Play

Housekeeping Play. ♣ If your environment permits, let children set up "houses" in the nature area. Branches, leaves, and stones are the ingredients for imaginative house play that encourage children to value natural objects. If you can, trim bushes so that children can use them for refuge and privacy. (Drooping branches of a large forsythia bush work well for this.) When children interact with nature in a way that is meaningful to them, they can develop the attitudes that later lead to responsible stewardship. Read "Shop" in *The Big Alfie Out of Doors Story Book* by Shirley Hughes to inspire new play ideas. Alfie and Annie Rose set up a store selling leaves, sticks, and such.

Directions for making sunflower-and-morning-glory houses are in Sharon Lovejoy's *Sunflower Houses.* Bean tepees are another possibility.

Fairy Houses. ♣ Read *Fairy Houses,* by Tracy Kane. Some children might want to construct their own fairy houses in a corner of the schoolgrounds. If that is not practical, provide shoe boxes and natural materials for them.

Creative Thinking

Ask children to imagine what our world would be like if it never rained or if we had sunshine all the time and no night. Accept all answers. Encourage children to listen to one another and build on others' ideas, if possible.

Jacqueline Horsfall's *Play Lightly on the Earth* has several guided imagery texts to help children visualize being a tree in the forest, going to the center of the Earth, being a flowing river, and being a bubble above the Earth.

Food Experiences

♣ Having children gather and prepare food that nature provides can be an appealing and challenging prospect for nature-loving teachers. In our regions, lucky teachers will find mulberry trees nearby to provide an edible wild treat in early summer. Some may know where an accessible wild grape vine or elderberry bush has ripened fruit ready to harvest in fall. Both of these fruits are too tart to eat freshly picked, but an ambitious teacher can gather them (both are out of reach of young children) and make jelly to share with the class. Photographs of the teacher at work could authenticate the harvesting from the wild state.

Children love to gather fallen nuts and attractive berries. They do so indiscriminately, often sampling their treasures. When a puffball unexpectedly erupted in our school playground, it seemed repulsive to the children, though it is edible and prized as a delicacy. Conversely, they were attracted to the bright red nightshade berries and lush blue pokeberries that were clearly visible beyond the playground fence. Both are poisonous. **As a safety precaution, always check with a local naturalist before offering any food from the wild to children.** (See the note on p. 68 regarding common poisonous plant materials.) A reliable resource for learning more about foods in the wild is *Stalking the Wild Asparagus,* by Euell Gibbons. (See Resources.)

For the longer range, see Robin C. Moore's *Plants for Play: A Plant Selection Guide for Children's Outdoor Environments.* He offers many ideas for landscaping the schoolyard with edibles. Tell children that many early Native Americans relied only on wild fruits and plant foods to add to their food supplies because few groups cultivated crops. Later settlers also made use of abundant wild fruits, as it was more important to grow grains and other kinds of crops at first. Grocery stores heaped with cultivated fruits and vegetables came into being much later in our history.

Field Trips

Creek Walk. ♣ If there is a creek nearby to walk along for a way, make the trip by yourself in advance to be sure it is suitable for your group. Take plenty of time to notice things that can be seen along the way: plants, insects, rocks, clay outcroppings, and trees. Creeks tend to be low in the fall, which makes them safer for young children. As we have said earlier, keep the science focus simple. There will be too many exciting things to see to make lengthy explanations bearable for the children. Be sure that the adults who accompany the class understand this. Children's previously constructed knowledge of elements of the environment may come to light here and in classroom discussions afterward.

Sewage Treatment or Water Treatment Plant. Some children would like to know what happens to the dirty water after washing their hands or flushing the toilet. Ask for children's ideas about satisfactory ways of dealing with dirty water and ways to make water from lakes, rivers, or underground sources clean and safe enough for us to drink. It may be possible in your area to arrange a visit to water and sewage treatment plants. Make the process more concrete by exploring the concepts of filtering and sedimentation. Collect a jarful of muddy water from a puddle or create some by adding a scoop of playground soil—gravel and other flotsam included—to a quart of water. Line a funnel with a coffee filter and pour some of the muddy water through it into a smaller container. Check the results. Identify the filtered water as *cleaner,* but *not drinkable.* Let the remaining water stand for a day in the quart jar to observe how the dirt and other "stuff" settles to the bottom as sediment, with the water above clearer and cleaner.

Asphalt transformed into a natural area: The Washington
Environmental Yard in Berkeley, California.

Read aloud *The Magic Schoolbus at the Waterworks,* by Joanna Cole, or *Flush: Treating Wastewater,* by Karen Miller Coombs.

Landfill. Some children might be interested in seeing where solid waste is contained. Children will have to stay on the bus for this experience. The utter blandness and extensiveness of the area can facilitate discussion of recycling and reusing.

Follow-up play in the sand table can occur with toy trucks and things to bury. Joanna Foster's book, *Cartons, Cans, and Orange Peels: Where Does Your Garbage Go*, has good photographs and information.

PROMOTING CONCEPT CONNECTIONS

Maintaining Concepts

1. Have children work in cooperative learning groups structured so that children are truly interdependent. Remind them that they are like the environment, where every part is connected and each part depends on other parts being there and functioning.

2. Assign different children each day to care for classroom pets and plants, maintaining the necessary microenvironments.

3. As children begin to appreciate trees as living things and begin to understand that trees play a part in the oxygen cycle, offer an important statistic from Project Learning Tree: "A 12-year-old child needs to plant and maintain 65 trees in order to offset the amount of carbon dioxide that child will put in the atmosphere during the rest of his or her lifetime." (See Resources.) Try to arrange to plant a tree seedling for the class, and plan for watering and maintaining the new trees. Our schools have done this for many years, so today's youngsters have shadier, screened-off playgrounds.

Improving Schoolgrounds

Rehabilitating Schoolyards for Children's Learning and Play. The most effective environmental teaching occurs in an outdoor environment rich with examples of ecological systems with which children can interact repeatedly. Although good outdoor environments used to be accessible to children, this is no longer true in many areas. Furthermore, many children today spend very little time outside, for a variety of reasons. Teachers who believe that children need outdoor experiences find that they must join with others in the school and community to create good outdoor environments at school. Administrators, the science coordinator, parent groups, the school board, community associations, and businesses all need to get involved in the major work of rehabilitating schoolgrounds.

A worldwide movement for this work began in the 1990s. It encourages teachers and colleagues who wish to replace the typical asphalt and turf schoolgrounds with natural elements such as trees, water, flowers, shrubs, vegetables, brush piles, bird houses, and compost piles. There also need to be places for children to sit and play among or near these elements.

Many resources have been generated. Some of the best written resources come from Great Britain, available in North America from the Green Brick Road. (See Additional Resources.) *Natural Learning* by Moore and Wong tells the story of an asphalt schoolyard transformed through school and community work into a "compact countryside," in one child's words. *The Great Outdoors: Restoring Children's Right to Play Outside* by Rivkin describes other good schoolyards for young children and provides design guidance. Many local and regional organizations are knowledgeable about fixing and using schoolgrounds for teaching. The National Wildlife Federation and the Center for Environmental Education, Antioch College–New England have extensive lists of organizations on their Web pages. (See Additional Resources.)

Gardening. A good beginning project is beds for flowers, vegetables, and native plants. Many kinds of gardens are possible. "Native American" gardens typically feature corn, beans, and squash (Caduto & Bruchac, 1996). "Pizza" gardens grow tomatoes, peppers, and herbs. "Butterfly" gardens use a variety of plants identified for your area as providing nectar for regional butterflies and food for their larvae. "Cultural roots" garden (Mannes & Rehns, 2001) provide concrete evidence of history and geography links to what we eat. To ensure children's interest in and care for the garden, involve them from the beginning in deciding where and what to plant, and how to maintain the garden. Here are some guidelines:

1. Locate beds where they won't be built over in the next year. Check this with school and school district buildings and grounds people. Consult with the maintenance staff to prevent the garden from being mowed down, sprayed with pesticides, used as a dump, or allowed to appear unsightly to neighbors. Reviving the outdoors is a collaborative effort. Consultation is crucial.

2. Locate flower and vegetable beds where they will receive 6 hours of sunlight. If a sunny location isn't possible, shade gardens can be mossy, ferny havens for children, especially with rocks or logs to sit on.

3. Choose a spot close to a water source, preferably a faucet and hose, or only the most devoted gardener will help the beds through droughts and summer vacations.

4. If there is any chance of lead being in the soil, have it tested. Land where people have lived for a long time in buildings is likely to have lead contamination, as is land close to highways used by lead-emitting vehicles. To avoid contaminated soil, construct a raised bed with stones, bricks, recycled plastic-wood timbers, logs, or untreated wood timbers. Fill the bed with fresh soil. Wood pressure-treated with CCA (chromated copper arsenate) is no longer used around children because of the arsenic in it. The EPA banned it for home and school use in 2002. Another preserving compound, ACQ (alkaline copper quaternary ammonium) appears to be safer and equally effective in protecting wood. Children, however, would benefit from seeing wood rot. Used tires may be used for gardens, although there is some concern about the safety of old rubber for children's use.

5. Plan to use Integrated Pest Management (IPM), which minimizes the use of pesticides (including herbicides, insecticides, rodenticides, and fungicides). There is growing concern over the widespread use of numerous toxins that, in killing pests, probably also harm children. Consult the county extension agent, the library, or a knowledgeable nursery for more information. Some states now require that schools use IPM, and federal legislation has been proposed. The Children's Environmental Health Network maintains a very informative Web

site, as does the U.S. Environmental Protection Agency (see Additional Resources). Celia Godkin's *What About Ladybugs?* is a useful way to introduce children to this important idea.

The American Horticultural Society and the National Gardening Association (see Resources) have many helpful materials about gardening at schools. There are fine home gardeners in your community who may be eager to share their knowledge and love of gardening with the next generation. You could start an intergenerational project for satisfaction beyond the plants, as Molly and Dirck Brown have with their "Roots and Shoots" project.

Composting. An important project to accompany garden-planting is building a compost bin or pile. It will reassuringly demonstrate to children how natural processes break down material into rich soil; otherwise we would be drowning in garbage. Use these guidelines.

1. Locate the compost pile where it will be convenient to throw weeds and cuttings, but not where it is unsightly or where the occasional smell will bother people.

2. Attractive wood or plastic compost containers can be purchased, but a simple structure of chicken wire and posts will suffice. The county extension agent can offer advice here.

3. Occasionally add a light layer of dirt to the plant material. Avoid adding heaps of grass clippings without mixing in leaves and stems. Solid layers of grass clippings become slimy from lack of air, instead of rotting nicely. Consult with school maintenance persons to enlist cooperation here.

Wildflower Meadows. Meadows abounded in this country before we fell in love with lawns. Restoring meadows of tall grass and wildflowers is both delighting and environmentally sound. Once the meadow is established, it provides children with plenty of flowers to pick. Native plant nurseries and county extension agents can be helpful with seed selection.

Providing Water. A water feature is a more ambitious project that provides incredibly diverse learning opportunities. Children love to play in water, and wildlife requires it. Imaginative ponds and wetlands can be constructed in a school courtyard where access can be controlled. Even in an open schoolground, a shallow wetland, thickly ringed with plants, presents little hazard to children. Many people in the United States seem unduly fearful of allowing children near water, but schools are starting to provide naturalistic water features. In Maryland, schools throughout the state now have wetlands, often created from altered storm-water drainage ponds. Begin with a birdbath for children to observe, and convince others to join in creating something more extensive. The West Nile virus is a new reason to worry about ponds because mosquitoes breed in standing water. However, in a well-balanced pond, fish and other larger life thrive on eating mosquito larvae. Bats and birds delight in eating mosquitoes. Work toward a healthy, diverse habitat.

Establishing Shrubs and Tree Areas. A longer-term project is planting a hedgerow of mixed shrubs in which birds can find shelter and nest. A hedgerow will also provide shade for seated children. Let children help research a variety of native species to plant.

The prospect of picking food off shrubs or trees is irresistible to most children, as well as educational. Pear trees and blueberry bushes are good choices. A school we know has its children plant a tree every year. The trees then bear fruit for edible math lessons.

Trees are the big structures of the environmental yard. Because they provide valuable shade, wildlife habitat, and play materials like cones, pods, and leaves, start with the biggest affordable size. Plant them in the most carefully chosen places, and maintain them scrupulously throughout the entire first year. Native trees have evolved to survive in your climate, so they will require the least maintenance after getting established. Moore's *Plants for Play* is useful for selecting plants that will do well and also provide play materials or structures for children.

Involving Everyone. Whatever you decide to undertake, involve the children and the community. Children will learn lessons about the environment and how to care for it that can last a lifetime. Community members will protect your efforts when you are not there. Involve community professionals who can give their expertise in landscape design and plant selection. The outdoor classroom is "the biggest classroom" (Humphries & Rowe, 1994). It is a profound link between the school building and the neighborhood—one that can enhance the lives of all children and their families.

Connecting Concepts

Generally speaking, the environment encompasses every element and every *thing* that exists in and around our planet. It would be easy to overwhelm youngsters by trying to pull together a multitude of possible connections in classroom discussions. For this reason, concept connections in this chapter have been limited to concepts found in Chapters 4 through 10. The topics of endangered species of animals, large-scale pollution, and depletion of nonrenewable resources have been avoided deliberately. It is our belief that issues of such scope needlessly burden and sadden young children who are helpless to remedy them. The concepts in this chapter focus on the positive connections in nature because children and adults are more likely to take care of what they truly appreciate.

Family and Community Support

Encourage families to model environmentally sensitive values. They can buy bulk foods at the store to reduce the amount of material needed for packaging. Children can help with the measuring and weighing to gain experience in valuable math processes. Children can participate in energy conservation by turning out unnecessary lights, not letting faucets run needlessly, and walking or biking instead of expecting to be driven short distances.

Children can participate in community recycling programs by washing and flattening empty cans and stacking newspapers. Newsletters to families can announce the dates and locations of community stream, roadway, or beach cleanup programs.

Families might visit the dump and observe the landfill operation, check out visitor displays at the sewage treatment plant, and find the water source that serves their home, be it a private or town well, a river, or a lake. Older children can look at maps to see the path of the river, noting reservoirs and dams.

Nature centers may have marked nature trails and displays about local plants and animals. Botanical gardens and zoos often feature environmental exhibits. Older children are often deeply interested in space, and some would enjoy a planetarium visit. In this context, they can see evidence that our planet, big as it is to us, is a tiny part of a vast system. This is both provocative and reassuring: "We are part of a larger design, and will be safe."

RESOURCES

BARRETT, K., & WILLARD, C. (1998). *Schoolyard ecology*. Berkeley, CA: GEMS, Lawrence Hall of Science. Good background information can be used for schoolyard study. Some activities are useful with young children.

BOSTON SCHOOLYARD INITIATIVE. (2001). *Landscape manual for on-site personnel*. Boston: Author. This is the most basic book ever on refurbishing a schoolyard. For example, a shovel is pictured and instructions on how to use it are provided. Many projects in gardening, landscaping, and maintenance are described in infinite—but somehow not boring—detail.

CADUTO, M.J., & BRUCHAC, J. (1996). *Native American gardening: Stories, projects and recipes for families*. Golden, CO: Fulcrum Publishing.

CORNELL, JOSEPH. (1979/1999). *Sharing nature with children*. Nevada City, CA: Dawn Publications. Classic in the field of connecting children to nature, especially through their feelings.

EARTHWORKS GROUP. (1990). *50 simple things kids can do to save the Earth*. Kansas City: Andrews and McMeel. This book has many wide-ranging ideas for making everyone feel he or she can do something useful for the environment.

EARTHWORKS GROUP. (1994). *50 simple things kids can do to recycle*. Berkeley, CA: EarthWorks Press. This very accessible book will get your classroom going on a variety of useful activities.

FRY-MILLER, K., & MYERS-WALL, J. (1988). *Young peacemakers project book*. Elgin, IL: Brethren Press. This project book links stewardship with peace.

GIBBONS, E. (1988). *Stalking the wild asparagus*. Brattleboro, VT: Allen C. Hood. This classic field guide to finding edibles in the wild is too hard for children, but authoritative for teachers.

HERMAN, M., SCHIMPF, A., PASSINEAU, J., & TREUER, P. (1991). *Teaching kids to love the Earth*. Duluth, MN: Pfeifer-Hamilton. This thoughtful book provides many resources.

HORSFALL, J. (1997). *Play lightly on the Earth: Nature activities for children 3 to 9 years old*. Nevada City, CA: Dawn Publications. Teachers will find usable, emotionally in-tune activities here.

HUMPHRIES, S., & ROWE, S. (1994). The biggest classroom. In P. Blatchford & S. Sharp (Eds.), *Breaktime and the school: Understanding and changing playground behavior* (pp. 107–117). London: Routledge. One of the best-known British schoolyards and its integration into the curriculum is described here.

KASPERSON, J., LACHECKI, M., & HOLLMAN, K. (1994). *More teaching kids to love the Earth.* Duluth, MN: Pfeiffer-Hamilton. The original book is extended in useful ways.

KOHL, M. A., & GAINER, C. (1991). *Good Earth art: Environmental art for kids.* Bellingham, WA: Bright Ring Publishing. Many recycling ideas and directions for homemade materials are found in this book.

LOVEJOY, S. (2001). *Sunflower houses* (2nd ed.). New York: Workman.

MANNES, J., & REHNS, M. (2001). *Seeds of change: Learning from the garden.* Parsnipanny, NJ: Dale Seymour.

MOORE, R. (1993). *Plants for play: A plant selection guide for children's outdoor environments.* Berkeley, CA: MIG Communications. Many ideas are suggested for landscaping the schoolyard to provide children with edibles and play materials.

MOORE, R., & COSCO, NILDA. (2002). *Developing an earth-bound culture through design of childhood habitats.* A thoughtful statement on the urgency of reconnecting children with nature. At *www.naturalearning.com.*

MOORE, R., & WONG, H. (1997). *Natural learning: The life history of an environmental schoolyard.* Berkeley, CA: MIG Communications. This rich account of making and using a naturalized urban schoolyard will make you want to change your grounds. The photographs are very convincing.

ORION SOCIETY. (1998). *Stories in the land: A place-based environmental education anthology.* Great Barrington, MA: Author. Teachers tell their stories of environmental studies with children. If the story inspires you to action, lesson plans have the nitty-gritty details.

PROJECT LEARNING TREE. (1993). *Environmental education activities, grades K–6.* Washington, DC: American Forest Foundation. The origin of the beloved environmental credo attributed to Chief Seattle is examined on pages 344–347.

PRINGLE, L. (1997). *Taking care of the Earth: Kids in action.* Honesdale, PA: Boyds Mill Press. Accounts are given of successful action by schoolchildren to study and improve their environment, with useful tips for teachers.

RIVKIN, M. (1995). *The great outdoors: Restoring children's right to play outside.* Washington, DC: National Association for the Education of Young Children. The author argues for children's needs and rights to have good outdoor play, and offers ideas for playspace improvement.

RIVKIN, M. (2000). *Outdoor experiences for young children.* ERIC Digest EDO-RC-00-7. Available on Internet from ERIC Clearinghouse on Rural Education and Small Schools.

RUSSELL, H. R. (1990). *Ten minute field trips* (2nd ed.). Washington, DC: National Science Teachers Association. This book emphasizes using the urban schoolground for environmental science. The chapter on interdependence of living things is excellent.

TUFTS, C. (1988). *The backyard naturalist.* Washington, D.C.: National Wildlife Federation. This basic handbook describes how to create a habitat for small creatures: birds, butterflies, and more.

VANDER MEY, B.J., McDONALD, S. I., HICKS, K.L., & FEINDT, K. L. (2001). *Printed resources for gardening with children and youth.* Clemson, SC: Landscapes for Learning, Clemson University Extension Service.

WILSON, RUTH. (1996). The development of the ecological self. *Early Childhood Education Journal, 24* (2), 121–123. An affinity with the natural world usually begins in childhood; so Wilson explores the research and advocates for more natural experiences for young children.

Additional Resources

American Horticultural Society
7931 E. Boulevard Drive
Alexandria, VA 22308-1300
1-800-777-7931

Center for Environmental Education
Antioch College–New England
http://weblinks.schoolsgogreen.org/links/weblinks_schlgrnd/

Children's Environmental Health Network
110 Maryland Avenue NE, Suite 511
Washington, DC 20002
 (202) 543-4033
http://www.cehn.org

U.S. Environmental Protection Agency
www.epa.gov/pesticides/ipm

Green Brick Road
c/o Dumas Court
Don Mills, Ontario, Canada M3A, 2N21
800-473-3638

National Gardening Association
180 Flynn Ave.
Burlington, VT 05401
(802) 863-1308
http://www.kidsgardening.com/grants.asp

Natural Learning Initiative
School of Design
North Carolina State University
http://naturalearning.org

National Wildlife Federation
111000 Wildlife Drive
Reston, VA 21090
www.nwf.org

Project Wild
707 Conservation Lane Suite 305
Gaithersburg, MD 20878
(301) 527-8900

Resources for Music, Recordings, Poetry, Creative Movement, and Equipment Ordering

MUSIC

Cassettes

BANANA SLUG STRING BAND. *Adventures on the air cycle.* Music for Little People. "Air Cycle Swing," "Lizard," "No Bones Within," "Animals," "Ecology."

BERMAN, M. *Rabbits dance: Marcia Berman sings Malvina Reynolds.* B/B Records, 1985. 570 N. Arden Blvd., Los Angeles, CA 90004.

BERMAN, M., & ZEITLIN, P. *Spin, spider, spin: Songs for a greater appreciation of nature.* Educational Activities. Includes songs about lizards, birds, snakes, frogs, and insects.

CHENILLE SISTERS. *1 2 3 Kids.* Red House Records. Includes "The Kitchen Percussion Song": Making music with things found in the kitchen.

CROW, D. *A friend, a laugh, a walk in the woods.* Includes "Walking on My Wheels," in which a child uses a wheelchair to get around; "The Zucchini Song," "Blowing Up Balloons," "The Shape of My Shadow." Sony Kids Music.

MICHE, M. *A kid's eye view of the environment.* Star Trek. Includes "Spiders and Snakes," "You Can't Make a Turtle Come Out," "Bug Bits," "Dirt Made My Lunch."

MICHE, M. *Kid's stuff.* Star Trek. Includes "The Cat Came Back."

MICHE, M. *Nature nuts.* Star Trek. "Recycle Blues," "Pollution," "Hey, Ms. Spider."

PALMER, H. *Walter the waltzing worm.* Educational Activities.

RAFFI. *Evergreen, everblue.* Shoreline/MCA.

RAFFI. *Raffi in concert.* Shoreline/MCA.

ROGERS, F. *Won't you be my neighbor?* Family Communications, Inc. Audiocassette MRV 8106C.

ROGERS, F. *You are special.* Family Communications, Inc. Audiocassette MRN8103C.

ROGERS, S. *Piggyback, planet: Songs for the whole Earth.* Round River Records.

SEEGER, P. *Birds, beasts, bugs, and little fishes.* Smithsonian Folkways.

TROUT FISHING IN AMERICA. *My world.* Music Management Productions, 1997.

TWIN SISTERS. *I'd like to be a marine biologist.* Twin Productions, Twin 423, 1998. Includes songs about whales, dolphins, and sharks. A marine life fact booklet is included.

ZAMFIR, G. *Romance of the pan flute*. Cassette #32150. Polygram Classics: 810 Seventh Ave., New York, NY.

Compact Discs

BANANA SLUG STRING BAND. *Penguin parade*. (1996). Includes songs about raccoons, ants, otters, fish, and moose. American Library Association Notable Children's Recording Award.
BANANA SLUG STRING BAND. *Goin' wild in Yellowstone and the Tetons*. (2000). Includes songs about beavers, bears, and bisons. National Park Service Excellence Awards.
ROUSE, J. *Around the world with Earth mama*. Rouse House, 1997.
SMITHSONIAN FOLKWAYS. *Children's music collection*. (1998). Includes Woody Guthrie's "Riding in My Car," and Pete Seeger's "One Grain of Sand."

Music Books

CARLE, E. (1993). *Today is Monday*. New York: Putnam & Grosset. Splashy illustrations capture the fun of singing this simple song about favorite foods.
HAINES, J., & GERBER, L. (1992). *Leading young children to music* (4th ed.). Upper Saddle River, NJ: Merrill/Prentice Hall.
LEVY, MICHAEL. (2001). *La tierra el mar*. This Spanish/English songbook of compositions by the Banana Slug String Band includes "I'm a Tree," "Roots, Stems, Leaves," "Decomposition," and "Dirt Made My Lunch."
MALLETT, DAVID. (1995). *Inch by inch: The garden song*. New York: HarperCollins.
RAFFI. (1987). *Singable songbook*. New York: Crown.
RAFFI. (1989). *Everything grows*. New York: Crown.
READER'S DIGEST. (1985). *Oats, peas, beans*. Pleasantville, NY: Author.
REY, M. (1986). *Over in the meadow*. New York: Penguin. Paperback.
SMITHSONIAN FOLKWAYS. (1988). *Childrens' music collection*. Washington, D.C.: Author.

Resources for Ordering Cassettes and CDs

Music for Little People
P.O. Box 1460
Redway, CA 95560-1460
Tel: (800) 346-4445

Order information and Real Audio clips of songs can be heard on this Web site: *www.bananaslugstringband.com*.

POETRY

CYRUS, K. (2001). *Oddhoppers opera: A bug's garden of verses*. San Diego: Harcourt Brace.
DEREGNIERS, B., BROWN, M., & DILLON, D. (1988). *Sing a song of popcorn: Every child's book of poems*. New York: Scholastic.
FISHER, A. (1986). *When it comes to bugs*. New York: Harper & Row.
FLEISCHMAN, P. (1988). *Joyful noise: Poems for two voices*. New York: Harper & Row. Awarded the Newberry Medal, this fine collection of poems captures the movement, sound, and essence of selected insects. Exquisite drawings by Eric Beddows reflect the imagery evoked by the poems.
FLORIAN, D. (1998). *Insectlopedia*. San Diego: Harcourt Brace.
FLORIAN, D. (2000). *Mammalabilia*. San Diego: Harcourt Brace.
FLORIAN, D. (2001). *Lizards, frogs, and polliwogs*. San Diego: Harcourt Brace.
GRAHAM, J. (1999). *Flicker flash*. Boston: Houghton Mifflin.
HOBERMAN, M. A. (1998). *The llama who had no pajama*. San Diego: Harcourt Brace.

HOPKINS, L. B. (Ed.). (1994). *Weather.* New York: HarperCollins. An I-Can-Read book. Brightly illustrated, carefully chosen, enjoyable poems about the weather.

HOPKINS, L. B. (1995). *Blast off! Poems about outer space.* New York: HarperCollins.

HOPKINS, L. B. (Ed.). (1999). *Spectacular science: A book of poems.* New York: Simon & Schuster

HOPKINS, L. B. (2000). *Yummy eating throughout the day.* New York: Simon & Schuster.

HUGHES, S. (1988). *Out and about.* New York: Lothrop, Lee, & Shepard. Includes poems about water buoyancy and a rainbow seen through a garden hose spray.

KENNEDY, DOROTHY (Ed.). (1998). *Make things fly.* New York: McElderry. A fine anthology of read-aloud poems about the wind; breezily illustrated.

KENNEDY, D. (Ed.). (1993). *I thought I'd take my rat to school: Poems for September to June.* Boston: Little Brown. Humorous poems about school realities include the topics of light, animals, plants, and nutrition.

KENNEDY, X. J. (2002). *Exploding gravy.* Boston: Little Brown.

LEVY, CONSTANCE. (2002). *Splash! Poems of our watery world.* New York: Orchard.

LEVY, CONSTANCE. (1998). *A crack in the clouds.* New York: McElderry.

LEVY, CONSTANCE. (1994). *A tree place.* New York: McElderry.

MILNE, A. A. (1961). *Now we are six.* New York: E. P. Dutton.

MOSS, J. (1989). *The butterfly jar.* New York: Bantam Books. Includes "The First Musician" and "The Banana King."

MOSS, J. (1997). *Bone poems.* New York: Workman.

PALADINO, C. (Ed. and illus.). (1994). *Land, sea, and sky.* Boston: Little, Brown. Fine color photographs of nature accompany the well-chosen poems.

SHANNON, G. (1996). *Spring: A haiku story.* New York: Greenwillow.

SILVERSTEIN, S. (2000). *Where the sidewalk ends.* New York: HarperCollins. Reissued.

SILVERSTEIN, S. (2001). *A light in the attic.* New York: HarperCollins. Reissued.

SILVERSTEIN, S. (1996). *Falling up.* New York: HarperCollins.

SINGER, M. (1989). *Turtle in July.* Upper Saddle River, NJ: Prentice Hall.

STEVENSON, R. L. (1999). *A child's garden of verses.* New York: Simon & Schuster.

THOMPSON, J. M. (1957). *Poems to grow on.* Boston: Beacon Press.

Creative Movement

CHERRY, C. (1985). *Creative movement for the developing child.* Washington, D.C.: National Association for the Education of Young Children.

PICA, R. (1991). *Special themes for moving and learning.* Champaign, IL: Human Kinetics.

SINCLAIR, C. (1976). *Movement of the young child ages two to six.* Upper Saddle River, NJ: Merrill/Prentice Hall. (Out of print; obtain copy from library.)

Equipment Sources

Reasonably priced, sturdy science equipment for classroom use is sold by mail from:

Delta Education, Inc.
P.O. Box 3000
Nashua, NH 03061-3000

HearthSong, A Catalog for Families
P.O. Box B
Sebastopol, CA 95473

The Nature Company Catalog
P.O. Box 2310
Berkeley, CA 94702

Lawrence Hall of Science
University of California
Berkeley, CA 94270

Exploring at Home Activities

EXPLORING AT HOME*

Plants

Plants are important. Without them, nothing else could live on Earth. Encourage your child to talk with you about what she or he has discovered about plants, how they grow, and how we use some of them. Then enjoy sharing some simple plant-growing activities with your child.

Home activities with seeds and plants have a big advantage over school activities. At home, your child can watch with you the beginning-to-end happenings. Together you can watch the whole life cycle of plants, from seed to plant to seed again. If you have use of a small, sunny piece of ground, plant a few dried beans. Let your child keep them watered. Watch for and talk about first sprouts, blossoms, and tiny beans. Eat some of the beans. Save some to dry. Then shell out the beans to plant next year. Bury the vines after they die down. Let them decay and renew the soil for next year's plants. Consider starting a compost bin for recycling yard wastes.

Bottle Botany. Suspend a fat, single clove of garlic in a small bottle of water,

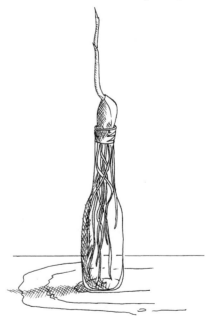

FIGURE B–1

*These suggestions may be duplicated and sent home to families.

From *Science Experiences for the Early Childhood Years*, 8th ed. Copyright 2004 Merrill/Prentice Hall Publishing Company. All rights reserved.

with the pointed tip out of the water. If the clove is too small to wedge firmly into the bottle top, poke three toothpicks into the clove to hang it across the top with the bottom half in the water. Keep the bottle filled with fresh water each day, so the clove stays in the water. Watch for fast, dramatic sprouting and root growth (Figure B–1).

Windowsill Gardening. Anytime you prepare fruits for meals, show your child the seeds you find. Soak some citrus seeds in water for a few days. Plant a few in potting soil in a small container. Put it on a sunny windowsill. Let your child give it a little water daily, and watch patiently. Plant a dried bean, a few lentils, or popcorn seeds in other containers. See which seeds grow faster and which plants live longer. Encourage thinking and talking about what happens.

EXPLORING AT HOME*

Animals

We share our planet with millions of animal species. All species of animals share some features in common. Encourage your child to talk about the animals she or he has observed closely in school. Here are some ways you can help your child's interest in animals grow.

Watch and Wonder. Pause for a moment to watch the commonplace small animals you see when you are outdoors with your child. Ants, worms, pigeons, and squirrels exist nearly everywhere, even near city sidewalks. When you share that time together, you are teaching your child to respect our wild-animal neighbors. With some coaching, even a lively toddler can learn to be still and watch.

Children can observe only at home the insects, birds, and other small animals that come out at night. Some can be seen or heard in the city. Others can be seen or heard in the country or woods. A nature center near you might offer night hikes to observe signs of those animals. This is a special adventure that school cannot provide your child. Good books on nature at night include *Nightprowlers,* by Jerry Emory, and *The Night Book,* by Pamela Hickman.

Try attracting birds to your yard or windowsill with a simple feeding arrangement. To learn more about how to do this, check with your area U.S. Fish and Wildlife Service for these free booklets: *Attract Birds* and *Homes for Birds.* (Also obtainable through the U.S. Consumer Information Center, Pueblo, CO 81009.)

Consider creating backyard habitats for birds and butterflies. To do so, include some native plants, as they provide food for native creatures. Try to arrange for shelter, water, and places to rear young. The Backyard Habitat Program at the National Wildlife Federation has print and Web resources to guide you, or consult your county extension agent. The same habitat that attracts little creatures is also a very nice place for young children to play. Your child will enjoy working on this project with you.

---

*These suggestions may be duplicated and sent home to families.

EXPLORING AT HOME*

Human Body

Your child has been gaining new knowledge about the marvelous, complex systems and structures in his or her body. Encourage your child to respect and care for these remarkable gifts. Enjoy sharing these simple but meaningful activities with your child.

Measuring Up. Your child is eager to grow. Children mainly grow taller as their long bones grow longer. Let your child gauge his or her growth against your full-grown size by comparing leg bone length with yours. How much do his or her leg bones need to grow to match yours? Do the same for hands, fingers, and feet. Let your child try on your sweatshirt or jacket. Is there still growing to be done to reach your size? Talk about the milk your child needs to drink to help those bones grow longer. Mention that the bones grow fastest during sleep when our bodies aren't moving much. (A good reason for getting enough rest.) If possible, make a growth record inside a closet by penciling a mark at your child's present height. Record the date and inches on a piece of tape beside the mark. Do this each birthday.

Mark That Growth. Some parts of mature bodies continue to grow. Remind your child that even though you have stopped growing taller, your hair and nails are always growing and need cutting many times each year. Together, observe the slow growth of your fingernails. Mark a dot of ballpoint ink next to the cuticle on one fingernail. Preserve the dot with a coat of clear nail polish, if you have some. Find out how long it takes for the mark to move away from the cuticle. Compare your nail growth with your child's. Mention that skin can continue to grow throughout our lives.

Check This Out. Join your child in checking some interesting body measurement comparisons. Your child should stand with arms and hands outstretched. Cut a piece of string the length of the span from fingertip to fingertip. Now compare that string length with your child's height. They are probably about the same. Compare these two measurements on yourself and other family members. Next, compare the length of your child's foot with the length of his or her forearm, from wrist to elbow. Are the measurements about the same? Let your child measure and compare your foot and forearm. They are probably about the same, also.

---

*These suggestions may be duplicated and sent home to families.

EXPLORING AT HOME*

Air

Your child has been exploring some of the properties of air—that invisible, vital element essential to all life. Listen to what your child has discovered in science experiences. Then be a partner in doing a simple experiment in your kitchen.

Impressive Pressure! Enjoy sharing this surprising air pressure experience with your child. You'll need a clean, lightweight plastic jar with a lid. (An empty peanut butter jar, ready for the recycling bin, will be just fine.) First, carefully punch a small hole about 1/2 inch above the bottom of the jar. (The hole should be about the diameter of a drinking straw.) At the sink, let your child fill the jar with water. Ask: "What happens?" (A small stream of water pours out the hole.) Quickly screw the lid on the jar. Ask: "What changed?" (The flow of water stopped.) "What could be touching the sides of the jar keeping the water from flowing out?" Give your child time to figure this out. (This is the same substance that helps to press down on the water, pushing the water out the hole when the lid is off: air!) Let your child continue to play at the sink with the jar of water with the lid on, with the lid off. Talk about the experiment you shared later on: tomorrow, next week, next month. Air pressure will become a permanent part of your child's fund of information this way.

---

*These suggestions may be duplicated and sent home to families.

EXPLORING AT HOME*

Water

Water is the most common compound on Earth, covering almost three quarters of the planet. This fascinating substance is critical to the survival of all living things. Listen to what your child has discovered about water. Then take a little time to have some water fun with your child.

Icy Shapes. Families have better access to year-round freezing temperatures in your kitchen than we have at school. Enjoy discovering with your child that water freezes in the shape of its container. For this experience, freeze water in assorted plastic or metal containers of different sizes and shapes: thimble-size plastic tops for spray cleaner bottles or nesting measuring cups, for example. You could have fun devising a way to fill, fasten tightly with a rubber band, and freeze a plastic glove almost full of water. Find out together what happens to a damp mitten in the freezer. See what happens when you drape a wet paper towel over an inverted plastic bowl and freeze it. Then remove the stiff, bowl-shaped paper towel. Enjoy the beautiful results when you carefully squeeze drops of water from a medicine dropper onto a piece of foil and freeze them. Do the same with a light coat of water droplets from a spray bottle.

Slippery Safety. (A winter lesson for children in northern climates.) Fill a deep, clear container with water. Put it in the freezer, or outdoors in below-freezing weather. See what's happening to it every few hours. When it has formed a layer of ice across the top, let your child look carefully to see that there is still water beneath the ice. The ice forms from the outside edges before it freezes in the center. The same is true when ponds or streams freeze outdoors. The ice might look safe enough to slide on near the edge, but it might not be thick and strong enough to hold a person near the center. Talk about your family rules about safe sliding and skating places.

Uplifting Discoveries. The next time you swim together, help your child feel the effect of water's upward push. Have your child stand in shoulder deep water, with both arms a few inches away from his or her sides, not pressing tightly to the body. Ask if those arms will stay just where they are. What happens in a short while? (Water's natural upward push begins to move the arms upward. It takes some effort to push the arms back down.) Let your child predict what will happen if he or she curls into a tight ball in the water. Compare this with what happens when he or she stretches out on top of the water. Water's upward push helps us float.

---

*These suggestions may be duplicated and sent home to families.

From *Science Experiences for the Early Childhood Years,* 8th ed. Copyright 2004 Merrill/Prentice Hall Publishing Company. All rights reserved.

EXPLORING AT HOME*

Weather

The sun warms the Earth. Air rises when it's heated by the Earth, and sinks when it cools, causing the movement we call *wind*. Together with the moisture it carries along, it makes all the conditions we call *weather*. Your child has been exploring some parts of the fascinating way that the sun, air, and water act together to make the weather. Share some weather-related investigations at home.

Ups and Downs of Air. Find out together if there is moving air in your house or apartment. Tape a small strip of thin paper to one end of a piece of thread. Tape the other end of the thread to a doorframe to let the paper dangle loosely. Quietly watch with your child as the paper drifts on the air current. Next, explore the ups and downs of air movement. *Carefully,* let your child hold his or her hand just above a lighted 100-watt lightbulb to feel the warm air. Then, hold a 1/2-inch strip of crisp tissue paper by one end, horizontally above the bulb. Watch the free end of the paper strip flutter up as the warm air rising from the glowing bulb pushes the paper up. Next, let your child hold the strip of paper just below the freezer or refrigerator door as you open it a crack. The cold air pushes the paper end down. Talk with your child about how wind happens: All over the world some air is being warmed by the sun, and some air is cool. The cool air moves down under the warm air as the warm air rises. All that pushing and rushing air is what we call *wind*.

Dry Facts. Join your child in noticing and pointing out common, everyday ways that air picks up moisture: a withered carrot or apple from the back of the refrigerator; a piece of dried-out bread; once-damp mittens, now dry; air-dried dishes on the kitchen counter—all are examples of how air takes moisture from things it touches.

Getting It Together. Point out to your child how moisture from warmed air condenses into droplets when it meets a cooler surface: under the lid of a carry-out cup of hot beverage; on the bathroom mirror after someone's warm shower.

Freeze some water in a wide and deep plastic bowl. Check the freezing process every hour to notice how the water begins to freeze from the edges of the bowl long before the middle freezes. Mention that this also happens outdoors when ponds or streams freeze. This is important safety information for children living in cold climates. Ice may be thin and unsafe to walk on in the middle of a pond, even when it is thick and safe to walk on near the shore.

*These suggestions may be duplicated and sent home to families.

EXPLORING AT HOME*

Rocks and Minerals

What are the oldest things your child can collect? Rocks! From the smallest grains of sand to the mammoth ball of rock we live on, rocks are an important part of our lives. Support your child's pleasure in collecting rocks. If you have a yard, let your child help you improve the soil.

Help a Rockhound. If the child in your home is an avid rock collector, help him or her enjoy organizing and thinking about these wonderful finds. Ask your child to tell you about favorite rocks: What is special about their appearance and where they came from? Help your child identify favorite rocks by using a library book or buying an inexpensive paperback nature guidebook like *Rocks and Minerals* by Zim and Shaffer. Try to find a place to display as many rocks as possible. An egg carton makes a simple display box. Use the surplus rocks around the house in different ways: in the bottom of a soap dish to keep the soap dry; under potted plants; outdoors under a downspout.

Start a Soil Time-Capsule. Dig a shallow hole, about a foot square, in a little-used spot of ground near your home. Put a layer of leaves or grass clippings on one side of the hole; a piece of aluminum foil on the other side. Cover these materials with soil. Mark the space with rocks so you can find it and dig it up in 1 year. Circle the date on the calendar, so you won't forget to check the results. (You'll find that the natural materials have started to rot, and perhaps get moldy. The foil will not have changed.) Let your child tell you as much as possible about what happened to the two kinds of material, and why we need to recycle or reuse things that won't decompose in garbage landfill sites. Make this a family rule: "We don't waste and we don't litter. We save the Earth and make it better."

*These suggestions may be duplicated and sent home to families.

EXPLORING AT HOME*

Magnetism

Your child has enjoyed discovering some ways magnets act. All magnets have two opposite poles: north and south (even that giant magnet, our Earth). Let your child share with you what he or she knows about magnets. Then have some magnet fun with your child.

A Scrap-Dance Box. Put together a magnet toy with your child. You'll need a small but strong magnet of any type, a shallow box, some plastic wrap, tape, and a steel wool pad. Shred very small bits of steel wool from the scrubbing pad. Heavy kitchen shears work best for this job. Cut enough steel wool scraps to barely cover the bottom of the box. Stretch the plastic wrap over the top to make a cover, and secure it to the box with tape. Together, enjoy making the scraps dance and creating patterns by pulling the magnet beneath the box.

A Hidden Magnet Hunt. Go on a hidden magnet hunt through your house with your child. Discover useful but unseen magnets in paper clip holders, cupboard door catches, flashlight holders, and message holders. Examine the magnetized plastic strip that holds the refrigerator door tightly shut. Talk about the invisible magnets that are important parts of car motors, electric motors, radios, speakers, computers, telephones, television sets, and tape recorders. Show your child the magnetized strip on the card that you slide into automatic bank teller machines to activate them, or on the credit card you use at the gas pump or grocery checkout. Let your child know that we need magnets and use them every day!

*These suggestions may be duplicated and sent home to families.

EXPLORING AT HOME*

Gravity

Your child has been investigating gravity: the force that pulls everything toward Earth's center. Encourage him or her to share these new ideas with you. Then have some fun with gravity.

A Balky Balloon. Blow up two small balloons of the same size and color, if possible. Tie one; let the air out of the other. Using a small funnel, put a tablespoonful of uncooked rice or a few small pebbles into the emptied balloon. Now blow it up again and tie it. Let your child try to blow the two balloons over the edge of a table. Which one rolls off? Which one tips, but stays put on the edge of the table? Can your child figure out how gravity made the difference? Compare the weight of each balloon to find out.

A Balancing Act. You'll need a ball of play dough or a potato you are going to fix for dinner, and two metal forks to have a neat gravity experience. First, see if you or your child can balance the play dough or potato on the tip of one finger. Then, insert the tines of the forks so the forks angle downward on opposite sides of the ball or potato. They should be stuck in about 1/3 of the way from the bottom. Now try the balancing act! Most of the weight is below the finger now, so the potato or play dough stays balanced. (see Figure B–2.)

FIGURE B–2

*These suggestions may be duplicated and sent home to families.

EXPLORING AT HOME*

Simple Machines

"What's inside?" "How does it work?" These are very familiar questions your child asks. We have been exploring simple machines in school. Simple machines are the basic designs for lifting and moving things. All the complex machines used around us are made up of one or more simple machine concepts. Now your child will enjoy discovering the devices you have in your house that are simple machines.

> *What and How?* Find out together about the simple machines you use:
>
> A screwdriver becomes a lever when you pry open a paint can with it.
>
> Inclined planes are easy to find: curb cut-outs and other ramps for wheelchair users, parking garage ramps, playground slides, spiral charity coin-drops in malls, and fancy gumball machines with spiral chutes.
>
> Traverse drapery rods or certain kinds of blinds have small pulleys inside the top rod.
>
> A hand-operated eggbeater uses gears that are easy to see.

Lift the hood of your car to reveal the belts that let various shafts in the motor turn together, then explore the system with your child, discussing how each belt works. Gears are wheels that turn other wheels. Many can openers have small gears. Hand-wound clocks are full of gears. If you have one that's no longer being used, try to take it apart with your child, using the smallest screwdrivers you can find. (You should be the one to remove the flat, coiled spring. It may spring up instantly and its edges are sharp.)

Explore the workings of gears on bicycles. Encourage your child to compare how the chain and gears help a bicycle go faster with less effort than does a tricycle.

Watch for simple machines like gears, pulleys, and other wheels if you visit a science or historical museum with your child.

> *Easy Rollers.* Check for small wheels that help you move things around the house. You may find them at the base of your refrigerator, vacuum cleaner, luggage or shopping cart, or outdoor grill. Take a close look at roller skates, roller blades, and skate boards. Make a game of counting all the wheels you see on the trucks you pass on the road.

---

*These suggestions may be duplicated and sent home to families.

From *Science Experiences for the Early Childhood Years*, 8th ed., copyright 2004, Merrill/Prentice Hall Publishing Company. All rights reserved.

EXPLORING AT HOME*

Sound

Your child has been making some discoveries about sound: the energy form that travels through air, water, and solids as vibrations. Listen to his or her new information about sound, then do some informal experimenting together at home.

Touch and Watch to Tell. Join your child in making some discoveries about the sounds of home. He or she already knows that sounds are made by vibrating things. First do a *touch* test to find out if something is making a sound: Holding your ears shut with your fingers, touch a washer or dryer with your elbow when the appliance motor is on, then when it is turned off. Could you tell when it was making a sound, even with your ears shut? Let your child tell you about vibrating things causing sound.

Now put a small jar of water on top of the appliance. Close your ears again. *Watch* the water in the jar when the motor is on and when it is turned off. You can see the water vibrating in the glass—the effect of the motor's vibration and sound. Unstop your ears while you *hear* the sound of the motor and *see* the effect of the vibrating appliance.

Louder, Please! Some things make sounds louder. Have fun with your child listening to yourselves whisper "Hello." Then close your ears with your fingers and whisper "Hello" again. The sound is louder when you hear it inside your head. The vibrating air inside your mouth and nose, and the vibrating bony parts of your head amplify the sound. Enjoy listening to yourself!

---

*These suggestions may be duplicated and sent home to families.

EXPLORING AT HOME*

Light

Your child has been discovering some intriguing ideas about light: the energy form that makes plants grow and makes our world visible. Listen to what he or she has to say about how light behaves. Then have some informal fun together with shadows, the absence of light.

Sharing Shadows. One of the best places for your child to learn about shadows is at home with you after dark. Your child already knows that shadows form when light can't shine through something. So find a strong flashlight or a spotlight-style lamp that you control, and join your child in a darkened room to try to share these explorations.

1. Shine the light on your child's back as he or she stands close to the light. Notice the shadow on the wall ahead. Notice how the shadow changes as your child slowly walks toward the wall.

2. Do the same thing, but this time with the light at floor level. Try it again with the light held high above the child's head. Enjoy noticing how each change makes a difference in the shadow size or location.

3. Add a second light source, shining from a different direction. How many shadows are there now? (Remember to point out shadows of players if you go to a ball game under the night lights.)

4. Hold two layers of waxed paper in front of the light. Notice how your child's shadow changes when some of the light is blocked by the cloudy paper. Mention that shadows change like this when clouds block the sunlight from us.

5. Have fun making shadows of familiar objects: toys, forks, combs, and whatever else you think of. Make the shadow shapes you learned to make as a child.

6. Find out what happens to your child's shadow in a dark room.

When you are outdoors together on a sunny day, you might want to protect your face from too much sunlight by wearing a shadow maker: a visor or sun hat!

When you walk down a lighted street at night with your child, notice how your shadows are sometimes in front of you, sometimes in back, and sometimes front, back, and sideways. Figure out the directions light is coming from to make such different shadows. Your bodies are blocking the path of the lights. You can have more than one shadow when the lights come from several directions. Notice shadows in your home at different times of day. See if you and your child can figure out what blocks the light to make these shadows.

---

*These suggestions may be duplicated and sent home to families.

EXPLORING AT HOME*

The Environment

Our class has been learning about some of the many ways children can help to improve their environment. They have a clearer understanding now that every person's cooperation is needed. Let your child put that learning about the 4 Rs—Restoring, Reusing, Repairing, and Recycling—into practice at home with you. Allow your child to help wash cans for recycling and stack old newspapers for bundling. Give your child responsibility for removing lids, caps, and rings from glass and plastic containers before recycling. Let your child remember to be in charge of taking your cloth or string bags to the grocery store when you go shopping.

Gardening can be a wonderful family project to beautify the environment, or to grow a healthy crop of vegetables. If you lack outdoor space, you could make a quick garden in a 50# bag of potting soil to keep on a porch or balcony. Plop the bag down where there is at least partial sunshine. Cut several holes in the bag. Stick seeds or small plants into the soil through the holes, and water as needed. The soil won't dry out fast, because it's so well-covered with plastic. It won't have any weeds, either!

If you have space and energy, create a habitat for small wildlife in your backyard or neighborhood. The National Wildlife Foundation has a program to help you attract birds, butterflies, and other small creatures by creating special plantings and water arrangements. Write: Backyard Wildlife Habitat Program, National Wildlife Federation, 11100 Wildlife Center Drive, Reston, VA 21090, or consult *www.nwf.org*.

---

*These suggestions may be duplicated and sent home to families.

REFERENCES FOR FAMILIES

ALLISON, L., & WESTON, M. (1994). *Pint-size science: Finding-out fun for you and your young child.* Boston: Little Brown. A nice array of activities for two- to four-year-olds. Paperback.

EMORY, J. (1994). *Nightprowlers: Everyday creatures under every night sky.* San Diego: Harcourt Brace. Families are the best guides to animals at night. This book will help you do that guiding. Paperback.

HARLAN, J., & QUATTROCCHI, C. (1994). *Science as it happens: Family activities with children ages 4 to 8.* New York: Henry Holt. Everyday events in home life are explored to uncover the science that makes them work. Paperback.

HIRSCHFIELD, R., & WHIET, N. (1995). *The kids' science book.* Charlotte, VT: Williamson. Paperback.

HICKMAN, P. (1999). *The night book: Exploring nature after dark.* Buffalo, NY: Kids Can Press.

PAULU, N., & MARTIN, M. (1992). *Helping your child learn science.* U.S. Department of Education. Stock #065-000-00520-4. U.S. Government Printing Office Order Desk #202/783-3238. Paperback; very low cost.

VANCLEAVE, J. (1996). *Play and find out about science.* New York: John Wiley. Easy experiments for young children. Paperback.

VANCLEAVE, J. (1999). *Play and find out about bugs.* New York: John Wiley. These activities to help young children get acquainted with insect features may need some help from you.

Free Resource

Coping With Children's Reactions to Earthquakes and Other Disasters. Write to: Federal Emergency Management Agency, P.O. Box 70274, Washington, D.C. 20024. Ask for Bulletin FEMA #48.

C

Relating Concepts to Established Benchmarks[*]

Benchmarks for Science Literacy criteria propose the concepts and understandings of science and social science children should have by the end of second grade.

The Benchmarks are categorized and presented somewhat differently than the concepts in this textbook. The chart below states each of the textbook's concepts from Chapters 4–16 and indicates in which category of Benchmarks the same or very similar concept is located. Some concepts lead to a Benchmark rather than being one.

CONCEPT	BENCHMARK
Chapter 4. Plants	
There are many kinds of plants; each has its own form.	Living Environment—Diversity of Life
Most plants make seeds for new plants.	Living Environment—Flow of Matter and Energy
Seeds grow into plants with roots, stems, leaves, and flowers.	Living Environment —Diversity of Life
Most plants need water, light, minerals, warmth, and air.	Living Environment—Flow of Matter and Energy
Some plants grow from roots.	Living Environment—Diversity of Life
Some plantlike forms do not have seeds or roots.	Living Environment—Diversity of Life
Many foods we eat are seeds.	Human Organism—Physical Health and Diversity of Life Living Environment—Diversity of Life

[*]Project 2061, American Association for Advancement of Science. (1993). *Benchmarks for Science Literacy*. Washington, DC: Author. Readers may access the Benchmarks at http://www.aaas.org.

CONCEPT	BENCHMARK

Chapter 5. Animals

There are many kinds of animals.

Living Environment—Diversity of Life

Animals move in different ways.

Living Environment—Diversity of Life

Each animal needs its own kind of food.

Living Environment—Flow of Matter and Energy

Many animals make shelters to rear their young.

Living Environment—Interdependence of Life
Physical Setting—Processes That Shape the Earth

Humans and animals often live together.

Living Environment—Interdependence of Life

Chapter 6. The Human Body: Care and Nourishment

Each person is unique.

Human Organism—Human Identity

We learn through our senses.

Human Organism—Basic Functions and Learning

Bones help support our bodies.

Human Organism—Basic Functions

Muscles keep us moving, living, and breathing.

Human Organism—Basic Functions

We help ourselves stay healthy and grow strong.

Human Organism—Physical Health and Human Identity

Strong, growing bodies need nourishing food.

Human Organism—Physical Health

Chapter 7. Air

Air is almost everywhere.

Physical Setting—Structure of Matter

Air is real; it takes up space.

Physical Setting—Structure of Matter

Air presses on everything on all sides.

Physical Setting—Structure of Matter

Moving air pushes things.

Physical Setting—Motion

Fast-moving air keeps planes aloft.

Physical Setting—Motion

Air slows moving objects.

Physical Setting—Motion

Warm air rises.

Physical Setting—Motion

Chapter 8. Water

Water has weight.

Physical Setting—Structure of Matter

Water's weight and upthrust help things float.

Physical Setting—Forces of Nature

Water goes into the air.

Physical Setting—Earth

Water can change forms reversibly.

Physical Setting—Earth

Water is a solvent for many materials.

Physical Setting—Structure of Matter

Water clings to itself.

Physical Setting—Structure of Matter

Water clings to other materials.

Physical Setting—Structure of Matter

Water moves into other materials.

Physical Setting—Structure of Matter and Motion

CONCEPT   BENCHMARK

CONCEPT	BENCHMARK
Chapter 9. Weather	
The sun warms the Earth.	Physical Setting—Energy Transformation
Changing air temperatures make the wind.	Physical Setting—Energy Transformation
Evaporation and condensation cause precipitation.	Physical Setting—Earth
Raindrops can break up sunlight.	Physical Setting—Structure of Matter
Weather can be measured.	Physical Setting—Earth: Mathematical World—Numbers
Lightning is static electricity.	Physical Setting—Structure of Matter
Charged electrons make sparks when they jump.	Physical Setting—Structure of Matter
Chapter 10. Rocks and Minerals	
There are many kinds of rocks.	Physical Setting—Processes That Shape the Earth
Rocks slowly change by wearing away.	Physical Setting—Processes That Shape Shape the Earth
Crumbled rocks and dead plants make soil.	Physical Setting—Processes That Shape Shape the Earth
Old plants and animals left prints in rocks.	Physical Setting—Processes That Shape Shape the Earth
Minerals form crystals.	Physical Setting—Living Environment Evolution of Life
Chapter 11. Magnetism	
Magnets attract some things, but not others.	Physical Setting—Processes That Shape the Earth and Structure of Matter
Magnets vary in strength.	Physical Setting—Forces of Nature
Magnets pull through some materials.	Physical Setting—Structure of Matter
One magnet can be used to make another magnet.	Physical Setting—Forces of Nature
Magnets are strongest at each end.	Physical Setting—Structure of Matter
Each end of a magnet acts differently.	Physical Setting—Structure of Matter
Chapter 12. Gravity	
Gravity pulls on everything.	Physical Setting—Structure of Matter
Chapter 13. Simple Machines	
Friction can heat, slow, and wear away objects.	Physical Setting—Forces of Nature
A lever helps lift objects.	Physical Setting—Structure of Matter
A ramp shares the work of lifting.	Designed World—Materials and Manufacturing
A screw is a curved ramp.	Designed World—Materials and Manufacturing

CONCEPT	BENCHMARK
Simple machines help move things along.	Designed World—Materials and Manufacturing; Common Themes—Systems
Some wheels turn alone; some turn together.	Designed World—Materials and Manufacturing; Common Themes—Systems
Single wheels can turn other wheels.	Designed World—Materials and Manufacturing; Common Themes—Systems
Single wheels can help us pull down to lift up.	

Chapter 14. Sound

Sounds are made when something vibrates.	Physical Setting—Motion
Sound travels through many things.	Physical Setting—Motion: Designed World— Communication
Different sizes of vibrating objects make different sounds.	Physical Setting—Structure of Matter

Chapter 15. Light

Nothing can be seen without light.	Physical Setting—Universe
Light appears to travel in a straight line.	
Shadows are made when light beams are blocked.	

Chapter 16. The Environment

There is an interconnectedness among things: plants, animals, air, water, weather, rocks, and ourselves.	Physical Setting—Processes that Shape the Earth Living Environment—Interdependence of Life and Flow of Matter and Energy Human Society—Global Interdependence
The environment is where we are. We can study it as well as live in it.	Living Environment—Interdependence of Life Habits of Mind—Values and Attitudes
We can work together to sustain the environment by restoring, reusing, repairing, and recycling.	Designed World—Energy Sources and Use Designed World—Energy Sources and Use Living Environment—Interdependence of Life and Flow of Matter and Energy

National Science Education Standards: Science Content Standards K–4

Science as Inquiry

Content Standard A:
As a result of activities in grades K–4, all students should develop

- Abilities necessary to do scientific inquiry
- Understanding about scientific inquiry

Physical Science

Content Standard B:
As a result of the activities in grades K–4, all students should develop an understanding of

- Properties of objects in materials
- Position and motion of objects
- Light, heat, electricity, and magnetism

Life Science

Content Standard C:
As a result of activities in grades K–4, all students should develop understanding of

- The characteristics of organisms

- Life cycles of organisms
- Organisms and environments

Earth and Space Science

Content Standard D:
As a result of their activities in grades K–4, all students should develop an understanding of

- Properties of earth material
- Objects in the sky
- Changes in earth and sky

Science and Technology

Content Standard E:
As a result of activities in grades K–4, all students should develop

- Abilities of technological design
- Understanding about science and technology
- Abilities to distinguish between natural objects and objects made by humans

Science in Personal and Social Perspectives

Content Standard F:
As a result of activities in K–4, all students should develop understanding of

- Personal health
- Characteristics and changes in populations
- Types of resources
- Changes in environments
- Science and technology in local challenges

History and Nature of Science

Content Standard G:
As a result of activities in grades K–4, all students should develop understanding of

- Science as a human endeavor

Index